# MUSIC IN
# ELEMENTARY EDUCATION

John W. Flohr

Valerie L. Trollinger

D1444906

## Prentice Hall

Boston   Columbus   Indianapolis   New York   San Francisco   Upper Saddle River
Amsterdam   Cape Town   Dubai   London   Madrid   Milan   Munich   Paris   Montréal   Toronto
Delhi   Mexico City   São Paulo   Sydney   Hong Kong   Seoul   Singapore   Taipei   Tokyo

Library of Congress Cataloging-in-Publication Data

Flohr, John W.
 Music in elementary education / John W. Flohr, Valerie L. Trollinger.
   p. cm.
 ISBN-13: 978-0-13-241396-1 (pbk.)
 ISBN-10: 0-13-241396-5 (pbk.)
  1.  School music—Instruction and study—United States. 2.  Music—Instruction and study--Juvenile.  I.
Trollinger, Valerie L. II. Title.
 MT1.F536 2010
 372.87—dc22

                                                    2009035154

**Editor in Chief:** *Sarah Touborg*
**Executive Editor:** *Richard Carlin*
**Editorial Assistant:** *Tricia Murphy*
**Director of Marketing:** *Brandy Dawson*
**Senior Marketing Manager:** *Kate Mitchell*
**Assistant Managing Editor:** *Melissa Feimer*
**Project Manager:** *Jean Lapidus*
**Composition/Full-Service Management:**
  *Macmillan Publishing Solutions/Jill Traut*
**Senior Art Director:** *Pat Smythe*
**Rights and Permissions Manager:** *Charles Morris*
**Senior Operations Supervisor:** *Brian Mackey*
**Color Scanning:** *Cory Skidds*
**Lead Media Project Manager:** *Rich Barnes*
**Senior Media Editor:** *David Alick*

**Creative Design Director:** *Jayne Conte*
**Cover Design:** *Bruce Kenselaar*
**Manager, Visual Research & Permissions:**
  *Karen Sanatar*
**Image Permissions Coordinator:** *Cathy Mazzucca*
**Foldout piano keyboard, Designer:**
  *Electra-Graphics, Inc.*
**Cover Photo:** *Madeline Drayer playing a metallophone.*
  *Courtesy of Jennifer Drayer, Union City Area School*
  *District, Pennsylvania*
**Printer/Binder:** *Edwards Brothers*
**Component: Foldout piano keyboard:**
  *Edwards Brothers*
**Cover Printer:** *Lehigh-Phoenix Color/Hagerstown*

This book was set in 10/12, Palatino.

Credits and acknowledgments borrowed from other sources and reproduced, with permission, in this
textbook appear on appropriate page within the text.

10 9 8 7 6 5 4 3 2 1

**Prentice Hall**
is an imprint of

www.pearsonhighered.com

Student Edition
ISBN 13: 978-0-13-241396-1
ISBN 10: 0-13-241396-5

Examination Copy
ISBN 13: 978-020-576035-0
ISBN 10: 020-576035-X

# TABLE OF CONTENTS

**Website**

For more materials visit the book website at: www.pearsonhighered.com/flohr

# PREFACE

The history of this book's development is long, labored, and exciting. We wanted to write a music method book that was geared for all possible music educators (not only music teachers, but general elementary specialists as well), and that emphasized a more current approach to teaching music in context to the general school curriculum, music's place in the world, music's place as an equal partner with other disciplines, current understanding of human growth and development (both cognitively and physically), and college students' need to develop the critical thinking, problem-solving, and group work skills that are so essential for success in the education field. This book is especially unique in that it addresses learners with special needs, basic fundamentals of world music characteristics, vocal development, performing arts medicine concerns, curriculum development and the ADDIE model of instructional design, and musical experiences that are illustrated in a sequential manner to show how many of the same concepts and music can be used but developed and expanded from kindergarten through Grade 6. We also include science, language arts, art, social studies, and math lesson plans partnered with music. Teachers and students can also use the book's open access website (www.pearsonhighered.com/flohr) to access video examples prepared by the authors for this text and, by using many of the resources available on the Internet, students and instructors can also pick and choose music and materials best suited for individual needs and interests rather than be limited to what is available on an accompanying CD of music.

The strongest philosophic principles driving this book are the ways of knowing: one can know something on an ephemeral level, or one can know something at a deeper, contextual, and meaningful level. Our emphasis is on the latter in that we encourage our students, and instructors using this book, to expand, modify, and take advantage of activities and materials to develop their own materials. If that happens, we will know we have been successful in this endeavor.

This logo indicates that a video is available for viewing on the book's website or on the DVD (available separately at an additional cost).

# ACKNOWLEDGMENTS

The authors wish to thank the contributors to this book, especially in the area of world music, and all of the colleagues and public school teachers who read, critiqued, and commented on the book as it was being written. We also wish to thank our many students, from kindergarten through graduate school, past and present over the last 30 years, who were the best students any authors could ever want.

We wish to acknowledge special people in particular without whom this book could not have been written: Richard Colwell, Lillian Katz, Robert Smith, and the late Mary Hoffman and Charles Leonhard—all part of the University of Illinois at one time; Robert Abramson, Juilliard School of Music; Jane Frazee, formerly of St. Thomas; Estelle Jorgensen, Charles P. Schmidt, and the late Jean Sinor from the Indiana University School of Music; Robert Appelman, Michael Molenda, Elizabeth Boling, and Barbara Bichelmeyer from the Indiana University Department of Instructional Systems Technology; and Laree Trollinger, Emeritus Professor of Voice and Music Education, Kutztown University of Pennsylvania.

For their review of the first edition, we would like to thank the following people: Amy Chivington, Otterbein College; Patricia St. John, Teachers College—Columbia University; Elaine Bernstorf, Wichita State University; Dr. Kimberly Inks, Ball State University; Kimberly Councill, Susquehanna University; Alan L. Spurgeon, University of Mississippi; Gwenneth J. Threadgill, Troy University; Susan Kenney, Brigham Young University; and Dr. Robin Swanson, Western Kentucky University.

We dedicate this book to the very important children in our lives: Amanda, Christine, Elisabeth, Genia, Ian, Jake, Justine, Karl, and Kevin.

# LIST OF CONTRIBUTORS

Melinda Cowart, *Texas Woman's University—Denton*

Phap Dam, *Texas Woman's University—Denton*

C. Victor Fung, *University of South Florida*

Gladys M. Keeton, *Texas Woman's University—Denton*

Gabriela Montoya-Stier, *Northside Independent School District, San Antonio, Texas*

John Osburn, *Texas Woman's University—Denton*

Diane C. Persellin, *Trinity University, San Antonio, Texas*

Joseph Pinson, MT-BC, *Texas Woman's University—Denton*

Shahanum Mohamed Shah, *Universiti Teknologi MARA, Shah Alam, Malaysia*

Maria T. Spillane, *Allentown School District, Allentown, PA*

Pamela Stover, *Southern Illinois University*

Nancy Sugden, *Bowling Green University*

Christopher M. Wenger, *North Penn School District, Lansdale, PA*

Sheila C. Woodward, *University of Southern California*

# TO THE STUDENT

## ORGANIZATION OF THE BOOK

This book is organized into three parts: (1) Foundations, (2) Music Elements, Curriculum, and Avenues to Music Learning, and (3) Musical Experiences. Because our emphasis in this book is presenting the learning and teaching of music as an intertwined experience with other disciplines (for example, science, social studies, mathematics, language arts), you will find that we see and experience music as part of the total human experience of living and learning. Each chapter includes references to the national standards in music and other disciplines, research background, the subject matter, cooperative learning and group activities, chapter conclusions, and references or resources. A unique aspect of this book is that we direct you to online resources, such as the Smithsonian Global Sound library, iTunes, National Geographic, and a host of other sites recommended by contributors, so you can investigate and choose music and materials. We have made the book as user-friendly as possible for both music majors as well as elementary education majors.

## HOW TO USE THIS BOOK

The purpose of the book is to provide both music and elementary professionals with an approach to teaching music in the school, and to help music educators obtain a stronger grasp on the holistic structure of the public school environment. In turn, elementary education majors will better understand how to teach music in the classroom. To further your own growth and development in teaching and learning music, we hope that you refer often to the materials in this book, and to the accompanying open access website (www.pearsonhigher.com/flohr), in your teaching career.

# TO THE INSTRUCTOR

## ORGANIZATION OF THE BOOK

This book is organized into three parts: (1) Foundations, (2) Music Elements, Curriculum, and Avenues to Music Learning, and (3) Musical Experiences. Because our emphasis in this book is presenting the learning and teaching of music as an intertwined experience with other disciplines (for example, science, social studies, mathematics, language arts), you will find that we see and experience music as part of the total human experience of living and learning. Each chapter includes references to the national standards in music and other disciplines, research background, the subject matter, cooperative learning and group activities, chapter conclusions, and references or resources. A unique aspect of this book is that we direct you to online resources, such as the Smithsonian Global Sound library, iTunes, National Geographic, and a host of other sites recommended by contributors, so you can investigate and choose music and materials.

## HOW TO USE THIS BOOK

There is a lot of room for flexibility in using the materials in this book to meet the needs of your students. We do suggest, however, that the first part—Foundations—be covered first. The second and third parts of the book can be used concurrently, as the Avenues to Learning and the Musical Experiences work very well together. The book is supplemented by an open-access website at www.pearsonhighered.com/flohr, that provides videos featuring live-action information on the voice and working with the voice, and will be especially helpful for students in your classroom who may be vocally challenged. Other materials on the website also serve as great lesson plan materials, not only for instructors but also for students. We hope that you will use this book as a core source with your students, but please feel free to modify and adapt materials as needed.

# PART I

# Foundations

# Why Music in the Elementary School?

**This chapter addresses the following:**

- Why Music in Elementary Education?
  *Four Styles*
  *Links Among the Arts and Other Subjects*
- National Standards
- Chapter Conclusions

## WHY MUSIC IN ELEMENTARY EDUCATION?

Whether you plan to be a music or elementary teacher, the current and future education climates indicate that distinct lines among education subject areas are blurring.

Education is moving toward a more global approach that implies knowledge of multiple subject areas is interdependent and often necessary for a child's success in school and life. This book does not present music as a single isolated discipline but rather as part of the larger educational picture.

What function does music fulfill in children's elementary education? This section covers several ways in which music may enrich elementary education throughout the day (Calogero 2002; Flohr 2006; Hansen et al. 2004). Music surrounds us—on the radio, television, movies, streets, concert halls, and iPods. How do children benefit from music in the classroom?

Three good ways music benefits and enriches instruction include the following:

1. *Self-expression.* Music is misused when employed solely as a means of enriching other instruction. Broudy (1972) used the term *cherishing* when writing about arts education. When we value and cherish the arts, we desire to preserve and care for them for their intrinsic properties, which provide delight. In an essay on arts education, Broudy defined "enlightened cherishing" as "a love of objects and actions that by certain norms and standards are worthy of our love. It is a love that knowledge justifies" (Broudy 1972, 6). Although arts education may significantly benefit a child's development, we should be cautious about views that emphasize music as a tool to teach other subjects or to provide relaxation. Many activities may serve as tools to teach other subjects or provide relaxation. What makes music and the arts different? Chapter 2 contains a thorough examination of meaning and music.

2. *Efficient, enjoyable learning.* Music may help teachers and students to achieve goals efficiently and enjoyably. Subjects partnered with music may help children acquire information with ease and speed. When other strategies fail, children, including those with special needs, may retain information carried by **melody** and/or rhythm; in this way, music can help children learn counting, names of states, colors, grammar—all nonmusical ideas.

3. *Professional growth for teachers.* Bresler (2002) outlines five major points of impact on teachers who integrate and collaborate with other teachers: They experience

(1) a role change as they develop curriculum, not just implement it; (2) focus that moves to broader issues of educating children; (3) exposure to a large array of sources; (4) a major shift in teacher self-image, from isolation to part of children's whole education, particularly for music specialists; and (5) a change of instructional role for music teachers who now become central rather than marginal to general instruction.

Chapter 2 contains a detailed discussion of music enrichment, music and the brain, parallel objectives, and social benefits of music.

## Four Styles

Classroom teachers studied by Bresler (1995) often used one of four styles for integration with the arts. In this chapter, we rename Bresler's styles as enrichment styles rather than integration styles. The most frequently used style, *subservient enrichment*, involves music to enrich other subjects without encouraging aesthetic growth in the arts. For example, during cleanup time, a teacher may sing the words, "This is the way we clean up our blocks" to the folk song "Here We Go 'Round the Mulberry Bush." Another example is enriching storytelling time with music.

The least used style, *coequal cognitive enrichment style*, was identified as the most advocated in arts enrichment literature. Classroom teachers who worked with arts specialists or had an artistic background usually used this style. Schools may invite artists for short-term instruction or ongoing arts instruction with classroom teachers. For example, a brass quintet visits a preschool and performs music from a standard repertoire and music based on children's folk songs (for example, "This Old Man"). Before the visit, the preschool teacher may begin a unit on brass instruments, with listening, pictures, making instruments, and children moving and pretending to play brass instruments. The musicians demonstrate each brass instrument, and then allow children to touch them and try to make sound on a mouthpiece. The brass quintet example involves listening and perceiving, interpreting and analyzing sound, synthesizing individual brass sounds into a quintet, and evaluating characteristics of the instruments.

The third enrichment style, *affective style*, was identified by the way it set a mood and was the most prevalent in grades K–2 in Bresler's study. For example, music in the background provides a relaxing mood during individual reading time.

The fourth style, *social enrichment*, linked the arts to the general curriculum. For example, all of the primary grade students of a school system join together to sing "America" for a patriotic event. This type of activity, usually championed by a principal, may draw public and media attention to the school. Another example is illustrated by a group of preschool teachers asking a music specialist to help with a song for the kindergarten graduation activities in the spring. Finally, children singing a "hello" and "ABC" songs for parents' day portray the school as involving music in the curriculum.

## Links Among the Arts and Other Subjects

Deasy (2002) writes that music and other arts—dance, theater, visual, language, and media—are unique yet connected. Two or more art forms may overlap. For example, movement and music are often combined for children. Each art form is unique in medium of **expression** and symbolic system, but connected to one another by the expression of aesthetic qualities. Concepts and terms relating to form often cross the arts. For example, repetition in music (a repeated rhythm pattern) may be linked to repetition in dance (a repeated movement). In addition, repetition in music may be linked to repetition in theater (a recurring part of a dramatic story) and in visual arts (repeated colors or shapes in a painting). For more information, visit the Arts Education Partnership website at: http://aep-arts.org/.

Good vocal modeling by the teacher is important in teaching singing.

*Photo courtesy of Kelly Riccio*

**Pitfalls to Avoid.**    Two important pitfalls need to be avoided. First, for thoughtful enrichment, teachers should retain the unique benefits of music when joining music with other subjects to create a beneficial learning environment. Although music may influence and enhance other learning, it is prudent to remember that music has worth in and of itself and should be used to achieve its own numerous purposes. Second, all music is not of the same quality; music of poor quality is far less effective.

## NATIONAL STANDARDS

A major U.S. national policy act gives the arts a firm position in schools and additional reasons for teaching music to young children. Public Law 107–110, entitled Elementary and Secondary Education Act or No Child Left Behind of 2001, includes the arts in the definition of core academic subjects. Title IX, part A–definitions, Section 9101 (11) of the law defines core academic subjects: "The term *core academic subjects* means English, reading or language arts, mathematics, science, foreign languages, civics and government, economics, arts, history, and geography" (U.S. Department of Education 2003).

National, state, district, and local school standards are available for organizing teaching. National and state content area associations (for example, mathematics, language arts, music, and dance) list standards on their websites. The national music standards from the National Association for Music Education (which uses the acronym MENC) are used for the music purposes of this book. The national standards are voluntary guidelines; there are no national standards for inspectors to use while visiting and reviewing schools. School district and state standards are often included in teacher evaluation. The following are MENC content standards:

1. Singing, alone and with others, a varied repertoire of music
2. Performing on instruments, alone and with others, a varied repertoire of music
3. Improvising melodies, variations, and accompaniments
4. Composing and arranging music within specified guidelines
5. Reading and notating music
6. Listening to, analyzing, and describing music
7. Evaluating music and music performances
8. Understanding relationships between music, the other arts, and disciplines outside the arts
9. Understanding music in relation to history and culture (MENC 1994b)

For a complete listing of achievement standards, see "Opportunity-to-learn Standards for Music Instruction: Grades PreK-12" (MENC 1994a).

---

## Chapter Conclusions

There are many reasons why music is valuable for elementary classrooms. Three reasons for enriching instruction with music are (1) benefits such as self-expression; (2) teachers and children reach goals efficiently and enjoyably because music is a good vehicle for learning information; and (3) music provides professional growth for teachers. National and state education standards include music and the arts as part of the core curriculum.

# Meaning and Music

**This chapter addresses the following:**

## VALUES IN MUSIC

This section of the book introduces relationships among humans, music, and meaning. These relationships are not simple, nor can they be investigated or defined simply. Rather, you will be introduced to dynamic and intricate convolutions of how humans, music, and meaning interact, and subsequently how they affect how you teach and how your students learn. We encourage you to investigate references listed throughout this chapter, read articles and books by music philosophers we discuss, and find your own meaning in music. Many have a great deal to contribute to what we generally accept as meaningful and valuable in music education, but ultimately your values and meanings will drive your teaching career. However, there is a caveat. To logically derive your beliefs about music and music education requires that you be informed about what actually has been going on in the fields of music and education that have a direct impact upon what we eventually teach in our classrooms.

## HUMAN VALUES AND PHILOSOPHY IN MUSIC

The term *value in education* has been bandied around in a number of contexts, from the late 1980s into the 1990s, as value-based education to the current No Child Left Behind model that promotes the values of science, mathematics, and reading. There are many meanings for one small word, *value*. As a culture, the term *value* implies

Playing an instrument can be a positive experience.

*Photo courtesy of Lorraine Trollinger*

worth, importance, usefulness, or even monetary gains. *Value* can also imply a moral, ethical, or ideal construct. In the study of attributes that comprise beauty, aesthetic value is determined by perceived and agreed upon beauty found in each art. Wars start over values, economic contracts are made or broken over values, and governments rise and fall over values. One person or culture may believe something is valuable, whereas another person or culture may not.

Within this framework, we make the following statement: Music has value in our schools. As musicians and music educators, we fight for quality music education under metaphorical banners bearing this statement. We have conferences, from local to international, to help promote and solidify the value of music education in schools worldwide. The belief that music has value seems to be inherent, because why would we want to teach something that has no value? As musicians, would we ever admit that what we do for a living has no value? The notion that some people out there believe that music has no value is something we find abhorrent, which is why we may often feel that we are continually required to justify ourselves, our career choices, and our existence. What we view as full of value, especially when viewing music from a monetary set of values, others may not. Sometimes these naysayers are our own educational colleagues in the schools in which we teach.

What *is* a value? Values are defined as something important, relevant, worthwhile, or useful. However, the manner in which value can be measured can be tricky. Economic values are measured by the exchange of money (such as on the stock market). Emotional values are measured by how a person feels in response to something. These two measures, for example, can even be mixed together, especially on a good day for the stock market, or conversely on a bad day for the stock market. The addition of a moral dimension—of good or bad—creates further complexities, because who is the official arbiter of what is good or bad? If I consider past performance, my entire portfolio and current economic conditions, I may feel fortunate. These three values—economic, emotional, and moral—plus others too numerous to name, play a part in what we do in the classroom.

## Philosophical Foundations of Music

The philosophers in music education present themselves at humble stance, yet their work is paramount in that it provides the underpinnings for what we do as educators. Philosophical inquiry is based upon logical reasoning and extrapolation in that one logical idea can be the gate to other logical, well-reasoned ideas. This is why many of our music philosophers refer back to early great thinkers, such as Plato and Aristotle, to show the logical progression of their theories. Although this particular point suggests that emotion is not a part of the philosophical process, it is indeed considered, especially in the arts.

It is best to build a foundation of beliefs and values about the function of music in the daily lives of children. It would be folly to build a house without an adequate foundation or expect a tree to grow with a weak and undernourished root system. Why would anyone want to start teaching children without a foundation? The way people think about music affects their teaching.

Over the past thirty years, a number of philosophical approaches have been considered, developed, argued, and revised. However, several have moved to the forefront and have stayed there, solidifying not only their own place in music education but also giving rise to other philosophies that may or may not be related.

Two philosophies that held the spotlight in the last thirty years have been the aesthetic approach, primarily associated with Bennett Reimer, and the praxial approach, primarily associated with Dr. Reimer's former doctoral student, David Elliot. Simply put, the aesthetic approach suggests music is understandable by all humans, and no special in-depth training is required to understand the inherent human qualities of music. The praxial approach emphasizes that humans must be engaged in the creation of music to understand it—that is, they learn by doing. The truth probably lies somewhere in the middle—the more we are engaged in music, the more we value and understand it. For example, philosophers have moved into this strong middle-ground area and have fleshed out more recent viewpoints.

With the establishment of the International Society of Philosophy of Music Education (http://www2.siba.fi/ispme_symposium/), world viewpoints are further contributing to a constantly evolving modern international philosophy of music education, value, and meaning. For further reading about the various philosophical viewpoints, readers are encouraged to peruse the *Philosophy of Music Education Review*, published by Indiana University Press, for the most contemporary and cutting-edge articles. Many people, too numerous to list here, are making great contributions to music education. In addition to the philosophers mentioned previously, some current music education philosophers worth reviewing are Randall Allsup, Estelle Jorgensen, Paul Woodford, Wayne Bowman, and David Carr, for a start. As you read one philosopher's work, you will likely want to research out their ideas, which will introduce you to more philosophers and their works.

Philosophy also seeks to investigate human knowledge: what it is, where it comes from, why it exists, and perhaps its value. This investigation is undertaken via logical reasoning of theories and ideas. Another branch of inquiry, psychology, also does the same, but uses empirical or qualitative measurements of the human experience to determine the answers of what knowledge is. We will discuss psychology in the next part.

But first, what is knowledge? An understanding of how knowledge is defined for this book in relationship to how it is defined in philosophy and psychology is important for readers of this text, as it provides the underpinning for everything in it. There are many kinds of knowing *something*, but for simplicity's sake, we will deal with the most basic for a start. For our purposes, we will stick to the basic three: (1) knowing that, (2) knowing how, and (3) knowing why.

For example, suppose you are driving down the street and you see two cars pulled over to the side of the road, both of them obviously damaged. From simply driving by, you *know that* an accident occurred, and that's all you can know. You don't *know how* it happened, unless you see the cars in particular positions that indicate one came from one direction, and one from the other, but there is still much you don't pick up in a simple drive-by. Finally, you certainly wouldn't *know why* the accident happened simply by driving by. Perhaps one driver had a colicky baby in the back of the car and was distracted, or was talking on a cell phone. Maybe it went deeper in that one driver recently left the veterinarian where the family dog just died. In music education, it works similarly. For example, sixth graders can *know that* Mozart was a classical period composer. It takes much more work for them to *know how* Mozart was a classical composer (meaning they would have to know characteristics of classical form and composition) and to *know why* he was a classical composer (which would include knowing more about his background and the culture of his time).

In music education, the most sophisticated and inspiring teachers avoid the drive-by approach to music education that emphasizes the lowest level of knowledge, and instead aims for students to have deeper levels of understanding of what music really is all about. That is the approach we use in this book. We embrace both the philosophical and psychological inquiries into knowledge to better inform you as a music educator, and to emphasize that these fields are not exclusive of each other, and ultimately enhance our ways of knowing.

## PSYCHOLOGY OF MUSIC

Compared to the field of philosophy, psychology is a relative newcomer because it really is only a little over a century old. As stated earlier, whereas philosophy emphasizes logical reasoning to derive and develop theories related to knowledge, meaning, and value, psychology measures indicators of knowledge, meaning, and value via quantitative reasoning (mathematical/statistical) and/or qualitative reasoning (prose or other verbal records of experience) to get to the facts. Psychology grew out of philosophy as another way to investigate human perception of experiences. Psychology first emerged in the late 1880s to the early 1900s, with the work of Herman von Helmholtz and Carl Seashore, who were both interested in investigating human perception of sound. Perception via sight, sound, smell, taste, and touch are included in psychological inquiry, along with internal mental representations of knowledge and human understanding of that knowledge. In psychology of music, we include studies into how sound is produced as well as how it is perceived, and we will be citing and referring to many of these kind of studies throughout this book. Brain research is often included in psychological studies as it provides a quantitative analysis of how the brain functions via the data provided from various kinds of imaging or studies of brain waves.

Neither field (psychology nor philosophy) holds keys to all the answers in our quest for knowledge, but they work together, sometimes in an antagonistic relationship, to better inform us as musicians and teachers. As you read this book, you are urged (1) to look at the philosophical and sociological viewpoints from not only a logical rational stand, but also from a hard science stand (Are there any research studies that support this as well?), and (2) to look at the scientific studies with a logical and rational view (Does this have a philosophical viewpoint that matches?). You may find out that, by thinking in these other ways, you will come up with new ideas that you may wish to investigate on your own. This is what learning and knowing are all about.

## MUSIC AND THE BRAIN

The brain is only part of a much larger system that includes the central nervous system (brain and spinal cord) and peripheral nerves (afferent nerve fibers and their receptors, which send messages to the brain, and efferent nerve fibers and their muscles and glands, which take messages from the brain). In addition, the brain regulates the release of hormones into the bloodstream, so that, in effect, the brain extends throughout the body.

The brain appears to be more malleable during the first decade of life than in adulthood. According to Thatcher (1998), studies have shown that 40 percent of short-term and 70 percent of long-term connections in the brain are influenced by heredity. Therefore, 30 percent to 60 percent of the brain's connections come from environmental influences or an interaction of heredity and environmental influences. Nelson and Bloom (1997) cite numerous demonstrations that show how positive or negative early experiences can alter both the structure and function of the brain. Also, it is important to remember that a child's brain is not the same as an adult brain. There is agreement that, during the first decade of life, a child typically has up to twice as much neural activity and connections compared to adults. The brain makes connections during the prenatal period and throughout life. Some connections are found to be predetermined genetically, and others develop from environmental influences. Much brain development occurs in early childhood, but the brain is far from completed even at the end of adolescence.

Although many findings into the intricacies of how the human brain works were made in the past fifteen years, research gives us more questions than answers and more fascinating what-if scenarios than provable learning strategies. It is important to keep results of recent brain research in perspective, because neuroscience findings can be overstated. On the other hand, it is easy to discount neuroscience findings because of problems with the use of new technology, difficulties interpreting data, and unproven brain theory. The neuroscience technologies are complicated and in a state of constant evolution. Researchers and consumers of research need to be familiar with limits of each technique to properly assess the value of the research. However, the information gathered from brain research has so far helped educators identify principles of best practice in teaching to aid more efficient and effective learning.

Early care and nurturing have a decisive, long-lasting impact on how people develop, their ability to learn, and their capacity to regulate their own emotions (Flohr, Miller, and Persellin 2000). Currently, general findings from research on the brain reveal the following:

1. Human development hinges on the interplay between nature and nurture. Recent brain research challenges old assumptions about talent and innate ability—that the genes humans are born with determine how the brain develops. In general,

neuroscience research has shown that nature or nurture alone do not determine brain development. The complex interaction among innate abilities, environment, and also the variability inherent in individual differences influences brain development. Although much growth and activity occurs during the young years, evidence shows that the brain has room for change during the later years.

2. Early care and nurturing also have a decisive, long-lasting impact on how people develop, their ability to learn, and their capacity to regulate their own emotions. Children as young as one day of age are able to make preferential choices about their environment, including musical choices.

3. **Experience** changes the physiological structure and operation of our brains. Music and music instruction have an effect on brain activity. Studies using various brain imaging techniques have documented some of these changes and also differences between trained and untrained musicians.

4. The human brain has a remarkable capacity to change, but timing is often important and at some points crucial (Flohr and Hodges 2006).

5. Evidence is accumulating that what most readily transfers between humans and their brains are the **dynamics** of intentions and emotions implicit in other people's forms of movement (Flohr and Trevarthen 2008; Gallese 2003; Schilbach et al. 2006).

## Interaction of Philosophy, Psychology, Teaching, and Learning

Philosophical inquiry and psychological investigations into the human mind have led to a plethora of theories on how we should teach so our students learn effectively and efficiently. In addition and from these theories, the field of instructional design addresses specifically how this interaction can best occur. All of these fields cycle around and foray into one another, searching for new and improved methodologies and approaches. Some are old, well worn, and successful with moderate changes made as needed, whereas newer ones are tested and investigated. The remaining section of this chapter will address primarily the learning theories derived in the interaction of these fields, with additional information on instructional theories that will be further applied in Chapter 11.

How does one know that learning has happened? The most obvious indication that learning has occurred is that learners have a new approach to problem-solving behavior, due to the application of the new knowledge. There are primarily three approaches to learning: behavioral, cognitive, and social-emotional. We are using this kind of classification to organize how they are presented in this chapter. The behavioral approaches are associated with the basic stimulus-response model in that a teacher would do one thing, and the children would do something in response. Simple music examples would include echo-clapping and **echo-singing.** Cognitive approaches try to reach the internal workings of the brain's thought processes and how it organizes, categorizes, and adds knowledge. Social-emotional approaches (our term for this) include the social and emotional aspects of learning and acquiring knowledge.

Although it is easy to categorize these theories and the consequent instructional approaches featured in Chapter 11 to help the learning process, you need to know that many of these theories overlap, and multiple theories could be active simultaneously in any learning situation. This is a good thing due to the rise of differentiated learning strategies in the schools—the hard thing is to make sure that, when you set up instruction, you design the instruction with as many of the relevant theories as possible in mind, with awareness that theoretical approaches may collide or confuse students.

## LEARNING THEORIES[1]

These following learning theories are some of the most well known. Many others are in current development, and some of the ones you read about here are continually adjusted to meet contemporary concerns and needs.

---

[1]Parts of this section were adapted from J. Flohr's *Musical Lives of Young Children,* Chapter 2. Thanks to Diane Persellin.

## Behavioral Approaches

Three early behaviorists were John Watson (1878–1958), the psychologist who is credited with coining the term *behaviorism*, Ivan Pavlov (1849–1936), and Edward Thorndike (1874–1949). Pavlov is best known for his work with dogs and meat powder. The classic conditioning experiment investigated the degree to which dogs would salivate to a stimulus (a bell) instead of meat powder. This was accomplished when the dogs were presented simultaneously with meat powder and the sound of a bell. Eventually, the dogs salivated when they heard only the bell, and without presenting meat powder. This is an example of a classically conditioned response—the dogs learned to salivate at the sound of a bell, because they associated the bell with the subsequent presentation of the yummy meat powder.

Thorndike's original interest was in how children learned, but he found out that was particularly difficult to study. So he turned his interests to studying chicks, cats, mice, and dogs and how they dealt with navigating mazes. Later in his life, he was able to resurrect his interest in how children learned. His studies laid the groundwork for B. F. Skinner's research.

Watson was interested in human stimulus-response reactions to situations. In his most famous experiment, he presented a white lab rat to a baby named Albert. Initially, Albert was unafraid and tried to touch the rat. A few months later, when Albert was 11 months old, he was again presented with the rat. This time, however, just as he touched the rat, a loud metal clang sounded behind his head that made him cry. This was repeated several times over a few weeks. Before long, just the sight of the rat made Albert cry. In fact, any furry item—a stuffed toy or a fur coat—made Albert cry because he was associating the fur with the rat and the accompanying loud clang that likely hurt his ears. This rather cruel experiment showed the behaviorist idea of stimulus response and later association with a child (Lefrançois 1994). Interestingly, Dr. Watson left his academic position at Johns Hopkins University and pursued a career in advertising in New York City, becoming quite wealthy.

B. F. Skinner (1904–1990), another behaviorist, extended the early stimulus-response studies of Pavlov, Watson, and Thorndike that had become known as classical conditioning. His continued work on animal and human behavior has had a strong impact on both psychology and education. Some of Skinner's key principles are summarized as follows:

1. *Operant conditioning.* This is a three-step process: stimulus, response, and another stimulus or consequence that reinforces the response. It differs from classical conditioning in that the voluntary behavior of the subject is modified through different consequences of *reinforcement* or *punishment*.
2. *Successive approximation.* Also referred to as shaping of behavior, successive approximation takes place when small progressive steps are taken toward a model. Music teachers use this technique by teaching parts of a song through singing one **phrase** at a time and asking children to repeat each phrase.
3. *Behavior modification.* Children are given external reinforcement for appropriate or inappropriate responses or behavior. Learning is affected by both positive and negative reinforcement. The behaviorism model views children as passive, and their development is largely determined by environmental influences. Behavioral modification is useful in the classroom for targeting and changing unwanted behaviors. The field of special education finds behavioral modification useful.

*Summary of behaviorism:* In music education, we use behavioral approaches for most of the simple activities, such as echo-clapping, echo-singing, having sudden-death rounds with flash cards, and taking dictation, to name a few. Much drill and practice with computer programs are also behavioral-based. In many cases, this represents the lower level of knowledge—the knowing or identification level. Although it is a great place to start our teaching, we have to avoid becoming bogged down at this most basic level.

**TABLE 2.1 Overview of Theories Relating to Children's Education**

| Theory | Theorists | Key Principles and Models | Instructional Strategies |
|---|---|---|---|
| Behaviorism | Skinner, Pavlov, Thorndike, and Watson | Positive and negative reinforcement, operant conditioning, successive approximation, and transfer of knowledge and skills to learners (does not consider mental processing). Learner must give correct response to stimulus. | Teachers use reinforcement (drill and practice, and cueing) for correct response. |
| Eight psychosocial stages of human development | Erik Erikson | Humans must resolve key conflict during each of eight stages before proceeding to the next stage of development. | Teachers need knowledge of child development and children's needs, interests, and abilities. |
| Social learning theory | Albert Bandura | Children see models of behavior that can be replicated. This is behaviorist theory, but more cognitive than previous theories. | Modeling; reinforcement of modeling; and personal evaluation |
| Piaget's stage dependent theory (cognitive) | Jean Piaget | Children progress through four stages of thinking: sensorimotor (0 to 2 years), preoperational (2 to 7 years), concrete operations (7 to 11 years), and formal operations (11 years to adult). | Teachers carefully observe learners to determine the stage of learning and to plan appropriate strategies. |
| Modes of representation (cognitive) | Jerome Bruner | Children move through three stages of learning: (1) enactive (sensing and doing), (2) iconic (imaging the experience), and (3) symbolic (representing experience through language, music notation, or other system). | Enactive: moving, touching, and doing Iconic: charts, graphic images, and line drawings Symbolic: language and musical notation |
| Maslow's hierarchy | Abraham Maslow | Children are motivated by five basic stages of needs: (1) physical needs, (2) safety and security, (3) belonging and affection, (4) self-esteem, and (5) self-actualization. | Strategies can include observing to see that children are well-fed, safe, and welcomed in the classroom; learning names; and encouraging children to succeed. |
| Bloom's taxonomy of cognitive domain | Benjamin Bloom | Six levels of thought processes in a hierarchical taxonomy from simple to complex encourage teachers to use higher-order thinking skills (more of a classification than a theory). | Teachers use all six with emphasis on more complex levels when planning teaching strategies and asking questions. |
| Meaningful reception (cognitive) | David Ausubel | Learning takes place when information is stored in an organized, meaningful way. Advance organizers help prepare learners for lessons. | Explanations and demonstrations, advance organizers, and well-organized learning strategies |
| Multiple intelligences | Howard Gardner | One learns through one or more of eight intelligences: (1) linguistic, (2) logical/mathematical, (3) spatial, (4) body/kinesthetic, (5) musical, (6) interpersonal, (7) intrapersonal, and (8) naturalist. | Instructional strategies for each intelligence are created: Children learn and demonstrate understanding through each specific intelligence. |
| Learning styles | Rita Dunn and Kenneth Dunn | Learning is affected by environmental, emotional, social, and physical factors. | Learners are more successful when teaching takes into account these four factors. |
| Learning Modalities | Walter Barbe and Raymond Swassing | Learners process information through one or more preferred learning channels: auditory, visual, and/or kinesthetic. | Teachers teach through the child's strongest channels, and reinforce through the other two: auditory (spoken word), visual (reading and charts), kinesthetic (moving, hands-on learning). |
| Constructivism | Lev Vygotsky, John Dewey, Neo-Piaget, R. DeVries, and Lawrence Kohlberg | Learners develop their own understanding of the world through their experiences. | Problem solving, scaffolding, learning from environment, peer interaction |
| Sociocultural constructivism | Lev Vygotsky | This can be seen as an extension of constructivism: Discussion and problem solving between children and adults help children become culturally socialized; the importance is placed upon children's pretend play. | Teacher participates and guides children in the learning and playing process, leading to independence. |
| Discovery learning | Jerome Bruner | Learners develop a deep understanding of ideas by experimenting and forming their own concepts before they are labeled (a constructivist strategy). | Children problem-solve by exploring. They are gradually guided to understanding and then are given the label for the concept. |
| Ecological psychology | Urie Bronfenbrenner | Interactions with others and the environment are key to development. | Importance is placed upon supporting a child's various social environments such as family, school, and community. |

## Cognitive Approaches

**PIAGET'S STAGES OF COGNITIVE DEVELOPMENT** The studies of Jean Piaget (1952), a Swiss biologist, about the intellectual development of children resulted in a stage theory of cognitive development. Children progress through the following four stages of cognitive development:

1. *Sensorimotor* (birth to age 2). Children in this pre-language period are egocentric (they think the world revolves around them), and they learn through direct sensory experience with their environment.
2. *Preoperational* (ages 2 to 7). Children use simple symbols or words to represent objects, but are unable to engage in abstract mental operations, to conserve (or recognize) a quantity after a change in shape or position (for example, if water is poured from a short squat beaker into a tall slim beaker, the child will think there is more water in the slim tall beaker), or to reverse an action. Children in this stage can play a sequential melodic pattern on six tone bells but have difficulty reversing their action and playing the pattern backwards.
3. *Concrete operations* (age 7 to 11). Children are capable of reversing an action, can conserve, and can order and classify objects. For example, they can hear and recognize a rhythmic pattern in its original form and also played twice as fast (more likely after listening several times).
4. *Formal operations* (age 11 to 15). At this highest stage of intellectual thought, children can reason abstractly and can analyze thoughts of others.

Piaget also conducted studies on how children learn new concepts and make sense of this new information. He proposed the theories of *accommodation* and *assimilation* to explain a child's learning process. Assimilation is the attending to and taking in information via the senses (for example, hearing, touch, and sight). Accommodation is a change in thinking or behaving to fit the new information children are trying to assimilate. Children strive to establish equilibrium when assimilating and accommodating new sensory information. When children receive new sensory information, they assimilate or try to fit this information into their already existing understanding of reality. If the new information can be immediately incorporated without the need for accommodation, then a sense of balance or equilibrium occurs. If they are unable to incorporate the new information, they try to accommodate and change their way of thinking to account for the new data and restore equilibrium. If they can't assimilate or accommodate the new data, they may reject it altogether. Piaget believed that children must discover relationships and ideas through play and in classroom situations that involve activities of interest to them. Understanding is then built through active involvement in the learning process. Piaget's ideas have generated both positive and negative criticism in the past twenty years. However, his ideas remain useable for music in elementary education (Serafine 1988; Sims 1988; 1991; Zimmerman and Sechrest 1968).

Since Piaget's death, there has been continuing work on his theories. A group of scholars who have continued this work are known as "neo-Piagetians," and they have brought up a number of interesting ideas. First, they have added stages in between the ones that Piaget originally identified, but more interestingly, they have added stages that extend into adulthood (Commons and Richards 2002). They make clear that the stages are sequential, and one stage must be completed before another one can be entered. This presents an interesting notion: Is it possible to be stuck in a cognitive stage of development? We will visit this idea briefly at the end of this chapter.

**MULTIPLE INTELLIGENCES** A theory of multiple intelligences was developed and modified by Howard Gardner (1983; 1999b). Earlier, Guilford (1967) proposed a structure of intellect comprising 120 different intellectual abilities, adding many more before his death. The work of Guilford and Gardner suggests that the traditional notion of intelligence, based on IQ testing, is far too limited. Gardner proposed seven and later eight intelligences to account for a broader range of human potential in children and adults (Gardner 1993). They include the following abilities:

1. Verbal/linguistic—the ability in acquisition, formation, and processing of language
2. Logical/mathematical—the capacity to think logically, use numbers effectively, and determine relationships and patterns between concepts and things
3. Spatial—the ability to create internal mental images or pictures
4. Body/kinesthetic—the capacity to use one's body skillfully as a means of expression or to work expertly to create or manipulate objects
5. Musical—the recognition of tonal and rhythm patterns
6. Interpersonal—the understanding and communicating with others
7. Intrapersonal—the self-reflection and understanding of one's strengths
8. Naturalist—the ability to sense patterns in and to make connections to elements in nature and to place ideas and things into discrete categories

Gardner continues to develop his theory on multiple intelligences. He adds, "While I am not yet ready to proclaim a ninth intelligence, I am willing to accept the possibility that a proclivity for pondering ultimate cosmic or existential concerns constitutes a distinctive human intellectual capacity" (Gardner 1999b, 68; the paperback publication is often listed as 2000).

**BRUNER'S THEORIES OF LEARNING**    Jerome Bruner (1966) described three stages or modes of learning in which learners translate experiences into a model of the world: enactive (sensing, doing, and acting on the environment), iconic (imaging the experience through visual or other sensory icons that look like the meaning of the concept), and symbolic (representing the experience through language or another system). Bruner stated that learners translate experiences into these sequential models. His theory is used extensively in music education. For example, children learning to read melodic notation would first show the high and low pitches with their hands or bodies (enactive), then would read high and low line drawings or icons that represent pitch (iconic), and finally would read the melody on a musical **staff** (symbolic).

Bruner was also an advocate of the discovery method of learning. This method encourages children to explore and manipulate ideas. Children are challenged to problem-solve by taking risks and experimenting, and are then guided toward an understanding and the name of what they have been doing. Bruner also stated that, although some topics are best learned through the discovery method, others are not. A decision about when to use the discovery method and when to use a more direct or expository approach is a difficult decision and part of the craft or art of teaching. Much direct or expository instruction has behavioral or semibehavioral objectives, goals, or aims. In one of his more recent works, *The Culture of Education* (1996), Bruner adopted an approach that is somewhat the opposite. Meaning is more constructivist, aligning Bruner less with psychologists but perhaps more so with educational philosophers such as Maxine Greene and Michael Apple.

*Summary of cognitive learning:* When dealing with behaviorism, it is quite simple to see how the various theories actually contribute to each other. The same cannot be said for cognitive learning theories. However, it is logical to assume that somehow they all can work together in some way. We will push the boundaries a bit, and encourage you to experiment that same way with these and other learning theories.

Is a combination of Piaget's learning theory and Gardner's theory of multiple intelligences possible? One idea proposed at the end of the section on Piaget and the neo-Piagetians was that we could get stuck in a particular stage of development. For example, in the 1960s and 1970s, a number of public school students were subjected to an instructional experiment called "new math." The goal of new math wasn't to focus on getting the correct answers; instead, it was on demonstrating an understanding of the process. As simply stated in the classic Tom Lehrer song, "New Math" was "so very simple, that *only* a child can do it." Tragically, due to this experiment, a generation of adults may not feel as secure in higher math ability as they likely would have under a more traditional approach. Some colleagues of that generation, familiar with neo-Piagetian research, have wondered—jokingly—if maybe they got stuck in the concrete operations stage of their mathematic intelligence. Joking aside, is it possible to be at a formal operations level in some areas of intelligence, while being stuck at other levels in other intelligences? This can be very possible in music, because it is not difficult to identify adults who can't keep a **beat** or can't carry a tune. Although this hasn't been investigated at a rigorous level of research, the idea is enticing, and perhaps an investigation into this overlapping phenomenon could reveal more aspects of learning along multiple dimensions that we have yet to discover.

## Cognitive Processing Styles

Cognitive processing styles deal with how humans prefer to process information and the environment that they choose when doing so. Dunn and Dunn (1984) proposed a theory advancing the idea that several factors affect learning. These factors include emotional, sociological, physical, and environmental influences such as sound, light, temperature, and food. For example, if children are uncomfortable or distracted, they may not be interested in singing as effectively as they could. Notice that the idea is similar to Maslow's hierarchy of needs (later in this chapter).

Barbe and Swassing (1979) suggest that learning modality preferences are a specific type of learning style. They state that learners prefer to process information through one or a combination of several sensory channels: *auditory* (one child learns best by hearing and prefers verbal instructions and other aural input from the teacher or other students), *visual* (another child learns best by seeing and prefers to see a presentation and read instructions), and/or *kinesthetic* channels (yet another child learns best by moving, participating, touching, and being physically involved in the learning process). Effective teaching involves all three modalities. Teachers are encouraged to teach to a child's strongest modality and reinforce through the other two modalities. If faced with twenty children with various strongest modalities, using several modalities in all instruction is best (Persellin 1993). The kinesthetic modality is especially appropriate for young children and music. Gardner's multiple intelligence theory (discussed previously) is related to learning styles, in the sense that each of the intelligences may be thought of as a learning modality.

There has been a great deal of interest in field dependency and independency in cognitive processing over the past fifteen years or so, and its effect on learning and teaching in the schools. However, the actual theory behind it goes back many years and was applied in the air force during World War II. Men who wanted to be pilots had to undergo a test in which they were required to keep their physical orientation in check the whole time, useful when pilots are required to execute barrel rolls or to pull an airplane out of a spin. Pilots who were able to keep their visual bearings were generally referred to as more field independent (FI), whereas those who could not—and therefore were not able to become pilots—were more field dependent (FD).

Field dependency refers to a cognitive processing style that is generally set in place in our very youngest years of existence, so unlike the Myers-Briggs personality profile, it generally doesn't change during life, although people can learn to modify their field dependence-independence (FDI), especially as teachers. Simply put, people who are field dependent tend to prefer group learning, step-by-step instructions, and to know exactly what is expected from them. For example, a learners who are field dependent would want very detailed review sheets for a test, would read the step-by-step instructions on how to hook up a DVD or VCR player before attempting to hook them up, and would likely enjoy working in group situations to solve problems. People who are field dependent would look at all the trees in the forest and appreciate them on how they all look together before looking for unusual trees. On the other hand, people who are field independent would prefer to figure out what is supposed to be learned, would ignore the instruction manual for the DVD or VCR and only look at it if there is a problem, and prefer to work alone. People who are field independent would most likely ignore all the trees in the forest and fixate on the scraggly looking crape myrtle that somehow got in there by accident.

Field dependency is a matter of degree rather than two simple types. There are tests that can be taken to help determine the degree to which you are more FI or FD (the *hidden embedded figures test* by Witkin et al. [1971] is standard, but is out of print), and most people are somewhere in the middle, encompassing cognitive-processing characteristics from both extremes. A reason why field dependency has come to the forefront is that most children learn best from a FD-structured teacher. Teachers who are field dependent would be very detailed in how they present the learning and assessment, whereas teachers who are field independent would generally not be. Teachers who are field independent can learn how to be field dependent, however. Readers who are interested in this area are urged to start by reading Saracho and Spodek (2007).

## Personality

Children's personalities may have strong impacts on their learning and learning styles, and the same will also affect teachers' teaching styles. The Myers-Briggs Type Indicator (Briggs-Myers and McCaulley 1992) measures preferences by generating sixteen personality types based on four scales: extroversion/introversion, sensing/intuition, thinking/feeling, and judgment/perception. Each of the learning style type theories may be valuable in adjusting instruction to the needs of individual students. In education, results from studies have indicated that music teachers with more extroverted personalities tend to gravitate toward elementary teaching and those with introverted personalities tend to gravitate toward secondary or college teaching. A number of interesting research findings concerning musicians and personality have emerged over the years, and readers who are especially interested in this aspect are urged to investigate *The Musical Temperament* by the noted British psychologist Anthony Kemp.

*Summary on cognitive-processing styles:* In music education, information on teaching with cognitive-processing styles in mind indicates that we need to consider not only the cognitive ability of our students based on their ages but also the manner in which they process information and turn it into knowledge, which leads to the development of knowing how and knowing why discussed earlier in this chapter. Examples of cognitive approaches would include discovery learning, essay writing, composing, improvising, presenting group reports or compositions, engaging in problem-solving compositional activities where there is more than one answer, and the like. Furthermore, teachers need to consider their own cognitive-processing styles and how they affect their teaching styles, and modify them if necessary. Ultimate teachers can accommodate a multitude of learning styles successfully.

## Social-Emotional Approaches

These two approaches represent two of the most well known, but that doesn't mean those are the only two that are referenced in education. The contemporary authors Maxine Greene, Michael Apple, and Nel Noddings detail other comprehensive approaches.

**BANDURA'S SOCIAL LEARNING THEORY**  The social learning theory of Albert Bandura is also considered a behaviorist theory. Bandura stressed the importance of children observing models of behavior that they can later replicate. A primary mode of learning for children is through imitation. For example, teachers can model music behaviors for children such as singing with good posture, keeping a steady beat on a drum, and listening carefully while music is being played. Bandura (1977) proposed the theory of reciprocal determinism, in which a person's behavior is based on an evaluation of the situation. This behavior changes the situation, requiring a new evaluation and a new behavior decision. For example, children enjoy the challenge of playing a new pattern on an instrument. Once they learn that pattern, they are ready to learn a more challenging pattern and raise the expectations of their performance. If they are unsuccessful in mastering the new pattern, they lower their standards of performance. Bandura objected

Student playing steady beat on conga drum.
*Photo courtesy of Union City School District, Pennsylvania*

to psychology's behavioral focus on powerful external forces and broadened the focus of behaviorism. He began to make a distinction between learning and performance. His theories are a bridge between behaviorism and cognition.

**MASLOW'S BASIC LEVELS OF NEEDS**    Abraham Maslow (1998) stated that humans are motivated by five basic levels of needs: (1) physical needs, (2) safety and security, (3) belonging and affection, (4) self-esteem, and (5) self-actualization. Maslow believed that people had to have their basic needs met to be truly self-actualized. If children are hungry, they are going to be thinking about food rather than learning and initiatives. The government program Head Start addressed the need with breakfast and lunch for students. If children have a low sense of self-esteem, they will be defensive or compensate in some other way. Only if the first four needs are met can they fully devote themselves to fulfilling their potential. The idea of self-actualization is related to the idea of flow (Csikszentmihalyi 1990). In music, flow or self-actualization is often achieved during **improvisation.** Flow can be achieved during improvisation when the task is not too easy or too difficult and the feedback is immediate.

## INTERSECTION OF LEARNING AND INSTRUCTION

Instructional strategies refer to formulas or sequences that work with the various cognitive, behavioral, and social-emotional theories. Their goals are to provide blueprints for effective instruction. It is important to note that the following instructional strategies represent only a few of many available, and that these strategies can be mixed and matched to work with others. The idea to keep in mind is that people learn many ways; one strategy may work for some students, but may not work for others, so varying strategies can be beneficial to effective teaching. Chapter 12 on Designing Instruction further expands the application of these theories within the development of effective instruction.

### Bloom's Taxonomy

Benjamin Bloom's original taxonomy of educational objectives is used extensively in public schools. The schools stress the importance of higher-level thinking skills rather than rote or drill-and-kill exercises. Bloom identified six levels of thought processes in a hierarchical taxonomy, from simple to complex (Bloom and Krathwohl 1956). The following six levels encourage teachers to use higher-order thinking skills in their questioning and when creating teaching strategies:

1. *Knowledge*—simple recall of facts or labeling ("Who were the characters in the story about instruments that we heard yesterday?")
2. *Comprehension*—ability to manipulate, reconstruct, and summarize knowledge ("Let's tell that story again from the beginning.")
3. *Application*—ability to take information and apply it to another task ("This time, let's add instruments as we tell that story.")
4. *Analysis*—ability to break knowledge into parts and show relationships among parts ("What instruments should be played when the three bears walk upstairs?")
5. *Synthesis*—ability to take parts of a whole and reorder or create a new product ("Lets create a song for the ending of our story using tone bells.")
6. *Evaluation*—ability to assess the value of a product ("What would you change about the way we told the story with instruments?")

Recently, educational researchers have revised Bloom's original taxonomy to contemporary terminology and understanding. In one of these revisions, the nouns (for example, knowledge, comprehension) were changed to verbs (for example, remembering, understanding, applying, analyzing, evaluating, and creating) (Anderson et al. 2000).

Ideally, teachers are engaging children in all six levels, with more emphasis on the complex levels (four through six). Classroom observations indicate, however, that

99 percent of questions that teachers ask are lower-level questions (Watkins 1993). The upper levels also work with the *knowing how* and *knowing why* levels of knowing, whereas the lower levels (one and two) work with the *knowing that* level.

## Constructivism

The underlying idea of constructivist theory is that children learn best when they are active learners and interact with the environment. These experiences and ideas become meaningful as children process learning and develop their own understanding of the world through their experiences. The role of the educator is that of a facilitator setting up an environment conducive to learning. Children become active seekers of knowledge from many sources (DeVries and Kohlberg 1987; Vygotsky 1962).

John Dewey was among the first to write about ideas promoting a constructivist approach. He advocated a child-centered curriculum in which active learning, music, and the other arts played an important role. Intellectual development was encouraged through problem solving, discovery, and exploration (Dewey 1966). Other constructivist principles have been summarized in the following material (DeVries and Kohlberg 1987; Kamii and Ewing 1996; Vygotsky 1962). It is also important to note that constructivism is a strong educational influence, and much of it is based not only on psychological research, but on philosophical inquiry as well. The principles of constructivist learning, laid out many years ago, have also been investigated, revised, queried, and researched under contemporary context (Anderson et al. 2001; Bruner 1996; Fostnot 2005; Israel et al. 2005; Rockmore 2005).

The following are principles of constructivist thinking:

1. Constructing meaning is learning. Learners construct knowledge for themselves.
2. Learning is an active process in which learners use sensory input and construct meaning out of it. Learning is not the passive acceptance of knowledge in the sense that children process information. It is an active process that engages learners. Physical actions and hands-on experience are necessary, but activities that engage the mind are also crucial to the learning process.
3. Teachers provide learners with opportunities to interact with sensory data, and to construct their own world. Children's prior knowledge and interests should be used when planning instruction. The development of independence is a primary aim of education.
4. Vygotsky (1962) refers to the zone of proximal development. This is an area of development between a level in which the child has achieved competence and a higher level in which the child is not yet competent. The zone is the in-between area from which children may reach out to an adult for help in understanding. The teacher can then plan activities within this zone to scaffold (Vygotsky's term) or provide structure to learning.
5. Learning involves language, and the language used influences learning. Vygotsky described the importance of language in learning and creating new thoughts and acquiring new knowledge. Norm Chomsky also supported this theory by stating that all children are born with the ability to acquire language and tend to acquire skills in language at the same age (Chomsky 1957; Standing 1957).
6. Learning is a social activity. Conversation, interaction with others, and the application of knowledge are all integral aspects of learning.
7. Learning is contextual. We learn in relationship to what else we know, what we believe, our prejudices, and our fears.
8. Learning is sociocultural. Discussion and problem solving between children and adults help children become socialized within their culture (Vygotsky 1978).
9. Play is important in learning. Teachers need to provide children many opportunities to play. Musical play may include making up **chants** or songs to go with games or movements, instrumental exploration, singing with puppets, ordering and classifying sounds, and improvising music. Through various types of play, a child's conceptual abilities are stretched.

## Process Learning

There are many different learning theories and little definitive research on how different learning theory strategies affect learning. As more studies of learning strategies and learning theories become available, we may someday reach agreement on the best or correct learning theory. For now, we do not have agreement on an overarching learning theory, but we do have agreement on principles of best practice.

The idea of principles of best practice is an effective way to use the best and most valuable ideas from several learning theories. For example, one idea from behaviorism is the idea of positive reinforcement. When a teacher reinforces a behavior with positive comments, the child's behavior tends to increase. Conversely, if a teacher does not reinforce a particular behavior, that behavior tends to decrease. We also find that positive reinforcement of behavior is usually more effective than negative reinforcement. For example, reinforcing a child who is behaving correctly is more effective at changing long-term behavior than giving negative reinforcement such as yelling, "Stop that!"

Another example of a best practice is present in several learning theories. Among several theories, including Montessori, Piaget, and constructivism, we find the idea that children usually learn more readily when engaged in active learning. For example, an objective may be to understand how the length of a vibrating string is related to the highness and lowness of pitch, and the mathematical relationships of length and pitch. A lecture with the children passively listening is not terribly effective. A more effective learning strategy would be to organize the environment to engage each child in active learning. An example of such a strategy would be a project to experiment with a small box and rubber bands of different lengths.

In the 1990s, the National Association for the Education of Young Children (NAEYC) and other organizations collected ideas regarding developmentally appropriate practice (DAP) and principles of best practice gleaned from research and common strategies of effective teachers. Much of what we have already discussed in this chapter is assimilated and accommodated into the DAP model.

## Developmentally Appropriate Practice

There is no single accepted theory in child development, probably because development and learning are so complex that no present theory is adequate to explain these phenomena. There are, however, principles that inform practice. Developmentally appropriate practice is an extremely important concept. The broad-based review of the literature on early childhood education by the NAEYC generates three dimensions of information or knowledge for developmentally appropriate practices and a set of principles to inform early childhood practice:

1. *What is known about child development and learning*—knowledge of age-related human characteristics that permits general predictions within an age range about what activities, materials, interactions, or experiences will be safe, healthy, interesting, achievable, and also challenging to children
2. *What is known about the strengths, interests, and needs of each individual child in the group*—the ability to adapt for and be responsive to inevitable individual variation
3. *Knowledge of the social and cultural contexts in which children live*—ensuring that learning experiences are meaningful, relevant, and respectful for the participating children and their families (National Association for the Education of Young Children 1997)

**NATIONAL ASSOCIATION FOR THE EDUCATION OF YOUNG CHILDREN**   The National Association for the Education of Young Children (NAEYC) lists twelve empirically based principles of child development and learning that inform and guide decisions about developmentally appropriate practice. NAEYC defines principles as generalizations that are sufficiently reliable to be taken into account when making decisions (Katz 1989; Katz and Chard 1995). The following italicized list resulted from a broad-based review of the early childhood literature (NAEYC 1997). Musical examples are added to the NAEYC's principles.

1. *Domains of children's development—physical, social, emotional, and cognitive—are closely related. Development in one domain influences and is influenced by development in other domains.* This principle is important to music education because music touches several domains of children's development. For example, a music singing game involves domains of the physical (movement), social (group in a circle), and emotional (expressive import of music). The cognitive domain may be used in games such as "Lucy Locket," where the child is required to deduce where the pocket is hidden (Forrai 1974).

2. *Development occurs in a relatively orderly sequence, with later abilities, skills, and knowledge building on those already acquired. Human development research indicates that relatively stable, predictable sequences of growth and change occur in children during the first nine years of life.* The *relatively orderly sequence* helps with organizing and planning experiences for children. For example, before a musical ability such as clapping eighth and **quarter note** patterns develops, the basic ability to keep a **steady beat** needs to be present. Basic musical understandings such as faster and slower or louder and softer belong in the early childhood curriculum and need to be mastered as a foundation to later musical abilities.

3. *Development proceeds at varying rates from child to child as well as unevenly within different areas of each child's functioning. Each child is a unique person with an individual pattern and timing of growth, as well as individual personality, temperament, learning style, and experiential and family background.* There is a wide range of variation among an individual child's musical development. Any development schedule is at best approximate, and a child's age is only a crude index of developmental maturity. It is important to recognize individual differences in children and adjust the educational environment to meet the child's needs.

4. *Early experiences have both cumulative and delayed effects on individual children's development; optimal periods exist for certain types of development and learning.* An *optimal* period refers to those periods in which development will be faster or easier. For example, learning to sing in tune is easier during the ages between 3 years and 6 years than between 25 years and 28 years of age. Over 100 years ago, Maria Montessori wrote about *sensitive periods* (when children may learn specific skills more easily). Authors often write about *optimal* periods as if they were *critical* periods. An optimal period is used to refer to those periods in which development will be faster or easier. *Critical* periods are defined as time frames in which no development or stunted development will occur if requisite stimulation is not present. The brain may be open to experience of a particular kind only during narrow periods of time (Flohr and Hodges 2006).

5. *Development proceeds in predictable directions toward greater complexity, organization, and internalization.* Learning in music proceeds from what Bruner called enactive (concrete) learning to symbolic or representational knowledge (Boardman 1988b, 1989; Bruner 1983). For example, children move to very fast music and slow music long before they understand that the musical term *presto* means faster than *lento*. Developmentally appropriate music programs provide a variety of musical experiences where the children *do* music. The children are actively engaged in listening, singing, moving, creating, and playing. Gradually, children are helped to acquire symbolic knowledge through representing their experiences through improvising, creating, dramatic play, and prior to music reading experiences such as moving their hands to show the contour of the music.

6. *Development and learning occur in and are influenced by multiple social and cultural contexts. Development is best understood within the sociocultural context of the family, educational setting, community, and broader society.* For example, a child in a musically rich family may be negatively affected by an educational setting with no music in the curriculum. Young children are influenced by the pop music culture in society. The NAEYC also makes the point that, because culture is often discussed along with diversity or multiculturalism, parents and teachers often do not recognize

the powerful role that culture plays in influencing the musical development of all children.

7. *Children are active learners, drawing on direct physical and social experience as well as culturally transmitted knowledge to construct their own understandings of the world around them.* The principles of developmentally appropriate practice are based on several constructivist, interactive theories (for example, those of Dewey, Piaget, and Vygotsky). These ideas support the use of music centers and free music exploration where children are free to form their own hypotheses and try them out through physical manipulation of sound sources and through social interaction. The active learning approach of Montessori may be used to enrich active musical experience and give children an opportunity to try out their thought processes by observing, reflecting on their findings, asking questions, and formulating answers.

8. *Development and learning result from interaction of biological maturation and the environment, which includes both the physical and social worlds that children live in.* A long and lively debate on nature versus nurture is still alive among behaviorists who focus on the environmental influences for development and the maturationists who focus on an unfolding of predetermined, hereditary characteristics. New advances in neuroscience have addressed the ancient debate of nature versus nurture. Nelson and Bloom (1997) cite numerous demonstrations that show how positive or negative early experiences can alter both the structure and function of the brain. Development is affected by interplay between environment and heredity. Human brains at the prenatal stages are already interacting with the environment (Standley 2002). Also, it is important to remember that a child's brain is not the same as an adult brain. There is agreement that, during the first decade of life, a child typically has up to twice as much neural activity and connections as adults. The brain makes connections during the prenatal period and throughout life. Some connections are found to be predetermined genetically, and others develop from environmental influences (Flohr and Hodges 2006).

9. *Play is an important vehicle for children's social, emotional, and cognitive development, as well as a reflection of their development. When teachers provide a thematic organization for play, offer appropriate props, space, and time, and become involved in the play by extending and elaborating on children's ideas, children's language and literacy skills can be enhanced.* A day and environment can be organized for music play. Sociodramatic play for 3- to 6-year-old children is addressed in storytelling with music and dramatizing books with music. Music centers filled with sound sources offer children an opportunity for play. Also, music singing games may be used for group play. For a summary on play, see *Early Childhood Education Today* (Morrison 2006).

10. *Development advances when children have opportunities to practice newly acquired skills as well as when they experience a challenge just beyond the level of their present mastery. Moreover, in a task just beyond a child's independent reach, adults and more competent peers contribute significantly to development by providing the supportive scaffolding that allows children to take the next step.* Best practice includes minimizing the chance of repeated failure and giving children a chance to practice musical skills. A preservice teacher once asked 5-year-olds to play a game with a song about north, south, east, and west. The children were asked to point to the four directions and move. The lesson crashed (the children lost attention and began to misbehave), but provided a good example of a challenge too far above the present level of student competence. The Manhattanville Music Curriculum Project (MMCP) described in the methods and creativity chapters provides a good example of sequencing experiences with the supportive scaffolding that allows children to take the next step. The techniques of free and guided exploration help children practice acquired skills and challenge them to move beyond their present level.

11. *Children demonstrate different modes of knowing and learning and different ways of representing what they know. The principle of diverse modalities implies that teachers should provide more than one mode for learning. Each child needs to use a preferred mode of learning to capitalize on individual strengths. Children need opportunities to develop in the*

*modes or intelligences they need to strengthen.* Earlier, this chapter examined concepts of learner modalities (for example, visual and aural) and Gardner's theory of multiple intelligences. An example of good practice is shown in collections of bounces and other techniques (Feierabend 2000). Although children are bouncing and singing, they are offered stimulation for their hearing, tactile (kinesthetic), and visual senses. A common technique in music education is to ask children to sing, to watch the teacher move, and then to move their own arms to show the contour of the music, thereby engaging the auditory, kinesthetic, and visual sense modalities. Music experiences are capable of addressing several of Gardner's intelligences including musical, spatial, bodily or kinesthetic, intrapersonal, interpersonal, linguistic, and logical or mathematical.

12. *Children develop and learn best in the context of a community where they are safe and valued, their physical needs are met, and they feel psychologically secure. In addition, children's development in all areas is influenced by their ability to establish and maintain a limited number of positive, consistent primary relationships with adults and other children.* Music experiences address social and emotional needs of children. Chapter 1 examines self-expression as an intrinsic benefit of music. A good example of how music experiences nurture social needs is found in singing games. As the children play a game such as "Here Comes a Bluebird" (Forrai 1974), they engage in a community where everyone forms a circle and each child in turn invites children through their "window." As children experience singing, moving, and playing instruments together, they form a musical community not unlike a band or orchestra. This musical community is a powerful force in the lives of children. High school graduates often speak of their musical community in statements such as, "If it were not for band, I don't know what might have happened to me in high school."

**BELIEFS ABOUT CHILDREN AND DEVELOPMENTALLY AND INDIVIDUALLY APPROPRIATE MUSICAL EXPERIENCES**    In addition to the twelve NAEYC principles, MENC lists ten beliefs about young children designed to guide decisions about developmentally appropriate practice (MENC 1991):

All children have musical potential. Every child has the potential for successful, meaningful interactions with music. The development of this potential, through numerous encounters with a wide variety of music and abundant opportunities to participate regularly in developmentally appropriate music activities, is the right of every young child.

Children bring their own unique interest and abilities to a music learning environment. All children will take away that bit of knowledge and skill that they are uniquely capable of understanding and developing. Children must be left, as much as possible, in control of their own learning. They should be provided with a rich environment that offers many possible routes for them to explore as they grow in awareness and curiosity about music. This belief is related to constructivist theory (see the previously cited NAEYC principle number 7) and promotes a child-centered view of the learning process.

Very young children are capable of developing critical thinking skills through musical ideas. Children use thinking skills when making musical judgments and choices. Possible critical thinking skills include grouping instruments or rhythms according to common attributes, classifying (for example, large and small maracas sound similar), identifying similarities and differences (for example, two rhythm patterns are the same or different), finding patterns, recognizing patterns (for example, simple musical forms, rhythm patterns, or melodic patterns), placing music items in an order, and sequencing (for example, animal sounds in the song "Bought me a Cat" or short phrases in a computer composition program). Brophy offers a review of critical thinking skills in music (2000, 234–45).

Children come to early childhood music experiences from diverse backgrounds. Their home languages and cultures are to be valued and seen as attributes that enrich everyone in the learning environment. Music from various cultures is shown to be valued when we, as parents and teachers, play examples and sing songs from other cultures. Music styles from all cultures, especially styles from cultures in the school community, are appropriate.

Children should experience exemplary musical sounds, activities, and materials. Children's learning time is valuable and should not be wasted on experiences with music or activities of trite or questionable quality. For example, young children find singing pitches below middle C physically difficult. Giving children models of singing below middle C is not developmentally appropriate. In the same way, many recordings of children's music are of questionable quality. The recordings often use only synthesized sound sources and singing models that may promote vocal damage as the children try to match the recorded sound. Although MENC advocates diverse styles of music, the performances and recordings should be of the highest musical quality and developmentally appropriate for the child. Feierabend points out, "If children are to grow to appreciate good music, they must be nurtured with excellent examples of children's music literature sung with sensitive expression" (Feierabend 1996, 20).

Children should not be encumbered with the need to meet performance goals. Opportunities should be available for children to develop accurate singing, rhythmic responses to music, and performance skills on instruments. Each child's attainment of a predetermined performance level, however, is neither essential nor appropriate. Although part of music education is performance-based, the major objective for young children should not be performance. Children need time to develop without pressure to achieve set goals. Instruction should not be willy-nilly; good instruction uses goals and objectives. Also, children develop musical skills and concepts at different and individual paces, so that predetermined performance goals should be viewed with some skepticism.

Children's play is their work. Children should have opportunities for individual musical play, such as in a music corner, as well as for group musical play, such as singing games. Children learn within a playful environment. Play provides a safe place to try on the roles of others, to fantasize, and to explore new ideas. Children's play involves imitation and improvisation. See NAEYC principle number 9.

Children learn best in pleasant physical and social environments. Music learning contexts will be most effective when they include (1) play, (2) games, (3) conversations, (4) pictorial imagination, (5) stories, (6) shared reflections on life events and family activities, and (7) personal and group involvement in social tasks. Dominant use of drill-type activities and exercises as well as worksheet tasks will not provide the kind of active, manipulative, and creative musical environment essential to the development of young minds. Repetition of songs, rhythms, and drill-type activities are not necessarily examples of bad instruction. However, the dominant theme of instruction for young children should be one of exploration rather than drill-type activities.

Diverse learning environments are needed to serve the developmental needs of many individual children. Children interact with musical materials in their own way based on their unique experiences and developmental stages. One child may display sophistication and confidence in creating songs in response to dolls. Another child, in the same setting, may move the dolls around without uttering a sound, but leaves the area content in having shared the music play. The silent participator often is later heard playing in another area, softly singing to a different set of dolls—demonstrating a delayed response. A recurring theme in this book is about the unique nature of individual children. Generalizations about children often fail in their breadth to inform parents and teachers about the wide variation in children's musical characteristics and development.

Children need effective adult models. Parents and teachers who provide music in their child's life are creating the most powerful route to the child's successful involvement in the art. A major mode of learning for young children is imitation. Young children need the best possible adult models. We need to remember that early care and nurture have a decisive, long-lasting impact on how people develop, their ability to learn, and their capacity to regulate their own emotions.

## Processing Multiple Objectives

When we think about how we process information, another principle is evident—children (as well as adults) learn multiple items during a period of instruction. Experiences are rich in content. However, intending that students will learn an objective during a period of instruction does not guarantee that they will achieve that objective. Children may learn more than the objective of a lesson. A child's brain does not always learn or work on the objective of the teacher. A 7-year-old child in a class of twenty-five children may miss the main objective of the lesson while learning that it is fun to tease class neighbors or make a paper airplane. Intending that students will learn an objective during a period of instruction does not stop them from learning items other than the intended objective. The item children learn may be the name of a new child in class rather than the mathematics objective. In a thirty-minute class period, a child may grasp nothing, only the main objective of the teacher, or any number of knowledge items—related or unrelated to the main objective.

## Enrichment

The integration of music and other fine arts into the entire curriculum is a current educational topic. Often a word such as *integration* becomes a buzzword that carries multiple meanings and connotations. Integration is usually thought of as a good idea and is used to help justify the place of music in the curriculum. The utilitarian view of music is not new.

The categories of extrinsic musical benefits and intrinsic musical benefits are helpful in discussions about the idea of integration. Extrinsic benefits are those benefits that are outside of music. Extrinsic music benefits for young children include fostering motor development, promoting cultural heritage, providing a release of tension, teaching language development, and utilizing music as a carrier of information (for example, the "ABC" song), as a cue for nap time, and to help teach other subjects such as reading or mathematics.

One philosophical concern with extrinsic benefits is that there are usually other ways of achieving these benefits. For example, the "ABC" song helps children learn the alphabet, but the alphabet may also be learned from a game, oral drill and practice, or a writing activity. Although extrinsic benefits may be very important in a child's development, views that emphasize the ability of music to teach other subjects or provide relaxation should be viewed with caution. Music has important worth in and of its own self, in addition to its use to achieve academic and personal purposes. Music clearly belongs in the young child's life as a distinct discipline and as an art form.

What are often called intrinsic benefits of music education include self-expression (Peery et al. 1987), as well as emotional expression and aesthetic enjoyment (Leonhard and House 1972; Merriam 1964; Reimer 2002). The extrinsic benefits are like frosting on the cake (Flohr, Miller, and deBeus 2000). The intrinsic beliefs are the cake and are satisfying even without the frosting. The intrinsic benefits are those benefits accomplished so well by music that other subjects are clearly less effective. Imagine a motion picture without music. Or rent a movie, turn off the volume, and watch a scene or two. What would that movie be like without music? Would the danger, chase, scary, or love scenes produce the same emotional impact in viewers?

Many thoughtful music educators find the idea of using or integrating music with little regard to the intrinsic benefits of music problematic. We propose the idea of *enriching* music with other subjects and *enriching* other subjects with music. Two important concepts outlined in the next part support the idea of enrichment—parallel objectives and teaching the whole child.

## Parallel Objectives

Earlier in this chapter, we visited the idea of how the human mind learns multiple items within a period of instruction. Now we are ready to view how we can design a period of instruction to contain at least two objectives. For example, in a music lesson, the music objective might be to sing a song with a pleasing tone quality and accuracy of pitch. The lesson may be enriched by the addition of a book about the song. The term *parallel objectives* refers to two objectives addressed simultaneously by the same experience. The experience could be taught for either of the objectives alone or both of the objectives together. A music teacher might teach an experience while enriching the experience with mathematics and a mathematical objective. A mathematics teacher might teach the same experience while enriching the experience with music and a musical objective.

For example, a book and song may be used simultaneously to create a parallel learning objective experience (Flohr and Smith 2008). Jez Alborough wrote a delightful book about a bear and little boy titled, *It's the Bear!* (Alborough 1994). Two possible parallel objectives from music and language arts for kindergarten or first grade can be threaded through an experience with this book: (1) music—to sing in a group with pleasing tone quality, and (2) language arts—to listen to stories being read aloud and to participate actively (react, speculate, join in, read along) when predictable and patterned selections are read aloud.

During the lesson, a music teacher's primary objective might be the singing and the music objective might be enriched with the language arts experience of the book. In the same way, the language arts teacher's main objective might be enriched by the experience with the song. Both teachers would *not* be using music nor using language arts, but rather enriching the instruction with both subjects.

We know from brain research that music and language arts, for example, activate different parts of the brain. By incorporating music and language arts into one experience, teachers are able to enable more activation. The increased brain activity serves to engage children.

We also know that different children have different learning styles. Designing engaging experiences helps address the children's learning style preferences. For example, the music aspects of the experience can help to engage aural learners whereas the language arts aspects of the experience can help engage visual learners.

### The Whole Child

The second concept important to the idea of enrichment through use of parallel objectives is the concept of teaching the whole child. Consider that children are born with certain physical, cognitive, social, and emotional potential rather than cognitive potential alone (Hodgkinson 2006).

No effective teacher works entirely with one aspect of a child's learning. Do effective music teachers consider only musical development? Do language arts teachers consider only language development? If we think back to our own childhood, to those teachers who had the greatest impact on our learning and development, we think of those teachers who enriched instruction with multiple ways of knowing and those teachers who exhibited concern about our entire development.

### Social Concerns

Teachers can bring students to more efficient learning by enriching instruction with parallel objectives. If music teachers can add a language arts objective to a lesson without jeopardizing the learning of the music objective, there is no reason why they should not do so. In addition to helping the child's overall learning, music teachers will become more valued by students, parents, and other teachers. If music teachers express interest in only the music achievements of the children, then the school community will not see them as vital parts of the school community.

### Summary and Relationship of Music Learning and Instruction

This section addresses the psychological aspects of how music learning occurs. Music learning (including listening, playing, singing, moving, and creating) generally develops in a sequential manner, rather than in isolated and unconnected experiences. Teachers wishing to use music in the classroom need to be aware of how children perceive, process, and apply musical knowledge, not only to music but also to other areas of inquiry. Future elementary classroom teachers and music specialists are required to take education classes about learning theory. This chapter will provide a bridge from those classes to music learning. Recent brain research includes findings applicable to music learning that have gained interest in the past few years.

## Experiences for Groups or Individuals

Let's see how you can apply what you have just read. The following activities will require some thought, and answers may not come easily. However, long and hard thinking is a requirement for becoming an excellent teacher.

1. Compose a hierarchal list of ways of knowing (that, how, and why) in the following fields of music:
   a. Music theory and composition
   b. Music history
   c. Music education
   d. Music performance
   e. Jazz
2. Do an online search to find out more about field dependency and independency. In which direction do you suspect you lean? How would you work with students whose cognitive-processing styles are the opposite of yours?
3. Define and describe your philosophical beliefs about music and music education. Do they correlate with the information presented in this chapter?
4. Think of a class in which you may not be doing well this semester. Apply your knowledge of cognitive-processing styles, personality, and developmental stages to see if you can find a strategy that can help *you* find a way to make the course work for you so you could do better.

## Chapter Conclusions

The most obvious conclusion of this chapter is that knowledge, teaching, and learning are all intertwined. A one-size-fits-all approach does not work. Teachers need to be aware of the many ways that not only their students learn, but also how they learn as well. Finally, we are promoting deeper levels of knowledge for music teachers and also for music students. The cycle of teacher as learner and learner as teacher is the strongest dynamic of education.

## CHAPTER 3

# Elements of Music

**This chapter addresses the following:**

## INTRODUCTION

Basic **elements of music** need to be thoroughly understood to appreciate and teach aspects of music. Although most people understand music at an emotional and aesthetic level (see Chapter 2), this isn't really all there is to it. To elementary teachers, music can be used to teach many aspects of science, particularly in the physics subfield of acoustics. So, before we begin, we'll give you a brief background on the development of musical sound from a theoretical and scientific context.

The performance of music was not always viewed as noble and admirable. As far back as the European medieval period, the performance of music was sometimes associated with wickedness, evil, and savagery. The devil himself was known to be a very fine violinist, illustrated in particular techniques, such as the "Devil's Trill" Violin Sonata by Tartini (1749), and the depiction of the devil as a violin player in pieces such as Stravinsky's "The Soldier's Tale" (1918) and Gounod's opera *Faust* (1859). The honorable way to study music was through its mathematical relationships and vibrations, which eventually gave rise to the field of acoustics, and the human perception of sound called psychoacoustics. One of the most prominent theories of the medieval period was the "music of the spheres," attributed to Pythagoras and further developed by Boethius, which proposed that everything in the universe (planets, people, trees, and so on) vibrated in harmony (Schrade 1947). Today, we see an application of this in current physics theory. Dr. Brian Greene of Columbia University wrote the book *The Elegant Universe*, introducing string theory to the general public, which led to a NOVA special series on string theory (Greene 2003). The relationship between the ancient music of the spheres with current string theory is undeniable. Sound and vibration have always enthralled humankind, and finding ways to organize it into a recognizable medium with meaning has been a goal since the invention of **solmization** and music notation.

You are probably familiar with solmization, although you may not recognize it by that term. If you have ever sung "doe, a deer, a female deer" from *The Sound of Music,* then you have sung the **notes** of the Western eight-note musical scale. The system of solmization we use in the United States was developed by a Catholic monk named Guido d'Arezzo around A.D. 1020 (Miller 1973). Although the current system we use differs a bit from the one developed then, it is unique in that we still widely use the system in teaching music. Father Guido wasn't content to just come up with this; he also strongly influenced the foundations of written musical notation, which led to what we use now to notate and preserve music (ibid.). With solmization, we have a basis for understanding melody. In notation, we have a way to write down the music so it can be shared, printed, and published easier. In acoustics, we study how sound is created and extended; in psychoacoustics, we study how people perceive sound. The foundations we discuss in this chapter have a basis in science and math. However, when we throw in the variable of culture, then certain sounds can have specific meanings attached to them that may be meaningful in one culture but have no value in another. All music, no matter what kind it is, from European medieval to Javanese gamelan to American hip-hop, is all based on the same elemental building blocks. What are the differences among these kinds of music? We will find the blocks are arranged differently, as is human meaning attached to the resultant sounds as they are processed by the human brain.

In our discussion of building blocks, we will differentiate between unique single blocks (primary blocks) and terminology used when they are combined in specific ways (secondary blocks). These will be addressed to help you understand ways to teach them successfully.

## ELEMENTS OF MUSIC: PRIMARY BLOCKS

The primary building blocks include rhythm, pitch, and melody.

### Rhythm

Rhythm is a primary component of music—either the perceived presence of it or the perceived lack of it, especially in contemporary music. Before any discussion on rhythm can proceed, we first have to look at the most important part of it—the underlying steady beat.

The steady beat is the heartbeat of music. Beats can be easy or difficult to perceive, depending upon the way the composer wrote the music and how the listener perceives it. For example, such works as the "Octet," "Petroushka," and "The Soldier's Tale" by Igor Stravinsky and "The Chairman Dances" by John Adams are very deceptive in the use of Audiences listening to both works definitely get a sense of the beats moving in a strong-weak, strong-weak sense (musically, the sense of the meter or timing of the beats) but the composers actually wrote the music much differently, requiring the performers to play it (and count very carefully) to give that sense of rhythm to the listeners.

Many natural phenomena move in a sense of a steady beat or vibration. If you sit on the beach and watch ocean waves, you may notice that particularly strong waves are often followed by several weaker waves. One can hear this with closed eyes while listening to the breaking waves. Solar waves work the same way. Animals and humans run in a beat—with one for bipeds, such as humans, and another for quadrupeds, such as wolves being stronger and contributing more energy. Our own language, English, also relies on groupings of beats, especially when reading poems in iambic pentameter or in reciting limericks. Read the original Middle English prologue to *Canterbury Tales* by Geoffrey Chaucer out loud for an excellent example of strong and weak beats in the English language. The sense of beat is innate to humans, but the rub is that humans may each have a different sense of the steady beat's speed (that is, **tempo**).

### The Research Base

We begin life with our mother's heartbeat. By the third trimester, babies in the womb are able to hear their mother's heartbeat, which is within inches of developing ears and hearing. Ability to keep the steady beat and preference for tempo are affected by the interaction of age, type of instrument or movement used, individual differences, whether the child is asked to keep a tempo to the music or without hearing music, tempo of the music, and culture. It is too simplistic to say that all 4-year-olds prefer a tempo of 130 beats per minute (bpm) or that children can keep the steady beat by age 8. Research gives guidance for steady beat and age, type of instrument or movement task, and individual differences:

1. Age—As children grow older, they are on average better able to keep a steady beat to music (Flohr 2000; Frego 1996; Malbrán 2002).
2. Type of instrument or movement task—Loong (2002) found the average tempo performed by sixty young children aged 5 years and below was 112 bpm for scraping or rubbing, 132 bpm for walking or stepping, 141 bpm for striking, and 164 bpm for shaking a maraca. It is easier for young children to keep a steady beat using certain movements (for example, chanting or tapping) than other movements (for example, marching) (Flohr, Suthers, and Woodward 1998; Frega 1979; Rainbow 1981; Schleuter and Schleuter 1985). Rainbow and Frega reported that matching a steady beat while marching and marching while clapping to music were extremely difficult for 3- and 4-year-olds. Rainbow found that only 10 percent to 14 percent of 3-year-olds were successful at clapping a pattern or a steady beat to recorded music. The easiest steady beat task for 3- and 4-year-olds was not moving but rather chanting rhythm syllables (for example, rat-a-tat-tat or ta-ta-titi-ta). In light of the research, a developmentally inappropriate practice would be to expect 3- and four-year-olds to march or march while clapping because most of them will not be able to do so. However, children enjoy moving to music (including marching to music), and the experiences are viable as long as teachers and parents do not expect them to match the steady beat until 6 or 7 years of age. Experience shows that if teachers instruct children to stay with the beat and model the behavior, they do better than if they just tell them to move.
3. Individual differences—Tempo preference is often identified as personal tempo and refers to the natural tempo that exists within individuals. Personal tempo is often determined by asking a child to move without listening to music. The preferred tempo or personal tempo generally decreases as children age (Frego 1996; Walters 1983). Frego found that there was also an increase in the personal tempo of walking speed between 5 and 6 years of age. The peak tempo of 149 bpm at first grade gradually decreased to 134 bpm in sixth grade.

As people age, this natural chosen tempo tends to slow down a bit. It can also be difficult for some people to perceive a beat to music, not as much in music that moves with a strong-weak, strong-weak sense, but more sophisticated music that groups the strong and weak beats differently (for example, strong-weak-weak, strong-weak-strong-strong), especially in contemporary classical and non-Western music. When teaching anything about rhythm, no matter the age of the students (and this extends into adulthood), we have to make sure that students can demonstrate they perceive and perform a steady beat by clapping, tapping, playing instruments, or in other overt, physical ways.

### Applying the Research to Teaching

The beat can be broken down into parts, fractions that will add up to one whole beat when added together. This is where an understanding of math comes in, especially when studying fractions in the second or third grade, or reinforcing them later on. However, caution is suggested here because children often confuse **time signatures** in music with fractions. (The top number indicates the beats in a **measure,** and the bottom indicates the kind of note equal to one beat. The top number occupies the top two spaces of the staff whereas the bottom number occupies the bottom two spaces; if this was a fraction, there would only be one line between the numbers.) It is best to keep the fractions in relation to the smaller values of notes that equal one beat in a piece.

To further help illustrate and teach this concept, the following is a scientific example. When one turns on a light, we see a simple perceived color—a result of the colors available in the spectrum. However, if we were to put that same light through a prism, then we would see that single color broken into the colors of the visual color spectrum. All those colors together make the light, and if one color changes in intensity, that can affect the color or shading of the light. This can also be demonstrated by playing with a color picker and changing hues, saturation, and CMYK (which allows one to subtract color) or RGB values (which allows one to add color) in a computer graphic program such as Adobe Photoshop®. In music, the fractions of the beat must mathematically and aurally add up to the perceived **duration** of one beat.

When teaching beat and rhythm, it is important to make sure the foundation of steady beat is strong. After that, layering experiences that introduce rhythm patterns that are consistently reinforced, reviewed, and refined are important. Do not try to do too much in one lesson; for example, it is not uncommon to spend the entire first grade year working on steady beat, **rest,** and **eighth notes.** Among two of the strongest music methodologies for teaching and reinforcing rhythm are the Kodály method and the Orff-Schulwerk (see Chapter 11). African drumming has also become very popular and helpful as a strategy to help teach rhythm. Reading rhythm notation is very different from keeping a beat or echoing a pattern by ear. Information on designing instruction is presented later in this book, and sample lesson plans for analysis are available on the authors' website (www.marvinmusic.org).

## Pitch and Melody

Melody has been defined many ways by different philosophers, psychologists, theoreticians, and musicologists. For our simple purposes here, we will define it as a set of mathematical frequencies (which humans perceive as **pitch**) that usually has some linear organization behind them. Whether a melody is pleasing or displeasing to a listener, whether it has a value to a listener, or whether it has a particular meaning to a listener are all subjective qualities. Humans do not hear as well as most of our nonhuman colleagues in the animal kingdom, although humans hear within the range of approximately 20 Hz to 20,000 Hz. Our most accurate **range** of hearing fundamental frequencies for music ranges roughly from 500 Hz (which is the C above **middle C**) to about 2000 Hz (Backus 1977; Butler 1992). We hear sound outside the range of 500 Hz to 2,000 Hz less accurately because the loudness of the frequency needs to be adjusted for our perception (see Fletcher and Munson 1933). Needless to say, this limits the available frequencies we choose to organize melodies. Through the centuries, some composers who had an inkling that something wasn't quite right with our human hearing would use this to their advantage in composing. For example, Giuseppe Tartini noticed that, when he loudly played two simultaneous frequencies on the violin that were close together, a low buzzing sound was added to the two frequencies he was generating (Joachim 1932). In acoustics, this is a type of combination tone. More information on the acoustical aspects of melody will follow, as they make great science experiments for both music and classroom teachers. Later, nineteenth- and twentieth-century composers added some perceptually deceptive melodic and acoustical characteristics, resonating to and bridging music with findings in the new fields of psychology and psychoacoustics.

## The Research Base

This section introduces the interaction of science, acoustics, and meaning. The field of acoustics investigates scientific aspects of sound, with the field of psychoacoustics investigating the manner in which humans perceive and process sound. Included in psychoacoustics is sound processing in the brain, which we then attach to human meaning. Although not comprehensive, this section will illustrate to you how these all interconnect and are relevant to you as educators.

**RELATIONAL PROCESSING OF PITCH AND MELODY**    Very young children are able to process musical pitch and melody. In some ways, preschool children may be better listeners than later elementary-aged children. Systematic research has revealed that infants are surprisingly proficient music listeners. After relatively brief exposure to a sequence of tones, they retain global information about its pitch contour (Trehub, et al. 1984) and rhythm (Chang and Trehub 1977a; Trehub and Thorpe 1989). Like adults, they treat transpositions of a melody as equivalent to the original (Chang and Trehub 1977b; Trehub, et al. 1987), and they recognize the invariance of rhythm across changes in tempo (Trehub and Thorpe 1989). In other words, they engage in relational processing, which is at the heart of music and its appreciation. As we might expect, the musical culture in children's environment is also important in their music development. What children hear is often preferred later in life, while other music is often not preferred.

**APPLYING THE RESEARCH—ORGANIZING PITCHES: THE MUSICAL STAFF, GRAND STAFF, AND NOTE NAMES**   Referring back to the first part of this chapter, we remember that Guido d'Arezzo was the individual responsible for the first real attempt at organizing musical pitches in a way that they could be read instead of being taught aurally (Miller 1973). This structure (which first consisted of four lines and, over the years, notes of various shapes) has been reworked considerably on its path to today's system. This doesn't keep contemporary composers from creating new notation systems.

It is perhaps with the teaching of the musical staff that we run into some confusion, as it is often seen as something concrete and static instead of a representation of dynamic pitch relationships in the musical fabric. Often, and effectively, the staff can be introduced without a **clef** at the beginning, and it can also be stripped down to two lines, with more added as needed. The Kodály methodology does this very well, but one need not be a Kodály specialist to use this kind of approach. See Figure 3.1 for an example.

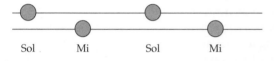

FIGURE 3.1 Simple Beginning Staff Presentation

The lack of a clef at the beginning and of the rest of the staff lines allows students to concentrate on the visual perception of the distance of the notes, and on how they sound and are perceived aurally and produced vocally. Gradually, more lines are added, and the **interval** is also moved into spaces, again to reinforce the visual, aural, and vocal distances. The lack of stems takes away the concern with rhythm (just as note heads aren't used when first working with rhythms of quarter and eighth notes). Children are allowed to concentrate on one piece of information at a time.

After teaching the basic pitch relationships, often by singing, students in general music are introduced to the treble staff, then the bass clef staff, and finally they view it in context as the grand staff.

As you see in the staff of Figure 3.2, we use the letters of the alphabet: A, B, C, D, E, F, and G. This is not arbitrary—the origin in using these letters goes back many centuries, and are plainly seen in the use of solmization (Rainbow and Cox 2007). In current notation, we use some other symbols to help figure out if the pitch is performed au naturel or if it needs to be raised or lowered a bit as part of a particular scale. When the pitch is to be performed a **half step** higher, a sharp (♯) is placed in front of it on the staff or in the **key** signature. Conversely, when the pitch is to be performed a half step lower, a flat (♭) is placed in front of it on the staff or in the key signature. Strategies on how to teach reading music notation follow in Chapter 10.

**Scales** are specifically arranged pitches that are often the base of a tonal system for a piece of music. The use of scales goes back to the medieval period in Western

FIGURE 3.2 Treble Clef and Grand Staff

music where it started out as a hexachord, or six pitches, and later grew to the eight pitches now used, the last note in the scale being repeated at the octave. However, this eight-note scale is not the only kind we have in the world. Others exist, with different interval relationships between the pitches, such as the Indian raga, the Arabic maqam, the Chinese Han scales, and the Indonesian slendro scale, which are also rich in cultural value and history. One commonly used in Kodály methodology and the Orff-Keetman approach is the pentatonic scale, often composed of the pitches C, D, E, G, and A. Pentatonic scales are often associated with early music and Chinese music (some Han scales are pentatonic). This scale is highly versatile and multifaceted—simply meaning that it never sounds wrong, even if someone accidentally plays a wrong note in an accompaniment. Scales are often used in Western classical music to help provide or set the foundation of a desired emotional meaning (for example, sadness, happiness).

A child picks out pitches on the piano.

*Photo courtesy of Christine Stratton*

**SCALES**   Although scales differ from one culture to another, the feature of unequal scale steps is ubiquitous (Sloboda 1985). For example, the Western **major scale** consists of two semitone steps (for example, do-re) and one semitone steps (for example, ti-do). In one study (Trehub et al. 1999), infants were required to detect a mistuned tone (three-quarter semitone change) in ascending-descending scales of various types. Interestingly, they succeeded in the context of the major scale and an invented, unequal-step scale, but they failed when the mistuned tone occurred in an invented scale with equal steps (that is, division of the octave into seven equal steps). This finding implies that unequal steps in scales facilitate perceptual processing and the retention of melodic information, just as consonant intervals do. Techniques for teaching reading, writing, playing, and singing of melody occur later in this book.

**TONE COLOR (TIMBRE)**   Tone color, also known as **timbre** (French, pronounced closer to "tamber"), is another fundamental building block of sound and, by extension, musical sounds. A particular tone color allows us to distinguish one sound from another, one voice from another, and one instrument from another. Tone color is a result of a number of complex vibratory and resonance events of a sounding medium, which makes this particular aspect of music very open to all sorts of experimentation and examination. You will see in this section that timbre isn't limited to the sounds of the human voice and musical instruments.

Before discussing timbre and tone color in terms of their physical properties, it is important to describe the acoustical phenomenon of periodic and aperiodic motion, because these have a great impact on the production of an identifying tone color. The manner in which the pressure wave motion moves through a resonating material, such as wood, metal, water, or the vocal tract creates an identifiable tone color.

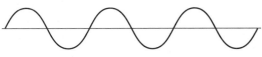

**FIGURE 3.3** Periodic Motion

Periodic motion is continuous, fluid, and repeated motion. Figure 3.3 shows an example of how it may look on an oscilloscope (a scientific device that measures pressure waves and provides a visual interpretation of them).

Aperiodic motion is the opposite: there is no repeated organization in how it looks (see Figure 3.4).

Environmental sounds or timbres are those that primarily occur in nature. Often these sounds are of an acoustical nonperiodic nature, meaning that if you look at them on an oscilloscope, they would not look like the typical sine wave motion, such as illustrated in Figure 3.3. These sounds can be of ocean waves, sand moving across dunes (a phenomenon known as "booming"), wind moving through leaves, and running water, for example.

**FIGURE 3.4** Aperiodic Motion

Body sounds or timbres include controllable, socially acceptable sounds such as clapping, patting, and all other kinds of body percussion, as well as sounds made by voices. For our purposes, we include nonhuman voices in this category. The sound waves can be aperiodic (environmental sounds) and also periodic (they have a wave shape represented on an oscilloscope that can resemble movement similar to a sine wave).

Sounds made on musical instruments and the human voice are pitched sounds or timbres. Some nontraditional musical instruments (such as a saw played by a bow) also fit in this category. These sounds produce pressure waves that are usually periodic in motion, but it is important to note that the shapes of sound waves are often less smooth than a sine wave, creating shapes closer to sawtooths and squares. Nonpitched sounds or timbres include, but are not limited to, musical **percussion** instruments such as drums, triangles, and wood blocks. These instruments make aperiodic sound pressure waves. Chapters 9 and 18 feature techniques for teaching the concept of tone color.

## ELEMENTS OF MUSIC: SECONDARY BLOCKS

By combining primary building blocks in different ways, we can create music. If we think of the primary blocks as the ingredients, then the secondary blocks can serve as a variety of recipes or techniques that can be combined or retooled in multiple ways.

### Expressive Elements

Expressive elements of music include tempo, dynamics, articulations, slurs and ties, and fermatas. There are two different aspects to consider: (1) helping children learn to listen for elements (if they are indeed perceptible), and (2) helping children learn to perform expressive elements on an instrument or vocally, two separate skills. Because students hear expressive elements doesn't mean that they can perform them. Often when children learn to perform them, they may do so at a level that they alone perceive but no one else does. For now, we concentrate on framing the elements for teaching in the elementary classroom.

Tempo refers to the speed of the steady beat. The tempo of music can go fast, slow, faster, and slower. By changing the tempo, sometimes for very short periods of time, the expressive quality of a piece of music can be drastically affected. For example, in Gustav Mahler's Symphony no. 1 ("Titan"), the third movement is based on "Frére Jacques," with a change to a very slow tempo. In our experience, the first graders who heard this piece, after being adequately prepared, were very surprised and pleased when they recognized the song performed in a very different way.

Dynamics refer to the perceived loudness or softness of the music. Like the perception of tempo, it is also a very subjective aspect of music (what is loud to one person may not be loud to another), but is also an aspect that has led to serious health concerns regarding hearing (Chesky et al. 2002). When we teach children to listen for dynamics, we begin with loud and soft (at reasonable levels) and then move to louder and softer. Young children often confuse pitch with dynamics: they confuse higher with louder and lower with softer. This is not a sign of cognitive confusion, for it is actually a phenomenon that is somewhat supported by research in hearing perception (Fletcher and Munson 1933).

Articulations, slurs, and ties are techniques of how melodies can be played. As a nonmusical simile, the word *articulation* refers to pronunciation. You might say to someone, "Articulate your words more precisely so I can understand the directions. Indicate where words start and end clearly." This is not much different from music. Some articulations are short and precise, such as in a march, and others are slow and languid, as in a lullaby. Although skill in articulation production is learned in music lessons, children are able to perceive effective and ineffective articulations. Slurs and ties are also skills learned in music performance lessons, but child listeners easily hear them. These techniques deal with the way tones are joined together to create perceived seamless transitions from one pitch to another. A slur is used to combine notes of different pitches by playing them with one breath or one bow stroke, if one is playing a stringed instrument. A tie is used to combine notes that are of the same pitch, although they may be of different durations. It is performed the same way as a tie, one breath or one bow.

Instead of a long tie, a composer may opt to use a fermata, also known euphemistically as a bird's eye because of its looks. A fermata over a particular note or group of notes vertically lined up indicates that these are held as long as the performer or conductor wishes. Ties and fermatas are often found at the end of compositions or songs where a transition, often in tempo, will take place.

Expressive elements can be combined with primary blocks of music in many ways, and ultimately can give birth to numerous pieces of music reflective of many cultures. Two more secondary building blocks, texture and form, are manifestations of various combinations in longer pieces of music, from a nursery song to a lengthy opera.

## Texture

Texture in music is not unlike texture in art, dance, and theatre. Textures can be thick or thin; they can be complementary or not. In visual art, texture is demonstrated in numerous ways, such as the layering techniques of watercolor (Monet's *Water Lilies* is an example of this), oils (Jackson Pollock did this well; one sees oil paint jutting out of the canvas, giving it a rough texture if touched), to pottery and sculpture, and to multimedia in which textiles, paint, wood, and sequins can all be combined in one piece of art. In dance and theater, texture is represented when one group of dancers performs one movement while another group performs a complementary movement at the same time, versus a solo dancer who has the entire stage. In theater, two or more characters talking at the same time, rather than one at a time, is a dramatic strategy used to build tension. Lack of texture or complexity gives a sense of simplicity and/or directness, whereas multiple textures give a sense of complexity and/or cloudiness.

In science, particularly chemistry, there is a strong bond to texture. One of the pleasures of high school chemistry is to be handed a test tube full of an unknown solution and assigned to conduct experiments to determine the chemicals actually present in the solution. By taking apart the solution and extracting the components, students understand the structure. In addition, students understand and appreciate why the solution didn't blow up in the test tube, because a number of chemicals are volatile when mixed together. A teacher has to know how to mix them precisely so as to not cause problems. The same goes for music. When we mix melody, rhythm, expressive elements, and various tone colors together, we are essentially combining a solution not unlike one in chemistry class. These mixtures can be complex and volatile, or they can be simple and subtle. This is when a quick review of texture in music is helpful.

Although music has many kinds of textures, there are three that we generally teach in elementary school: monophonic, homophonic, and polyphonic. These are not difficult to teach as long as the teacher is a good musical mixologist and uses music selections that allow students to extract the components: simple at first, to complex.

Monophonic music is the easiest to understand. The Latin foundation, mono, means "one," and phonic means "sound." This means one melody that everyone sings or plays in unison without accompaniment. Examples of monophony are found in medieval chant practices of the Roman Catholic Church. Another example is a single child singing, or a class singing the same song at the same time without accompaniment, such as when a teacher teaches a rote song.

The next two textures developed complexity between A.D. 1200 and the twenty-first century. Homophonic, again from the Latin, means "like or same sound." This refers to a single melody supported by a chordal accompaniment. The old chestnut, "Heart and Soul," the elementary school standard two-child piece performed on a piano, is a prime example. One student picks out the melody; the other plays the **chords** underneath, lower. On advanced levels, Orff pieces often use homophonic texture. Mozart, Haydn, and other composers of the classical period of Western music history wrote a number of symphonies with primarily homophonic texture. Church hymns and Jewish synagogue music also are primarily homophonic. Much rock music, especially classic rock, is homophonic. Visual imagination may help explain homophonic texture. Imagine sixteen circus dogs lying on their backs in a line. Each one has its legs up in the air where it supports another dog lying on its back. In turn, each of those dogs has a ball balanced on its hind feet. Along the top of this line, a particularly agile dog runs, hops, and skips gracefully from ball to ball as the other dogs support it underneath. In music, that's the purpose of the accompaniment chords—to give support to the melody.

Polyphonic texture is the most complex; poly refers to "many sounds." This means more than one melody is performed simultaneously. A simple example of polyphonic texture is a round, such as "Row, Row, Row Your Boat." Rounds are inherently polyphonic. Polyphonic texture can get out of hand if it isn't handled correctly, because unrelated melodies cannot be thrown together and result in good music. The Baroque composers (Bach, especially) were masters of polyphonic writing; they adhered to certain mathematical rules (which we call counterpoint in music) that helped create orderliness and understandable structure. However, compare Baroque with composers of the late medieval period, who could put (1) part of a religious Mass, (2) a drinking song, and (3) a totally new song all together at one time and came up with a new piece of music. In our experience, students in introduction to music literature classes have referred to this medieval period phenomena as polyphony behaving badly or polyphony gone wild; because it's so difficult to choose what to listen for, comprehension suffers.

All of these textures can be mixed together in unique and inspiring ways. Although monophony really can only be performed by itself, the same isn't true for the other two, which can be mixed together quite successfully. A famous example of this is the Canon in D by Johann Pachelbel. He set up this piece with a continuo (a pattern of low notes that repeats over and over) with the canon (the musical term for a round) layered over the continuo.

## Form

**Form** goes one step further as the grand organizing principle. Say that you heard a piece of music in which you noticed the first part was monophonic texture but then it was followed by homophonic texture with a different melody. Listening further, you hear the monophonic section returning. You heard a form of music that was monophonic-homophonic-monophonic (m-h-m), or more simply put in common music, ABA. If you had heard only the first two parts, you would have heard AB form. The letters are simply used to designate the same or different aspects of a piece.

Teaching and listening to music to identify form takes time. Children need to be taught to listen carefully for form and, like the chemistry references earlier, how to extract musical characteristics to understand why and how the A section differs from the B section. Visually identifying form is usually used as a stepping-stone in the process. For example, in class, you could alternate boy, girl, boy standing in line—as an example of ABA form. You can do the same with clothes, hair colors, eye colors, and so on—to get to the point where children are able to figure out similar and contrasting features. In music, we also use the letters C, D, E, F, and so on, in designating sections of music in a larger form.

There are many kinds of forms; the ones traditionally taught are AB, ABA, ABC, ABACA (rondo form), and theme and variations. We already discussed AB, ABA, and by extension ABC; the next two are easier to understand. ABACA, called rondo form, occurs when the A section returns after each contrasting section, working as sonic glue to hold everything together. Theme and variations is a bit more complex. The main melody, that is, the theme, stays almost the same, although it gradually changes each time it returns by tweaking various elements of the building blocks we discussed. Accompaniments are changed as well. Using your visual imagination, think of visiting a home-building website, where you choose a basic stock floor plan. Then you choose extra features for the house (Florida room, extra garage, and a breakfast room), the building materials (laminate versus granite countertops), and external features—a deck, pool, or special landscaping. The theme you chose is the stock building plan; by adding and changing some characteristics of the house, you change it to something that no longer looks like a stock plan. Along the way, you have had the guidance of an architect and a structural engineer to make sure that all changes are up to local building codes. Theme and variations works pretty much this way in music—there is a stock plan (the melodic theme), then you add, subtract, and/or change features of the piece. As in building a house, there are structural aspects concerning the building blocks already discussed; some need to stay consistent, or the musical structure—like a poorly built house—will collapse.

## GROUP EXPERIENCES IN COOPERATIVE LEARNING

The following activities will help you become more familiarized with musical forms, styles, and composition skills.

*Group activity 1:* Form and order are characteristics of human desire for organization and symmetry. You may be considering form to define a living space, specifically a dorm room. Spend time sitting in your room, analyzing it to see how you have placed belongings, books, computers, and bed pillows. Do you see any visual representations of AB, ABA, ABC, ABACA, and the like in your dorm room or apartment? How would you describe the form of your room? Compare your room with some of your classmates' rooms. Do you all tend to use formal orders in visually designing your living space, or do you eschew it all together?

**Extended activities:**

*Group activity 2:* Walk around the neighborhood and see how people have organized the form of their gardens. The famous writer Goethe referred to architecture as "frozen music." Investigate architectural history from early architects (such as Andrea Palladio) to the current work of Frank Gehry. Architects rely heavily on form to design buildings; however, the preferred form of one architect may be more easily perceptible than the preferred form of another. Each building shares common characteristics yet looks different. How would you relate this to music that is not frozen?

*Group activity 3:* Using simple sequencing programs such as GarageBand (available on Mac computers) or Audacity (http://audacity.sourceforge.net), a free program for both Mac and PC/Windows computers, compose a simple piece of music by pasting together different sound samples in different orders, but still represent a musical form. By experimenting, you may be surprised with the results. Each group member should contribute one MP3 or MP4 audio clip that can be imported into the computer.

*Group activity 4:* Using the demo version of CSpeech (http://userpages. chorus.net/cspeech/), analyze a number of sounds of humans, animals, and music. Sample sounds and simple directions on using the CSpeech program are available on the website for this book at www.pearsonhighered.com/flohr.

## Chapter Conclusions

This chapter presented a basic introduction to the elemental building blocks and structure of music to help nonmusicians grasp these concepts and also help future music teachers use nonmusical metaphors and similes when teaching children. Music of all cultures is made up of the same building blocks of rhythm and melody. However, the manner in which building blocks are arranged gives all music uniqueness, meaning, and recognizable cultural identity.

## Resources

For working with music fundamentals and other subjects, see the following websites:

*Math:*

Go to http://www.iit.edu/~smile/ (at the Illinois Institute of Technology) and click on the link for mathematics. From there, the lessons on creative math, especially the lesson on fractions and origami—or paper folding—are especially relevant.

*Science:*

Go to http://www.iit.edu/~smile/ (at the Illinois Institute of Technology) and click on the link for science. Particularly good plans, in relationship to this topic, are the ones that deal with ball bouncing and ones further down the page about waves, sound, and optics. See also http://www.teachnology.com/teachers/lesson_plans/science/physics/waves/. For overall information, one of the best websites is the Physics Classroom (http://www.physicsclassroom.com/), which was first developed and is maintained by scientists and science teachers. It is an excellent resource.

The National Institute on Deafness and Other Communication Disorders (NIDCD) website (http://www.noisyplanet.nidcd.nih.gov/) contains a program to help protect the hearing of children. The program is designed for parents to teach their children how to avoid hearing loss from overexposure to loud noise.

*Social Studies:*

A good place to start is http://www.ancient-future.com/; click on the link for World Music Education. There, you are introduced to rhythmic and melodic aspects of world music that are unique and identifiable to particular geographic regions of the world. After perusing this site, you will have improved your ability to search for others that provide interesting information for teaching and learning. Another excellent resource is the Smithsonian Global Sound project (http://www.smithsonianglobalsound.org) for authentic samples of music from around the world.

CHAPTER **4**

# Kinds of Music

**This chapter addresses the following:**

## WHY DIFFERENT KINDS OF MUSIC? NATIONAL STANDARDS

We can all agree that music is a part of most human cultures; we cannot always agree on its purpose. We know that it exists, but not why and how. The national standards in music education state that students need to have an understanding of music in relation to history and culture. This implies that culture refers to both macrocultures and microcultures existing within macrocultures. Although the great majority of music presented in this book is primarily of a European classical music tradition, many equally important musical cultures and traditions need to be considered and investigated in the classroom.

This chapter is a basic introduction to music of the world, and is by no means comprehensive. It provides examples of various musical traditions and how they may be taught in a classroom. To enhance understanding, musicians from around the world contributed sections about their personal musical heritages. At the end of the chapter are a number of resources to help you teach and understand music from around the world. We emphasize that music always needs to be introduced within the cultural context in which it resides. No study of world music should be undertaken without studying traditions, beliefs, language, history, food, dress, and other equally important characteristics. Understanding the mechanics of how the music was composed is only one aspect of knowledge; understanding why it was composed and how it was and is used is just as important.

Several points need clarification as to how music is viewed on an international scale. First, consider the saying, "Music is a universal language." Viewing music across the world, nothing could be further from the truth. Music, if it is even called music in a culture, serves numerous purposes and carries with it meanings that may not be understood by nonmembers of that culture. Language is composed of particular, clearly defined words and phrases that carry obvious meaning to members of a particular culture. These meanings may not be understood by nonmembers, who may actually misinterpret the music (Letts 1997; Nettl 2000). Here is a linguistic example. A colleague of ours many years ago accepted a position in the Mexico City Philharmonic Orchestra. Our colleague felt he needed to work on his Spanish language skills, so he enrolled in Spanish classes in Mexico City. In the first class, students needed to introduce themselves. He did the best he could with the Spanish he knew, but tripped up when it came to saying he was embarrassed by his lack of language skills. Instead of using the appropriate conjugation of "avergonzadar" for "embarrassed," he announced to the class "estoy embarazada"; everyone broke out laughing, because he announced that he was pregnant. He made the mistake of assuming that "embarrassed" would be similar in Spanish, but it was much different. Color works the same way in meaning. For example, in the United States, we associate white clothes, such as gowns, with weddings, whereas white in Japan was historically the color worn by mourners to funerals. Music has the same problem; it can be misinterpreted or misunderstood.

This chapter addresses how music fits into culture, but not to the depth we would like. It concentrates on the mechanics of the music: its similarities to and contrasts with music the children and teachers know and ways to introduce it at levels they can understand. Remember that the great majority of world music traditions are based on creations by *adults* in a particular culture, so not all of the music is suitable for children to perform due to vocal and physical difficulty, but they can still learn about it. For in-depth study of the richness and diversity of world music, start by exploring the resources and references at the end of this chapter.

## SOCIOLOGICAL RESEARCH IN WORLD MUSIC

Research in world music has often been undertaken by ethnomusicologists, musicologists, and anthropologists, primarily because music has been studied to see how it is present in particular cultural traditions. Several researchers and writers have truly been outstanding in their contributions to our understanding of world music and traditions.

### Where to Start?

Our starting place is music of our own macroculture of the United States; it makes sense to clarify its place. When teaching music of another culture to new or inexperienced listeners, it is a good idea to start by comparing it with music that is already known. The known is a point of departure; it does not imply superiority to other music, only that it is familiar. Chapter 5 addresses learning to listen to music in great detail, as students need to have a strong understanding of the characteristics of their own musical culture before analyzing and critiquing music of other cultures. In this way, similarities and differences are better understood. For our purposes, similarities and contrasts may be addressed along several continuums, featured in Table 4.1.

Note that many musical traditions within one culture include characteristics that run from very simple to complex. This table is useful for comparing two or more musical traditions that are both similar and different in many ways (for example, comparing and contrasting traditional European opera with traditional Chinese opera). The table can easily be simplified for the needs of the teacher and students and helps students to listen and gain a preliminary grasp using known terms. It isn't meant to provide an easy labeling system for world music. World music is complex on a grand scale, but beginning learners need to start as simply as possible by connecting with music systems already familiar.

There are musical traditions that are unfamiliar to many in the United States, and several of them will be discussed. These aren't chosen arbitrarily; the United States is becoming very diversified due to increased immigration and international adoptions. Several authors in this section have used the terms *Western classical music* or *Western classical tradition* to help readers grasp the differences and similarities

**TABLE 4.1** Listening Similarities and Contrasts

| | |
|---|---|
| Vocal use: simple, speechlike, narrative | Vocal use: singing, complex narrative |
| Vocal use: simple songs, no special techniques | Vocal use: complex songs, extended techniques |
| Timbre: one or two instruments and kinds | Timbre: many instruments and kinds |
| Melody: simple | Melody: complex |
| Texture: thin, monophonic | Texture: thick, polyphonic |
| Tuning: simple scales | Tuning: complex scales |
| Harmony: none | Harmony: complex |
| Beat: no really obvious beat | Beat: complicated meters |
| Rhythm: simple and repetitive | Rhythm: complex and overlapped |
| Dynamics: none | Dynamics: many |
| Use of the music | Function of the music |
| Indigenous origin | Adapted from other cultures: synthesized origins |
| Dramatic components: none | Dramatic components: many |

found in cultural musical styles. These terms are meant to refer to music that is generally associated with tonal systems, forms, and performance practices that originated in Europe. They do not imply superiority or higher value, but are a means to aid readers' comprehension.

## Music of the Caribbean

The Caribbean consists of a number of island nations that stretch from the Bahamas to off the coast of Venezuela. Many of the islands were colonized by European nations and the United States; some of these countries still influence or rule these islands. Many colonizing Western nations have influenced language and culture, resulting in a plethora of musical traditions. Languages spoken in this area include French, Spanish, English, and Dutch. Prior to colonization, most of the islands were populated by the Arawak and Carib peoples, who intermarried with Africans, Caucasians, and Asians who came to these islands. The history of the Caribbean is a bit bloody, with pirates, slave traders, and unsavory types, as well as merchants supplying sugar, molasses, and rum to Europe and American colonies. Due to this blending, a myriad of musical traditions developed, too numerous to include in this short section. Readers are encouraged to consult the numerous books and websites that are dedicated to presenting in-depth information on the various kinds of music.

Native Caribbean music contributes rich vocal and strong instrumental traditions. An Internet investigation to find how many different kinds of music were considered traditional to the Caribbean revealed a total of ninety-six. This section is limited to several that are authentic but perhaps unfamiliar.

**VOCAL MUSIC**    Vocal music of the Caribbean tends to be political and/or spiritual. According to Miller and Shahriari (2006), most of the reggae music exported to the United States is sanitized and simplified in the commercial realm (for example, Bobby McFerrin's "Don't Worry, Be Happy" from 1988). Caribbean reggae is far more complex. Originally associated with Rastifarianism after 1950, the music was known for its verbal challenges to the social order, including European hegemony of Jamaica. The music became popular in the Jamaican underground and for dancing. Disc jockeys turned it into performance practice in dance halls. Here, they softened the melody track and boosted the rhythm and bass tracks, which allowed them to talk over the music into a microphone rather than sing. The roots of reggae are traced to *mento* (creole) and *ska* music.

Another vocal performance tradition is the "rhyming spiritual" (Miller and Shahriari 2006), which, unlike reggae, has a lyrical and melodic core, with plenty of room for embellishment. The primary voice is a tenor, known as the "rhymer," who uses a **call-and-response** technique. The rhymer works with a lower-voiced singer, the "baser." Other voices may be added to flesh out the harmony (ibid.). Many of the songs are related to spirituals sung in the southern United States.

**INSTRUMENTAL MUSIC**    Instrumental traditions of the Caribbean are vast and varied. Many are related to dancing or drumming activities. Seldom subservient to the voice, instruments definitely hold their own.

Perhaps the most popular instrumental music is steel drum or pan, which originated in Trinidad and Tobago (Miller and Shahriari 2006). These instruments were probably the first with staying power, made out of trash left behind by British and American militaries. Originally made of 55-gallon oil drums, the heads are beaten into a number of tuned convex circles (either many for higher-sounding drums with numerous pitches or only a few for lower-sounding drums with only a few pitches), and have been popular for over 50 years. Bands can vary in size from a few players to many. A rhythm section is included, composed of a conventional drum set, conga, automobile brake drums, maracas, and other West Indies instruments. Collectively, this ensemble is referred to as the "engine room" (ibid.). Much of this music is fast, melodic, syncopated, and highly rhythmic. On the other hand, with these same instruments, musicians are perfectly capable of producing slower ballad-type pieces.

Another instrumental style common in the Bahamas is the "rake 'n' scrape" music, characterized by the use of a saw. Cat Island holds a rake 'n' scrape festival yearly. The origins of this music are from the ripsaw genre of the Turks and Caicos Islands, but it is now more popular in the Bahamas. Other instruments included in the rake 'n' scrape performances are the goatskin drum and accordion. Common characteristics of this music include an emphasis on the weaker beats or notes in a rhythm pattern, an overall rhythmic drive and fast tempo, a recognizable form (ABA, for example), much repetition, and improvisation (Nettl et al. 2008).

**RELEVANCE**    Interestingly, much of the music that will be discussed in the following sections is primarily of a vocal tradition, usually spiritual and ceremonial, with little emphasis placed on the independent development of instrumental ensembles and music. In the Caribbean, we see a very different twist in that much vocal music is political and spiritual, and that there is a great development of instrumental music. More interesting is that many instruments are contrived from waste material or building tools. This invites endless possibilities for lessons on the imagination and creativity of humankind in music making.

**INTRODUCING CARIBBEAN MUSIC TO STUDENTS**    As with many of the music cultures in this section, comparing and contrasting vocal and instrumental Caribbean music with vocal and instrumental performance styles already familiar, can pave the way to a deeper investigation of the ways Caribbean music is similar to yet different from music of the United States. Calypso, salsa, and reggae are commonly found in the United States, but are quite different when placed in the cultural context of their origin.

To explore scientific aspects of vibration, teachers may associate steel drums with Chladni figures, an acoustical set of vibratory figures that emerge as a steel plate is vibrated. This experience will reinforce acoustical science with creating music (Murr et al. 1999). A lesson where children create instruments or an instrumental band using classroom objects with vibratory or sound-making capacity may result in a very interesting music ensemble. Adding words that take a stand on a particular school issue such as the lunch menu, late starts on snow days, or dress codes, illustrates how music has been historically significant in times of human conflict.

## Music of China

*[This section was contributed by C. Victor Fung, University of South Florida.]*

China is a big country with highly diverse ethnicities from within. It has about one-fifth of the world's population (1.3 billion of 6.6 billion) (Central Intelligence Agency 2008). In the United States and probably in many other nations, the most frequent personal contact points with the Chinese culture are likely to be Chinese restaurants, or the Chinatowns in some major cities (for example, Chicago, New York, San Francisco, and Washington, DC). However, these Chinese cultural contact points tend to present a homogenized picture of the Chinese culture. The decorations, menus, people, and language tend to look alike to non-Chinese, and oftentimes even to Chinese. This homogenized picture is illusive, because it does not represent the spectrum of rich cultural varieties in China.

China is also a country with one of the longest histories. It dates back to at least seven thousand years ago (Lau 2008, xiv). It went through tremendous changes. Many artifacts and documents through the millennia can be found in museums outside of China. In China, many of the historic artifacts remain in sight to the public, both inside and outside of museums. If one considers construction as a large artifact, then the Great Wall is a prime example, which could be traced back to at least the third century B.C.

To understand Chinese music, one should know about the diversity and history of China. With fifty-six different Chinese ethnicities (although over 90 percent of them are Han) and over 200 Chinese dialects (Mandarin or Putonghua being the official dialects) (Gordon 2005), it is impossible to claim Chinese music as *one* type of music. The diversity of cultures within China allows for a wide range of music to be created and developed. One could find vocal music in all dialects, each with a unique musical style. There are vocal and instrumental musics for all Chinese ethnic groups, in all historical periods, and in all social strata (for example, court, elite, and the common people). In addition, there are over 200 types of operas, with Peking (or Beijing) opera being the most well known outside of China.

**VOCAL MUSIC**    China has a wide range of vocal music: folk song, storytelling, art song, and opera, to name the major categories, with many subcategories under each. Storytelling tends to have highly localized styles. Folk songs and art songs may include choral arrangements with Western influence. Art song is a twentieth-century phenomenon influenced by the West. Depending on the region and tradition, operas may incorporate other art forms, such as face painting, gesture, dance, acrobatics, costume, and scene design. Operatic settings tend to contain rich symbolic meanings in all aspects of the performance. Interestingly, the traditional articulation of Chinese songs requires many of the sounds to be created in a different way than in English, with more sounds requiring activity in the middle to the back of the mouth, which is very different from most European languages, adding to the unique sound of Chinese singing (Trollinger 2006).

**INSTRUMENTAL MUSIC**    Due to the long history of China, many musical instruments adopted from outside of China hundreds or thousands of years ago have become "traditional Chinese instruments" today. A best-known instrument as such is the *erhu*, a two-stringed fiddle with the bow placed between two strings. The *pipa*, a pear-shaped lute with four strings, and the *yangqin*, a hammered **dulcimer,** are also adopted Chinese instruments. Other well-known Chinese instruments today include the *zheng*, a plugged string instrument with eighteen to twenty-three strings played on a stand or table; the *dizi,* a bamboo flute; the *xiao,* a vertical end-blown flute; the *sheng,* a wind instrument with multiple pipes, known as the mouth organ; plus a range of drums and other percussion instruments. Wind instruments made of bamboo and string instruments once made of silk became the "silk and bamboo ensemble," or *"Jiangnan sizhu,"* originating in the Jiangnan region in and around Shanghai. This type of instrumental musical ensemble is one of the most popular in China.

**RELEVANCE**   Music of contemporary China continues to evolve from its traditions and continues to be influenced by music outside of China. For example, the Chinese orchestra consisting of Chinese musical instruments is modeled after the symphony orchestra but produces a uniquely Chinese sound. Chinese popular songs adopted the Western style, yet maintained a Chinese identity in song contents and some musical characters. Contemporary Chinese composers may apply Chinese musical idioms to Western musical media. Music continues to change in China, incorporating outside influences using its rich and long history as a foundation.

**INTRODUCING CHINESE MUSIC TO STUDENTS**   Using the names of the Chinese music instruments provided in this text, locate video or audio recordings of these instruments, in solo or in an ensemble. Ask students what the music describes, using words or pictures. Most of the Chinese instrumental music pieces have descriptive titles, such as "Colorful Clouds Chasing the Moon" or "Horse Race." Pictures of the Chinese instruments are easily available on the Internet. After the children become familiar with the instruments aurally and visually, have them identify the musical instruments as they listen. Students may also tap along to determine the tempo characteristic of the music. Some tempos may be steady throughout the piece; others may start slow and become slightly and gradually faster.

Students can also compare various qualities of the music between a Chinese piece and a Western piece. One may consider melody, **harmony,** rhythm, timbre, dynamics, texture, and form of the pieces. For operatic pieces, students may also compare settings, makeup, costumes, and movements of singers and actors through video viewings.

Singing a Chinese song can be both challenging and enjoyable. Most published Chinese songs available in the United States are sung in Mandarin or Putonghua with pinyin, which is a Romanized pronunciation guide for the Chinese language. It would be best if teachers identify a native Chinese locally to assist with the pronunciation. Breaking down the lyrics to learn individual words would be most beneficial. In addition, listening to recordings sung by Chinese helps. Students may imitate the pronunciation of the lyrics and stylistic interpretations of such recordings. "Jasmine Flower" (*"Mo Li Hua"*) or "Flower Drum Song" (*"Feng Yang Hua Gu"*) could be good songs to begin.

## Music of Hawai'i

Hawai'i is considered part of the larger group of islands known as Polynesia that include Easter Island, Tahiti, the Samoan Islands, and the Cook Islands. Hawai'i was likely settled by ocean-faring explorers from what is now called Tahiti and the Marquesas Islands between the seventh and thirteenth centuries (Miller and Shahriari 2006). Along with the settlers came the musical and societal traditions. Although the United States annexed Hawai'i and it eventually became a state in 1959, it retains much of its traditional musical practices.

Mainlanders who have visited the Hawai'ian Islands may have noticed some aspects that affect the way the music is discussed in this section. The most obvious is the continued use of the Hawaiian language, along with the use of punctuation in the spelling of numerous words. Like in some Polynesian languages—Tahitian for one—there are limited consonants and vowels; these limitations require the voice be used in a manner unfamiliar to most non-Hawaiian mainlanders. After the colonization of Hawai'i by Americans, many Western music influences intertwined with Hawaiian traditional music, much of it resulting in entertainment provided at "traditional" lua'us, which include slack-key and steel guitars, neither Hawaiian in origin. Following American settlers, numerous Japanese and Chinese immigrants came as laborers at the turn of the nineteenth century, further contributing to the musical and cultural diversity of Hawai'i. This section introduces aspects of traditional music originating with early Polynesian settlers.

**VOCAL MUSIC**   Hawaiian music, like much Polynesian music, is primarily vocal, with mostly percussion instruments (for example, *kilu* and *pahu* drums) used to accompany the voices. Much vocal music is of religious or ceremonial nature, and can be both chantlike and songlike. Often, vocal music can be accompanied by a traditional *hula*, the dance of Hawai'i that tells a specific story. For excellent samples of traditional and ancient chant, hula movements, and a compendium of historical archived interviews, visit the website of the Hula Preservation Society (http://www.hulapreservation.org/).

Some vocal performance characteristics are prevalent in Hawaiian chants. One is the extensive use of what may be a wide fabricated vibrato, usually a bit more pronounced than in healthy singing voices. Another aspect is the technique of vocal sliding between pitches (Miller and Shahriari 2006). An extensive use of hard glottal attacks when pronouncing successive vowels may be heard in chants, separated by apostrophes. This is a normal aspect of the Hawaiian language (Trollinger 2006).

**INSTRUMENTAL MUSIC**   Like much traditional music of the Polynesian region, the instruments used are often there to accompany singing. In Hawai'i, *kilu* and *palu* drums are often used, the kilu being smaller and the palu being larger. Like drums of Southeast Asia, they are struck many different ways to create a variety of sounds that carry different meanings.

**RELEVANCE**   Traditional Hawaiian music, as presented to mainlanders, is usually convoluted and contrived, limited to that often seen on television. Because much of this music is associated with music performed to entertain tourists at lu'aus, a sense of authenticity is lost with respect to the rich musical traditions of the Hawaiian peoples.

**INTRODUCING HAWAIIAN MUSIC TO STUDENTS**   For children who do not regularly hear or see Hawaiian music performed, one may begin by asking children to describe chants or even "raps" they know. Do they have meaning? Use their responses as a bridge to discuss the cultural context. Children can create chants with accompaniments on a drum. Stipulate that they must play in a nontraditional fashion. After the children are familiar with the creation and performance of chants, listen to a traditional Hawaiian chant to compare and contrast. They may also add dance movements, then compare and contrast Hawaiian chant and hula with other cultural chants and dances (for example, traditional Javanese and Malay court gamelan that is accompanied with dancers). Comparing world traditions of chant and dance with current ones will help provide cultural, historical, and contextual understanding of music and how it is used across a number of cultures.

## Music of Mexico

*[This section was contributed by Gabriela Montoya-Stier, Northside Independent School District, San Antonio, Texas. From* El Patio de Mi Casa © *2008 GIA Publications, Inc.]*

The music of Mexico, like its people, is a mixture of pre-Columbian cultures and European and African influences that have developed into its own unique music. In this article, appropriate musical material for young children will be discussed along with different types of popular instrumental groups. This includes Mexican children's folk songs, corridos, mariachi, norteño, tejano, banda, as well as music of the Western art tradition.

**VOCAL MUSIC**   The Mexican culture has a rich body of children's folklore. Thanks to the published works of Mexico's great ethnomusicologists Vicente T. Mendoza and his protégé Francisco Moncada Garcia, many children's folk songs, games, chants, and

**FIGURE 4.1** "A las Estatuas de Marfil" ("The Statues of Ivory")

A las es - ta - tuas de mar - fil,   u - no,   dos   y   tres   a - si.

rhymes are preserved. The folklore content reflects children's lives and includes themes like: (1) religion, where children refer to saints or the Virgin Mary; (2) occupations, where students act out adult occupations like dancers, laundry workers, lumbermen, and so on; (3) animals, like cats, mice, rats, or cockroaches; (4) historical events or figures, like the story of Mambru; and (5) celebrations, like the annual Christmas Las Posadas or Dia de los Muertos (Day of the Dead). Most music is in major or implies major tonality. It is rare to find children's folk songs in a minor tonality or mode. Although there are simple two-tone folk songs like "Tortillitas de Manteca" or "Aserrín, Aserrán," most simple folk songs have so-do-mi intervals. Rhythmically, folk songs reflect the rhythm of the Spanish language, including duple rhythms in combination with triplet rhythms (for example, "A las Estatuas de Marfil" ["The Statues of Ivory"]).

Figure 4.1 starts with an eighth note triplet combination while the rest of the song has eighth note duple combinations. The song uses a tone set of sol, do, and mi. This particular singing game is a freeze game where students walk around in a circle with a person in the center, and the children freeze into a statue at the end of the song. The child in the center chooses the "statue" he or she likes best and trades places with that student. The vocal range of a children's folk song tends to be within an octave. It consists primarily of skips with some stepwise motion. Rhymes are usually meant for very young children—babies and infants—where parents can wiggle their children's toes or fingers or tickle them. For example, in "Una Viejita," a parent gently says the rhyme and walks the pointer and middle finger up a child's or infant's arm and tickles the child underneath the armpit at the end.

| | |
|---|---|
| Una viejita juntando su lenita, | A little old lady was gathering wood, |
| Le agarro el aguacerito, | A storm took her by surprise, |
| Y se metio a su covachita. | And she ran to her little cave. |

In most chants, the next person is chosen for the next game, like "Tin Marin," or for elimination, like "Zapatitos Blancos," ("Little White Shoes"). In Figure 4.2 "Tin Marin," the student or teacher says the chant while pointing to the possible players. Whoever is pointed to at the end of the chant is the next person to start the game.

Another category more adult in content is the *"corrido,"* which is a form of storytelling. According to Chew-Sanchez (2003), the corrido is a narrative song that is often danced. Composed in Spanish, it recounts historical circumstances surrounding a protagonist whose conduct may serve as a model to a community or whose history embodies everyday experiences and values of the community. A common historical theme among corridos is immigration, which describes and reflects the struggles that Mexican people face in the United States.

**INSTRUMENTAL MUSIC**    The most popular and well-known instrumental music is *mariachi.* The ensemble usually consists of four violins, *guitarrón* (a large fretless

**FIGURE 4.2** "Tin Marin"

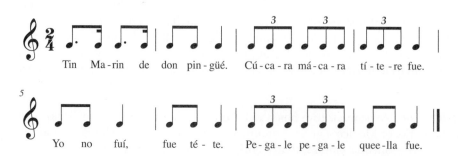

Tin   Ma - rin   de   don   pin - güé.   Cú - ca - ra má - ca - ra   tí - te - re fue.

Yo   no   fuí,   fue té - te.   Pe - ga - le pe - ga - le   quee - lla fue.

six-string bass guitar), *vihuela* (a guitar with six double courses of strings), *guitarra sexta*, harp, and trumpets. The musicians are dressed in *charro* uniforms that consist of boots, tight trousers that are ornamented along the outside seams, a short ornamented jacket, often a white shirt and a wide bow tie, and sombreros. There is still much speculation about the origin of the mariachi, but it is certain that it already existed by the early 1800s in west central Mexico, particularly in the states of Jalisco and Michoacan. It was considered party music for dancing in the rural areas of these states. During the twentieth century, mariachi was transformed to its current artistic status of careful orchestration and composition. The repertoire usually includes instrumental music and songs like *rancheras* that accompany a singer. One of the most respected and well-known groups is the Mariachi Vargas de Tecatitlan, founded in 1898.

Other regional musics include banda, norteño, and tejano. All of these types of music exhibit strains of German music brought in the 1800s by German immigrants to Texas and Mexico's west coast. Banda is originally from the Mexican state of Sinaloa. It is known for its big, brass band sounds. Bandas use trombones, trumpets, tubas, clarinets, saxophones, and percussion; it is dance music that incorporates polka, waltz, and bolero rhythms. A long-standing group that is known for its banda music is Banda Recodo. Norteño (or music from the north) refers to the music played along northern Mexico and along the border of the United States. Norteño features the accordion, the *bajo sexton* (twelve-string guitar), electric bass, drums, and often vocals. Tejano has almost the same instrumentation, but varies with the group. Tejano also has its roots in Texas; its well-known and loved artists were Selena and Los Dinos.

Like any other popular music, norteño, corridos, and so on, can have language or themes not always appropriate for children. It is important to obtain a reliable translation of all music prior to introducing it in the classroom. Although the lyrics of these genres are meant for adults and are usually inappropriate for the school setting, children will likely be familiar with them due to their popularity in Mexican and Mexican American communities. This music is usually played at dances and celebrations.

Western art music was introduced with the arrival of the first conquistadores to the Americas. As part of their plan to convert as many native people as possible, the Spanish conquistadores quickly went about building churches and cathedrals. The cathedrals became musical centers for performance and training. The most active cathedrals were in Mexico City, Puebla, and Oaxaca. Opera and instrumental music were very popular, especially in the nineteenth century, along with piano and salon music. Both European sacred and secular music had a major impact on Mexican folk music and dancing, especially in its harmony, choice of instrumentation, and song structure. Through the nineteenth century and part of the twentieth century, nationalistic music emerged; composers integrated contemporary art music compositional techniques with folk, popular, or indigenous tribal music. At the forefront were Mexico's famous composers Carlos Chavez, Silvestre Revueltas, and Manuel M. Ponce. For example, in Sinfonía India (1935–36), Carlos Chavez tried to re-create sounds attributed to indigenous tribes within the framework of a symphony.

**RELEVANCE**  Much of the music from Mexico has found its way into the United States and is quite popular. A large part of the population of the United States has roots in Mexico and other Latin American countries, indicating that there is a need to be familiar with the authentic music, rather than the commercially marketed music that may give a convoluted impression of the multiple styles and complexity of Mexican music.

**INTRODUCING MUSIC OF MEXICO TO STUDENTS**  The Mexican culture has a rich repertoire of traditional singing games, chants, rhymes, and folk songs that have been preserved by dedicated ethnomusicologists and educators. When choosing Mexican music for the classroom, always be mindful to have an accurate translation, especially when selecting instrumental music like norteño, banda, and tejano meant for adults.

## Music of Appalachia

*[This section was contributed by Maria T. Spillane, Allentown School District, Allentown, PA.]*

The cultural roots of the southern Appalachian region are rich and deep. English, Irish, and African traditions passed down and newly introduced shaped the developing forms of music and dance as the region grew (Inscoe 2005). The rough and wild nature of southern Appalachia isolated residents, so music was an essential part of the settlers' lives (Seeger 2003). They depended on mothers to teach the songs of their heritage, and they depended on the songs of their neighbors to keep them informed of the world outside the "holler." Fathers brought out their fiddles to keep their feet stepping and lighten the burden of day-to-day life. The rare public gathering always guaranteed a dance where tunes and steps could be traded along with stories and songs (ibid.). Many of the songs and tunes of southern Appalachia have been adapted for wide use in the classroom, and many more are still performed today as they were in the early nineteenth century.

To understand the multitextured cultural history of the southern Appalachian Mountains, it is important to understand the settlement of that area and the background of settlers themselves. The mountains run over a 1,500-mile stretch, from Maine to Georgia. Southern Appalachia includes most of West Virginia and parts of Alabama, Georgia, Kentucky, Tennessee, Maryland, North and South Carolina, and Virginia. The terrain is marked by impassable ridges and tangled overgrowth that would have made traversing the area extremely difficult in the days of early settlers. The ridges were four thousand feet high and only passable where rivers had cut valleys (Williams 2002). The multitude of crossing ridgelines created a maze-like terrain that often forced travelers back the way they had come. Settlement in the Appalachians started in Pennsylvania, where the landscape was less threatening, and headed south along the valleys.

Southern Appalachia remained unsettled for many years due to the existence of understandably hostile Native Americans, violent conflict over fur trade between the English and the French, unsettled land rights, and poor planting soil. However, a few strong, brave, and independent souls did venture into those hills to make homes for themselves. Most of these settlers were too poor to buy more hospitable land (Seeger 2003). They found their living in fur trade, making brandy wine, and hunting and gathering (Williams 2002).

There are two distinct types of music that can be traced to the roots of Appalachian culture. The Appalachian ballad centers on storytelling and the passing of information. Its roots are English and Celtic, and may be broken up into two categories: the traditional ballad and the broadside ballad (Riddle 1970; Wolfe 1977). Influences from early African American gospel music can also found in the Appalachian ballad, such as the tradition of adding verses (for both interest and necessity) and including call-and-response sections. Traditional Appalachian dance music (also referred to as old-time, jig music, hop, and flatfoot music) borrows its instruments from England, France, and Africa (Seeger 2003). This instrumental dance music found its beginnings in the traditional jigs and reels brought to this country from Ireland, England, and Scotland (McClatchy 2000). The introduction of the banjo by African slaves changed the way the people of southern Appalachia approached rhythm, and traditional Appalachian dance music was born.

**VOCAL MUSIC**    The voice was the most prominent instrument in early Appalachian homes. Most families could not afford instruments, so they sang together for entertainment and for educational purposes (Riddle 1970). The primary purpose of singing was to pass information. The subject matter of traditional ballads was sometimes adapted from bawdier versions of English songs about lost love (McClatchy 2000). In other cases, traditional ballads centered on life lessons learned the hard way as told to a composer by a neighbor or friend (Riddle 1970). Often the songs were about depressing subjects. The responsibility of passing ballads of the old world, and those created in the new, was left primarily to women of the household (McClatchy 2000). In some cases, ballads would transform themselves over time as new verses were added or deleted, and as new versions sprouted up in another area. In addition to traditional ballads, which were passed down from voice to voice, there also existed the broadside ballad, many of which can be accessed via the Bodleian Library at the University of Oxford. These songs were composed by professional musicians and were distributed by traveling minstrels on note cards referred to as ballad cards (Riddle 1970; Wolfe 1977). This form of ballad was also inherited directly from England. Broadside ballads were usually composed to depict current events such as train wrecks, sensational murders, and other disasters. Ballads that originated in England or Scotland are generally referred to as Child ballads (Wolfe 1977). This is in reference to Francis Child, who collected 305 ballads published by Houghton Mifflin in England between 1882 and 1898. American ballads are categorized according to the collector, some of which include Smithsonian Folkways and Malcolm Laws.

**INSTRUMENTAL MUSIC**    The most prominent stringed instrument in southern Appalachia was the fiddle, probably brought over during immigration (Lornel 1993). The man of the house was usually responsible for this instrument. Initially, the fiddle music of early southern Appalachia imitated the sound of the ballad. Later, as immigration continued, the Irish and Scottish influence became more prevalent. The jig (6/8 time) and the reel (4/4 or 2/4) were developed in the mid 1700s in Scotland. The characteristic and rhythmically powerful "saw-stroke" bowing style of southern Appalachia can actually be traced to a Scottish fiddler of that time period by the name of Neil Gow (Blank 1994). The drone of the Irish uilleann pipes later influenced the developing style even further, adding the tension-filled "sliding double stop" to the palette of the Appalachian fiddler (McClatchy 2000). The introduction of ragtime music added a rocking motion to the bow that has also become characteristic to the genre. Several dance forms resulted from mixing genres. Clogging or flatfooting is a distinctive collaboration between Irish step dancing and African dance (Charlton 1997). Later, square dancing developed as well with the addition of a dance caller to the musical ensemble (McClatchy 2000).

**RELEVANCE**    The multicultural history of the southern Appalachian region of the United States carries traditions from England, Ireland, Scotland, and Africa. The combination of these influences and the resilience of the mountain people created the high, lonesome sound that has by far been the most influential contributor to the world of modern country music, which remains the largest-selling genre of music in the United States today.

**INTRODUCING MUSIC OF SOUTHERN APPALACHIA TO STUDENTS**    By introducing students to the music of southern Appalachia, educators can instill an understanding of the multicultural heritage of that region and of the United States as a whole. By exploring Appalachian ballads and dance music, students gain an understanding of music in relation to the history and culture of the United States, an appreciation for the relationships between music and other arts and disciplines, and a deeper understanding of the importance of multiculturalism in a developing society.

## Music of the Middle East

*[This section was contributed by Christopher M. Wenger, North Penn School District, Lansdale, PA.]*

Arabic culture enjoys a widespread influence on Western culture, evident particularly in its formative adolescence, both in musical and other spheres of life (Farmer 1978). The music of the Middle East, like the cultures it reflects, is rich and diverse, characterized by a lack of standardization and regional variations.

**VOCAL MUSIC**    People more familiar with Western music who initially approach music of the Middle East find that the attention to vocal timbre is less developed than that of the tonal concept of Western classical music. Vocal presentations tend to be highly melismatic and ornamental, as the voice is used very instrumentally, rather than merely as a vehicle for text, sometimes using neutral syllables. Although text is certainly of primary importance in many genres, for example *qasidah* and *muwashshahat*, the communication of the lyrical idea never completely eclipses the importance of a beautiful melody.

This melodic focus, novel to Western ears, is a major facet of Middle Eastern music. Traditionally devoid of harmonic elements, exemplars feature an ensemble of solo instruments, all playing the melody simultaneously. This heterophonic accompaniment is then often paired in alternation with a vocalist. It is rare to find written examples of Middle Eastern music, as it is primarily an oral tradition and also highly improvisatory in nature (Racy 1998). Melodies in Middle Eastern music are derived from complex formulae known as *maqâmât*. Although maqâmât may initially seem like the scales or, more accurately, modes, found in Western music, the sound comprises much more than a mere collection of notes (Touma 2003).

An individual maqâm encompasses the pitch classes normally associated with its subsidiary patterns, but also expresses the traditional mood and character evoked in the listener by the performer. These moods are often rather vaguely and poetically described, such as "distant desert" or "eastern breeze" (Racy 1998). Bundled into this package as well are the nuances of intonation historically applied in performance in the form of microtonal variations: the bending of tones lower or higher to soften the aural impact of a larger melodic interval. Performers are guided further by characteristic patterns that function as a common starting point for the artist's own innovation in developing a maqâm in a *taqsim* (instrumental improvisation) or *layali* (vocal improvisation) (Hayes 1992).

Rhythmic forms in Middle Eastern music are formalized as well, though they are not as complex as their melodic counterparts. The majority of *iqâ'ât* (metric modes) are based on simple, duple patterns, with compound or complex iterations found increasingly in Turkey and eastern Europe. Many compositions have little or no rhythmic framework, or alternate between highly ordered rhythmic patterns and free melodic improvisation. Still others, especially folk and dance genres, are completely metrically ordered. Artists' creativity is also measured, in part, by their intentional lack of reconciliation to the **pulse.**

**INSTRUMENTS**   Instruments commonly found include the ubiquitous and popular *oud* (or *'ud*) the "amir al-tarab" (prince of enchantment). The *nay*, a reed flute; *buzuq*, the ancestor of the Greek *bouzouki; kamân*, a retuned Western violin; and *qânûn*, a plucked box zither are other melodic instruments typically found in Middle Eastern ensembles. Rhythmic instruments are the *tablah* (or *doumbek*), a very common ceramic drum, the *riqq*, a single-headed tambourine, and the *târ*, a large, single-headed frame drum.

**RELEVANCE**   Traditional elements of Middle Eastern music over the past thirty or forty years have been diluted by the influence of Western popular music. The number of common microtonal maqâmât in use today is approximately half that which were practiced in the first half of the twentieth century. Harmony, once completely absent, has infiltrated, removing much of the microtonal nuance of melody that is so vital to the uniqueness of this culture's music. Also, with the advent of fretted or tuned (well-tempered) instruments like the guitar and **piano,** shadings of tuning are clearly impossible, further stripping melodies of their richness. Traditional examples are still available but harder to find as the vast majority of what is commercially available retains mere inferences of the rich heritage, more as a flavor than as a distinct idiom (Touma 2003).

**INTRODUCING MUSIC OF THE MIDDLE EAST TO STUDENTS**   Patricia Sheehan Campbell and Amy Beegle (2003) write that, of all the world's cultures, Arabic styles seem to have been neglected in the American musical classroom, a situation that needs to be remedied. Middle Eastern genres, especially those of the folk traditions, are certainly novel to

Western ears, but can be very exciting, especially when introduced early. Arabic music is in large measure an amalgam of the cultures that surround it: a bit of the rhythmic intensity of continental Africa and a bit of melodic complexity of the Far East. Exploring scale structures different from Western music is a good starting point, perhaps on a Western string instrument like the violin. If it is possible to procure a Middle Eastern instrument, children can explore a different scale structure. For children not regularly hearing or seeing Middle Eastern music performed, it may be best to start with listening and video examples.

## Music of Native North Americans

The traditional music of Native Americans of North America is as diverse as the number of tribes; however, current ethnomusicologists agree that specific characteristics are shared in the following seven particular music areas (Miller and Shahriari 2006; Nettl et al. 2008):

1. Plains
2. Eastern United States
3. Southwestern United States, parts of southern California (Yuman)
4. Navajo and Apache
5. Nevada and Utah (Great Basin)
6. Pueblo (Four Corners region of the southwestern United States)
7. Northwestern coast and some of Alaska

According to Nettl et al. (2008), similarities among these various music areas are that the music is primarily vocal, and tends to be quite short due to the oral tradition of teaching songs. Drums, rattles, and scraping instruments are used to accompany voices. Singing often occurs with large groups, and individual ability is not as highly valued as group participation. The singing style often has a tense, pulsed sound to it, and there is a wide use of "vocables," or words that have no specific meaning. The traditional view of music was that it was from the gods, not created by man, and that it was to serve as a mediator between man and the supernatural world. To clarify, if a particular weapon was to be used for hunting, the assigned song for the weapon would need to be sung to activate its strengths.

A student shows how to stroke the surface of a hand drum to create a sound.

*Photo courtesy of Christine Stratton*

**VOCAL MUSIC**   Each of the seven areas previously mentioned have different vocal traditions: the Plains area has the singing style most distant from classical Western style; it emphasizes high pitches, tension, and harshness along with manufactured pulsations (Nettl et al. 2008, 343). Other music areas emphasize nasality (for example, the southwestern United States), low, harsh, and pulsing sounds (Pueblo and Yuman) or relaxed vocal sounds (for example, eastern United States). Some areas use wider ranges for singing (Navajo and Apache), whereas some use a narrower range (Great Basin) (Nettl et al. 2008). All areas include formal structure in music, either by sections (A, B, C, and so on) or phrases that are repeated. The eastern area uses a call-and-response style. Music of some Eskimo peoples is characterized by complex rhythmic structures and recitative style (Nettl 1954). However, there are many differences among the various tribes in Alaska so this description is not uniformly applicable.

**INSTRUMENTAL MUSIC**   The seven music areas also share a variety of instruments, similar in function and structure due to materials available for construction. Drums, rattles, and scraping instruments are common. An instrument closely associated with Native American music is the flute, which has various forms and shapes and may be made from numerous materials, depending upon availability. Instrumental ensembles or solos are not common in traditional Native American music, which is true for other world cultures with vocally based music.

**RELEVANCE**   Like Hawaiian music, traditional Native American music has largely been marginalized or commercialized for non-Native Americans in ways that are not always respectful to historical authenticity. With the opening of the National Museum of the

A student improvises rhythm patterns using a hand drum.

*Photo courtesy of Christine Stratton*

American Indian in Washington, DC, authentic performances and presentations of these cultures will be available on a broader scale.

**INTRODUCING NATIVE AMERICAN MUSIC TO STUDENTS**    Presenting Native American music follows the same recommendations made in previous sections. A sense of authenticity needs to be present by having students engage in an actual performance with Native Americans who specialize in performing traditional music. One venue for this is via a *powwow*. According to Nettl et al. (2008) and Miller and Shahriari (2006), the powwow culture developed in the latter half of the twentieth century as a visible strategy to build intertribal relations. Powwows happen in numerous places, for numerous reasons; many times they are open to the public as educational opportunities. Numerous activities, including powwows, have been planned nationally in coordination with the National Museum of the American Indian (http://www.nmai.si.edu/).

## Music of Russia

Although Russian music is often considered European, we have included it. Until recently, Russia permitted American families to adopt 62 percent of the Russian orphans adopted worldwide (Russian adoption statistics 2006). Many children entered the United States quite young, and as a result, may lose or have lost their native language and their traditional music. Some adoptive parents may have been surprised to hear their new 4-year-old child break into a sad and vocally stressful Russian folk song. After a few years, the child may forget it entirely. For those reasons, we include it here.

Although most of us think of the great Russian classical composers such as Shostakovich, Tchaikovsky, Prokofiev, and Stravinsky, the traditional folk music of Russia provided inspiration for many symphonic music works. Characteristics at a basic level follow.

**VOCAL MUSIC**    Because there are many cultures included in Russia, identifying each one cannot be discussed in this small section. However, some vocal styles are shared across much of Russia. Folk songs of Russia tend to be pitched somewhat low and are of a fairly narrow range, with a great deal of repetition. The melodies tend to be minor modal, giving listeners a sense of great weight and sometimes sadness. Two singing styles are familiar to Russian culture, although they are not limited to Russia. One style, mostly heard in female singers, is very pressed and a bit strident, and is anecdotally referred to as a "hard voice style." This is heard in many Russian folk songs recorded by Russian female folk groups. Although interesting to hear, it is not a style children should imitate due to the stress it places on the vocal mechanism. Another traditional voice associated with Russia is the very low Russian bass. Found in male ensembles, Russian basses are able to relax their vocal mechanisms so much that they can turn a vocal fry sound into an actual pitch, used for held tones or a "drone." A vocal style found in the Tuvin region and also in other parts of East Asia involves "throat singers." Throat singers, typically male, are able to create two pitches simultaneously.

**INSTRUMENTAL MUSIC**    A well-known instrument associated with Russian folk music is the balalaika, a triangular stringed instrument plucked similar to a guitar. Balalaikas can range from small ones to very large sizes that need to rest on the floor or ground to be played. Currently, balalaika orchestras abound in Russia, with many authentic recordings available.

**RELEVANCE**    Many Russian folk songs have been used in symphonic music. For example, Tchaikovsky used "The Little Birch Tree" in his Symphony No. 4, and three Ukrainian folk songs in Symphony No. 2. Several folk song traditions also include a dramatic component as parts of plays or holiday rituals and celebrations. Unique performance aspects of Russian music include pressed singing for females, a modified vocal fry (the Russian bass) for males, and, in the Tuvin region, two simultaneous pitches produced by one person through throat singing.

**INTRODUCING RUSSIAN MUSIC TO STUDENTS**    For a compare-and-contrast activity, use the sample chart provided in Figure 1: the children sing a simple American folk song and analyze it for musical characteristics (melodic similarity, contrast, **meter,** form, and so on). Next, compare it with a Russian folk song along the same lines. Balalaika orchestra music will provide a good contrast to a Mozart string orchestra.

## Music of South America

Like neighbors to the north, South America is a melting pot of many cultures ranging from indigenous peoples to current-day immigrants. Current research indicates that people were living in Brazil from 30,000 years to 50,000 years ago and about 13,000 years ago in Chile and Venezuela (Miller and Shahriari 2006). The Spanish and Portuguese arrived in the late 1500s, and added another dimension of culture. African slaves arrived in Brazil via the Atlantic slave trade, consequently adding African characteristics. Miller and Shahriari (2006) describe three musical traditions most prevalent in South America: (1) indigenous, from a native population descended from pre-Columbian and Incan peoples; (2) European derived music; and (3) music with African influences. Music of this section will focus primarily upon the indigenous music, but will briefly address the influence of European and African traditions.

**VOCAL MUSIC**    Both Brazilian rain forest and Andean peoples used vocal sounds in their music making; currently they are sung the same way they were thousands of years ago. Vocal music of the rain forest in Brazil is primarily monophonic, but it can be accompanied by flutes, rattles, and drums. The melodic contour descends, text is syllabic, and there is a strong use of rhythmic vocal pulsations to help give melody a sense of motion because text of the music drives the phrasing rather than meter, which is uneven. Males and females sing separately (Miller and Shahriari 2006). Vocal music was primarily associated with rituals of a spiritual nature, or when communicating with forces of the natural world.

In contrast, Andean peoples are recognized for a style of vocal music known as "yaraví," a song of sadness, usually concerned with death and/or the end of a love affair, sung in Spanish (Nettl et al. 2008). This music, although primarily associated with Peru, is a distant relative of the "triste" songs of Argentina and Bolivia (ibid.). Excellent examples of vocal music of the Brazilian rain forest and Andean peoples are available via the Smithsonian Global Sound website.

**INSTRUMENTAL MUSIC**    Andean music has a strong Incan heritage, greatly influenced by Roman Catholicism of the Spanish conquistadores. Like vocal music discussed previously, it is often performed the way it was hundreds of years ago. Miller and Shahriari (2006) describe characteristics of this music as having a pervasive amount of drumming along with the use of the *siku,* also called *zampoña,* and in English, pan pipes. Sikuri ensembles are found all over the Andes. Multiple sikus are used, as a solo siku cannot play all of the required melodic tones. Performers need to interweave and coordinate their playing so melodies sound seamless. There is use of parallel polyphony (Miller and Shahriari 2006), two melodies following the same melodic line, but not composed of identical pitches, which often results in parallel fourths and fifths. Melodies are short and repeated, but with little variation. Accompany drums have a drum head made of alpaca or llama skin. Several other kinds of instrumental music need brief mentioning because of inextricable connection with South America. For example, tango comes from Argentina, samba from the lambada dance, and bossa nova from Brazil. These dances are probably most familiar to North Americans; two are discussed in some detail.

Tango is a dance of passion that portrays two men vying for the attentions of a single female. The music is in a minor key when dancers are separated, but moves to a

A child shows how to play the Guiro.

*Photo courtesy of Rountree Elementary, Texas*

major key when the man and woman are united. There is much **syncopation,** and a strong steady beat with which the dancers flirt, but never commit (Miller and Shahriari 2006), so most melodic and rhythmic interest occurs on offbeats. Tempo is slow so dancers show off controlled movements and dramatic poses.

In contrast, Brazilian samba is pure joyous energy. The beat and rhythm of this dance music is drawn from African influences; therefore, many of the instruments are percussion. Yelling is also an essential part of the samba; when there is singing, call-and-response is the most common style. The strongest characteristic of the samba is the paused, stretched third beat (out of four) that is easily recognized. An excellent example of a samba is available on the Lost Safari Drummers CD (available via iTunes).

**RELEVANCE**    Music of South America shares many commonalities with music of the Caribbean and North America. Investigating similar influences adapted in different ways can help students recognize these same musical roots in other cultures.

**INTRODUCING SOUTH AMERICAN MUSIC TO STUDENTS**    This music would fit nicely with a social studies unit on the history of South America, and for lessons contrasting the music of Native Americans of North America. In music class, it may be compared and contrasted with Latin American music already familiar to students, such as "Livin' La Vida Loca," likely familiar to those who saw the *Shrek* movies. Although "Livin' La Vida Loca" is a salsa rather than a samba and is Cuban influenced, it would be a familiar place to start for many students.

## Music of Southeast Asia

*[This section was contributed by Shahanum Mohamed Shah, University Teknologi MARA, Shah Alam, Malaysia.]*

The region of Southeast Asia is made up of eleven countries, specifically Brunei, Cambodia, East Timor, Indonesia, Laos, Malaysia, Myanmar (Burma), Philippines, Singapore, Thailand, and Vietnam. Together, these countries contribute to the rich tapestry of music found in this region, each with its own diverse musical tradition. The music found in Southeast Asia is very different from the Western music tradition in the sounds, instruments, and philosophy. So diverse is the music found in this region, that not only is it different from one country to another, but the music can differ from region to region even within one country. This diversity is shaped by many internal and external influences such as animism, migration, religious movements, and social, economic, and political factors. The influence of surrounding cultures such as India, China, the Middle East, and the West are also evident (Malm 1977).

However, in diversity there is also homogeneity, uniting the music of this region. Southeast Asians themselves were responsible for the diffusion of cultural elements (Taylor 1990). Many great empires existed in this region, and with the extension of their rule, trading relations and marriages between royal families contributed to cultural diffusion and integration. For example, similar instruments and ensembles are found in certain countries although these instruments may be called different names and have different uses.

Besides popular music genres, much of Southeast Asian music is described as traditional in the sense that its scales, idioms, and repertoires do not in any obvious way derive from European, American, Middle Eastern, or other foreign music. Traditional music of Southeast Asia comprises court music, folk music, music for religious ceremonies, dance and theatre music; as well, it may be instrumental, vocal, or a combination. Although some music is unique to a country, some music of Southeast Asia is also syncretic in nature in that the music combines both native and foreign influences (Matusky and Tan 1997).

Although different types of scales are widely used, one main feature of Southeast Asian music is the use of the five-note or seven-note (or both) scale systems. However, their constituent intervals are not like the exact tones and semitones of Western scales, as the intervals between notes vary. Much of Southeast Asian music is nonharmonic with a horizontal organization but also homophonic in that it consists of a single line melody, not necessarily played on a single instrument, but often with a drum accompaniment. The musical texture referred to as heterophony evolved from this principle; that is, elaborations are carried out by two or more voices in various ways above the basic melody.

As with instrumental music, Southeast Asian vocal music is also found in a variety of styles, whether sacred or secular, such as classical court music, folk music, theater performances, and poetry (Malm 1977).There are many different styles of vocal production, and voices are used in different ways. For example, voices can be used for their color qualities rather than being used in the European music concept of dividing voices into ranges. In shadow puppet theater, a narrator assumes many singing and speaking qualities to depict different characters and scenes (Matusky and Tan 1997).

**VOCAL MUSIC**   Vocal folk music, which is sung with or without accompaniment, is found throughout Southeast Asia. The folk songs vary according to country and may be identified according to their function (Santos 2007). Most of these songs are an expression of a way of life and are associated with life, religious and community events, or daily labor. In Laos, folk music is known as *lam,* which is improvised or extemporaneous singing accompanied mainly by a bamboo mouth organ (*khaen*), although other instruments are also used. There are different styles of *lam: lam saravane* is the most popular. The various styles may have more than one singer and other instruments accompanying as well, including fiddles, flutes, and bells. Similar forms (for example, the *luk thung* and *mor lam)* are also found in Thailand, accompanied by the *khaen.* The Javanese vocal music, *tembang,* and the *Thai say pha* are both purely vocal (Malm 1977). In the Philippines, indigenous vocal music is performed in a solo or responsorial manner. Instructional pieces such as the *kyo* songs of Myanmar are also taught to beginners but are considered to be part of the country's repertoire and worthy of public performance.

Choral singing is also found in this region. The Malaysian *dikir barat* is a form of unison choral singing in which a soloist leads two groups in call-and-response in matching the verses of their competitors (Nasuruddin 2003). A form of chorus singing, but for a different context, is the *Kecak,* or monkey chant of Bali, which is a reenactment of an episode from the Indian epic *Ramayana.* The *Kecak* is performed by a large group of men who chant interlocking vocal patterns. Southeast Asian singing in large groups is also heard in religious chanting.

**INSTRUMENTAL MUSIC**   A rich variety of instruments are found in Southeast Asia. These instruments are typically made of metal (bronze or iron), bamboo, or wood and comprise percussion, wind, and string instruments. More commonly, these instruments are categorized as idiophone, membranophone, chordophone, and aerophone instruments, depending on how sounds are produced. Solo instrumental music is played everywhere in Southeast Asia; however, instruments are typically used in an ensemble setting, and Southeast Asia is famous for its rich orchestras that favor the blending of timbres over solo instruments (Music of Southeast Asia 2007).

Most music ensembles found in this region may be of mixed instruments or dominated by a single type of instrument, depending on the ensemble. Southeast Asia is noted for its gong tradition; in many instrumental ensembles, gongs are fundamental to the local music, particularly in Thailand, Laos, Cambodia, Myanmar, Indonesia, southern Philippines, and Malaysia. Three major ensembles belonging to the gong culture are the gamelan, *kulintang,* and *pi phat* orchestras in which the gongs carry the melodic part of the ensemble. The most famous of these ensembles are the Javanese and Balinese gamelan orchestra of Indonesia, consisting primarily of gongs and drums (Titon 2009). Depending on the region, other instruments such as the *rebab* (a two-string bowed instrument), bamboo flutes (*suling*), and even vocals are found in gamelan orchestras (Lindsay 1990). The gamelan ensemble is also found in Malaysia; a variant of the

Playing frog instrument from Southeast Asia.
*Photo courtesy of Christine Stratton*

Javanese gamelan, the Malaysian gamelan has no other accompanying instruments (Matusky and Tan 1997; Nasuruddin 2003).

The Thai equivalent to the gamelan orchestra is the pi phat. Originally to accompany traditional theater and religious rituals, the pi phat orchestra is an ensemble of bulb-shaped gongs, xylophone, drums, and the oboe (*pi*). Cambodia, Laos, and Myanmar also have ensembles similar to the pi phat ensemble. The *kulintang*, an ensemble of kettle-shaped gongs and drums, is found in the Philippines and Malaysia, and is similar to the *talempong* ensemble of West Sumatra (de Jager 2005).

Other ensembles in which a single category is heavily predominant are the bamboo gamelans used in Central and East Java and the *angklung*. In the northern part of Southeast Asia, ensembles consisting exclusively or mainly of strings can be found in Vietnam as well as ensembles of instruments like the lute, zither, and fiddle and the khruang sai ensemble of Myanmar, an ensemble of stringed instruments, drums and hand cymbals, and flute (*khlui*). The *mahori* ensemble of Thailand and Cambodia is largely string-based, with percussion instruments, xylophones, gong circles, and flute (Philippine arts: Indigenous music 2007).

Ensembles comprising wind and percussion instruments are other types of instrumental combinations found in Southeast Asia. The *nobat* ensemble of Malaysia, connected to certain royal courts, uses brass, reed, and skin instruments such as the kettledrum (*nengkara*) and a long silver trumpet (*nafiri*), two double-headed drums (*gendang*), oboe (*serunai*), and a suspended gong (Taylor 1990). In Myanmar, the *hsaing waing* orchestra that accompanies various kinds of theatrical performance is made up of a double-reed instrument (*hne*), cymbals, gong, and tuned drums. There are two categories of the classical orchestra found in Laos, *Sep Nyai* (or *mahori*) and *Sep Noi*. The Sep Nyai is ceremonial and formal music; it includes two sets of gongs (*kong vong*), a xylophone (*lanat*), an oboe (*pei* or *salai*), two large kettledrums, and two sets of cymbals (xing). The *Sep Noi* includes two bowed string instruments, the *So U* and the *So I*. Laotian music is dominated by its national instrument, the *khaen*, which is a type of bamboo pipe. A typical band (*mor lam*) includes a *khaen* player, fiddlers, and other musicians. *Pinpeat* ensemble of Cambodia is mainly a wind- and percussion-based ensemble of approximately nine or ten instruments.

Some of the ensembles found in Southeast Asia fulfill a variety of contexts and functions that include accompaniment for various forms of dance, theater (sung, shadow puppet, or marionette), martial arts, religious ceremonies, ceremonial music, weddings, or entertainment. The shadow puppet theater of Indonesia, Malaysia, and Thailand provides a case in point. In Indonesia, the shadow puppet is accompanied by the gamelan whereas, in Malaysia, it is accompanied by a small but distinctive ensemble made up of percussion instruments and a double-reed instrument (*serunai*). *Pi phat* and *mahori* ensembles are also used to accompany theater. The *kulintang* ensemble functions in social entertainment for a host of different occasions such as large feasts, festive or harvest gatherings, weddings, and official celebrations. Music used to accompany dance is the Spanish-influenced *rondalla* of the Philippines, *kantrum* of Myanmar, and *ronggeng*, among others.

Much of Southeast Asian instrumental music is used for vocal accompaniment (Malm 1977). Instrumental ensembles, which may include vocal solo or ensemble, are the gamelan, pi phat, and mahori ensembles. Different forms of theater also include vocal music such as the shadow puppet theater, ma'yong, and menora.

A detailed explanation of Southeast Asian music is beyond the scope of this section. There are many more genres of music in this region, including popular music and Western classical music.

**RELEVANCE**   One of the most obvious relationships we have in the United States to music of Southeast Asia is seen in the Orff Instrumentarium. Carl Orff was strongly influenced by gong and barred instruments and patterned the Instrumentarium after them. Music for Southeast Asians is reminiscent of gamelan style characterized by repetitive rhythms and passages. However, that's where the similarity ends. Playing in a gamelan ensemble requires a number of other physical skills that take time to learn, especially in striking the gongs, drums, or bars, and the cipher notation system that is used has nothing in common with music notation that you see used in this book (for an excellent description and examples, go to http://www.efn.org/~qehn/tutor/notation.htm). Gamelan ensembles are becoming popular in the continental United States, and combining gamelan with traditional symphonic styles has been done (for example, the Suite for Violin, Piano and Small Orchestra: First Gamelan by the American composer Lou Harrison).

**INTRODUCING MUSIC OF SOUTHEAST ASIA TO STUDENTS**   In selecting materials for classroom use, select music of countries that share similar concepts and instruments to compare and contrast. Students can compare **Orff instruments** and music with gamelan music. There are also podcasts available about gamelan music via *Gongcast Gamelan* (see Resources).

## Music of Sub-Saharan Africa

*[This section was contributed by Sheila C. Woodward, University of Southern California.]*

The danger of trying to provide an introduction to sub-Saharan African music in such a short manuscript is that the complex may be simplified, the diverse misrepresented by necessary selection, and the detail smudged by awkward and insufficient labeling. Nevertheless, in an attempt to provide small glimpses of a magnificent array of musical richness, it is hoped that these few words will inspire students and teachers to continue on a lifelong journey of exploring African music. Before embarking on that journey, it would be advisable to consider that national divides across the continent are not ethnically based and that music is more ethnically than country-based. Within each of the over fifty countries, multiple languages are spoken, and over 800 ethnolinguistic groups have been identified across the country (Turino 2001, 174). The diverse social structures, lifestyles, and cultures among these groups are reflected in the vast diversity of the music.

In sub-Saharan Africa, music has traditionally been widely practiced as a community experience in which all take part (Blacking 1967/1995; Willoughby 1993; and Gibson et al. 1992), and through which one is believed to attain one's humanity (Levine 2005). Historically, it would not be performed by a few on a stage. To this day, it is commonly practiced in the open, with everyone joining in. Nevertheless, particular members of the community would specialize in the performance of certain instruments. Over time, global influences have brought about huge changes in musical styles and practice. Solo and group performers have become well known nationally and internationally, such as the South African male choral group, Ladysmith Black Mambazo, the trumpeter Hugh Masekela, and vocalist Miriam Makeba. The music has never been static, and its diversity reflects the diversity of the multiple ethnic and immigrant cultural groups that have populated this region. Many centuries ago, travelers, when meeting on the road, would stop to exchange new music of their cultures. As a result, variations of the same song may be found today in many different languages, with distinct alterations in melodic, harmonic, and rhythmic characteristics, as well as formal structure and arrangement. Centuries of immigration and recent technological innovations have helped those influences to attain a global level. In turn, African music has deeply influenced musical traditions across the world, particularly those of American gospel, rock 'n' roll, and jazz. The music, of course, has always continued to develop within a context of social change. It has moved and altered in response to the social milieu. It is the "the voice of a culture—the narrative of its poetry, ideologies, beliefs, and lifestyles" (Loots 1997, 279). Yet, in a more dramatic direction, it not only reflects changes, but it is also a "force for change" (Woodward 1994, 198), and acts as a powerful transforming agent.

**VOCAL MUSIC**   Although particular regions emphasize certain types of instruments, all communities appear to practice vocal music. It is generally practiced by every member of the community. However, some music may be performed only by certain groups, like children, adolescents, women, men, or leaders. There is music that is distinctly unique to children, not taught to children by adults, but music that is created by children (Blacking

1967/1995). Much of the music is ceremonial, tied to special events in the passage of life, such as reaching puberty, initiation into adulthood, marriage, harvest, war, political events, and death. Music is frequently practiced as a celebration of life, a means of amusement and recreation. In other cases, it is a solemn means of connecting with ancestors, praying, or paying reverence to an individual person. Each piece of music has a specific purpose (Willoughby 1993). Music also plays an important role in traditional medicine and healing. Music is often practiced as a form of storytelling, where the history and legends of the people are passed on to the next generation orally. Other purposes may be to teach and to inspire values. Music is viewed as "mimetic and prophetic, serving as a mirror and mediator" (Byerly 1996, i). It recounts and comments on current events while serving a powerful role in directing and bringing about change in society.

**INSTRUMENTAL MUSIC**    Although the entire community traditionally practices music, individuals might specialize in performing on certain instruments, and some instruments might even be restricted to performance by a certain group or gender. Traditionally, natural elements were used in the creation of instruments, but manufactured materials, such as bottle tops, nylon string, and metal cans have been increasingly incorporated. Eventually, instruments originating outside Africa became prevalent as well.

One of the earliest known instruments is the one-stringed bow of the San who have inhabited the African continent for over 100,000 years (Thompson 2001). This bow was probably derived from an early hunting tool. A huge variety of multistringed bows are found in ethnic groups across the sub-Saharan region. The sizes, shapes, numbers of strings, and tunings vary considerably. These instruments are mostly plucked with the finger or struck with a stick, incorporating strong rhythmic articulation. Resonance may be achieved through placing an open mouth beside the string and varying the oral cavity to produce difference timbres. Gourds are also used to obtain resonance. Applying pressure at points on the string achieves different tones.

Handheld percussion instruments include a wide variety of items found in nature, such as seed pods of all descriptions that rattle. Smaller varieties might be strung together and wrapped around the legs to create percussive sounds when musicians are dancing. Shells, log drums, and sticks are additional examples of using natural sources to create musical instruments. Iron is hammered into bells and gongs.

Traditionally, drums take on both musical and nonmusical roles, being used to carry messages over hills and mountains to tribes in the distance, informing them of a wedding, a call to battle, or the death of a leader. Not only different rhythmic patterns, but also different drums might be used in association with particular gods or leaders, such as in the Yoruba tribes of Nigeria. Drums of innumerable sizes might be carved out of a tree trunk—a hollow cylinder with a skin stretched over one or both ends. One end may be open or closed, and the drums may be played with sticks, the hands, or a combination of the two. The hand strikes the drum in various ways to produce different

Two ways to play a small conga drum.

*Photos courtesy of Christine Stratton*

tones, creating more rhythmic interest. The fingers, thumb, heel, or entire hand might strike the drum, using various types of arm, wrist, and hand motions. The interplay of pitches and rhythms within one drum or across drums creates intense musical interest. Furthermore, the weaving of strings on hourglass-shaped drums that tighten the skin head allows for drums to become melodic instruments. In some cultures, drums are used to imitate speech, particularly where languages are tonal, such as among the Yoruba of Nigeria.

A wide variety of horns and flutes are made of seaweed, bamboo, cane, ivory, animal horns, and other natural elements. They are often crafted without holes or valves, designed for vertical or horizontal use. These might be played individually, or in a group, with single or few notes of each instrument combining to form patterns across the group that develop within evolving rhythmic and melodic structures. Interlocked pipes, known as panpipes, are found among the Venda in the south and as far north as the Soga in Uganda.

Mbiras (common to the Shona people of Zimbabwe) are found with varied design and names in different regions, having from eight to thirty or more different-sized metal rods. These are secured to a metal bridge on a wooden base. Held inside a gourd that provides resonance, the rods are plucked with the thumbs. A string of bottle caps might be attached to provide a buzzing sound. The mechanics of this instrument resulted in it being the most highly developed lamellaphone in southern Africa (Turino 2001). Patterns are repeated continuously, and several melodic and rhythmic lines can be heard at any one time. By combining patterns in different ways or adding small adjustments, the ear hears these patterns in constantly changing ways. Common to central African areas and spreading to other regions, marimbas are relatively large in size and have wooden bars arranged across resonant wooden cavities or large gourds. Musicians strike the bars of varying lengths and pitches with sticks. Marimbas of various sizes are combined to provide rich melodic, harmonic, and rhythmic textures. The modes vary from region to region. The akadinda variety of the Baganda in Uganda is so large that many people can gather around to perform on one instrument.

**OTHER COMPONENTS OF MUSIC PRACTICE**    The music of southern Africa incorporates more than voice and instruments—it is often integrally interwoven with costumes, crafts, sculpture, and props (which all have specific meanings and messages), as well as speech tones, drama, and movement (Willoughby 1993). During performance of most African music, the body might be described as fluid—it moves naturally as an integral part of the expression of the music. Sometimes, this is spontaneous. Other times, it may be a formal dance, performed synchronously within a group. Some rhythms within the movements may involve visual perception only, whereas others contribute to the percussive sounds, such as stamping, swishing the body, or making sounds with shakers attached to the body. Either way, the movements do not necessarily mirror the rhythms of the instruments and voices. They add to the rhythmic complexity of the music.

A multiplicity of modal scales is found across the regions of southern Africa, and the concept of pitch is relative. Outsiders might wonder if performers in some regions might be singing out of tune because of the minute differences from the pitches used in the **diatonic** scale. In some cases, speech tones may be incorporated, adding richness to the spectrum of sounds. Some African languages are tonal—where the same vocalization will represent a different word depending on the pitch level at which it is spoken. Some of the music in these regions follows the melodic shape of the tonal sounds of the text.

Modes vary across sub-Saharan Africa, with multiple combinations of tones that might make up various combinations of pentamodes (five pitches), hexamodes (six pitches), or the heptamodes (seven pitches) found in Venda music (Gibson et al. 1992). In parts of eastern Angola, the equihepta scale was used with the octave divided into seven equal intervals, whereas the hexatonic scale, evident in Xhosa music (G, F, E, D, C, B flat), is a combination of two triads: C, E, G and B flat, D, F (Gibson et al. 1992). Parallel movement of the harmonic parts is common (unlike principals of some Western classical music where parallel fourths, fifths, and octaves are discouraged).

Frequently, melody appears through the interlocking of different instrumental and vocal parts (Turino 2001). In other words, different parts of the melodic line might appear in different instruments or parts of an instrument. Melodic contour in southern African music is often based on a descending motion, and it is common for a lead singer in antiphonal singing to begin on a note higher than the entry point for the group (Gibson et al. 1992). Melodic improvisations are characteristically harmonically based.

Much of African music has levels of rhythmic complexity that are remarkable to most outsiders. Offbeat, syncopated rhythms are evident even in unison songs of very young children. Rhythm in Africa is considered "more highly developed than melody or harmony and more highly developed than rhythm in the music of many other cultures, India a notable exception" (Willoughby 1993, 166).

Rhythmic interest is mostly achieved through layered textures of rhythmic patterns within and between instrumental and/or vocal parts, speech sounds (clicks and speechlike vocalizations), the visual rhythms of dance movements, and audible body percussion (stamping and clapping). Offbeat rhythms complement the strong rhythmic pulse. A typical component of African rhythms is the juxtaposition of meters. A three-beat pattern in one part may be complemented by a two- or four-beat pattern in another. Depending on the various combinations of textures or **accents,** the same patterns might be heard in multiple ways.

There are structural components that are common to much music across the sub-Saharan African region. One is the typical call-and-response form, which has interplay between a leader and chorus (vocal or instrumental). Cycles of core harmonic, melodic, and rhythmic patterns will repeat over and over for lengthy periods in a circular motion, with no time-dependent endpoint (Turino 2001; Gibson et al. 1992). The improvisatory nature of the music involves performers engaging in a continuous variation form until the group senses a natural ending to the musical development. Performances of any piece will never be exactly alike. Multiple threads of melodic and rhythmic interest are interwoven as textures are altered, different parts enter or withdraw, melodies are embellished, and rhythms are intensified in complexity. Among the Pygmies of central Africa, the basic structure does not include call-and-response, but we see the overlapping of **ostinato** patterns that create a dense, contrapuntal texture, each part possibly having different length cycles that interweave to create a whole (Turino 2001).

Expression and dynamics are particular to each style and performance practice. One might find gentle yet articulated sounds of solo bow instruments being complemented with soft, speech sounds and lilting vocal melodic motifs. Some choirs portray melting, tender sounds, like Ladysmith Black Mambazo. Other choral groups use powerful chest voices and piercing ululating. Some instrumental groups might portray high-energy sounds of loud stamping and drumming.

**CHANGING STYLES**   Over the last centuries, distinct styles have developed within sub-Saharan Africa, not replacing, but alongside the community music of the peoples. These have occurred within vastly changing social environments hugely impacted by immigration, urbanization, and the development of the recording industry. African hymnody, linked to early Christian missions, increasingly incorporated African elements into its choral part-singing, as churches gradually became more tolerant of altered syllabic accents and other traditional influences. Examples are the hymns of the nineteenth-century Xhosa composer, John Knox Bokwe (Coplan 2007). In the twentieth century, an explosion of musical styles and subcultures has crossed tribal, ethnic, racial, religious, or other cultural divides. Urbanized populations, particularly the youth, have been moving away from traditional music toward unique styles that fuse their own musical heritage with elements of Western popular and jazz music. Some of this emerged in the workplace, such as the energetic gumboot dancing of South African mine workers where the body and speech sounds create intense rhythmic patterns. Other forms developed in villages, such as the Zimbabwe jit style, but the most common venue was the nightclub. Furthermore, some musicians of Western classical backgrounds began to incorporate indigenous material, such as in the works of the South African composer Peter Louis van Dijk.

Among the urban, popular styles, basic western European harmonic structure has mostly prevailed. The infusion of traditional melodies and indigenous rhythms has given each region its distinct forms of dance, jazz, and popular music. The juju music of Nigeria has become internationally known, fusing electric guitars and amplified vocals with traditional percussion, such as the sekere and "talking drum" (Turino 2001). In the Congo-Zaire region, local sounds were combined with Caribbean influences, made widely renowned by vocalists like Franco, with extensive guitar solos and bold horn accompaniments (ibid.). During the 1920s and '30s, the South African choral traditions that had originated with the Christian missionaries developed into the isicathamiya style in the mines and cities. This also became known as mbube style, after the Solomon Linda song, "Mbube" ("The Lion Sleeps Tonight"), which became an international hit. Joseph Shabalala "set new standards in isicathamiya composition" (Erlmann 1996, 89), his works being performed by Ladysmith Black Mambazo. Around the same period, instrumental dance music developed rapidly in the shebeens (illegal bars) that mushroomed in black urban areas. With the sale of gramophones, American swing music began to be imitated in clubs, and a local version of swing, known as marabi, was based on repeated harmonic progressions (like blues music), its cyclical nature having roots in indigenous musical traditions (Ballantine 1993). It was initially pioneered by untrained pianists and seldom recorded because of its association with illegal activity (ibid.). Groups feature piano, horns, and drums, often mixed with pennywhistles, accordions, or violins. The style later became known as mbaqanga. The lighthearted kwela style was developed by children in slums playing pennywhistles, who were imitating jazz bands (ibid.). Despite years of repression, the demolition of racially mixed towns that were home to key musical activity in nightclubs, and the fleeing into exile of many musicians, urban popular and jazz styles have flourished in South Africa (Ansell 2004).

**INTRODUCING MUSIC OF THE SUB-SAHARAN AFRICA TO STUDENTS**    Introducing children to the music of sub-Saharan Africa should preferably be achieved through pedagogical practices that are common to the region. This mostly involves modeling and imitation, rather than learning through the reading of a score. Especially considering the integration of costume, dance, and other elements into much of the traditional music, live demonstrations and the use of film are highly recommended. Learning to perform the music of young children is a good starting point. The students might examine how the melodic and rhythmic styles compare with those of their own children's music. The music should always be presented with vivid explanation of the historical and cultural context, reflecting the nature and intention of the music.

## Jazz

Jazz is a true American music genre. Jazz was born during the turn of the twentieth century in the United States. Several cultural music influences were mixed together in the musical cooking pot of the New Orleans music scene.

**ORIGINS OF JAZZ**    Many influences helped shape jazz music during the rich cultural and musical scene of the late nineteenth-century New Orleans. One musical influence came from the African captives of the slave trade. The African people had a rich musical heritage, and African musicians were often present on the slave boats coming to America. African music qualities influencing jazz include call-and-response, riffs (short phrases repeated several times), rhythms (syncopation, polyrhythm, offbeats), cakewalks (high-kicking dance) of the southern plantations, and the blues. The **blues scales** were named for their *blue notes*—usually the third, fifth, and/or seventh step of the scale. These *blue notes* were often played out of tune by bending the pitch. Figure 4.3,

**FIGURE 4.3** Sample Blues Scale

Sample Blues Scale, shows a typical blues scale; the *blue notes* are quarter notes with solid note heads.

A second musical influence was the band movement, including the American band movement, French bands in New Orleans, and the funeral band. Other influences were ragtime music, European church music, minstrels, country music, and music of the Caribbean-born musicians living in New Orleans.

**TYPES OF JAZZ**    The first genres of jazz were known as New Orleans style music and Dixieland jazz. Musicians of the era include Louis Armstrong, Sidney Bechet, Bix Beiderbecke, Jelly Roll Morton, and Fletcher Henderson. Jazz was distinguished from other forms of music by the use of improvisations. Vocal jazz grew out of the gospel and blues traditions of singing styles. Representative early vocal jazz artists include the blues singer Bessie Smith, Ethel Waters, Sarah Vaughan, Billie Holiday, and Ella Fitzgerald.

Between 1920 and 1940, larger or big bands grew common on the jazz scene. Big bands play jazz, include improvisations, and are composed of three to four trumpets, three to four trombones, five saxophones, and rhythm. Bands of the era included Count Basie, Tommy Dorsey, Duke Ellington, Benny Goodman, Harry James, and Glenn Miller. After World War II, many new styles of jazz developed, including Latin, bebop, cool, fusion, free, and smooth. Many experimental jazz styles that were known mostly to musicians are now commonly played in supermarkets and radio stations. Significant artists include Charlie Parker, Miles Davis, Dizzy Gillespie, Thelonious Monk, Stan Getz, Clifford Brown, Dave Brubeck, Quincy Jones, John Coltrane, Horace Silver, Oscar Peterson, Art Blakey, Herbie Hancock, Chick Corea, and Wynton Marsalis.

**RELEVANCE**    Jazz music influences many forms of popular music. Although jazz music is often heard in American culture, it remains less popular than other genres of music. In the late 1950s and later, many jazz musicians moved to Europe to find a more fertile ground for their art. Unique performance aspects of jazz music include improvisation and a musical language including syncopation, triplet feel, pitch bending, blue notes, and the use of riffs. The acclaimed album by Miles Davis, *Kind of Blue*, is recognized as the most popular jazz recording sold.

**INTRODUCING JAZZ MUSIC TO STUDENTS**    In American society, jazz music needs no introduction. Jazz is heard in the supermarket, and on television and radio, and the influence of jazz style is prevalent in many types of popular music.

For compare-and-contrast activities, use the sample chart provided in Figure 4.1. Ask the children to explore a blues scale on an Orff xylophone. Set up the xylophone with the pitches C, D, E, F, G, A, and Bb. Then listen to a recording on *Kind of Blue*, and compare Miles Davis's music to the explorations on the xylophone.

## Kiddie Pop

We include what we call "kiddie pop" because many children hear this music and go to these concerts long before they ever enter a classroom. Therefore, this may have a strong influence on children's music education long before they begin any formal study, so it behooves savvy music teachers to know about this music.

**PURPOSE OF KIDDIE POP**    The phenomenon of kiddie pop is fairly recent and, because it lies outside the field of music education, its influence has not been studied. However, recent research, especially in voice development (see Chapter 6), suggests that a more critical study of this genre needs to be undertaken, and further inquiry as to what degree it influences children's singing development and vocal use needs to be explored. Information presented here is to help you, as future music educators, investigate how this music influences your students.

A foray into iTunes brought up over 300 pieces of music that were designated for children. Several groups, singers, or music from TV shows seem especially popular (for example, Raffi, The Wiggles, *Sesame Street*, Alex & the Kaleidoscope Band, and VeggieTales). Music ranges from simple playgroup songs, to rock and roll. Topics are varied, from personal hygiene to religious instruction to developing appropriate social behaviors.

As we listened to and analyzed these kiddie pop pieces based on knowledge of child vocal and musical development, a number of interesting findings emerged. Adults write this music for children, and it is primarily sung by adults (surprisingly, many of them are male), or by female adults pretending to be children, or by adults and children—real children as opposed to electronically enhanced children's voices. Younger children love repetition, which we know to be an important developmental step in learning. They will play recordings or watch DVDs over and over. Perhaps what has truly emerged is a genre of children's music for adults. Examples of this particular phenomenon can be found on some web pages marketing children's music to parents. The selection text says something like, "If you like music of the Beatles and Paul Simon, then you will like this particular CD." Sadly, there is no mention of the children liking the music.

**RELEVANCE**    Most kiddie pop music is innocuous from a music education standpoint; however, a few concerns do need to be raised in relation to vocal modeling, and these need to be researched. The music is fine to listen to and to sing along with occasionally. Problems may arise when children try to sing entire songs that are not in their comfortable vocal range and don't fit their developing voices. These problems include vocal pressing; this happens when trying to produce pitches that are too high or low for healthy singing. Scooping or sliding pitches are also problems. Often heard in country and western music, sliding or scooping is not bad to do occasionally for an effect, but can become an unhealthy singing habit, especially if it is done with vocal pressing. Young children, who try to sing along with songs in an adult voice range, may yell or use a pressed speech sound in an attempt to reach pitches out of their singing range. This may explain why we sometimes have kindergarteners who equate yelling with singing. Needless to say, this is an area that needs research to see how it affects children's singing development before they enter school.

## GROUP EXPERIENCES AND COOPERATIVE LEARNING ACTIVITIES

The study of music of other cultures opens doors to a better understanding of the way music fits in daily life, special occasions, or traditions. Being able to put music in appropriate context is an important aid to understanding included activities.

*Activity 1:* Design a learning unit (approximately eight sequential lesson plans) based on the music of one culture. Include activities that are nonmusical. For example, share food, legends, stories, history, drama, and fashion or traditional dress of the culture if relevant.

*Activity 2:* Explore the Smithsonian Global Sound website (http://www.smithsonianglobalsound.org/) and the Smithsonian Folkways website (http://www.folkways.si.edu/index.html). Assign each group member to compile a selection of representative pieces from a single culture of the individual's choice. The students then share the list with their groupmates. This compilation can serve as a fundamental resource for teaching world music.

*Activity 3:* Search out and explore kiddie pop websites. Investigate the songs or song samples to see how well they work with child vocal development and vocal pedagogy (see Chapter 6 for more information). If you were to buy five songs for your own children to interact with, what would they be and why?

## Chapter Conclusions

The study of music and world music requires teachers and students to investigate the contexts in which music is utilized. Teaching world music to elementary-aged children requires teachers to design listening activities that allow children to compare and contrast musical characteristics using musical terminology, with which they are already familiar, before moving into unfamiliar characteristics. Designing lessons about these kinds of music requires preparation and thought on the part of teachers. Due to increased travel and sharing of ideas around the globe, many world musical traditions have adopted characteristics of other cultures. Although these similarities are interesting to investigate, each musical culture has its own unique history and identity, and this needs to be addressed whenever teaching music of any culture. This chapter is not exhaustive, but it presents basic information about a number of world musical traditions, including some important ones of the United States. Its intent is to help educators to use this information as a starting point for investigating music from differing cultural traditions.

## Resources

*For audio recordings (downloadable MP3 and other formats):*

Smithsonian Global Sound: http://www.smithsonianglobalsound.org

Smithsonian Folkways: http://www.folkways.si.edu/index.html

iTunes: http://www.itunes.com

*For podcasts:*

http://www.gamelan.org/gongcast for gamelan music

National Geographic Music: http://worldmusic.nationalgeographic.com/worldmusic/view/page.basic/home

*For further information about world music:*

Alan Lomax Collection: http://www.loc.gov/folklife/lomax/

Bakan, M. 2007. *World music: Traditions and Transformations.* New York, NY: McGraw-Hill.

Hula Preservation Society: http://www.hulapreservation.org/

Introduction to Gamelan Music: http://www.efn.org/~qehn/tutor/

Lindsay, J. 1990. *Javanese gamelan: Traditional orchestra of Indonesia.* Singapore: Oxford University Press.

Musical Traditions Magazine for Traditional Music: http://www.mustrad.org.uk/

Music of Cambodia: http://www.emusic.com/album/Traditional-CAMBODIA-The-Music-of-CAmbodia-Vol-2-Royal-COur-MP3-Downliad/10976745.html

Music of South America (National Geographic World Music): http://worldmusic.nationalgeographic.com/worldmusic/view/page.basic/region/content.region/south_america_6

Music of Southeast Asia: http://www.cartage.org.lb/en/themes/arts/music/Worldmusic/msoueastasia/msoueastasia.htm

*Rough Guide to World Music.* vols. 1, 2, and 3. London, UK: Rough Guides Publications.

U.S. Library of Congress: http://www.loc.gov/index.html

# PART II

# Music Elements, Curriculum, and Avenues to Music Learning

CHAPTER 5

# Listening

**This chapter addresses the following:**

- Why Listening?
- Listening and Cognitive Growth
  *Melody and Harmony*
  *Rhythm and Issues of Interaction with Other Musical Elements*
  *Preferences*
  *Age-Related Differences*

- Steps to Successful Listening Experiences
  *Effective Listening*
- Cooperative Learning Activities
- Chapter Conclusions
- Resources

## WHY LISTENING?

Listening is a basic life communication skill and an especially important musical skill. We are born listeners, as long as our auditory development isn't compromised during time in the uterus. The auditory system is the first sense to develop in the human fetus (Deliège and Sloboda 1996). Skill in listening permeates all music activities; it is difficult to think of a musical activity that does not have a listening component. Listening includes various experiences, ranging from identifying a single musical aspect such as a trumpet or a clarinet timbre, to determining a composer, period, and style as well as analyzing a composition's musical characteristics.

Many aspects of listening are simple responses, such as listening to a conversation; however, effective, efficient, and successful listening, especially to music, is a skill that needs to be taught and practiced over a long period of time. MENC national standards include "Listening to, analyzing, and describing music;" this is not a simple task, but a multidimensional one. For example, it is not unusual for children to hear a piece of music in music class and pronounce that they simply do not like it. Effective music teachers will ask the children to explain why, or help the children discover, in analytical and musical terms, why they do not like the music, instead of accepting the answer of "I just don't like it" without a reason. It isn't a problem when children do not care for a particular piece of music; however, children who have learned to listen critically will be able to support likes and dislikes using appropriate terminology that shows they understand. This chapter will aid music teachers in guiding students to think carefully and critically when listening to music.

## LISTENING AND COGNITIVE GROWTH

Much of listening research deals with infants and comparisons of children to adults. Our ability to listen begins before we are born (see a brief review in Chapter 3). This chapter includes listening research for children after the first year. More detailed information is contained in several general reviews (Flohr 2001; Flohr and Hodges 2006; Haack 1992; Hedden 1980; 1981; Lewis 1989; Thompson and Schellenberg 2002), a review for hearing disabilities (Darrow 1989), and a review about music therapy for infants (Standley 2002).

## Melody and Harmony

Research exists on key, harmony, and the intervals contained in melody.

**KEY AND HARMONY**   As indicated in Chapter 3, infants are able to detect out-of-key changes (Trainor and Trehub 1992). Trainor and Trehub (1994) gave 5- and 7-year-olds the listening task of hearing a half-step change, a whole-step change that went against the harmony but stayed in the key, and a two-step change that worked with the key and harmony. The 5-year-olds found the half-step change easiest to detect, whereas the 7-year-olds found the whole-step change against the harmony was easier to detect than the two-step change. The researchers postulated that the 7-year-olds showed awareness to the key as well as to the implied harmony. Krumhansl and Keil (1982) played an auditory stimulus to children between 6 years and 11 years old that defined a key and then offered a single pitch. The children rated how each single pitch of the chromatic scale fit into the set key. Between the ages of 6 and 11, the children's performance dramatically improved, probably as a result of maturation and enculturation.

Children listening to piano playing.

*Photo courtesy of Union City School District, Pennsylvania*

**INTERVALS**   Schellenberg and Trehub (1996) found that both adults and 6-year-old children were able to detect changes in interval of a chromatic note or **half step** (for example, on the piano moving from middle C to the black key C# directly above). However, the success was limited to consonant intervals (C and C an octave higher, C and F or C and G played simultaneously).

## Rhythm and Issues of Interaction with Other Musical Elements

We normally think of music elements such as rhythm, melody, pitch, and intervals as independent and divisible parts of music. Some studies support independence (Thompson 1994), and others point toward a lack of independence among elements (Flohr and Hodges 2006; Jones et al. 1982; Schellenberg et al. 2000). For young learners, a generalization might be that, depending on conditions of the task at hand, musical elements may interact with each other. For example, experienced teachers often note confusion that young children find in the process of learning the concept of high and low. As children listen for high and low pitches, several elements interact. Those elements may include pitch, loudness (loud has more energy and is higher), spatial orientation (for example, if a child is familiar with the piano, high on piano is to the right and low is to the left), and rhythm (for example, a child may confuse fast music with music that is higher, because fast music may be heard as having more energy than slow music).

## Preferences

Young children are able to demonstrate preference for musical styles described as march-like more than flowing sounds (Abel-Struth 1981). Peery and Peery (1986) found that preschool children's preference for classical music as opposed to popular music was influenced by a ten-month exposure. Even day-old infants make choices about what music they wish to hear. One team of researchers gave neonates the choice of listening to excerpts of classical and rock music (Flohr, Atkins et al. 2000). Neonates were able to manipulate which sound they heard by using a nonnutritive sucking pacifier and demonstrating preference for one type of music. Most of the thirty-four neonates chose the classical excerpt.

There are certain aspects of music that are preferred in music across international strata as well. In his study on preferences, Victor Fung (1995) found that people greatly preferred music that was loud, fast, tonal, and used many different pitches. Music least preferred displayed characteristics of being slow, dissonant, soft, and of a simple and limited nature. In adults, this may explain why parents can get so tired of listening to music that is very simply put together, such as a child constantly singing "Jingle Bells" or "Mary Had a Little Lamb." Young children like the repetition of simple songs, but adults may find it difficult. Children's music artist Tom Chapin commented upon this particular

| TABLE 5.1 Milestones in Listening | |
|---|---|
| **Months** | **Milestone** |
| 0–3 | Infants turn their head toward a musical sound; express satisfaction or distress with different kinds of vocal sounds; quiet to music (not all music, for example, most probably will quiet to music heard in utero); and respond to sharp sounds (for example, the click of light switch). |
| 0–12 | Infants are surprisingly proficient music listeners (for detail, see Trehub 2004). Infants demonstrate a preference for consonant as opposed to dissonant intervals (for example, P4 or C–F over A4 or C–F#). They are even able to detect a mistuned tone in ascending-descending scales of various types. They are more attentive to intact musical phrases than phrases disrupted by brief silent intervals of time. Infants may detect out-of-key or harmony changes better than adults. Infants prefer positive emotional tone. They also show more interest in singing than in speech. Maternal singing reduces infant arousal more than maternal speech. |
| 6–8 | Infants search for sound with eyes; and cry on hearing intense sounds or when music is withdrawn. |
| 9–14 | At this age, they orient to their name spoken or sung, and react to novel features of musical instruments. |
| Year 1 | At 1, children attend to music for several minutes. |
| 2 | They now can play music at various tempi, including those between 120 bpm and 200 bpm, and the child's natural response is to move or dance to the music. |
| 3 | They begin listening to tonal and rhythm patterns; they are ready to sing and/or play short, two- to four-sound patterns and can engage in games with step bells and other melodic instruments. There is wide variation in children's total listening time—individual children were very consistent in the time spent listening to each of four selections (Sims 1986). |
| | Children are acquiring many words. This age range is an optimum time for language development and musical development. For example, children hearing a language during this age period will retain their native speaker accent. In the same way, children hearing music during this age period will retain many nuances of musical sound. Just as children retain the nuances in language (for example, accent and tone), children will retain the nuances of sounds in music (for example, musical accent, duration of pitches, and timbre). |
| | Use good models of music for the children to hear and imitate. Both passive listening and active listening are beneficial for their musical development. |
| 4 | Exposure to a music style may increase preference for that style. |
| 5 | Children at this age are able to distinguish happy and sad emotions affected by tempo (Bella et al. 2001). Meta-analysis of listening studies show some positive effect but does not lead to a conclusion that exposing children to classical music will raise intelligence, academic achievement, or long-term spatial skills (Hetland 2000a). |
| 5–7 | Children at this age are able to identify instruments such as drum, trumpet, flute, clarinet, and violin as belonging to families of instruments (strings, woodwind, brass, or percussion). Several studies find a change or *shift* in listening (Bella et al. 2001; Flohr and Miller 1995; Moore and Staum 1987). |
| 6 | Children at this age are able to detect half-step consonant interval changes. Children aged 6 to 8 are affected by mode and tempo when listening for emotion in music (Bella et al. 2001). There is wide variation in total time an individual child listens to music, but children are consistent in their approach of time spent listening (Sims 1986; 2005). There seems to be no relationship between listening time and age or teacher ratings of attention. |
| 7–9 | Children are still open-eared early and interested in listening to various kinds of music. Interest in pop music starts around third grade, whereas interest in classical music decreases (Greer et al. 1974; LeBlanc 1981), as well as preference emerging for faster tempos. Fourth grade children are able to verbalize clearly about emotional responses to pieces of music (Paul 2003). |
| 10–11 | Children prefer music of faster tempos (LeBlanc 1981; LeBlanc and Cote 1983; LeBlanc and McCrary 1983); sixth grade students who receive instruction before and after or just before a concert will likely do better on music tests measuring presence of musical elements and styles than students who hear a concert with no preparation (Shehan 1986). Peer pressure is likely strong in affecting music preference, as sixth graders prefer pop music but have difficulty in verbally explaining why (Taylor 1985). |

phenomenon. In a concert series rehearsal with the Delaware Symphony Orchestra in February 1990, he remarked to the orchestra during the rehearsal that one reason he wrote children's music was to provide music that parents could listen to repeatedly. He wanted to make sure it was complex enough for adults to enjoy, yet simple enough for children to enjoy as well; he hoped that, as the children grew up, they would discover more about the song (the musical constructs as well as the satire) and continue to enjoy it.

An interesting concept that has gained some momentum over the last twenty years has been that of *open* and *closed-earedness* (Hargreaves 1982; LeBlanc 1981). This refers to the research findings that people are more receptive to particular kinds of music at certain stages of their lives, with a very likely variable including peer pressure, preferences, and enculturation. There are several stages in this phenomenon: children are quite open-eared from birth to approximately 9 years old. From there, they tend to stay closed-eared until middle adulthood. However, the closed-earedness returns in old age. This phenomenon suggests an explanation for older elementary up through college-aged children mostly preferring popular music, and for senior citizens also preferring the popular music of their younger years. Although this does allow one to imagine interesting implications when the current teenagers reach their advanced ages and take residence in various elder-care facilities, it doesn't quite explain everything about preference. A very significant variable in preference is familiarity. If a child is reared to listen to and critically experience all different kinds of music, from classical to pop to world music, then the open- or closed-earedness effect can be overridden to some degree.

### Age-Related Differences

Several studies (shown in Table 5.1; Mills 1989; Moore and Staum 1987; Flohr and Miller 1995; Bella et al., 2001) found age-related differences in listening ability. Two age spans are of particular interest. First, Mills (1989) reported most increases on a pitch and rhythm perception ability test occurred before age 10 or 11. Mills's findings support the idea that music aptitude develops in the early years of life, stabilizing around the age of 8 or 9, after which scores on music aptitude tests do not change to an appreciable degree. Second, the 5- to 7-year-old range correlates with Piaget's stage theories and findings in other fields (Janowsky and Carper 1996).

## STEPS TO SUCCESSFUL LISTENING EXPERIENCES

Techniques to enhance effective listening include clear goals and objectives, an efficient lesson plan, use of aids such as listening maps and props, electronic media, and live performance.

### Effective Listening

To become effective listeners, children need to be taught by effective teachers, whether they are parents, schoolteachers, or any other adults whom the children value as important. Although we will cover this aspect in more detail by grade level later, a number of cardinal rules and goals come into play when creating effective listening lessons for students. Above all, these lessons are never to be thrown together at the last second.

The following are goals and objectives for listening lessons:

- To help develop sensitive, interested, attentive music listeners
- To build an aural vocabulary and identification/discrimination skills (increased perception and consequent describing of aural phenomena)
- To help develop the ability to perceive and consequently explain how elements of music fit together and create an expressive medium
- To reinforce already learned musical concepts and vocabulary

The following are traits of an *effective* listening lesson:

- Does not exceed the child's attention span. A child's attention while listening to music is very individual and not as simple, as older children can listen for longer time periods (Sims 2005; Sims and Nolker 2002).
- Focuses the students' attention selectively on a particular aspect of music (for example, meter, tempo, dynamics, instrumentation, form, and style), *one at a time*.

Inexperienced child listeners are generally able to center on only one musical aspect at a time. Older children with listening experience may be able to handle two or three things at a time.

- Presents a piece more than once to help students fully grasp the objective. A child needs an average of seven to nine listening times to internalize and mentally process music. This also works for inexperienced teenage and adult listeners.
- Provides a hook that prepares the listener for the experience.
- Provides for an experience that takes place within a context with which students are already familiar. Listeners need to have some connection to previous knowledge (for example, a musical, historical, or literary connection).
- Provides listening experiences that are layered and multifaceted. As you play music over and over to help children internalize music, make sure to add a layer of new experience each time in the listening activity to help keep attention.

The following are traits of an *ineffective* listening lesson:

- Includes the teacher talking over the music. Although teachers may believe they are being helpful, this is actually distracting to listeners, and is also likely to result in the auditory phenomenon of "masking," in which one sound source is so concentrated upon or provides auditory information that supercedes the other, so that the other is masked and not attended to (Gelfand 2004; Moore 1986; 2004).
- Has the children read or draw how they feel while the music is being played.
- Is a one-time shot, without revisiting the piece of music.

To plan an efficient and effective listening lesson, the teacher must:

- Be totally familiar with the piece of music—no ifs, ands, or buts. There is a good reason for all that music history, appreciation, and theory that music students study in college.
- Be able to extract the salient musical qualities and highlight those for students to help guide them
- Be able to make *effective* listening maps and visuals, especially for young students. However, visuals can't be so overwhelming as to detract from the listening experience. More on this follows.
- Either have sections of music extracted to play as hooks or ideas to listen for in advance. There should be no digital hopping around on the CD trying to find something (this is where MP3s come in very handy); if one is technologically challenged, excerpts can be created using older technology such as a tape recorder.
- Be able to connect the piece of music to concepts and skills in the curriculum. For example, with older children, the famous "Dies Irae" ("Day of Judgment") melody can be first taught melodically and rhythmically as students play it on their instruments or actually sing it in Latin, and then the students can hear (over a period of time) how the same theme is used by different composers over the ages. You may hear the "Dies Irae" melody in movie sound tracks. Following is a list of music that uses the "Dies Irae" melody:
  1. "Symphonie Fantastique" (Movement 5) by Berlioz
  2. "Totentanz" by Liszt
  3. "Symphonic Dances" (Third Movement) by Rachmaninoff

**FIGURE 5.1**  "Dies Irae" Melody

Dies Irae Melody

Thomas de Celano, 13th Century

**4.** "Danse Macabre" by Saint-Saens

**5.** Music from the *Lion King* (when Mufasa is chased and dies)

With younger children (in kindergarten and grade 1, for example), you can point out that the melody from "Twinkle, Twinkle Little Star" is also featured in the following:

**1.** Mozart's variations on the same theme

**2.** The "Alphabet Song"

**3.** Fossils from *Carnival of the Animals* by Saint-Saens

The lesson must be well planned in advance. These are not the kind of lessons that are put together the night before teaching a class.

The following are possible teaching and learning approaches to assist in listening development, or preparing for a lesson:

- Song or melody. Use music with an embedded familiar song or melody.
- A musical concept (for example, higher, lower, fast, slow, faster, slower)
- Story-based (*Carnival of the Animals, Peter and the Wolf*)
- Playing and composing using melodies from the music (using, for example, Orff instruments, student-constructed instruments, found sounds)
- Music from TV shows, commercials, and movies. These are often good starting places, but you have to recognize the pieces. The following are some currently common ones:
  **1.** *Pirates of the Caribbean:* Notice that the themes for nearly all the pieces in the original movie are in d minor and start with do-re-mey. The variations among them are in rhythm and tempo.
  **2.** *Babe:* The theme song sung by James Cromwell is actually the main theme from the finale (Movement 4) of Saint-Saens' Organ Symphony No. 3.
  **3.** *Shrek 1, 2,* and *3* borrows from many musical artists using styles from classic rock to contemporary music.
  **4.** Verdi's "Dies Irae" from the *Requiem* is often used in movie trailers and athletic commercials, as is Orff's first movement ("O Fortuna") of *Carmina Burana*.
  **5.** Aaron Copland's "Hoedown" from *Rodeo* is used in commercials about meat and beef.
  **6.** "O Mio Babbino Caro" from Puccini's opera *Gianni Schicchi* is often used in Italian restaurant or pizza commercials.
  **7.** For National Public Radio listeners, the theme song used for election coverage segments is the 3rd Movement, "Allegro Vivace," from *Symphony in Brass* by Eric Ewazen.
  **8.** *Ratatouille* contains marvelous musical selections that lend themselves well to teaching and reinforcing form, rhythm, melody, and syncopation and jazz style. An earlier Pixar movie, *The Incredibles,* has a strong stylistic connection to big band jazz of the 1940s and '50s. The movie *Wall-E* also uses several pieces from American musical theater, while *Up!* uses musical styles closely associated with the middle 1900s. Michael Giacchino composed the music for all these movies.

**AIDS TO ENHANCE THE LISTENING EXPERIENCE**    Teaching an effective listening lesson also goes beyond telling the kids to listen to the music. Often, visual materials are implemented to help the process along. Although these are great tools to use, they can be overused and misused, and can cause more problems than be helpful. We will look at the pros and cons as we discuss several avenues of visual aids: listening maps, electronic media and live performance, and the use of props and worksheets. However, before we get into that, we need to give some background in the field of instructional systems design (ISD), now more commonly known as instructional systems technology (IST), which concentrates on, but is not limited to, visual and aural presentation of materials and consequent human perception and processing of them, and how they enhance or distract from learning.

Gerald Murch's (1984) landmark research clearly indicated that there are physiological principles of visual perception that drive our effective use of color and design, especially in the education process. Although much of this has been considered in computer interface design for instruction, the ideas seem largely ignored in music education. By using many fancy visuals, visual movement, and bright colors as possible to help teach music, we may be distracting from the music. For example, imagine that you are watching the evening national news, and the anchor is female. Now imagine, as she sits at her desk and seriously reads the news off the teleprompter, that her hair color, clothing, makeup, and background all change every ten seconds through the entire broadcast. At the end of the broadcast, you will more likely remember all the visual changes that were happening and very little news. This kind of situation can also occur with listening aids that are too stimulating—children will more likely remember visual aspects and not musical ones, and the younger the children, the more likely they will concentrate on the visual stimuli only and ignore the music. Use of visual aids needs to be carefully considered in detail, especially when teaching listening skills. With too much visual stimulation, there is a chance that there could be some cross-sensory modal processing confusion (Frassinetti et al. 2002; Godfroy et al. 2003; Schutz and Lipscomb 2007; Strybel and Vatakis 2004).

When looking at using listening maps, either the kind that are handed out or the kind that are on computers, music teachers need to be savvy enough about visual aspects of the map and how they relate to music to make sure the visual presentation doesn't distract from the actual listening experience.

**Listening Maps—Printed Handouts or Overheads**   These kinds of maps can take all different forms—from those that are simply of a linear nature, a pictorial nature, or as a chart, to those that are complex representations of a piece of music requiring a teacher to spend a lot of time helping children figure out how to use it. These kinds of maps are often included with major music series books, and there are a number of websites where music teachers upload their own to share.

To be effective, listening maps need to be quite simple and to the point. They need to be intuitive and user-friendly in that the children can simply look at the map and see how it will function in context of the piece. For example, the following listening map for part of the "Troika Song" from Prokofiev's *Lieutenant Kije Suite* can provide a useful sample. The goal of this lesson would be to reinforce understanding of same and different sections in music, moving to the terminology of A and B. This particular map also indicates that the beats move in groups of twos.

Figure 5.2 can be used to introduce the "Troika Song" (orchestral version, not vocal). Because one important design aspect of an effective listening lesson is to layer listening experiences, this could be used for the first level in which students simply tap an illustration to the steady beat. This would be done to find out if the music has a steady beat or no beat. The entire piece would not need to be played. The second layer of this activity would be to listen for form. When children start tapping the beat on the sleigh, they would change to the horse when they hear an instrument change: brass plays the B section, whereas strings and jingle bells play the A section. In a third experience, they would listen to see if melody changes along with instrumentation (it does). At this time, children would review, with the teacher, the concept of same and different sections of music, and use terminology to explain how the second section is similar but different from the first: Both sections have a steady beat. The first section has a longer melody and is played by strings, and the second section has a shorter melody and is played by brass. At this point, the children could be introduced to A and B at the beginning of the lines as the music terminology used to tell one section apart from another. A simpler version of the previous example could be just of one sleigh on one line, and one horse on another, and children would tap the corresponding illustration to the beat.

**FIGURE 5.2** Listening Map for Part of "Troika Song" from Prokofiev's *Lieutenant Kije Suite*

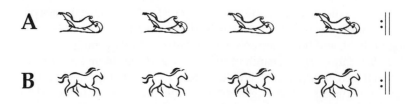

Those of you familiar with the "Troika Song" know that the piece is far more structurally complex than this; it's actually a rondo form with a spectacular fall in the C section. When it comes to introducing this music to new listeners-in-training, shorter is better. The next time this piece comes up, we would review what we already learned and continue. This would be a terrific piece to introduce rondo form, but only after the students are familiar with the A, B, and C sections. This piece also includes the introduction and ending, which are very different, and those might also be saved until later.

Now take a look at the map itself (see Figure 5.2). You see that graphics are relevant to the piece of music, which is about a sleigh ride, so that's why both a sleigh and horse are used as graphics. The style of the two illustrations is very similar, which provides visual continuity and doesn't need a whole lot of visual processing. The students spend less time mentally dealing with graphics and instead spend more time with music.

If this map were to continue (a later version would be handed out), it could look like Figure 5.3.

In this case, the C section is introduced with the horse upside down. When the horse slips and the sleigh threatens to fall over, there is what may be called a "whoa" moment to show that the section is different, but it's different primarily in melody, not in tone color. If it were drastically different in melody, instruments, tempo, and so on, a complementary graphic would be chosen to indicate that difference.

The previous are simple listening maps, and one of the best aspects about making your own is that you can make them to meet your students' specific needs and your instructional purposes. Other kinds of listening maps of this genre become more complicated, indicating a journey or procession through the music. A trend has been to make the maps more complicated, simultaneously indicating many aspects at the same time: dynamic level, rhythms, articulations, character connections, and story line. To use a metaphor, imagine that you are driving your car into an unfamiliar town, and you fleetingly glance at a GPS map in front of you to make sure you know the name of the street that you need to turn on. When you glance at the map, you need a clear marking of what is the most singular important aspect. If instead you glance at the map and see it obliterated by a mass of bright and crowded ads for restaurants that fight for your attention, in addition to narrated directions that may not be understandable, the chances are good that (1) you would miss your road, (2) you pull over to the side of the road to look at the GPS more closely, or (3) you scream in frustration.

Information overload can happen with listening maps as well when they are filled with too many pieces of information, especially when the information presented isn't

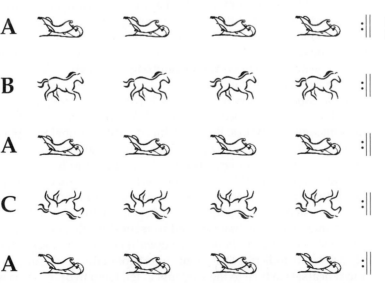

**FIGURE 5.3** Listening Map 2 for Prokofiev's *Lieutenant Kije Suite*

exactly relevant to the music activity at the time of instruction. When you peruse a listening map to consider whether or not to use it, consider the following:

1. Is it intuitive? Do you need to explain every symbol to students before listening?
2. If the graphics are representative of the musical story, are they actually relevant?
3. If the graphics are non-representational, are they simple and streamlined?
4. Are there repetitive elements that reinforce the concepts, or are there different graphic elements along the whole map?
5. Does the map encourage students to just sit and zone out—is an overt reaction (clapping, snapping, raising of hands when a section changes, and so on) possible?
6. Most importantly, does the map cover a very long piece of music with simply too much information? For example, are all of the possible layers of experience represented at once in a manner that may be more distracting than helpful?

A current trend is to have interactive listening maps that can be run on a computer. Although interesting and promising, these can serve to be more of a distraction than an enhancement, because the characters on the maps move. Adding movement, particularly of characters or instruments, can be an impediment to the listening lesson, particularly if the computer runs a bit slowly and the map motion is out of sync with the music, or if it stalls. These also need to be evaluated far more carefully for use in the classroom.

**Electronic Media and Live Performances**   Electronic media refers not only to the electronic interactive versions of listening maps mentioned previously, but also to videos or DVDs of live performances and materials prepared electronically by symphony orchestras, available online. Both of these serve different purposes and are important aspects of the layering process.

Videos and DVDs are available, but can be a bit expensive. Usually, these are prepared with an educational goal in mind (for example, the American Symphony Orchestra League has identified education as a prime concern), but that doesn't mean that the performance is constructed in a way to enhance the ability to learn to listen. This means that music educators need to prepare students well before they see the video, so they can not only watch musicians perform the piece, but also be able to identify major aspects of the music. These videos are best used as a culminating listening experience rather than as an introductory one.

A number of symphony orchestras are making listening guides and preparation materials available online for children to either interact with on their own, or for teachers to download and use to help prepare students to go to a youth concert or an open rehearsal. Creating effective materials for music educators is a new endeavor of many orchestra education departments. You may find they are filled with a lot of information that is not particularly relevant (for example, word searches, pictures to color, and so on). Some orchestras are moving toward the development of more relevant materials (such as Kodály- and/or Orff-based approaches, or materials that work with the school music curriculum), but these are exceedingly rare at this point. We developed samples of these kinds of materials for professional use that are available online for download. This is the direction these materials are moving toward in development; however, this doesn't need to stop you from developing your own.

One of the best ways to teach and enhance listening experiences is to take students to actual concerts or open rehearsals. Most symphony orchestras and opera companies offer student performances, and a number of the major symphony orchestras (for example, Philadelphia, Dallas, Boston, Chicago, the National Symphony) permit school students to come to open rehearsals. What needs to be emphasized here is that, for this kind of experience, students need to be prepared to listen and watch, so this entails a great amount of preparation on the part of music teachers. This experience would be the epitome of the listening lesson sequence. Students are expected to sit in the audience and listen and watch quietly, as they are actually watching musicians at work.

Some orchestras have started to reconsider this offering due to poor behavior of students who have attended these open rehearsals. On several occasions during open rehearsals, an audience of students interrupted the musicians, and the conductor had to stop rehearsals to turn to the students to tell them to be quiet, as witnessed by one of the authors of this book. There is no invisible screen separating musicians from the audience, and the musicians in the orchestra often see and hear the audience very clearly—an acoustical issue in the construction of concert halls. Preparing your students to enjoy a positive listening experience is integral to success of an open rehearsal for both musicians and students.

One of the best live performances you can give your students is your own. Play a piece of music or sing for them. If you perform professionally, invite them to your concerts. Have them put on class recitals. Often, small chamber ensembles are available to visit schools, but please note they are often on a tight schedule and the impetus to prepare students for the performance still lies with the music teacher.

**Props and Worksheets (Non-Mapped)**    Props and worksheets are perhaps some of the best vehicles to enhance listening lessons, as they require more student-centered behaviors. Students can't just sit and listen: they will need to overtly gesture, write down, circle, or point to an icon on a chart to indicate what they hear.

Props are especially good for young students, and can be as simple as holding up a particular colored stick in response to hearing a theme or repeated pattern. Props are effective in music that tells a story. For example, *Peter and the Wolf* has a cast of characters that can be converted into puppets (characters are cut out, colored, and pasted on wooden sticks) that students hold up when they hear the particular theme of the character. Props can also be actual instruments that are played—very softly, or the playing is pantomimed—at certain times in the listening lesson.

Listening charts work well for older students who have an extensive musical vocabulary, but they can be modified, made simply for younger students (see Table 5.2).

Although the sample in Table 5.2 is quite sophisticated, it can be easily reconfigured to be simple. For example, with younger children, the chart could be formatted as an either-or selection (fast or slow). These are very easy to make. Students would use these during a listening lesson and circle what they hear; the first listening would require

**TABLE 5.2  Listening Chart, Grade 6**

| Rhythm | Steady beat | Irregular beat | Slow tempo (largo, adagio, lento) | Moderate tempo (moderato, andante) | Fast tempo (allegro) | Very fast tempo (vivace, presto) |
|---|---|---|---|---|---|---|
| Meter | Moves in 2 | Moves in 3 | Moves in combination of 2+3 | Moves in combination of 3+2 | | |
| Melody | Generally moves by steps | Jumpy melody | Simple, songlike melody | Very elaborate melody | Same melody is heard often | |
| Dynamics | Loud | Soft | Gradually softer (decrescendo) | Gradually louder (crescendo) | Many dynamic changes | Few dynamic changes |
| Timbre | Solo instruments | Small ensemble | Large ensemble | Traditional instrumental | Traditional voice | Unusual or electronic timbres |
| Harmony | Consonant | Dissonant | Key feeling/no key feeling | Same texture throughout | Mixed textures throughout | Monophonic; homophonic; polyphonic |
| Form | Strophic (AA) | AB | ABA | ABACA | Sonata-allegro | Through-composed |
| Tempo changes | Gets gradually faster | Gets gradually slower | Gets suddenly faster | Gets suddenly slower | | |
| Style | Choral | Orchestra | Opera | Pop/modern | | |
| Period of music history | Medieval | Renaissance | Baroque | Classical | Romantic | 20th–21st century |

them to listen for rhythm. The second time they listen to the music, they may listen to another aspect of the piece (for example, melodic characteristics). This chart can also be used when listening to two or more sections of a piece of music. Students might circle the characteristics they hear in the A section with a green marker, then listen for characteristics of the B section and circle those with a red marker. This way, they are set up to compare and contrast how the sections are different and same. Although this kind of chart is the simplest, it has potential to be most effective.

**Other Strategies**   Students can create a piece of music out of fundamental building blocks and experiment with their own interpretations of it before they hear how a composer arranged the same building blocks. For example, W. A. Mozart is known for his "Musikalisches Würfelspiel," a composition game involving the rolling of dice for which he wrote out instructions in 1787. Although it is not likely that Mozart played this game himself to compose his pieces of music, many of the themes and ideas actually may be found in some of his pieces. Rules for this game are available online at a number of websites, and there is also an official game available.

Prior to listening to an example, compositional styles of minimalism and serialism most easily lend themselves to experimentation. Tone rows are easy to construct, and an entire class can create and perform one, with an accompaniment, on many kinds of instruments. The tones do not even need to be actual pitches, as they can also be tone colors of nonpitched instruments and unique rhythm patterns. In minimalist composition, taking apart a piece by the American composer Terry Riley and having the students put the small pieces of it back together in different ways before they hear how Riley did it is a very effective way for students to experience minimalism. The lesson plan example we use later in this book with John Adams's "The Chairman Dances" was a very successful strategy, which can be adapted to work with other pieces of music. This is a very good way to learn about similarities and differences among the world's music.

**No Maps, No Charts, No Props**   This can be done. It is indeed possible to have students listen quietly to a piece of music. However, use this as a culminating experience, not an introductory lesson. It can be used, on occasion, if you want to play a version of "Name That Tune," in which the children listen and identify the piece of music (for example, title, composer, style,), or if they listen and identify various characteristics of the music from memory. This will require them to listen critically and intently, with a purpose. This is the kind of listening one should do at a concert or any kind of performance, as the aural information discovered needs to be extricated from within one's personal knowledge rather than identified from a list of possibilities. This activity is the sign of a sophisticated and learned musical listener, a goal we have in music education.

**Sample Listening Experience**   The aids we discussed previously lend themselves to inclusion in many kinds of listening activities. In Part III, we will provide sample lessons that address age appropriateness. It is best that these activities be done within a contextual framework, whether it is historical, literary, scientific, or other subject matter. We provide one sample here, but Part III has others. This one gives an overall feel of how this is done, and encourages the use of your own imagination and knowledge of other disciplines to create interesting and fun units and activities.

In 1986, the National Aeronautics and Space Administration (NASA) instituted the "Teacher in Space" project that, as many of you know, turned out tragically. Fortunately, in the summer of 2007, the Teacher in Space project was reimplemented, although many schools were not in session at the time and were not able to participate to the degree they would have during the school year. However, in 1986 a number of teachers, not going into space, were still part of this project. Some public schools were designated as "Mission Watch" schools. They received not only satellite dishes directly from NASA to use for the week that Christa McAuliffe was to be broadcasting lessons from space but also a lot of preparatory materials. The materials from NASA concerning music were interesting, but weren't too useful, so the music teacher for one of the Mission Watch schools came up with other lesson plans that revolved around music and outer space. Another "Music in Space" plan (creating musical instruments for extraterrestrials) is available in Part III of this book.

The obvious connections are between science, literature, communication, and music for this extended activity. Music that invites use for the listening activity is Gustav Holst's *The Planets* Suite. In Holst's portrait of the planets—which included Mercury, Venus, Mars, Neptune, Jupiter, Saturn, and Uranus—the connections are easily made:

**Experience** *In science*    Pluto wasn't included because it hadn't yet been discovered, and then, more recently, it was ousted from its status as an official planet. This leads to investigations as to what makes a planet a planet in the classroom.

*In literature*    The portraits are based on the Roman gods and their characteristics, which lead to classroom investigations of literary portraits and how they are transformed from words into music ("Lincoln Portrait" follows later in this book).

*In communications*    Music is a form of communication. So strong is this belief that both spacecrafts *Voyager* 1 and 2 carry a "golden record" that was developed by Carl Sagan and a number of other scientists to serve as a communication device to introduce Earth and our various cultures to other cultures that may exist in the universe. On this golden record are a number of musical selections, such as the First Movement of Bach's Brandenburg Concerto No. 2, the Sacrificial Dance from Stravinsky's *Rite of Spring*, and many other world musics (for a complete listing, go to the official Jet Propulsion Laboratory Voyager website at http://voyager.jpl.nasa.gov/spacecraft/music.html). Also on the record are recorded greetings and sounds of nature. The record itself is etched with pictorial directions on how it is used. It is also available from the same website. These activities invite students to imagine what they might include as their *own* golden record (or perhaps, now a golden MP3 or DVD) if they were to send it into outer space, or, more locally, to an e-mail pal in a different country.

**When Music Is the Central Focus**    Important to remember is that the music, in this case, Holst's *Planets*, is the central theme from which the teachers work, not the other way around. The following is a basic outline of how this lesson was approached by a music teacher.

## LISTENING EXPERIENCE 1–TEXTURE, MELODY, DYNAMICS, TEMPO, AND RHYTHM

### Level

Grade 4 group project

### Project/Activities

How texture, melody, dynamics, tempo, and rhythm contribute to a composer's musical interpretation of a life stage

### Previous Knowledge and Skills

Students have already been working with three basic textures of music, namely monophonic, homophonic, and polyphonic. Activities have previously included art collages to visually demonstrate. Students are very familiar with and are able to use appropriate musical terms concerning melody, tempo, and rhythm to help describe a piece of music. They are also musically literate and can read and write music notation well, both melody and rhythm. In the previous lesson, students composed melodies and countermelodies, sharing compositional ideas. Students are experienced and comfortable improvising and composing individually and as a class.

### Parallel Objectives

### *Music Concepts and Objectives/Assessment*

**STANDARDS ADDRESSED:** Improvising melodies, variations, and accompaniments; composing and arranging music within specified guidelines; reading and notating music; listening to, analyzing, and describing music (MENC 2007)

**INSTRUCTIONAL OBJECTIVES:**  The student will show how texture, melody, dynamics, tempo, and rhythm contribute to a composer's musical interpretation of a life stage.

**ASSESSED BY:**  Observing children playing the game and moving

### Mathematics Concepts and Objectives/Assessment

**STANDARDS ADDRESSED:**  Recognize patterns and how many in sets of objects (NCTM 2008)

**INSTRUCTIONAL OBJECTIVE:**  Students will be able to count and view patterns in music.

**ASSESSED BY:**  Asking students questions about the patterns in the music they and others create

### Time for Lesson

Duration: This lesson will cover two class periods of forty minutes each.

### Materials/Resources

1. Simplified listening sheet
2. Colored markers
3. Recording of "Saturn, the Bringer of Old Age" from *The Planets* Suite (this particular recording is of the Chicago Symphony with James Levine, Deutsche Gramophone 429730-2, 1990)

### Procedure

### Anticipatory Set (Attention Hook)

**BRAINSTORMING ACTIVITY:**  Ask students if it is possible to have a melody that is made up of only two neighboring pitches (for example, G and A), and would it be interesting? Boring? Can you think of any songs we know that have melodies made up of only two neighboring pitches?

Select two neighboring pitches and put them on the board, in notation. The next step is to add a rhythm and, in this case, **half notes** and **quarter notes** are suggested. This leads to wondering what could actually be written using just these parameters if we brainstormed.

**COMPOSITION ACTIVITY:**  Students are given manuscript paper, and are permitted to compose a quick melody that is four measures long, includes four beats per measure in which the quarter note gets the beat. They can only use two pitches and combinations of half and quarter notes. Students have a five-minute limit, and then they turn in their results.

Take the compositions and play those that students gave permission to use on the piano. Students hear that melodies can be constructed in many different ways.

By themselves, the melodies aren't all that interesting, they decide. Because students have been studying texture, ask students to volunteer possible textures to be added. At students' directions, you can experiment with suggestions on the piano, or instruments can be distributed so students can play instead or along. The goal is to see how to make this simple melody interesting. Experimentations in tempo and also in octave placements, playing the melody low, high, fast, slow, or in any of those combinations are suggested. This part of the activity takes fifteen minutes, as long as the teacher keeps up the pace.

After students have exhausted possibilities, you may introduce a piece of music in which the composer did just that (that is, used the compositional techniques with which they experimented to compose a piece of music). Hand out a listening guide; the students are directed to circle what they hear in terms of tempo (fast or slow), melody (simple or complex) texture (monophonic, homophonic, polyphonic, or a mixture). They are permitted three listenings of the excerpt to complete answers. The teacher may play the two notes used (B and A above middle C) on the piano to "tune" students to the pitches used.

Play an excerpt from the beginning of "Saturn" for thirty seconds into the piece. Do this three times. Students can put what they find on the chalkboard. Most will agree the tempo is very slow, the melody is simple, and the texture is mostly homophonic, although some students will point out that the bass line could be a countermelody.

At this time, tell the students that this piece of music is portraying part of our own life cycle—is it birth, childhood, adulthood, or old age? They listen again to figure an answer. Then canvass students to get opinions, asking them to support their answers by using musical terms (for example, did the tempo give a clue?). Students will possibly submit every stage represented in their answers.

If the students do not agree on an answer, replay the excerpt—maybe adding a bit more, but don't go past a minute. Perhaps now they agree and support only one or two possibilities.

Ask students to list characteristics of the cycle(s) they decide upon—for example, how do people of this age move? Do they often tire? Do they appear strong or weak? What kind of TV shows and/or music do they like? Invite students to refer to the listening guide, but ask them to use a different colored marker for the next listening sample (4:36–5:20). Now they listen for melody, texture, and tempo, plus the most prominent instrumental family, and dynamics (loud, soft, or both). Permit from two to three listenings, as needed.

Students compare and contrast their findings. Most likely they will have circled a slow tempo as before; the melody is still simple, but most will notice it changed by the addition of more stepwise movement and that it was higher, that the music got very loud, and that brass instruments predominated. Replay the excerpt as needed.

Students review the list of characteristics chosen. Many are confused: loudness and brass aren't usually associated with old age, which is likely the age they chose.

At this point, tell them the name of the movement: "Saturn, the Bringer of Old Age." A brief discussion about the person named Saturn in Roman mythology may ensue. However, the teacher wants to point out that old age isn't a sign of weakness, but it happens to all of us, and we can't avoid it.

Then play the first three minutes of the piece, and have the students circle or note more about what they hear, and also come up with the timeline of aging that the composer used in this piece (basically the implication that one can't stop the march of time and age and that it gets stronger and stronger). If time permits, play the entire piece of music to see how the students' timelines intersect with Holst's music. For example, how does the music represent actual characteristics of old age? Could the louder music also indicate the loss of hearing in older people and therefore the need for hearing aids?

## Evaluation

Students share additional findings about this piece. Did they hear other instruments? More dynamic changes? More changes in texture?

## Continuing the Lesson

After completing the first lesson, you can go in several different directions. A good idea is a contrasting piece of *The Planets* Suite such as "Jupiter, the Bringer of Jollity." A similar format may be used relevant to this music. Should you want to present a contrast that uses half and quarter note rhythms, another work is excellent for this: the final chorus of faeries at the end of Benjamin Britten's Opera *Midsummer's Night's Dream*. Of special importance is that children sing in this chorus along with adults. This also demonstrates how simple quarter notes and half notes can be arranged to create syncopation. Possibilities are endless, but most important is that the teacher review the previous lesson, including the lesson, before moving to the next step. This is standard practice in effective instructional design. A third lesson is also possible, and even a fourth. It depends upon the goals of you and the students.

## LISTENING EXPERIENCE 2—MUSICAL PORTRAITS

*[This section was contributed by Dr. Nancy Sugden, Bowling Green University.]*

### Level

Grades 5 and 6 group project

### Project/Activities

Music can present a musical portrait of a person, place, or thing.

### Previous Knowledge and Skills

Students should be familiar with the American Civil War, Abraham Lincoln, and the Gettysburg Address. They should be able to listen to and describe compositional characteristics of a piece of music.

### Parallel Objectives

#### *Music Concepts and Objectives/Assessment*

**STANDARDS ADDRESSED:** Listening to, analyzing, and describing music; evaluating music and music performances; understanding relationships between music, other arts, and disciplines other than arts; understanding music in relation to history and culture (MENC 2007)

**INSTRUCTIONAL OBJECTIVES:** Students will define and describe various kinds of portraits (paintings, photos, verbal portraits, online portraits), aurally identify characteristics of music that create a portrait in this piece, and describe portraiture in historical contexts.

**ASSESSED BY:** Observing children answering questions and participating in class discussions

#### *Social Studies Concepts and Objectives/Assessment*

*Social Studies*

**STANDARDS ADDRESSED:** Social studies programs should include experiences that provide for the study of culture and cultural diversity, and for the study of the ways human beings view themselves in and over time (NCSS 1994)

**INSTRUCTIONAL OBJECTIVE:** Students answer questions about music in relation to history and culture.

**ASSESSED BY:** Asking questions about the musical portraits in relation to history and culture

### Time for Lesson

Duration: 30 minutes

### Materials/Resources

1. Recording of "A Lincoln Portrait," by Aaron Copland (the recording referenced in this plan is of the Seattle Symphony Orchestra conducted by Gerard Schwarz,

and narrated by James Earl Jones, Delos DE 3140, 2001). Length is 14:35 minutes. If using this recording, the teacher is encouraged to explain that the narrator is the actor, James Earl Jones, or students may think Darth Vader is narrating the piece.
2. Paper and pencils
3. Assorted pictures, paintings, drawings, photographs

## Procedure

### *Anticipatory Set (Attention Hook)*

Students are engaged in discussing "what is a portrait."

Many answers are possible. The usual answers often refer to photographs, but the teacher can help guide students to discover that portraits can also be painted and drawn. Students may also mention the current trend of online portraits that are composed of words (adjectives) to describe a person, often with an accompanying picture, which may or may not actually be the person.

Students are guided to investigate what a portrait tells them about a person (personality, place in history, place in family, and so on) that may go beyond the physical characteristics.

At this point, tell students that they are going to listen to a piece of music that is a portrait of someone famous. However, they are first going to hear three small parts of the portrait, and then list adjectives to describe the music and what it may represent. The goal is to see whether students can name the person portrayed before hearing the entire piece.

Play segment 1 (beginning to about 1:13): Possible descriptors that may arise are *sad, moody, pensive, melancholy* (help with this one), *angry, in conflict, worried.*

Play segment 2 (3:58 to about 4:31): Most students will recognize "De Camptown Ladies" as a clue to the part of the country referred to in the segment. Descriptors may be *happy, silly, fun,* and *the South* (primarily *Kentucky*).

At this point, you can guide students to the possible identity of the person described by the portrait.

Play segment 3 (5:02 to about 6:09): Most students will hear the dominance of brass, associated with military bands, then "De Camptown Ladies" repeated, and tympani and drums, meant to signify gunshots and cannon. Possible descriptors may be *war, anger, cannons,* and *battles.*

Students consider all characteristics they have discovered, and see if they can come up with a list of possibilities. List all these on the blackboard. Play the recording from 7:11 for about a minute. Here, the narrator identifies the portrait as that of Abraham Lincoln, and continues with quotes from the Gettysburg Address and biographical information.

Students discuss why the music indicates Lincoln and not someone else.
The recording is played, from beginning to end.

## Evaluation

Students decide if the musical portrait was accurate based on what they already knew about Lincoln. Asks, "Are there other musical portraits of famous people?"

## Continuing the Lesson

Students can create their own musical portraits. Students undertake a critical analysis of how Aaron Copland used musical elements to create the portrait: melody, rhythm, tone colors, and historical music quotations. Writing letters during the Civil War was the standard method of communication. Students can write letters describing a hypothetical portrait of their lives during that time. Students compile a selection of Civil War music as a portrait of that time.

## COOPERATIVE LEARNING ACTIVITIES

1. Select a piece of music that you would like to use as a listening lesson from the following choices: *The Planets* Suite by Gustav Holst, or *Carnival of the Animals* by Camille Saint-Saens. Both of these are suites, so you can select one or more pieces from them. Using the lesson plan format suggested by your teachers, construct a two-plan sequence for listening, and modeled after the examples.
2. As an extension of the previous plan, rewrite it to be appropriate for a different age level.
3. As another extension of the plan, have children engage in a compositional activity to prepare for the listening activity.

## Chapter Conclusions

Listening is a skill that is learned, and knowing how to do it well will greatly enhance the musical experience for you and for your students. Listening lessons need not be limited to playing a recording and have students listen quietly, but to actually engage them in the listening process. The more actively children are engaged in listening, the stronger they will become as listeners, and eventually as musicians and audiences.

## Resources

*Bowmar Orchestral Library*. This is the classic collection, now available on CD. The collection includes recordings for use in classrooms. It is possible that your future school or current university has this collection in album form if not in CD. This is a set well worth investigating and purchasing.

*Bowmar's Adventures in Music Listening*. This is another classic compilation, updated regularly and available on CD. This set covers all grade levels.

*iTunes* (http://www.apple.com/itunes). This website allows you to listen to various versions of music before you download the version you prefer for a low cost. iTunes has a large and diverse classical music library, and you can download directly into an iPod. The iPod can be inserted into a docking station that can be used in the classroom. This is also useful for students and parents who want to purchase a particular recording. These recordings can also be burned onto a CD. This is also a very fine resource for non-music teachers, although you would first need to research the kind of music you would need before you try to purchase it. "The Lincoln Portrait" presented in this lesson is one example of a piece of music that can be used in non-music classes.

*Smithsonian Global Sound* (http://www.smithsonianglobal sound.org/). This site, maintained by the Smithsonian Institution, works very much like iTunes, with the primary difference being that you are able to listen to and download (for a low cost) world music that is performed by authentic performers, often in authentic context. This is a great resource for non-music teachers as well, as it addresses social studies, world cultures, anthropology, and world music performance practice.

*Your music history or appreciation classes*. You are often required to purchase a set of recordings for these classes, with the two standard compilations being the *Historical Anthology of Music*, edited by Archibald T. Davison and Willi Apel from Harvard University, and the recordings that accompany *The History of Western Music* (Grout et al. 2005), known as the *Norton Anthology of Western Music*. The *Historical Anthology of Music* (aka HAM) is a classic set although it is dated, whereas the current Norton Anthologies are constantly updated. Both of these anthologies are valuable in teaching music listening, not only for college students but also for kindergarten through twelfth grade students as well. CDs that accompany music appreciation texts also work very well for these kinds of activities.

CHAPTER | 6

# Singing

**This chapter addresses the following:[1]**

## INTRODUCTION

As general classroom teachers or music teachers, you will be using your voices excessively, both in teaching and, we hope, in singing. The purpose of this chapter is to help you not only sing and use singing appropriately in the classroom, but also to give you information on how to take care of your voice. Teachers are among the highest-ranked groups prone to vocal damage, and we would like to see you get through your career with your voice intact.

The approach to singing in this chapter emphasizes that singing is personal and unique among individuals and cultures. Your own background, which we will explore later on, will be integral in helping you decide how you would like to use singing in

---

[1]Parts of this chapter were adapted from Joanne Rutkowski and Valerie Trollinger, *Musical Lives of Young Children,* Chapter 9, Prentice Hall, 2004.

your classroom. Students who plan on being music teachers need to have a healthy voice, and they need to be able to sing. However, if you are not planning on being a music teacher and feel you cannot sing—and provide evidence to show this—you should not be singing with your children. You will likely have a number of children in your classes who love singing and will delight in being the leaders for those activities.

The DVD is used heavily in this chapter: The icon indicates that the material is further addressed and demonstrated on the DVD. Additionally, this material may be viewed in streaming format at www. pearsonhighered.com/flohr.

## WHY SINGING? THE NATIONAL STANDARDS

Singing is the foundation of music education. The first music many children make is with their voices, by simply vocalizing. Until recently, singing was viewed as a natural activity in which all children could participate; however, recent research in the field of vocal health has indicated this simply isn't true. In this chapter, singing will be addressed as a health-based activity, which may change the way you have looked at singing in the past. Health-based singing is strongly promoted by MENC; children and youth who injure their voices by poor singing habits are a global concern. The national standards in singing require students to sing a variety of music, both alone and in groups. Teachers are encouraged to be models of vocal health during these lessons.

## RESEARCH IN VOCAL DEVELOPMENT AND ANATOMY

This section begins with an investigation of the nature of the very young voice, and then how this information can be applied to nurturing the voices of children. Children with healthy voices, and the neurobiological ability to process musical pitch (Ayotte et al. 2002), are capable of learning to sing, and many do so at an early age. For purposes of this text, singing refers to the ability to reproduce a recognizable melody with a healthy sound. Singing, as defined by a professionally trained singer or voice teacher, presents a far more complex definition than room allows. Singing is a complex muscular activity; readers are advised to review the vocal health section of this chapter to aid the development of healthy singing after the child is able to start reproducing melodies.

Most children seem to be natural-born musicians and singers, but, by the time some children enter kindergarten, they seem reluctant to sing and have difficulty matching the pitches of others. Without help and encouragement from singing teachers and parents, these children may never sing freely again, and their lives will be void of this natural form of music experience. Are educators and parents to accept this fate for them, or is there something that can be done? Research and practice indicate that most children with healthy voices can learn (or maybe relearn) to sing. It is hoped that this information assists adults in appropriately nurturing the young voices of children.

### Background

Before discussing singing and voice development research, theories of singing acquisition, and issues concerned with very young voices, it is important that readers have an understanding of the physiological nature of the vocal mechanism. With an understanding of how the voice grows and develops from birth to age 6 years, one may better understand how children's voices are different from adult voices and how to work with them. Because presenting a detailed analysis of the function of singing is beyond the scope of this chapter, the following text addresses the overall physiological nature of the voice and emphasizes how a young child's voice differs. For more information, readers are encouraged to refer to books such as Kenneth Phillips's *Teaching Kids to Sing* (Phillips 1992; 1996), Oren Brown's *Discover Your Voice* (Brown 1996), and the five-volume work *Excellence in Singing* by R. Caldwell and Joan Wall (2001). Being familiar with adult voices as well as young voices is vital to teaching singing. The following system for pitch is used throughout this chapter:

C4 = middle C (the middle note on the piano)

D4 = the D above middle C

C3 = the C one octave below middle C

C5 = the C one octave above middle C

## THE VOCAL MECHANISM IN ADULTS AND CHILDREN

The voice is not only the first musical instrument a child possesses, but also the only one that is *played as it develops,* from birth until death, inside the body. The way the voice works is difficult to grasp because it is within the human body. Using the analogy of singing as a kind of vocal ballet may prove helpful to your understanding. Both ballet and singing (1) are psychomotor skills; (2) require precision movements; (3) use cartilages, muscles, and ligaments; (4) aim for gracefulness in movement, not jerkiness; (5) make simultaneous use of vertical, lateral, and rocking movements; and (6) may result in physical injury if not executed properly. As ballet is an athletic event for the body, singing is an athletic event for the vocal mechanism. A ballet teacher needs to have a basic awareness of what the body can do physically for effective teaching and learning, and to prevent painful accidents. Likewise, someone who is going to be involved in teaching singing, even at a very basic level, should understand the physical workings of the voice.

Basic vocal sounds for both speech and singing are produced by way of the interactive functions of the respiratory system and the larynx. In this chapter, only the larynx is discussed in some anatomical detail, as it is assumed that readers are familiar with the anatomy of the respiratory system. The distance from the larynx to the mouth is referred to as the vocal tract. Also included in the vocal tract are the resonators—the mouth, sinuses, and throat.

The larynx is a complex organ in that it serves multiple purposes (Brown 1996) and is composed of very small muscles, cartilages, and ligaments (see Figure 6.1). Because the larynx is not attached to the skeleton, it is able to move in many directions, not all of them desirable in healthy singing. Observe this happen by watching a grown man as he speaks, sings, or swallows: in a man, the thyroid cartilage tips forward, creating the Adam's apple. As he speaks, the Adam's apple will move in a kind of front-to-back and raising-and-lowering motion. The same kind of motion happens with women's voices, too, but it is not as observable, as the thyroid cartilage is at a less pronounced angle. Although the actual production of pitch is accomplished by the vocal

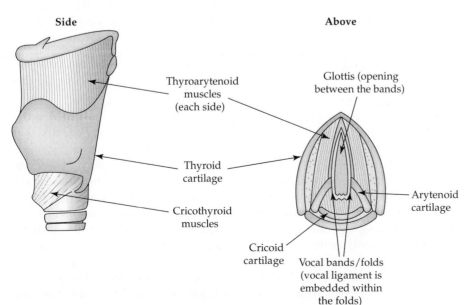

**Side**          **Above**

Thyroarytenoid muscles (each side)

Thyroid cartilage

Cricothyroid muscles

Glottis (opening between the bands)

Arytenoid cartilage

Cricoid cartilage

Vocal bands/folds (vocal ligament is embedded within the folds)

**FIGURE 6.1** The External and Internal Cross-Section of the Larynx Viewed from Side and Above (Simplified)

*Illustrated by V. L. Trollinger*

bands, raising and lowering the larynx (a behavior studied extensively in adult singing studies, but not yet in children) allows one to gain a few more pitches; however, this is a very unhealthy habit and needs to be discouraged as soon as possible in children, as it can contribute to vocal problems later on. The larynx should remain relaxed and in a stable position while singing (R. Sataloff, pers. comm., May 3, 2007).

The inside of the larynx is where the crucial task of sound production (phonation) takes place. This occurs when delicate muscular tissues known as the vocal bands (also referred to as vocal cords) are set into motion. When the bands are subjected to air pressure generated by the lungs, they will start to vibrate. The bands can vibrate in many ways, depending upon the size of the opening between the bands to let the air through, how long and stiff they are at the time, and the degree of power of the sound. Although many internal mechanisms contribute to how wide the bands are opened and how long and stiff they are, two particular muscle pairs are primarily responsible for these kinds of movement: the **thyroarytenoids (TA)** control the amount of opening between the vocal bands, and the **cricothyroids (CT)** control how long and stiff they become. For example, the more the bands are lengthened and stiffened, and the stronger the breath pressure, the higher the sound. The less the bands are lengthened and stiffened, and the lesser the breath pressure, the lower the sound. In addition, the physical length of the vocal bands affects the pitch of the sound: Longer bands will generate lower sounds, and shorter bands will generate higher sounds. In adult females, the bands can be from 11 mm to 17 mm in length, and for men, they can be 15 mm to 21 mm in length. The presence of longer bands is the primary reason why men have lower voices than women. The bands are attached in a parallel fashion to the **vocal ligament,** which is often referred to as the true vocal cord structure. The vocal ligament attaches the TA to the CT, which allows for wider ranges of high and low sounds produced for singing.

All of the muscles inside the larynx, along with many others directly outside of it, are attached to particular cartilages and ligaments so the entire mechanism can move in many different ways. As an adult, the cartilages ossify (become bones), giving the vocal mechanism more stability and control over the sounds it produces, but also requiring more muscular strength to make the mechanism work. Like any muscle, if these muscles are not exercised, they will loose the ability to function properly, whereas, on the other hand, if exercised regularly, they will result in a wide singing range with much control and agility that can last a lifetime, a reason why professional opera singers have very long careers.

The cartilages, ligaments, and muscles controlling the vocal bands and laryngeal movement need to interact with each other in a balanced manner (see Vocal Registers) for healthy singing and speech to occur. However, it is possible for an untrained singer to inadvertently work these mechanisms in a very unbalanced manner, by forcing one mechanism to work in resistance to the others. In ballet dancing, if a dancer moves a leg or arm out of balance, a nasty fall may occur. In singing, if the singer forces one mechanism to work against the others (for example, by forcing the larynx to move up too high or too low), then an audible cracking sound—the equivalent of a vocal fall—may happen. If this kind of vocal behavior occurs regularly, physical damage to the voice could result. Strategies on how to avoid these kinds of vocal behaviors in both children and adults are discussed in the Vocal Health section later in this chapter.

After speech or singing sounds have been generated via the interaction of the larynx and respiratory system, they are subject to the degree of *resonance* that is influenced by the throat, sinuses, and mouth cavities. An example of a voice that has a lot of resonance is that of the actor James Earl Jones, who provided the voice of Darth Vader in the original *Star Wars* movies. When one sings or speaks, the majority of the sounds produced move out of the mouth and into the resonating areas in sound energy waves. The physical sensation of the energy waves in the head in untrained teenage and adult singers may cause discomfort, as the person is not used to them and may not know that the sensations are completely normal. As a result, an untrained singer may try to avoid making the sounds that caused the discomfort in the first place. A goal of voice education is to adjust the resonators so that the sound is not destroyed or so the singer feels uncomfortable during production. Instead, a singer can modify the resonators so that the sound waves can work together to actually boost the power of the voice. For ideas on boosting vocal resonance, see Brown's *Discover Your Voice* (1996).

## The Child's Vocal Mechanism

The vocal function and anatomy previously discussed is primarily that of an adult. The child larynx differs greatly from an adult larynx, and is therefore not capable of functioning the same way in singing. At birth, the infant larynx more closely resembles that of a nonhuman primate like a monkey (Bosma 1975; Kent 1981). Over the first six months of life, the larynx undergoes dramatic change, along with the rest of the vocal tract, to more closely resemble the adult version (Sasaki et al. 1977). The primary function of the infant larynx is to protect the airway and to aid in swallowing (Hast 1985). Therefore, it is placed particularly high in the vocal tract to keep children from choking while eating. This high placement also allows children to eat and breathe at the same time. The high placement of the larynx, along with the very short vocal bands in the vocal tract, results in infants vocalizing in a fairly high-frequency range. After the first six months of life, the larynx begins a gradual descent, less dramatic for girls than for boys, that continues through life.

In addition to the high position of the larynx in the vocal tract, there are several other physiological differences from the adult larynx. Until age 2 to 3, the vocal bands of the larynx are composed of mostly mucosal (like mucous) rather than fibrous (like fibers in muscle) tissue (Titze 1992), as the vocal ligament is not yet present (Andrews and Summers 2001; Sataloff et al. 1998). These bands are also very short (6 mm to 8 mm in infancy) (Sataloff 1997). Due to the absence of the vocal ligament and the presence of mucosal vocal bands, young children may have difficulty controlling their voice sounds. At birth, the cricothyroid (CT) muscle pair is the largest muscle in the larynx, but the thyroarytenoid (TA) muscle pair is essentially an undefined mass of tissue (Sataloff et al. 1998). However, as the TA (which controls degrees of opening and closing of the vocal bands) begins to take shape around the age of 2 years, children begin to gain some consistent control over the range of pitches their voices make. The mucosal vocal bands that children possess at birth are not the true vocal cord structure (for example, the vocal ligament) that will begin to develop between the ages of 1 and 4 years (Andrews and Summers 2001; Sataloff et al. 1998). Because the vocal ligament is not present, many of the high and low sounds that infants and very young children make are primarily due to the manipulation of their very short vocal bands, which results in a limited number of controlled sounds that could be used for pre-speech and pre-singing. The vocal ligament remains weak as it develops until the age of 6 years. At that point, it starts to become layered and fibrous, adding more vocal stability and control, especially for singing. This layering process continues until approximately age 16 (Morrison and Rammage 1994). The degree of development of the vocal ligament in relationship to the growth of surrounding muscles and cartilage structures may have a direct impact on the development of singing **registers** and singing range in children. However, at this time, no research is available that directly addresses this relationship in children's singing development. Physiologically, a connection seems logical, as the vocal ligament allows humans to develop a wider singing range by providing the ability to create higher notes (Titze 1996). The vocal ligament, laryngeal musculature, and cartilages are all underdeveloped in infants and, throughout early childhood, begin to develop and take shape; they do not function together as an adult singing voice until the later teen years. The progression of physical vocal development in relation to speech and singing development is presented in Table 6.1. The information is physical and acoustical, with F0 indicating fundamental frequency of the voice at particular ages.

Another area of interest in relation to the young voice is the development of the respiratory system. Even though infants have smaller vocal tracts and shorter vocal bands—which means the sounds they make will be higher—they can make these higher sounds at a very strong amplitude (very loud). The primary reason for this is because the infant respiratory system is smaller than the adult system; research suggests that infants work 50 percent to 60 percent harder with their lungs than adults do to

**TABLE 6.1** Vocal Development Milestones for Birth—Prior to Onset of Puberty

| Age | Physiological Characteristics | Vocalization/Speech Characteristics | Singing Development |
|---|---|---|---|
| 0–4 months | Larynx situated very high in the vocal tract. The cricothyroid (CT) is largest muscle in larynx. The thyroarytenoid (TA) muscle is not developed. There is no vocal ligament. Tissues are mucosal rather than fibrous. Vocal fold length is approximately 6 mm to 8 mm in infants. The respiratory system is underdeveloped. | The birth cry is about 500 Hz (C above middle C) (Sataloff 1998). Infants have different cries or vocalizations for specific discomforts at 2 months (Stillman 1978). | |
| 4–12 months | The larynx begins to slowly drop. The respiratory system is still underdeveloped (and continues to grow and strengthen throughout childhood). | Infants vocalize to get attention (Stillman 1978). They may exhibit a wide pitch range (G3 to C6 found when measuring spontaneous vocalizations; (see Table 6.3). They imitate vocalizations of a teacher or adult with prompting at 9 months (Stillman 1978). | |
| 12–18 months | A very thin and nonlayered vocal ligament begins to appear (from ages 1–4 years). | Children vocally imitate others without prompting (Eilers and Oller 1988; Stillman 1978). Voice F0 at 340–470 Hz (E4 to A4) (Titze 1992; Wilson 1987). A wide vocalization range may still be evident. Vocal sounds may be closely identified to native language to be learned (de Boysson-Bardies et al. 1989; Kuehn 1985). | They play with vocal sounds (Davidson et al. 1981; McDonald and Simons 1989). |
| 19 months | | | Melodic and rhythmic patterns begin to appear in vocalizations (Davidson et al. 1981; McDonald and Simons 1989). |
| 19–24 months | | Children develop one- to two-word phrases, use their voice to impart emotional meaning (e.g., *no* said very loudly), develop a jargon, such as *wah* for water or *bah-bah* for blanket (Stillman 1978).<br>    A wide vocalization range may still be evident (not in singing). | Children this age create short, spontaneous songs with small melodic intervals and flexible rhythm patterns. Range used for vocalizing with intent to sing is quite small. They are able to learn to produce short repeating melodic patterns from simple songs closer to 24 months (Davidson et al. 1981; McDonald and Simons 1989). |
| 24 months | The TA begins to take shape; ossification of some cartilages begins (and continues until age 65 years). | Vocalization range may begin to narrow, or may continue to widen depending upon reinforcement of vocalization skill (Sinor 1984; Trollinger 2001; Wendrich 1981). Language acquisition begins (this may affect voice usage). Voice F0 average is 340–470 Hz (E4 to A4) (Wilson 1987). | Children this age use melodic patterns or bits from learned songs for spontaneous singing.<br>    They may start to confuse loudness with pitch (e.g., they will vocalize louder instead of singing higher (Titze 1992). |
| 2–3 years | Vocal ligament is still very weak, and the TA is developing. | By age 3, children can state their first and last name, gender, and recent happenings; they can express physical and emotional states and imitate the voices of characters in stories. Voice F0 average is about 255–360 Hz (C4 to F#4) (Titze 1992; Wilson 1987)s. | They imitate short songs or melodies, but not always accurately. They may change melody to better accommodate voice range. |

**TABLE 6.1** (*Continued*)

| Age | Physiological Characteristics | Vocalization/Speech Characteristics | Singing Development |
|---|---|---|---|
| 4 years | There is continued weak vocal ligament and TA development. | Children speak in complete sentences (Stillman 1978). Voice frequency is about B3 to F#4 (240–340 HZ) (Titze 1992; Wilson 1987). Vocalization depends on individual development and learned vocal habits (Sataloff 1997). | Learning songs generally follows this sequence: words, rhythm, phrases, and melodic shape (Davidson et al. 1981; McDonald and Simons 1989). Possible beginnings of vocal singing registration emerge (due to TA development and vocal ligament development); however, this may be very individualistic. Research directly addressing this relationship is not yet available. |
| 5–6 years | At 6, the vocal ligament starts to layer into three parts. | Voice F0 is generally about 225–325 Hz (A3 to D4) or so (Titze 1992; Wilson 1987). Again, this is highly variable. Physiologic vocal range is fairly stable (and remains so through childhood) (Sataloff 1997). | Children's sense of key is stabilized, and they can sing fairly accurately (Davidson et al. 1981; McDonald and Simons 1989). Increased singing range can develop (Sataloff 1997), if the voice is healthy. Musical range may increase due to physiological development and other maturation factors. |
| 7–onset of puberty | Vocal ligament continues to layer, and reaches the ability to function more as an adult's by age 13 (Hartnick et al. 2005), although it continues to develop until age 16. The larynx continues to drop, adding more vocal resonance, with the most drastic drop in males occurring in puberty. Physiologically, prior to puberty, male and female voices are the same (Kahane 1975). Vocal bands continue to lengthen, and the respiratory system moves closer to mature level (Stathopoulos and Sapienza 1991). | Voice F0 is significantly different by gender, emerging with males developing a lower F0 in speech (Hasek et al. 1980; Glaze et al. 1988). The overall mean vocal F0 is around 232 Hz (Glaze et al. 1988). | The vocal range continues to increase, with vocal ligament allowing upper register to emerge prior to puberty (Hartnick et al. 2005). Maturation of respiratory system allows for singing of longer phrases in songs. |

*Note:* The tables in this chapter use the following system: C4 = middle C; D4 = D above middle C; E4 = E above middle C; F4 = F above middle C; F#4 = F# above middle C; B3 = B below middle C; A3 = A below middle C. F0 5 fundamental frequency.

make these louder sounds (Stathopoulos and Sapienza 1991). Anecdotally, it has been observed that infants breathe optimally when they are crawling or sleeping (doing what a singer may refer to as abdominal breathing rather than clavicular breathing), but this phenomenon may disappear as the child becomes upright. This is one reason why voice teachers often have adult students practice breathing while they are on all fours so they can practice breathing correctly. Due to their underdeveloped respiratory system, young children have to take many breaths when they talk and sing.

The interaction of the child larynx and respiratory system allows for the production of sound that may be less resonant than that of an adult in speech or singing. With maturity and proper development of healthy vocal behaviors, healthy resonance can be developed in children. This, in turn, will affect the manner in which children use the voice to sing. It is not a good idea to push this concept too soon. Titze (1992) and Miller (2000) have cautioned that having young children sing songs in adult ranges and of adult length will do a disservice to their developing respiratory and vocal systems.

**CAVEATS IN VOICE RESEARCH, SINGING, AND CHILDREN** At this time, truly rigorous research in the physiological development of the child voice in relationship to singing development is almost nonexistent. Although a number of phenomena have been studied at the adult level, such as the behavior of excessive raising and lowering of the larynx in singing, the effect of visual vocal models in vocal training, and relationships of anatomical development or deterioration, have not been yet undertaken with children. There is evidence, primarily through the voice science field, that these relationships exist, but they have yet to be investigated in children, as it is known that vocal habits and behaviors are laid down in childhood rather than in adulthood. For example, adult untrained singers who engage in excessive vertical laryngeal movement in singing are likely to have learned this behavior when young. However, there is no research yet on how children learn this behavior, why they do it, and why they continue to engage in this behavior into adulthood. With this in mind, music teachers and all educators are encouraged to continue learning and studying about voice and to realize that what is presented here is the tip of the vocal iceberg. There is much we need to know.

**THE VOICE THROUGH LIFE** The voice is the only musical instrument that actually changes from birth to death. As children, our voices are very flexible, because the anatomy of the larynx is made of mostly soft, underdeveloped tissues and cartilages. As we age, our larynxes drop (making our voices more resonant), and the cartilages become bony and less flexible. This is one reason why, if we stop singing as children and then try again as adults, it feels much harder to do. As we get even older, our larynxes continue to show signs of aging. Although it may be appropriate for a woman in her eighties to have a low, gravelly voice if she hasn't taken care of it very well, it is a problem for a young woman in her twenties or a young child to sound the same way. This will be further discussed in the later section on vocal health. The DVD also presents an audiovisual presentation of the Lifelong Journey of the Human Voice. Additionally, this material may be viewed in streaming format at www.pearsonhighered.com/flohr.

## RESEARCH AND THEORIES CONCERNED WITH THE YOUNG VOICE IN SPEECH AND SINGING

This section addresses the research and resulting theories of how children learn to speak and sing, how they use vocal registration in singing, and how they learn songs. Issues that research and theories generate follow the discussion. The area of vocal development in the child voice has been investigated for a number of years. Although the research in anatomy and speech has presented consistent findings about development, the research concerned with singing development has provided less consistent findings, and has simply dropped off more recently. Newer research in singing development (Trollinger 2003; 2004; 2007a; 2007b) suggests that the vocal ranges of children are more likely to be varied from child to child, depending upon the variables of physical development, vocal use in singing and speech, and vocal health habits. More detailed and current information on the pediatric voice is available from *Pediatric Voice Disorders* (Hartnick and Boseley 2008).

### Speaking Voice Development

Very young children often exhibit babbling behavior, which is primarily seen as a precursor to language development (Blake and Fink 1987; Eilers and Oller 1988; Moog 1976; Vihman and Miller 1988). Although it is generally believed that infant babble sounds similar across cultural and linguistic boundaries until the age of one year (Kuehn 1985), some researchers have found that babble differs between these boundaries (de Boysson-Bardies et al. 1989).

Children who have moved beyond babbling and are verbal (around the age of 2 years) have been studied to determine mean speech frequency and the overall speech frequency range. As Table 6.1 shows, there is a lot of variability in the pitch level (designated by the note names of A, B, C, and so on) of children's speech voices, depending upon how they were assessed and how their voices matured. For an excellent summary of research concerned with children's voice frequencies (the acoustical measurements of vibration), see Wilson (1987). Children often imitate the speech patterns of parents and other important adults, and by doing so they learn to add intonations that may be perceived as having emotional context and meaning. However, in languages other than English, such as Cantonese and Mandarin, the pitch of the word also imparts the linguistic meaning. For example, *ma* in these languages can mean either mother, horse, flax, or serve as an expression of anger, depending upon where it is pitched tonally (DeMente 1995; Hu and Lee 1992). How children use their voices is highly individualized, and is strongly influenced by the native culture and familial vocal use in which they live.

Speech and singing research has, until recently, been conducted separately, with little attention paid to how one may directly affect the other. Research in this area undertaken by a number of researchers (Chen-Hafteck 1998; Rutkowski and Chen-Hafteck 2001; Rutkowski et al. 2002; Trollinger 2003; 2004) has indicated that the native language and personal speech characteristics of children may affect the manner in which the children consequently use their voices to sing. These findings have given support to Gould's (1968) assertion that the speech voice cannot be ignored when addressing singing skill development; often, poor speech habits will translate into poor singing habits, and good speech habits could aid the development of singing to some degree.

## Singing Voice Development

Research findings are often in conflict in the ranges found. These discrepancies may be due to the different ways in which children's voices have been assessed for pitch or may reflect the great variance in young children's singing behaviors. In studying infant and preverbal children's voices, all vocal sounds, including pitched sounds that likely would not contribute to the acquisition of singing, have been included. This may give an inflated view of range. A summary of observed vocal ranges of young children is presented in Table 6.2. Be reminded that these are ranges observed in varying situations and may not reflect ranges children would exhibit in nurturing musical environments, similar to nurturing language environments. For specific voice ranges found by each researcher and details regarding each study, please refer to the direct source indicated in Table 6.2.

Some researchers have also investigated the pitch that children select when they start singing a song on their own. Consistently, researchers have found that 4- to 6-year-olds begin songs on C4 or D4 (Plumridge 1972; Porter 1977; Thurloway 1977; Wilson

**TABLE 6.2** Observed Singing Ranges of Children

| Ages | Ranges | Research Sources |
| --- | --- | --- |
| 3–9 months | G3 to C6 | Fox (1990), Michel (1973) |
| 7–months to 3 years | A3 to G5 | Ries (1987), Simons (1964) |
| 2 years | D4 to A4 | Jersild and Bienstock (1934) |
|  | A3 flat to C5 | Alford (1971) |
|  | Lowest A3 flat | Michel (1973) |
|  | C4 to C5 | McKernon (1979) |
| 3 years | C4 to A4 or B4 | Jersild and Bienstock (1934) |
|  | G3 to C5 | Alford (1971); Updegraff et al. (1938) |
|  | B3 flat to G4 flat | Harkey (1978/1979) |
| 4 years | B3 to C5 | Jersild and Bienstock (1934) |
|  | A3 flat to C5 | Alford (1971) |
| 5 years | A3 to D5 | Jersild and Bienstock (1934) |
|  | B3 to G4 | Updegraff et al. (1938) |
|  | A3 to B4 | Cleall (1970) |
|  | B3 flat to G4 flat | Joyner (1971) |
|  | C4 to A4 | Plumridge (1972) |
|  | B3 flat to G4 flat | Young (1971) |

1973). However, Kostka (1984) found that the midpoint of 4- to 5-year-olds' singing appears to be around E4 flat. Interestingly, these pitches are within the mean speech frequency ranges of young children, perhaps indicating young children's lack of distinction between their speaking and singing voices, either cognitively, physically, or a combination of both.

Concerning older children, past research has been more interested in investigating instructional, cognitive, and psychomotor processes to help children learn to match pitch and sing in tune. To sing in tune, to accurately match pitches, and to comfortably use their singing voices, young children must progress through a series of kinesthetic, proprioceptive, and mental processes. To develop children's singing accuracy, Joyner (1969) outlined a series of three processes that required children to (1) be able to discriminate pitches from each other and in relation to a melodic contour, (2) remember the succession of pitches needed to sing a melody, and (3) have a vocal instrument capable of reproducing the sounds.

However, Joyner's processes require that children be able to perceive various organizational characteristics of pitch and melody, and also to have a vocal instrument capable of producing the required sound. There is no mention of children recognizing and attempting to differentiate between a singing pitch and a speech pitch, which could possibly include the perception of different timbres that may be vital in singing production.

A number of researchers have theorized that, as singers produce a vocal sound, they are guided by the physical sensation and the aural perception of the pitch they create. Anyone learning to sing must learn to attend to and remember both these kinesthetic sensations and aural feedback, and it has been speculated that the memory of specific aural and kinesthetic sensations and their consequences may play a role in preparing the human body for singing (Miller 1996; Moog 1976). Subsequent monitoring requires singers to compare their voice to a simultaneous external model or an internal representation of the melody (Bentley 1973; Goetze 1985). Goetze et al. (1990) have suggested that pitch monitoring skills for successful singing rely upon the individual's ability to discriminate pitches, reproduce them, and attend to the sensations created by the production of the sound. However, it must be added that perhaps children display these abilities at varying levels, and therefore may exhibit varying degrees of success.

Attempting to teach singing without first addressing vocal range and flexibility may result in failure. One of the most commonly used approaches to teaching singing is by using the "song method" (Phillips 1992). In *Teaching Kids to Sing*, Kenneth Phillips writes: "The song approach—which in recent years has been the one most widely used to teach young people to sing—places primary emphasis on expression, with secondary emphasis on technique. The student learns to sing by singing songs. This is not to say that vocal technique cannot be taught using this approach; rather, it is the song that serves as the vehicle rather than specific exercises or vocalises" (p. 4). One of the more prominent methods of teaching music literacy is the Kodály method, which emphasizes the use of **a capella** singing. Concerning this particular method, Phillips states: "Kodály stressed beautiful singing, but the method presupposed the ability to sing beautifully; there was nothing in the original Kodály method concerning vocal technique. Trying to teach music reading before the skill of singing is like the proverbial cart before the horse. Singing technique and music-reading skills must develop together" (p. 12). Because most music instructors who work with young children use either or both the song method and the Kodály method, these observations are important, as both methods assume that the child already has the vocal range and ability needed to sing the songs.

The difference in reported research is interesting and begs for further inquiry and validation, perhaps by using current technology, investigating multiple dimensions of voice use and development, and working collaboratively with voice science specialists.

## Vocal Registers

The terms **vocal registers,** *registration events, shifts,* or *breaks* are often used in singing. These words are attempts to give a name to what is thought to be physically happening inside the larynx when the quality of tone in a voice changes. Sundberg (1987) provides an analogy that the shifting of the voice is not unlike—at least perceptually—the shifting of a gear mechanism in a car. In a car, using an inappropriate gear at a certain speed is inefficient and may even damage the engine. Similarly, using an inappropriate register to sing at a certain pitch level is inefficient and, over time, will damage the vocal mechanism. Consequently, understanding vocal registers is necessary for anyone working with voices.

The problem with registration research is that it is impossible to know for sure what is happening. With a fiber optic scope inserted above the vocal bands, one is able to see what is happening inside the larynx from above—but what about from below? A number of factors contribute to registration events—the breath, the angle of the head, and the position of the body, which will affect the resonance, for example. In the last 150 years, numerous voice researchers and pedagogues have proposed and evaluated many ideas and theories, including the number of perceived register areas in the voice (Appelman 1967; Garcia 1841; Miller 2000; Vennard 1967). Because this is a confusing issue, the following paragraphs provide some basic information about vocal registers and how they are defined in this book. The field of pediatric vocal development is still growing, so you are urged to continue your own research and investigation in this area.

Registers in voice research refer to areas in which the sounds are perceived as being produced using similar adjustments of vocal mechanism and breath. For example, if you growl like a dog, and then meow as high as you can like a newborn kitten, you are using different physical adjustments (**registers**) of the larynx and the breath to do so. These vocal register areas are defined by the manner in which the vocal bands vibrate and the quality of the sound produced. Children, even in infancy, have demonstrated a wide use of these vocal registers (Keating and Buhr 1977), although not all of these registers will contribute to the development of singing. In fact, one of these registers used by infants and children, the highest **whistle register** (Zemlin 1988), more often called the *short register*, produces the "loud shrieks made by lusty, furious infants" (Miller 1996, 148). The whistle or short register generates sounds that are "not subject to control, are not of a pleasing timbre, and are not useful to the singer" (Miller 1996, 148).

Singers concentrate on the specific vocal register that is used for speech and singing: this particular area is referred to as the **modal register** or adjustment. The early voice pedagogue, inventor of the laryngoscope, and author of the 1841 book, *A Complete Treatise on the Art of Singing*, Manuel Garcia, broke this modal area into register subdivisions: chest (in which the sound feels as if it is vibrating the sternum), head (in which the sound feels as if it is vibrating in the head), and mixed or middle (a mixture of head and chest often referred to as the *zona di passigio* or the zone of passage between pronounced high and low register breaks). More recently, the terms *heavy adjustment* and *light adjustment*, which refer to degrees of control of the thyroarytenoid and cricothyroid muscles for singing, have been adopted. Changes from one register or adjustment to another are often difficult for untrained singers to control and may indeed convince them that they can't sing because the shifts may feel uncomfortable, and are therefore avoided. However, these shift areas are normal and can be smoothed out with training and practice (see Brown 1996). All these different registration terms (for example, *head, chest, heavy, light*) attempt to describe a particular perceived vocal adjustment; however, there is little agreement across the board on the validity of all of these terms, as well as others too numerous to mention for our purposes. For more details about the phenomenon of vocal registration, readers are encouraged to refer to Appelman (1967), Miller (1996), Titze (1994), and Vennard (1967). In this book, the terms *heavy adjustment* and *light adjustment* are used, as they are better descriptors of degrees of interaction between the TA and CT in the voice during registration. Other writers often use the older terms *chest voice* for *heavy adjustment* and *head voice* for *light adjustment*.

## Vocal Singing Registers in Children

Young children make most of their pitched vocalizations by engaging their very short vocal bands in vibration, and some children may engage in some raising and lowering of the larynx in a belief that it will further extend their ranges. Done excessively, this is a very unhealthy vocal habit; although this has not been researched in music education, music teachers observe it often (indicators include the jaw jutting out when the larynx is pulled too high, and the chin pulled in when the larynx is pushed too low). The registration events discussed previously can only logically occur following the development of a functioning vocal ligament structure (which allows humans to develop range in singing via interactions of the CT and TA). For very young children, the singing voice and the speech voice are likely the same, as they operate mechanically under the same principles of movement and sound production, at least where pitch production is concerned. Even more confusing is that current research indicates that the vocal ligament begins to function as an adult ligament somewhere between the ages of 10 and 12 (Boseley and Hartnick 2006; Hartnick et al. 2005; Ishii et al. 2000; Sato et al. 2008). This, however, can be highly variable among older children. With that in mind, be aware that the following registration research is likely not applicable to children under the age of 9 years. More research in this area is desperately needed.

Although it is natural for young children to change adjustments when they sing, a common practice for many young children is to actually speak in an elongated fashion instead of singing when they are asked to do so. These are children who are often called monotones or problem singers. Two possibilities exist here: (1) the child may be phonating healthfully yet is only able to do so in a limited range, or (2) the child instead engages the laryngeal structures in pressed phonation to produce that sound, thus also exhibiting a very limited range. Although remediation with a child who is phonating healthfully is possible, remediation with a child who is phonating unhealthily would be less successful in that a voice specialist, such as a school voice or speech therapist, would need to address vocal problems first. This is very tricky, as a number of vocal behaviors would need to be relearned. Although a music teacher may be able to help a child find a singing voice temporarily in a class, the older behavior will likely remain firmly in place unless the behavior to do so is reinforced daily. Children who exhibit healthy phonation habits, yet seem to have problems using the voice in singing, will likely be able to be remediated by the number of strategies that are demonstrated on the DVD and are also available at www.pearsonhighered.com/flohr. If these behaviors are not addressed in children while they are young, they will often attempt to sing in a higher range than is healthy with these adjustments (this is referred to as "forcing" the voice) as they get older. Why some children exhibit this kind of behavior has not been empirically investigated. However, practice suggests that the musical environment of young children, particularly the vocal models they have, influence their vocal development (Tonkova-Yampol'skaya 1973; Trollinger 2007a), and speech science research has established this relationship in learning vocalizations for speech (Andrews 1999; Andrews and Summers 2001). It is important that the voice never be forced. Children should never be placed in situations that will encourage them to sing loudly or push their voices, as damage may result.

The adult voice is anatomically and functionally different from the child voice in that (1) the ligament structure is fully developed, (2) younger children don't display vocal registration events for singing, (3) children can't physically sing the same way adults sing. The voice changes throughout life.

## Vocal Health

As stated earlier, teachers, like public speakers and actors, can be more susceptible to vocal problems than the general population. This means we need to be vigilant in taking care of our voices, but we also have to help our young charges in schools take care of theirs as well. Although parents and teachers may view the sight of a third grade class choir as charming, if the children are yelling instead of singing (sometimes heard over an accompanying CD that is either too loud or overorchestrated, or both), the reality is that their voices are being abused and/or misused, and if done too much and too often, can contribute to vocal damage. Children's singing voices are not going to be loud: they actually sound very light when they are singing the way their anatomy permits, but you will run across children who will have more of a vocal presence than others with no indication of misuse. In this section, we go over the fundamentals of vocal health for you and your students.

### Healthy Phonation Pointers

1. *Find the optimal vocal pitch speaking range of your voice*. The optimal vocal speaking pitch range of your voice is found by yawning and then vocalizing a sigh as you exhale. This is not the same as the singer's sigh, but instead is the sigh or vocalization you produce when you yawn when sleepy. You may be surprised to find that you may actually sigh at a pitch level that is higher than you normally speak. This exercise indicates the best vocalization area for your voice. If you normally speak much lower than your sigh indicates, then you may be forcing your voice too low, and that will catch up with you in time. This is also a good exercise to do if you think you are talking too low (from fatigue, for example). Although vocal rest is the best course, if you still need to talk, then find your vocal center again. Even if you don't speak where your yawn-sigh indicates, try to aim for the same relaxed feeling, and allow your voice to go where it wants to go, which hopefully will not be too much lower than or near your lowest yawn-sigh pitch. Please note that healthy voices use the entire speech range available, rather than staying within just one area all the time.

2. *Create balanced onsets*. One thing to be careful about is how we start our vocal sounds. Glottal attacks (which come from slamming the vocal bands together at the start of words that begin with vowels) are particularly damaging. To remedy this behavior, practice starting your vowels, in both speech and singing, with a soft "h" sound first, like *h*able, *h*art, *h*effect, and so on. These take practice, and eventually the *h* sound will not be audible, but this behavior will help save your voice. The *h* keeps your bands from slamming together. This is discussed in more detail later in the chapter.

3. *Posture*. When you sit or stand, you need to relax your body. If your body is tense, it will be reflected in your voice. When you stand, you should very gently tuck under your behind, keep your arms and shoulders back but relaxed, and your feet slightly apart. Beware of "duck butt," which is the incidence of standing but jutting your behind out, which throws your back out of alignment as you stand. When you sit, aim for the same—but don't sit at the edge of your chair; this also causes too much stress on your back, because it will tend to arch if you "sit up straight" on the edge of the chair.

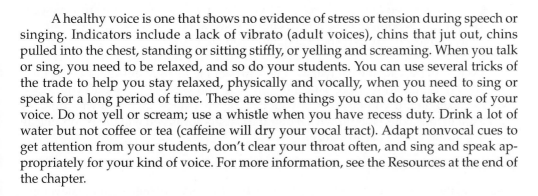

A healthy voice is one that shows no evidence of stress or tension during speech or singing. Indicators include a lack of vibrato (adult voices), chins that jut out, chins pulled into the chest, standing or sitting stiffly, or yelling and screaming. When you talk or sing, you need to be relaxed, and so do your students. You can use several tricks of the trade to help you stay relaxed, physically and vocally, when you need to sing or speak for a long period of time. These are some things you can do to take care of your voice. Do not yell or scream; use a whistle when you have recess duty. Drink a lot of water but not coffee or tea (caffeine will dry your vocal tract). Adapt nonvocal cues to get attention from your students, don't clear your throat often, and sing and speak appropriately for your kind of voice. For more information, see the Resources at the end of the chapter.

### Unhealthy Vocal Sounds

At times, you may suspect that what you are hearing, in both your voice and your students' voices, may indicate that something may be wrong. Indicators that a problem could be developing include, but are not limited to: (1) extended periods of hoarseness, (2) the voice cuts in and out while talking or singing, (3) two or more sounds are generated at the same time, and (4) the voice sounds like it is straining, perhaps indicated by your chin jutting out or pulled in. You may constantly fade into a vocal growl and get lower at the end of sentences. The last indication is the one that may be the easiest to remedy by modifying vocal behaviors. The first three may indicate that intervention by a physician may be necessary: None of those behaviors are normal, even if they occur over an extended period of time. If you suspect you or one of your students may have developed vocal problems, the best person to visit is your school district's speech specialist. This individual will be the best qualified to observe either you or the student in question and give you some feedback.

The DVD provides some audio samples of healthy and unhealthy vocal sounds in speech and singing. This material is also available at www.pearsonhighered.com/flohr.

## STEPS TO SUCCESSFUL SINGING WITH CHILDREN

Because children go through many sequential steps in learning how to walk, and then run, they do the same for singing in that the muscles required for singing need to go through the following sequential step process:

### Efficient Singing

Singing is an athletic skill, just like any sport. However, the muscles involved are much smaller and less observable. The purpose of this section is to help you come to grips with your own voice and how to get it ready to sing for children, as well as for your own enjoyment. The strategies presented here will also work with children, and they are all demonstrated on the DVD. Additionally, this material may be viewed at www. pearsonhighered.com/flohr.

Remember, singing is difficult with an unhealthy voice, and it has been our experience to send students to the voice clinic at the university to be evaluated if the voice sounds unhealthy. If you suspect you have a damaged voice, then take advantage of the voice clinic facilities that are likely offered at your school.

Before we start, several points need to be made clear:

1. *Singing is personal; every voice is different.* Although some of you may be voice majors, others may not be, but that doesn't matter. Even if you plan on being a high school band director or a general elementary education teacher, you need to be able to sing and phonate healthfully. This leads us to the following item.
2. *One does not need to have a great voice, but should have a healthy one.* Your voice is YOU. There is nothing to be shy or embarrassed about. Sing with pride. Your students will feel motivated about singing if you are yourself.
3. *Investigate your own singing habits.* Where do you sing the most? In the shower? On a stage? In the car? It's likely that, if you are singing in your shower or in your car, you are calm and relaxed. That's the attitude you want to carry into your classroom singing. If you do most of your singing on a stage, then you will probably want to tone your voice down a bit for the classroom, as you will tire if you sing all day as if it were a performance.

### Working with the Singing Voice

In singing, there are several behaviors to make habitual that will allow you to develop a nice, healthy sound, and these also can be taught to your students. These behaviors include the following:

Building free phonation and flexibility

Breathing and posture for singing

Singing without stress

Although the strategies presented here and on the DVD (the same material is also available at www.pearsonhighered.com/flohr) are widely accepted among current voice pedagogues, use of them will not remediate nor work with a voice (adult or child) that has undergone damage or misuse resulting in compromised vocal health. It is imperative to always watch yourself in a mirror or your students carefully for any signs of tension, which may indicate problems that are beyond the scope of this book and need to be addressed by a vocal specialist.

## Building Free Phonation and Flexibility

"Free phonation" is part of vocal pedagogy technique referred to as the "appoggio" approach, which is currently what professional vocal training emphasizes. Oberlin voice professor and tenor Richard Miller has written about it extensively in *The Structure of Singing* (1996). The appoggio technique, primarily used with singers in professional training, is defined as "a system for combining and balancing muscles and organs of the trunk and neck, controlling their relationships to the supraglottal resonators, so that no exaggerated function of any of them upsets the whole" (Miller 1996, 23). The most basic components of the technique can be taught to youngsters as they learn to sing, because it promotes ideals of vocal health and helps develop habits that can lead to a lifetime of healthy singing. Free phonation, part of this technique, allows one to sing without exaggerated stress, and several behaviors are part of the process. The techniques and strategies presented here are further fleshed out in *Solutions for Singers* by Richard Miller (2004) and *The Diagnosis and Correction of Vocal Faults* by James C. McKinney (2005). Although they are discussed here, they are demonstrated on the DVD with modifications shown as needed to address young voices. Our goal in this section is develop healthy singing, not create professional singers.

The way you start, continue, and end a singing sound is of paramount importance, and the primary component is the *balanced onset*. The balanced onset is directly related to breathing and consists of three parts: (1) inhalation, (2) suspension, and (3) exhalation. Most of us have no problems with inhalation and exhalation; however, suspension may be new to you, especially if you are a wind instrumentalist or an untrained singer. When we inhale in preparation for exhaling a few moments later, we tend to close the back of the throat—the glottis—and then, when it's time to blow through the instrument, the glottis is opened and a rush of air comes out; the air starts at the back of the throat, sometimes with an "Ah" kind of sound. From a vocal health standpoint, this is a problem because vocal bands have just been required to perform in a very rigid state and are slammed together, which is bad news for instrumentalists as well as vocalists. However, this problem can be easily rectified by suspending the breath, which means that when you hold it, you do not close the back of your throat—you just suspend the air while your throat remains open. In this way, vocal bands are not forced to slam against each other, and will be less prone to damage. In addition to the exhalation, if you find you need to start a word on a vowel (if you are singing) then add a little "h" sound to the beginning, audible only to you. This kind of phonating is stressfree and healthier for the voice.

Another aspect of free phonation is warming up and using sounds made at the front of the mouth. This is also very useful for choral rehearsals as well as your own singing. It means that you warm up singing, "Boo," "Bah," and "Boh." By putting those sounds at the front of the mouth using these forward vowels, pressure is taken away from the back of the throat, because you can't generate a *B* sound back there, or start the sound before making the *B* articulation. Make sure that the *B* sounds do not come out too forced and that the jaw is not clenched. When the sound is relaxed and free, and the jaw is not clenched, then changing to *M* and *N* sound at the beginning of the syllables also works, but make sure that you aren't starting the sound in the back of the throat first before you make the *M* or *N* sound. If you see clenching in the jaw at that time, go back to the *B* sounds to relax it. Many additional techniques are available, and you are strongly urged to take voice lessons to find strategies that work well with your own voice and help you investigate others you may wish to use. If you are a wind instrumentalist, you may also find that these kinds of techniques (not the *B, M,* and *N* exercises while you play) can help you achieve a more open sound and better breath support playing your instrument; we have found this to be true by applying these techniques to our own instrumental performing. It's worth a shot.

## Breathing and Posture for Singing

In the past, people were trained to sing and support from the diaphragm and often to push the lower belly out. This technique—called *Bauchaussenstütze*—was and still is a trend in some schools of German operatic singing, beginning at the end of the nineteenth century (Miller 1996; 2004). Fortunately, this style of breathing and support has fallen to the wayside because of the tension it produces in the body and especially in the laryngeal area (Miller 2004). However, some music teachers still instruct students to sing or support from the diaphragm with the belly out. We propose to eliminate this strategy from consideration when teaching breathing to children for both vocal and instrumental music, for the same reasons mentioned previously.

The diaphragm is primarily an involuntary muscle, so you really can't consciously control it when you breathe. However, muscles around it (transverse, oblique, and other abdominal muscles) can help control supported exhalation in singing. Between your ribs, you have intercostal muscles, which also contribute to inhalation and exhalation control. The free phonation approach to singing embraces a less tense way of breathing that engages abdominal and intercostal muscles when inhaling and exhaling; these muscles support breath in a controlled exhalation. This can be achieved in several ways.

If you feel you have difficulty breathing properly, then a simple way to engage your muscles is to bend forward at the waist as low as you can comfortably go and inhale. You will notice that your whole belly—not just the lower belly—will expand, as will the sides of your abdomen and even your back to some degree. This is what is supposed to happen. You can also try this strategy by leaning against a piano or bookshelf (see the DVD or www.pearsonhighered.com/flohr) or, if you want, you can get down on all fours in the privacy of your own home. The goal is to replicate this kind of breathing when you are sitting or standing.

To facilitate this kind of breathing when standing, stand in the typical singer's stance (feet slightly apart, one slightly in front of the other) and very gently tuck your behind underneath (but don't tighten it hard). It is important to do this gently so you do not add tension. The gentle tucking will line up your body and allow the muscles we just discussed to work properly when you inhale, suspend, and exhale the breath. The same can be done on a chair, with caution: Do not sit at the edge of the chair, as that will not give you enough support. Sit back, but do not slouch and do not allow your back to touch the back of the chair. Placing your legs in front with one out a bit more in the front may also help facilitate your posture. In both situations, standing and sitting, you need to feel that you have a string gently pulling you up by the head, not unlike a marionette string, so you are elongated but not tense at all.

### Singing Without Stress

Singing without stress can be achieved by following the previous tips. You will notice that your voice is less fatigued, and that your sound is much more relaxed and more likely in tune. This is a great habit to model and teach to your young students. Breathing and phonating comfortably is the key to singing efficiently, for children and adults.

### What To Do if You Really Cannot Sing

If you have a voice that is damaged, and you are a music education major, then you may need to seriously reconsider your career options or undergo voice therapy. Although some have tried to teach music while dealing with a vocal problem, usually damage is compounded and the culminating result is career ending, for general music, vocal, and instrumental teachers as well as general classroom teachers. Voice therapy can help music teachers with problems at the beginning, but engaging in it after your voice has undergone serious damage may not help very much. It is worth considering, though, as we have heard some wonderful improvements but also no improvements. Each voice responds differently.

If your concerns mostly arise out of not being able to match pitch well, or concerns about the quality of your voice, then you do have some alternatives, but they need to be used carefully. The first is to find a child model in your classroom who can serve as your vocal model. You need to help the child learn the song with everyone else, and then the child can help further teach and reinforce the song to the students. This also works well if you sing regularly but are having a bad vocal day. You still need to help, perhaps playing parts of the tunes on a piano or recorder, or doing a little bit of singing. Another option is to use a recording, which is generally the last possible resort. Too many recordings do not really present appropriate vocal models, especially if the model is an adult, male or female. A recording is *not* a good teacher of singing for children, mostly because the visual cues from the teacher that are needed in learning a song are not present. The recording will also not be able to diagnose inaccurate or unhealthful singing.

## Vocal Modeling

In direct relationship to what we have just discussed is the vocal model, which refers to not only the sound a music teacher creates when singing but also the manner in which the song is taught, the entire process from beginning to end.

There are some concerns for gender differences. Women usually do not have any major problems; however, men can have a bundle of them. The following are some guidelines to help if you are male and end up teaching elementary classroom music.

First, the younger the students, the more you need to do your initial vocal modeling in your **falsetto** range. Most young children will try to sing down where you are if you use your adult male voice, so you need to place it up in the same pitch range that they use. However, this is very fatiguing, and doing it for an extended period of time will compromise your own vocal health. It's suggested that you initially teach the song in your falsetto, and then have a child take over as the vocal model as soon as possible. From there, you can drop down into your adult voice. This strategy works with younger children, up to third grade, as long as you explain to them why you are doing it. In fourth grade and sometimes in third, most children are able to sing in an octave displacement but you have to help them learn that skill, and you may need to, on occasion, pop your voice back up to help them.

All music teachers, regardless of gender, need to keep the following considerations in mind when teaching a song, either by rote or by other strategies:

1. *You need to have the song memorized as much as possible.* Having a little cheat sheet when the song is new is OK, but you can't have your eyes glued upon it at all times.
2. *You need to have eye contact with the students while singing.* Children learn by watching singing as well as hearing singing.
3. *You need to enunciate your words very clearly and open your mouth.* Children have mislearned the words to a song, then gone home and sung it for the parents; what actually comes out are accidental obscenities or questionable topics. This guarantees a phone call by a parent to the principal.

## SAMPLE SINGING ACTIVITIES

Children who have healthy voices tend to be happily natural-born singers especially if they get ample opportunities to sing enough to strengthen and train their vocal mechanisms. Remember, everything grows during childhood, and the voice is in a constant state of growth and change, so these children may loose ability and become adults unable to sing as freely as they did in childhood. Now that you have found out how to work with your own voice, it's time to show you how to use it to help children in their own vocal and singing development. In this section of the chapter, we are going to explore the following in choosing appropriate songs:

- Range, length, difficulty, using and not using accompaniment
- Choosing songs you like
- Writing your own song or modifying an existing one
- Teaching a song by rote or by immersion

## Range, Length, and Difficulty

The younger or less experienced the child is with singing, the shorter the song needs to be. It is best to start with songs that have a limited range, such as from E up to A

Children singing from sheet music.

*Photo courtesy of Union City School District, Pennsylvania*

(both above middle C) and then moving to D to A. As you read in the earlier materials, singing is an athletic skill for the body, so it needs time and practice to learn efficiently. Due to smaller respiratory systems, children need to sing short songs with small phrases that will allow them to breathe as much as they need to. Concerning difficulty, beginning singers should not sing songs with unwieldy or wide pitch leaps (thirds or fourths at the most). These criteria generally indicate that many of the songs written for younger children (kindergarten through second grade) and marketed as children's music are really not appropriate for children to sing because they may be physically beyond what children's voices can do. However, if you have your heart set on having them sing a particular song (for example, one from *Sesame Street*), then have them sing one that has a lot of repetition in a simple refrain, and have them sing only the refrain.

As children get older and build more vocal stamina, then teachers can use longer songs with wider ranges, with these general caveats in mind. By the end of sixth grade, children should be able to sing in the range of an octave at least somewhat comfortably. However, a number of reasons, all discussed earlier in this chapter, could compromise that. Most music written for upper elementary children takes advantage of children's theoretically available singing ranges, but what is available may not be accessible. For example, if children really start singing in grade 4, their accessible pitches—the ones they can produce comfortably—may be of a smaller range by the time they are in sixth grade. Available pitches are those that are physically and theoretically possible based on known anatomical development of the vocal mechanism. The amount of experience the children have in singing will indicate what is actually accessible. Savvy music teachers will watch and listen to the children singing to aid the selection of music for concert or classroom singing. It is entirely possible to have your fifth and sixth grade choir sound like a middle school group one year, and the next year sound like a group of third and fourth graders. Teachers need to know the children's voices to make informed decisions as to music selection.

### Choosing Songs You Like

Music teachers spend a lot of time trying to find music that is good for the students to sing. To be an enthusiastic teacher of singing, you also need to like the songs you choose. However, if you can't find many that you like, and that meet the needs of your students, then you can do the following.

### Write Your Own Songs or Modify Existing Ones

This is not as hard as it sounds. You can take a folk song, or even a list of forty prepositions, and turn it into a piece of music (see the song activity with "Grammar in Rhyme" later in this chapter). You are not limited to what is available in a textbook or a song anthology, or by what you can purchase. In addition, if you find a song you do like, but you are concerned that it may be a bit difficult, you can modify it to work with your students. For example, you can change the key, or substitute notes that are too low with some that are higher but are still harmonically correct.

### Teaching a Song by Rote, Immersion, or Reading

With younger students, the rote teaching approach is generally the most used, based on the fundamental belief of "sound before symbol," a known aspect of language development. As students become older, they can actually learn songs by reading the notation. In between, sometimes an immersion approach works as well.

Rote teaching of songs is a cornerstone of the Kodály method, and teaching a song by rote is a skill that takes practice. The following shows a general sequence of how it is done, illustrated by using the song "Nanny Goat" (see also Figure 6.2):

1. The teacher provides a "hook," so the children have something specific to listen for (the younger the children, the smaller the list). For example, if the teacher is teaching "Nanny Goat," she may tell the children that she is going to sing a song about a particular animal, and what it can't do.

FIGURE 6.2 "Nanny Goat"

Nanny Goat

Traditional chase game

Nan - ny    goat,    Nan - ny    goat,

You    can't    catch    a    Bil - ly    goat!

2. The teacher checks the starting pitch, then sings the song with good diction and plenty of eye contact. It is important for the teacher to consistently sing the song in the same key when teaching it.
3. The students provide the answer to the hook (in this case, the song is about a nanny goat and she can't catch a billy goat).
4. The teacher gives the same starting pitch as before, then sings the first line so the children can repeat it.
5. The students sing back the first line.
6. The teacher sings the second line.
7. The students sing back the second line.
8. The teacher sings the entire song.
9. The students sing the entire song.

This approach is successful as long as the songs taught are not of a long length, and have phrases that are of an AA, AB, ABA, or ABAB kind of formal structure. Teachers need to consistently provide a starting pitch, which may even require them to give directions while singing the starting pitch (this is quite effective).

The rote approach will not work as well with songs that are "through-composed" or long, because they can be too difficult to break up into smaller and manageable pieces. This is when an immersion approach can be beneficial. The songs that work best in this circumstance have repeating refrains or phrases that come back. These phrases can be a starting point, as the children will only sing that part of the song, but will hear the rest of it. A sample song that is good for this is the song "Skin and Bones" (see Figure 6.3).

The "Ooo-oo-oo-oo" part is the repetitive portion that can be taught. As the children interact with the rest of the song, then they will learn the rest of the words. This is also a good approach when teaching choir music as well: children learn all the sections that are similar or the same before the sections that are different.

One caution needs to be addressed when using the immersion method. This approach does *not* include using a recording to teach a song by playing it over and over for the students. The recording can't efficiently teach a song in the way a teacher can.

Finally, children can learn a song by reading the notation. This is not far-fetched; children in first grade are able to read music notation and figure out simple songs. This

Skin and Bones

Traditional

FIGURE 6.3 "Skin and Bones"

Voice

There    was an old wom-an all    skin and bones, ooo    oo ooo    ooo!

2. She lived down by the old grave yard.....
3. One night she thought she'd take a walk.....
4. She walked down by the old grave yard.....
5. She saw the bones a-layin around.....
6. She went to her closet to get a broom.....
7. She opened the door and BOO!

is likely to happen with students who are taught a Kodály-based curriculum, because music literacy is a goal of that methodology. This activity has far-reaching advantages, especially if children learn to read music while young and continue to do so through elementary school. A choral program in the fifth and sixth grades really benefits from students developing this skill because the teacher will not need to rote-teach the choir all of the music. Children will be capable of rehearsing their own music at home, as long as they have access to correct starting pitches. However, this is a process that takes time and relies upon structure, sequencing, and practice. Trying to cram these skills in the later elementary years may be a bit more difficult due to time constraints. Information on teaching using Kodály methodology follows later in this book.

With children in primary grades, singing can happen at any time for almost any reason: to get children's attention, to segue to a new activity, or to settle them down to concentrate on class time. Music teachers will have more options, such as not only singing in the music class, but also by putting on age-appropriate musicals or shows, which can very easily translate into a cocurricular activity with another teacher as a way to enhance parallel teaching objectives. The following sample lesson addresses that possibility.

The song "Grammar in Rhyme" presents an example of how two people from different disciplines can work together to create something brand new. Instead of trying to find a prepackaged musical or show to purchase, creating one yourself allows you to tailor it for your students, and it also allows you to create your own music and exercise your imagination. This song is the result of collaboration between a language arts and a music teacher, and serves as a sample of what can happen. Possible additional songs might include lists of prepositions, songs about diagramming sentences, or recitations of works of literature. Possibilities are endless and extend to other disciplines as well. Student lyrics and poetry can also be used.

## LESSON 1: "GRAMMAR IN RHYME"

Words by George M. Meiser, IX: Music by Valerie Trollinger

### Level

Grade 5 and 6 (and older)

### Project

Sing the song, with correct words, correct pitches, and good diction.

Investigate the ways that formal structure is achieved in writing but also in music composition.

### *Music Concepts and Objectives/Assessment*

**NATIONAL STANDARD ADDRESSED:** Singing alone and with others, a variety of music; listening to, analyzing, and describing music; understanding relationships between music, the other arts, and disciplines outside the arts

**INSTRUCTIONAL OBJECTIVES:** Students are able to: (1) correctly recite the parts of speech, and (2) correctly sing the song set to the poem with good diction and correct pitches.

**ASSESSED BY:** Public performance, observing students singing to make sure it is done healthfully

Look for indications of vocal stress that indicate a need for melodic adjustment.

The students achieve the objective if not only singing the song correctly, but can also apply the words to their own writing in their English classes and compare and contrast how form is used in writing and music.

Sample questions: What are the parts of speech? Why are these important? Is there a way we can learn them that will help us remember them?

When using this to help reinforce formal structure in music: "We use the parts of speech to help us write in paragraphs and sentences, which are forms of writing. What do we use in music to help us create form?"

## Time for Lesson

The song would be taught over a period of rehearsals or music class meetings. If taught during class meetings, then one lesson would suffice for the concepts of form to be addressed and the song introduced. The song could be rehearsed as needed after that, for preparation as a final performance.

## Preparation for Lesson/Student Readiness

The students need to (1) have a demonstrated understanding of form in music, especially the forms AB, ABA, ABC, rondo, and theme and variations, (2) be literate in reading music, and (3) have a functioning use of solfège. They need to be able to discuss and demonstrate ways the sections of a form differ (for example, by rhythmic changes, melodic changes, tempo changes, and so on). This can be compared and contrasted with forms of writing, such as sentences, lists, paragraphs, essays, poems, and sometimes haiku, that occur in language arts classrooms in elementary schools. What is used depends upon what the classroom non-music teachers have covered. Finally, for performance purposes, students need to have a strong background in singing, as the song is primarily a pedagogical tool for building range in young voices that already have some flexibility, but is not very accessible to students who have limited singing ability or experience.

## Materials/Resources

1. Copy of the poem "Grammar in Rhyme" arranged by George M. Meiser IX in 1959[2]
2. Links for music with the words and audio recording are available at www.pearsonhighered.com/flohr.

## Procedure

Students are already familiar with various forms in music, so this class investigates the way the form can be achieved in writing as well. Teachers can start by asking students to describe and review the musical forms they know, and then having them identify how form appears in non-music fields (such as in biology, anatomy, art, stars, architecture, plants, and finally, language). When language arts are brought up, then the poem "Grammar in Rhyme" can be passed out. Students investigate and discuss how the parts of speech work to create form in writing (prose and poetry, if possible). This is followed by comparing and contrasting the form of the poem and the form of the music. A recording of the song is available at www.pearsonhighered.com/flohr Alternatively, teachers can simply demonstrate it by (1) singing the words, using the same melody (with needed adjustments for words) for each part (AAA form), and then (2) singing the first part of the song as written, followed by the second and third parts as written, helping the students discover that the form is primarily a theme with variations, and how each verse is varied in the music. Adding the accompaniment helps reinforce this concept further.

After the song is analyzed, teachers can begin teaching it to the students. This song doesn't work with a rote approach very successfully, nor an immersion one. Therefore, reading through the song first in solfège will be helpful, starting with the first verse. This can continue until the end of the class period. Further rehearsing can

---

[2]An 1867 version—the basis for the 1959 modernized version—included in the chapter "Elements of English Grammar" from the book *First Lessons in Language* by David Tower and Benjamin Tweed, is available from the 19th Century Schoolbooks collection, hosted by the University of Pittsburgh (http://digital.library.pitt.edu:80/n/nietz/).

take place in the next classes or in chorus rehearsals if the teachers have all the music classes that have chorus members completing this lesson.

### Extensions

Students could create a poem entitled "The Parts of Music" and set that to music, for example. Other possibilities are the parts of math, the parts of cells, the parts of humans, and so on.

## COCURRICULAR CONNECTIONS WITH VOICE AND SINGING

In addition to the activity previously addressed, other areas are compatible with the voice and singing. Investigating voices of animals and humans, such as in the field of acoustics, is very useful. Simple acoustical programs can be downloaded to help teachers and students analyze wave shapes and characteristics of not only human voices, but of animal voices. A link to a program (CSpeech) and detailed directions on using it are available on our website (www.pearsonhighered.com/flohr). This is an activity especially useful for older elementary students.

Another area of consideration is the sociological considerations of singing in non-Western cultures. Although this is addressed briefly in Chapter 4, it is of special importance here. Singing has many anthropological and sociological purposes in many world societies, and sometimes what we call singing in Western cultures is *not* singing in non-Western cultures, for example.

## COOPERATIVE LEARNING AND GROUP ACTIVITIES

Now that you have learned about singing, apply the knowledge and skills you have gained in these activities.

1. Practice analyzing and correcting singing with groups of classmates; this can be done by having a classmate deliberately sing incorrectly and see if you can catch and fix the problem.
2. Create a mini-musical or concert program of your own music that is based on cocurricular connections (for example, history, world music, language arts, mathematics, and science).
3. Take the previously created mini-musical or concert and adopt it for grades 1–2, then 3–4, then 5–6, so each version is grade-appropriate in content and in vocal considerations.

## Chapter Conclusions

The human voice is unique in the animal kingdom in that we use it for language and for singing. All voices are different and special. Recently, vocal health in teachers and in children has become a new focus in music education, with much research still needing to be done. As a result, new research and different approaches to working with voices have emerged, and more will emerge. Encouraging and teaching children to take care of their voices while young will result in happy and healthy voices through life.

## Resources

*Professional Websites for Vocal Health:*

The Voice Academy, designed for teachers: http://www.uiowa.edu/~shcvoice/

Chicago Institute for Voice Care: http://www.chicagovoicedoc.com/

National Institute on Deafness and Other Communication Disorders, "Taking Care of Your Voice": http://www.nidcd.nih.gov/health/voice/takingcare.htm

The VoiceCare Network: http://voicecarenetwork.org/

CHAPTER **7**

# Moving

**This chapter addresses the following:**

- Why Move to Music?
  *Developmental Milestones*
  *Steps to Successful Moving Experiences*

- Sample Movement Experiences
- Cooperative Learning Activities
- Chapter Conclusions

## WHY MOVE TO MUSIC?

Children are predisposed to move to the sound of music. They spontaneously move to recorded and live music. Émile Jaques-Dalcroze believed that rhythm is the primary element in music. The source for all musical rhythm may be found in the natural rhythms of the human body (for example, a heartbeat, a newborn's sucking rate, and breathing) (Fraisse 1982). Dalcroze identified the body as the first instrument to be trained in music.

Children usually experience some form of musical movement in the schools. They move to recordings, their own music making, the teacher's performances, physical education movement, and dance movement. Movement is a concrete way to learn about music. Bruner (1966) suggested three possible ways (enactive, iconic, and symbolic) that experiences are translated into a personal model of the world. Children respond to concrete experiences more readily than to abstract language or pictorial representation. Movement to music is an enactive or concrete mode of learning and helps children internalize music concepts of fast/slow, high/low, even/uneven, longer/shorter, and moving up/moving down. The national standards for music include children response through movement to music of various tempos, meters, dynamics, modes, genres, and styles to express what they hear and feel in works of music (National Association for Music Education 2007). Other standards include improvising melodies, variations, and accompaniments that can be addressed through movement (for more information, visit http://www.menc.org).

Be sure to review Chapter 11 sections about Émile Jaques-Dalcroze and Orff for many more ideas about moving to music.

## Developmental Milestones

Milestones of music are set to approximate ages. Individual children exhibit wide differences, and improve with age, experience, and instruction.

The musically adapted fundamental motor skill milestones in Table 7.1 may be helpful when designing music movement experiences in early childhood. There are at least thirteen milestones in the development of general locomotion skills: rolling,

**TABLE 7.1 Milestones in Motor Skill Development**

| Year | Milestone |
|---|---|
| Birth | Children have unsteady and generalized movement to music around 2 to 3 months; they engage in bouncing, tapping, and tickling music experiences; are able to shake small maracas and rattles; and put small instruments in their mouths. |
| 1 | Children at 1 year walk forward and backward; bounce and rock to music while standing; and imitate movements never before performed in music activities. |
| 2 | Children at 2 years run well, but not fast, without falling. They will move almost immediately to music with a steady beat. Teachers or parents should try to match the child's movement with a drum or other instrument to find child's preferred tempo. |
| 3 | Children at 3 years will respond to call-and-response tasks with movements. They imitate arm swinging across midline (for example, swing left arm across middle to the right side of body); will show steady beat, especially to chanting; may be able to clap or play sticks to the beat; will participate in simple circle games with movement; and will readily imitate adults and peers (Flohr and Brown 1979). This is a good time to begin giving children a repertoire of movements to music. |
| 4 | Children at 4 years will jump while running; skip with one foot forward (one-third of the children may be able to skip); exhibit one-foot balance; will move to music more complex; will often clap to the music (with spontaneous movements decreasing); and are able to perform simple movement experiences using arm swings, twisting, hammering fists, and shaking hands in front. Children's walking or stepping tempo is usually between 130 bpm and 140 bpm, with large motor locomotion. From between 4 years and 6 years, children experience faster walking and marching tempi, and then a gradual decline in speed occurs through age 12 (Frego 1996). Movement participation increases when children utilize a prop (Patrick 1998). |
| 5 | Children at 5 years skip alternating lead foot (two-thirds of the children may be able to skip); catch balls and other objects; and may engage in simple folk dances. |
| 6 | At 6 years, children's walking or stepping tempo increases to a peak of 149 bpm and then gradually slows to 134 bpm between 11 years and 12 years. |
| 7–11 | Children engage in sport related movement activities. Children's ability to keep the steady beat increases with age; most increase in ability to perform rhythm is from 4–7 years of age with smaller increase from ages 7–11 (Flohr 2000). |

Adapted with musical examples from (Jansma and French 1994). © Prentice-Hall. Used by Permission.

crawling, creeping, cruising (one hand on an object), walking, jumping, running, hopping, climbing, sliding, galloping, dodging, and skipping (Jansma and French 1994). Each locomotive milestone may be further subdivided.

**DEVELOPMENT OF STEADY BEAT** Several studies examine steady beat and young children. The ability to keep a steady beat is basic to musical performance. Keeping the steady beat is also referred to as synchronization to the beat of music or matching the heartbeat of music. The abbreviations **bpm** (beats per minute) or **m.m.** (metronome marking) are used to describe the speed of the beat. Both bpm and m.m. refer to the

Children engaging in movement is an important part of music classes.

*Photo courtesy of Kelly Riccio*

number of steady beats during a minute (for example, 120 bpm denotes a speed of 120 beats per minute). The ideas of macro- and microbeats are found in music. The **macrobeat** refers to the longer overall steady beat. The **microbeat** refers to the subdivided smaller steady beat of the same composition. When one listens to a march and is asked to perform the steady beat, the response may be to the slower macrobeat or the faster microbeat. For example, Duke (1989) found that, when tempo rates were greater than 120 bpm, adults tended to respond to the slower pulse, or macrobeat, whereas responses to tempo rates slower than 60 bpm tended to be to the microbeat.

In Chapter 3, we discussed how age, type of instrument or movement task, and individual differences affect rhythm performance. A child's ability to keep the steady beat is also affected by interaction of age, type of instrument or movement used, individual differences, whether they are asked to keep a tempo to the music or without hearing music, tempo of the music, and culture.

Children keep a steady beat to music best if the beat is close to their preferred or personal tempo (Smoll and Schutz 1978; Walters 1983). Vaughn (1981) recommends to "[S]tart with a tempo dictated by the children's own behavior and their ability to respond will increase dramatically." There is evidence that a child's cultural surroundings influence the ability to keep the steady beat to music (Flohr et al. 1998; Rose 1995; Vaughan 1981). For example, Rose (1995) found that children raised in a mountain culture where a dance called clogging was common were better at keeping the beat than children from a city environment.

## Steps to Successful Moving Experiences

**PITFALLS TO AVOID**    The major pitfall to avoid is possible injury to a child. As children move to music, they can become very excited. Set up the room for movement. Remove or place padding on all furniture and other objects that may injure children (for example, sharp corners of a piano). Make sure there is enough space for the type of movement being used. Each child should have personal space in which to move. Do not ask children to move in ways that are not developmentally appropriate (for example, advanced ballet moves in preschool).

**STEPS**    Pitfalls are avoided by careful attention to the following steps before beginning movement experiences:

1. *Set the environment and boundaries for movement.* Whether the children move to the music while sitting in their chairs or move through a room, it is advisable to set the environment to reflect boundaries for movement. Many movements to music may be done with limited space (for example, use only arms, hands, and head to move). Encourage positive experiences by setting rules for moving (stop/start with the music, respect each others' space). Move desks and chairs to optimize movement area. Find another space outside or in the school that will accommodate moving.

2. *Stop and start.* Do *not* start children moving around the room before you are able to control them. First work with the children until they are very used to stopping and starting their movement with the music.

3. *Use the many available ways to incorporate movement.* Basic elements of the music movement program for young children are feeling the beat, expressing the beat, synchronizing the beat, time/space awareness, expressive movement to music, and creative movement (for other movements, see Table 7.2). Following is a listing of general movement experiences:
   - *Action songs.* Movements (embedded in the text) accompany a song such as "Wheels on the Bus Go Round and Round" or "If You're Happy and You Know It, Clap Your Hands."
   - *Dance.* Movement formalized into dances with simple patterns
   - *Describe a movement.* Use words to talk about movements the children make. Also describe animal movements.
   - *Move to the beat and expressive movement* (expressing beat through movement). For example, "Show me the way music moves."

**TABLE 7.2** Basic Moving Repertoire

**Space**

*Locomotion:*

- Move into general space with others (walk, run, skip, slide, jump, leap, prance, hop, gallop, tiptoe, stomp). Encourage children to generally propel themselves in a direction like a locomotive.

*Nonlocomotion:*

- Move within limited space such as a desk or within self-space (stretch, bend, sway, rock). Encourage children to not propel themselves in a direction (locomotive at the station).

*Locomotion or Nonlocomotion:*

- Move in different directions.
- Move at different levels. Explore the activities of stretching, sitting, kneeling, lying down, and squatting. Use parts of the body to show level change. For example, "How high can you get your elbow into the air?"
- Move in different ranges. For example, start with a natural known movement like waving and "do it differently." The action may be done slower, faster, smaller, bigger, smoother, or more erratic. Also use a different body part.
- Move in different pathways. Explore directions of movement. For example, ask all the children to be on one side of the room, and designate a goal to reach (like a chair). Explore direct and indirect pathways to the chair. Explore moving with different orientations to others such as body facing, body sideways, or body backwards.

**Body Awareness**

- Move different body parts (hands, arms, feet, legs, fingers, head).
- Move by changing body shapes.
- Change relationships of body parts to each other.
- Change relationships of body to objects.
- Change relationships of one person to another.

**Force/Weight and Energy**

- Demonstrate tension and relaxation.
- Create force (for example, heavy, strong, light, weak movements).
- Absorb force.
- Make and hold still balances.
- Move on-balance and off-balance (gravity).
- Transfer weight by stepping, rocking, rolling, and sliding.

**Time**

- Move at different speeds/tempi.
- Move rhythmically to beat, accent, musical phrases, and rhythm patterns.

**Flow**

- Move with free flow and bound flow. Flow in this sense refers to the plasticity of the movements (for example, smooth, choppy, sudden, interrupted).
- Create movement sequences.

---

- *Movement with props.* Many objects may be used as movement props (for example, stick horses, scarves, puppets, or plastic aquarium figures) (Patrick 1998).
- *Movement with single sounds.* Move to isolated sound sources. For example, play a drum and ask the children to move their arms until they do not hear the drum any longer. Then play a triangle and move for the duration of the sound. Notice how much longer the triangle sound lasts. Use other instruments and found sound sources.
- *Sequences.* Several movement songs have number or word sequences. For example, "Band of Angels" sequences numbers and "Bought Me a Cat"

sequences animals and their sounds (Smith and Leonhard 1968). Other music describes events (for example, a sunrise described by Grieg's "Morning" from *Peer Gynt*) (National Academy of Recording Arts and Sciences [NARAS] 1999). Children could be asked to represent through their movements the gradual rise of the sun. There are also musical sequences where a pattern is repeated higher or lower. For example, in "Shoo Fly," the phrase "Flies in the buttermilk, shoo fly, shoo" is sung three times (the second time is sung lower than the first, and the last time is sung like the first phrase).

- *Singing game movement.* Many singing games incorporate movements such as passing ("Tisket Tasket"), creating movements ("Hey, hey, look at me"), and moving around the group ("Nanny Goat").
- *Wiggles, tickles, and tapping.* Feierabend (2000) collected and recorded many good experiences for children, particularly young children.
- *Word stimulus/interpretative movement.* Moving to descriptive words or phrases such as "Move as if you are a flower" or using imitative means of representation (*a mimetic dance*) "Move like an elephant."

4. *Consider tempo.* Select music of many tempi designed to match the preferences of the children in the classroom. Try grouping children into groups based on their "personal tempo." The children perform steady beat more accurately if the tempo of the music is close to their preferred tempo. Ability to keep the steady beat is affected by the interaction of age, type of instrument or movement used, individual differences, whether the child is asked to keep a tempo to the music or without hearing music, tempo of the music, and culture.

## SAMPLE MOVEMENT EXPERIENCES

Music can be taught in such a way that it supports how every child is motivated, from within, to form collaborative and creative relationships in moving, and to pick up new ideas and elaborate rituals of performance from other people. Experiences with music and movement should be at the center of children's music education. Movement experiences are also a very fertile ground for creating. Table 7.2 lists ways to move in space, body awareness, force, time, and flow. For example, refer to Table 7.2 for locomotive and nonlocomotive ways to move in space. Additional ideas are available from the work of Laban (Davies 2001). Feelings and the expressiveness of music may be united with movement. Use a variety of recorded music, improvised music, and rhythm instruments to supply the music for movement.

### MOVING EXPERIENCE 1–DURATION GAME

**Level**

Grade 3 group project

**Project/Activities**

Move to three rhythm durations in a game of tag

**Previous Knowledge and Skills**

Ability to start and stop to musical cues

**Parallel Objectives**

*Music Concepts and Objectives/Assessment*

**STANDARDS ADDRESSED:** Listening to, analyzing, and describing music (MENC 2007)

**INSTRUCTIONAL OBJECTIVES:** Students move to three rhythm durations while playing a game with other children.

**ASSESSED BY:** Observing children playing the game and moving

*Physical Education Concepts and Objectives/Assessment*

**STANDARDS ADDRESSED:**   Demonstrates competency in motor skills and movement patterns needed to perform a variety of physical activities (NASPE 2004)

**INSTRUCTIONAL OBJECTIVE:**   The students display competency in movement to the game.

**ASSESSED BY:**   Observing students moving

## Time for Lesson

Duration: 11 minutes. Set aside two to three minutes to practice the movement to the three durations and at least five minutes to play the game. Children enjoy playing the game for a long period of time.

## Materials/Resources

1. Large drum or prepared CD with music that moves with three durations (for example, half note, quarter note, and eighth note)
2. A piece of cloth, hat, or soft ball to be used to show who is "it"

## Procedure

### Anticipatory Set (Attention Hook)

Before starting, make certain that the children have learned to stop and start with the music so that, when they become very excited playing the game, control is maintained when the music stops. Play a marching drumbeat (a step = 120 bpm), and ask the children to move through space in a steady march. Decrease the speed by half (60 bpm) and then increase the speed to twice as fast (240 bpm). To stimulate the children's interest, use a visual picture of animals for each speed. The visual pictures should be images within the child's experience and modified if not current or unknown to the group of children. For example, use little mice feet for 240 bpm (very, very fast!), a marching band for 120 bpm, and bigfoot or the hairy mammoth from the current animated movie *Ice Age,* for 60 bpm.

Bigfoot or Hairy Mammoth is a controlled tag game; the teacher controls the beat and tempo. Start the tag game (no tag-backs). Use a piece of cloth, a soft ball, or a hat to identify the person who is "it." The rule is that everyone in the game can only move to the drumbeat. Stop the beat if the children are not moving with the beat. The children will quickly learn how to use time and space to take larger steps to catch another child.

## Evaluation

Ask questions such as the following:

Who can show us how to move to the three beats?

Who can show me how to stop moving when the music stops?

## Continuing the Lesson

Add more durations to the game. This game is also appropriate for children younger than third grade.

## MOVING EXPERIENCE 2–OPPOSITE MACHINE

### Level

Grade 2 group project

## Project/Activities

Move to show changes in music

## Previous Knowledge and Skills

Creative movement activity experiences and knowledge of simple music opposite concepts such as faster/slower

## Parallel Objectives

### Music Concepts and Objectives/Assessment

**STANDARDS ADDRESSED:**  Performing on instruments (through movement), alone and with others, a varied repertoire of music; improvising melodies, variations, and accompaniments (improvising movements); listening to, analyzing, and describing music (MENC 2007)

**INSTRUCTIONAL OBJECTIVES:**  The students demonstrate changes in musical concepts by their movement and identify the changes in other children's movements.

**ASSESSED BY:**  Observing children playing the game and moving

### Physical Education Concepts and Objectives/Assessment

**STANDARDS ADDRESSED:**  Demonstrates competency in motor skills and movement patterns needed to perform a variety of physical activities (NASPE 2004)

**INSTRUCTIONAL OBJECTIVE:**  The students display competency in movement to the game.

**ASSESSED BY:**  Observing students moving

## Time for Lesson

Duration: 10 minutes

## Materials/Resources

1. Piano, guitar, or prepared CD
2. A movable chalkboard or a large box for the opposite machine (machine gears and other pictures can be placed on the board or the box)
3. Either improvise music for the game or choose audio excerpts that illustrate opposite musical qualities such as faster and slower.

## Procedure

### Anticipatory Set (Attention Hook)

Before starting, make certain that the children have learned to stop and start with the music so that control is maintained when they become very excited playing the game. Demonstrate with at least one example how the opposite machine changes movements using the following procedures. Begin by playing an instrument or an audio excerpt.

Students enter one side of the machine, showing a musical concept by their movement. Then, for example, they enter the opposite machine where the music is fast. Inside the opposite machine, students are changed and exit moving to illustrate the opposite of the musical concept. In this example, children would exit moving slowly. Use recorded music for the concepts, or the teacher or children may improvise examples. Possible concepts include shorter/longer, even/uneven, faster/slower, higher/lower, and louder/softer. After the children are acclimated to the game, give a child or group of children a slip of paper showing a pair of opposites such as shorter/longer. The child or group moves through the opposite machine, and the class decides what concepts are being shown.

### Evaluation

Students achieve the objective if they participate in the game, improvise movements to musical concepts, and identify the musical concepts from the movements observed. The class may be formed into groups. Ask questions such as: Who can show us how short and long in music looks in movement? What qualities of music did that group of show with their movements?

### Continuing the Lesson

Add various concepts to the game. This game is also appropriate for children younger than third grade.

## COOPERATIVE LEARNING ACTIVITIES

1. Select an instrument that you would like to use for improvisation from the following: piano, guitar, percussion, or recorder. Using the lesson plan format previously mentioned or one suggested by your teachers, construct a two-plan sequence for movement modeled after the examples.
2. As an extension of the previous plan, rewrite it to be appropriate for a different age level.

## Chapter Conclusions

Movement and music in elementary education go hand in hand. Children spontaneously move to recorded and live music. There are many ways to incorporate movement. Experiences include action songs, dance, dance therapy, describing musical movement, expressive movement, movement with props, movement with sound, movement sequences, singing game movement, wiggling, tickling, tapping, and word stimuli movement. See Chapter 16, "Movement Lessons," for more examples. Experiences with music and movement should be at the center of children's music education.

CHAPTER **8**

# Creating

This chapter addresses the following:

- Why Create Music? National Standards
- Development and Creating
  *Theories*
  *Improvisation*
  *Composition*
  *Structure in Children's Creating*

- Steps to Successful Creating Experiences
  *Pitfalls to Avoid*
- Sample Creating Experiences
- Cooperative Learning Activities
- Chapter Conclusions
- Resources

## WHY CREATE MUSIC? NATIONAL STANDARDS

Of all the music experiences for children, creative experiences are sometimes the most forgotten in classrooms. Unfortunately, creativity is often vaguely viewed as some mysterious talent. Parents and teachers think of singing, movement, listening to recordings, and playing instruments before creative activities. Experiences offered in this chapter can assist encouragement of music creating.

Although researchers may agree on the existence of musical creativity in children, they disagree on the definition of creativity and whether the products of children should be labeled improvisations or compositions. What is creativity? Certainly creating involves the ability to generate new innovative ideas or products that are useful and valued by others. Children often improvise music in their free play. Improvisation is a spontaneous invention and shaping of music. Azzara identifies three key factors for defining the process of improvisation: (1) spontaneous expression of musical ideas and feelings, (2) making or making up music within specified guidelines (think of improvising in jazz to a twelve-bar blues), and (3) engaging in musical conversations (Azzara 2002). Folkestad (1998, 109) points out that time is a key distinction between improvisation and composition. The spontaneous invention of music exists in real time and may be called an instant composition. In addition, its creator performs the improvisation whereas a musical composition may be separated from its creator and performed by another person. A music composition involves creating music that is finalized in some way (for example, is written with a notational system so another person or group can play the composition). Creating may involve improvisation or composition. It is important to note that studies indicate that improvisation ability and experiences transfer to a child's comprehension of music performed from notation (Azzara 1993; Montano 1983). In summary, creating is the generation of new innovative ideas or products that are useful and valued by others.

Two kinds of experiences, free exploration and guided exploration, may facilitate improvisation. In free exploration, children are left alone to explore instruments, the voice, pots and pans, or any other sound-making object in the environment. In guided exploration, teachers or parents serve as a guide to the children's exploration by asking questions or engaging in parallel play with the children. Active exploration and interaction are parts of the MENC standards: improvising melodies, variations, and accompaniments (National Association for Music Education 2007).

Given the opportunity, children enjoy and engage in improvising music with their voices and instruments. Any experienced parent or teacher of young children will agree with Gardner's (1982) portrayal of the preschool years as being characterized by creative behavior. Children often exhibit an inherent desire to play with sound. One belief about young children is that children's play is their work. "Play provides a safe place to try on the roles of others, to fantasize, and to explore new ideas. Children's play involves imitation and improvisation" (Sims 1995, 91). Children may learn about music and a host of subjects more effectively through creative play than any other way (Gardner 1982; Piaget 1962). For further information about music creativity, reviews may be found in several works (Colwell and Richardson 2002; Sundin et al. 1998; Webster 1987).

## DEVELOPMENT AND CREATING

Young children are clearly creative, and musical creativity is an important field for research. There are three caveats about the creativity research to consider. First, if children's creating is approached from an adult perspective, it is easy to ignore how a child's mind is different from that of an adult. If the approach is trying to determine the child's view (for example, in a naturalistic setting), there is great difficulty in summarizing, categorizing, explaining, and often describing the musically rich, often complex, and unique products of children's music play. Researchers have various opinions not only on the definition of creativity, but also about the way in which the products of children are analyzed, what is process or product, and whether it is better to treat the creations from the child's view or as the development toward adult music. Second, the research definitions of creative activities are in conflict. For example, improvisation is usually treated as instant music where its creator performs the improvisation. On the other hand, Swanick and Tilman (1986) write about composition to include improvisation. Third, it is important to recognize that some studies observe only vocal creating and others examine only instrumental creating. It may be erroneous to assume that findings for vocal creating are applicable to instrumental creating or vice versa.

### Theories

Education often emphasizes logical and sequential learning. The field of psychology has spawned a number of ideas and theories about creativity (Amabile 1989; Csikszentmihalyi 1975; de Bono 1993; Guilford 1967; Sternberg and Lubart 1996; Webster 1992). This brief overview examines Guilford, Webster, and Sternberg and Lubart.

Guilford's concept of creativity is defined with a model *structure of intellect*, including 120 factors across three dimensions. The three dimensions are operations (what the child does); contents (the vehicle; for example, the musical instruments); and products (the forms in which the information is processed). Guilford's influential work includes the ideas of *divergent* and *convergent* thinking. Divergent thinking results when a teacher or parent asks a child for many possible answers to one question. Divergent thinking concepts include fluency (number of different responses), flexibility (different classes of responses), originality (novelty of responses), and elaboration (extension of responses). Convergent thinking is the type of thinking that results in a single best or correct answer to one question. In divergent thinking, a teacher may ask the children to think of many different ways of moving to a piece of music (see examples of experiences later in this chapter). In convergent thinking, a teacher may ask the children to find the best single way to move to the piece of music.

Webster (1987; 1990; 1992) provides reviews of musical creativity. He developed a theory of creative thinking in music that works with his assessment instrument, Measures of Creative Thinking in Music (MCTM) (Webster 1992). His theory utilizes the idea of divergent thinking as it interacts with convergent thinking. Besides the quantity of ideas a child might create, Webster's theory includes flexibility and originality. For example, when given a xylophone to explore, some children will try to reproduce a song such as "Twinkle, Twinkle, Little Star"; some will improvise on a known song; and others will create original and ever-changing improvisations.

Sternberg and Lubart (1996) have developed components of creativity that are part of an *investment* theory. A variety of intellectual resources—knowledge, cognitive style, personality, environmental, and motivational—combine to stimulate creativity. For example, a supportive environment serves to stimulate and promote special talents in music (Monsaas and Engelhard 1990; Trollinger 1978). The investment theory is promising for its ability to suggest instructional strategies such as good environment and motivation incentives for children.

## Improvisation

Age, development, and experiences make a difference in the ability to improvise and the products that are created (Flohr 1985; Laczó 1981; Moorehead and Pond 1978; Ott 1996). The work of Pond and others at the Pillsbury Company Foundation is an early study about musical improvisations of children. Pond found that children playing instruments and singing were not predisposed to making pretty, symmetrical tunes, but rather patterns, shapes, and structures whose elements are rhythmic figures and intervals. After the pioneering work of Pond, several studies examined the development of improvisation activities. Cohen (1980) and Shelley (1981) followed the naturalistic techniques of the Pillsbury studies and observed 3- to 5-year-old children's free explorations. The qualitative research of Cohen involved observation of kindergarten children's musical behavior in an unstructured music center. The study concluded that children's free exploration of instruments in an unstructured situation might be categorized under the headings of mastery and the generating of musical gestures. Intensive analysis of the gestures produced indicated that kinesthetic (movement) gestures are the source of musical gestures. Cohen found that children's improvisations including the gestures (or musical phrases and sentences) were dominated by ways the child moved. Until such time as children can produce *pure* musical gestures, they produce *hybrids* in which kinesthetic components compensate for aspects for which the child can as yet not produce an acoustic analogue. Through observation of free exploration, Shelley identified several factors that seemed to encourage creating on instruments (beautiful sounding instruments, supportive environment, free exploration within structure, and encouragement of teachers who observed and sometimes participated).

Flohr (1979) studied improvisation behavior of 4-, 6-, and 8-year-old children using Orff xylophones. Twelve children were asked to improvise in free and guided exploration activities. He found that the characteristics of the children's improvisations changed in relation to the child's chronological age: The older children maintained interest in exploring sound possibilities of a single instrument longer than 4-year-olds; tonal orientation and cohesiveness of form increased as the children matured; and young children are able to create musical images of verbal stimuli. Later, Flohr (1981) found that short-term music instruction including instrumental improvisation influenced children's developmental music aptitude as measured by the *Primary Measures of Music Audiation* (Gordon 1979). A longitudinal study was reported following children aged from 2 to 5 years; the 2-year-olds in the study participated to the age of 5 (Flohr 1985). Three continuous levels of instrumental improvisation for young children were identified in the study.

One study of children less than 3 years of age found that the youngest children's singing forms were "floating" in the sense that they sound much like scribbled drawings appear (Dowling 1988). Dowling's floating, spontaneous singing is similar to the motor energy that Flohr found in instrumental free explorations.

Child exploring the tonal qualities of a Xylophone.

*Photo courtesy of Jane Rivera*

Kratus (1991; 1995b) suggested seven developmental levels in instrumental improvisation that normally span a time period longer than early childhood. The levels include (1) exploration, in which students try out different sounds and combinations of sounds in a loosely structured context; (2) process-oriented, in which children produce more cohesive patterns; (3) product-oriented, in which children become conscious of structural principles such as tonality and rhythm; (4) fluid, in which children manipulate their instrument or voice in a more automatic, relaxed manner; (5) structural, in which children are aware of the overall structure of the improvisation and develop a repertoire of musical or nonmusical strategies for shaping an improvisation; (6) stylistic, in which children improvise skillfully within a given style, incorporating its melodic, harmonic, and rhythmic characteristics; and (7) personal, in which children are able to transcend recognized improvisation styles to develop a new style.

## Composition

In addition to the creativity theories and research about improvisation, several studies look at music composition in the elementary school. For example, Kratus (1985) found developmental differences among song compositions of children aged between 5 and 13. The 5- and 6-year-old children did not use formalized endings, and the 7-year-old children used logical resolutions (endings) to melodic or rhythmic motives. Kratus also found that, when students rush into a creative activity, the results are of less musical quality than if they take their time at the outset. Once they get started, the tempo of their work doesn't seem to affect the outcome (Kratus 1995a).

Tilman and Swanick (1989) suggested musical creativity involves spiral development. Spiral development was also described in the materials for the Manhattanville Music Curriculum Project. In spiral development, children may gradually progress to more stylized forms of composition or improvisation and then return to use characteristics of earlier development. For example, a child most often improvises music that incorporates four-measure phrases characterized by repetition and contrast, but at times returns to the plodding accented durations that characterized the child's early improvisations (Biasini et al. 1970). Tilman and Swanick identified a developmental sequence for instruments and singing based on Piaget's work and characterized by spiral development rather than discrete stages. The *sensory* mode (free exploration) describes the musical behavior of 3-year-olds. For example, children experiment with the sounds an instrument makes as in free exploration. The *manipulative* mode (motor skills) characterizes 4- or 5-year-olds. For example, children find skill to produce scales (especially if the instrument is shaped to produce a scale, such as an Orff xylophone that would work better than a piano). The *personal* mode (intense personal expression) was first seen to appear in songs of 4-year-olds. For example, a child may repeat one word such as *zoo* over and over again with different melodies and pitch ranges. The *vernacular* mode (music conventions of the culture) is characterized by musical cliché, symmetrical phrases, and ostinati. The *personal* and *vernacular* modes continue to age 9. The other modes identified by Tilman and Swanick, *speculative, idiomatic, symbolic,* and *systematic,* are labeled as occurring during ages 10 and above (Swanick and Tilman 1986).

## Structure in Children's Creating

Young children's musical creations contain structure. Several researchers note that 5-year-olds and younger improvise vocal and/or instrumental music that contains structure (Barrett 1998; Davies 1992; Dowling 1988; Flohr 1985; Moorehead and Pond 1978; Sundin et al. 1998). For example, Davies studied invented songs of 5- and 7-year-olds. She found the vocal compositions to be structurally organized and suggested that the urge to make meaning drives the developmental process. Flohr (1979) notated the exploratory instrumental improvisations of twelve subjects. He found that, of four 4-year-olds, two children's exploratory improvisations exhibited a number of structural elements including melodic repetition, variation, sequence, and inversion (45–49, 66). It is agreed that structure is present in children's created musical products, and the products of older children typically exhibit more structure. However, there is concern that what the children are asked to do and the analysis of the children's products help determine the found structure. For example, the structural properties of compositions evaluated with an imposed time limit of ten minutes may be different from composition without a time limit.

Pond's observation of children having their own personal world of sound is an important concept to remember. Adult perceptions of music, including concepts such as form or tonality, may have little to do with the child's world of sound. It is also important to remember that the environment is a significant factor in the child's creating. Much of the developmental differences found in children's creating—especially older children—may be influenced by the children's ability to absorb the musical culture that surrounds them. For example, when Kalmar and Balasko (1987) observed 6-year-olds while creating songs from text rhymes, they often improvised melodies that were similar to songs learned in preschool.

**DEVELOPMENTAL MILESTONES**    The following milestones are set for approximate ages. Individual children exhibit large music skill differences; their skills generally improve with age, experience, and instruction.

**TABLE 8.1  Milestones in Creating**

| Year | Milestone |
|---|---|
| 0–2 | Exploration of sound-producing objects in the environment. |
| | Children are not predisposed to make pretty, symmetrical tunes, but rather patterns, shapes, and structures whose elements are rhythmic figures and intervals (Pond 1978). Improvisations are characterized by plodding and accented durations (pendulum-like regularity) similar to scribbling in art (Flohr 1985). |
| 2–3 | The songs and instrumental improvisations of children less than 3 years have a quality much like scribbles in drawing (Dowling 1984; Flohr 1985). |
| | Factors to encourage creativity are beautiful sounding instruments, supportive environment, and free exploration within structure (Shelley 1981). |
| | Children experiment with their own capacity for sound production with instruments and their own voice. |
| | If given the opportunity for free play with instruments and sound-making objects, children will create spontaneous games. They engage in sound exploration, long periods of absorbed activity, unconventional use of instruments, and teaching of peers (Smithrim 1997). Families of highly creative women attended concerts, other cultural events, and traveled together (Trollinger 1978). |
| 4–5 | Improvisations are gradually characterized by melodic repetition, variation, sequence, and inversion. Improvisations are often dominated by the ways a child moves (Cohen 1980). Manipulative mode, personal, and vernacular modes continue past 8 years (Tilman and Swanick 1989). Children are able to create complete songs beginning at the age of 5 years (Davies 1992). Improvisations often contain creative transformation of learned musical material (Kalmar and Balasko 1987). |
| 6 | Songs learned in preschool are used in improvised melodies. They use more structure leading to decentered perception, attention to overall form rather than attention only to one element (for example, timbre) at a time. |
| 7 | Children's creative products are formally organized, contain more rhythm patterns, and exhibit increased motivic development, particularly during ages between 6 and 9 years (Brophy 1999). |
| 8 | As children become older, they use more composition strategies of development and repetition over exploration and silence (Kratus 1989). |
| 9 | By age 9, children are creating in vernacular mode (cultural influences) (Tilman and Swanick 1989). Children's creative products from between 6 years and 9 years (see age 7 years above) do not change much during between 9 years and 11 years (Brophy 1999). |
| 10–11 | Children composing with ten xylophone bars as opposed to five xylophone bars spent more time in exploration, composed longer songs, and were less able to repeat the song (Kratus 2001). Improvisation experiences transfer to a child's comprehension of music performed from notation (Azzara 1993; Montano 1983). |

## STEPS TO SUCCESSFUL CREATING EXPERIENCES

Techniques to enhance creative experiences include clear goals and objectives, ample free and exploratory experiences, and realistic expectations about the children's improvisations and compositions.

### Pitfalls to Avoid

Provide the opportunity for exploration of sounds. Thinking of the child's banging on pots, pans, or instruments as just noise is a mistake. Children are experimenting with sound and their creativity will be nurtured in a supportive environment. Be careful with compliments to children 3 to 5 years of age. A common behavior for a 4-year-old is to stop an activity if an adult interferes or calls attention to the music making. Take care to avoid distracting children from their improvisations or explorations. Children from birth through elementary age need opportunities to play, improvise, and compose.

Pitfalls are avoided by careful attention to several steps before beginning creating experiences.

1. Carefully introduce guided exploration experiences after children have ample opportunity to freely explore instruments. For example, give third graders an opportunity to freely explore the maracas, castanets, and guiro before using them in a guided way.
2. Use descriptive language to stimulate creating such as "Move like an elephant" or "Improvise sounds that are like a summer rain."
3. Do not expect children to create adult music. Young children are not predisposed to making pretty and symmetrical tunes. Their creations are more often patterns, shapes, and structures whose elements are rhythmic figures and intervals. Created songs by children under the age of 5 have several differences from traditional songs (smaller range, more repetition, chanting and singing, complex rhythms). Elementary aged children may also create music different from adult music styles.
4. Teachers should ask children to slow down and think about what they are doing in the first few minutes of creative work (Kratus 1995b).

## SAMPLE CREATING EXPERIENCES

Improvising and composing are excellent ways to learn about music. Children find creative experiences fun and satisfying.

### CREATING EXPERIENCE 1–CONVERSATIONS

#### Level

Grade 1 project for teacher and student or two students

#### Project/Activities

Create a conversation with instruments

#### Previous Knowledge and Skills

Ability to play xylophone or other instrument for the improvisation

#### Parallel Objectives

#### *Music Concepts and Objectives/Assessment*

**STANDARDS ADDRESSED:** Performing on instruments, alone and with others, a varied repertoire of music; improvising melodies, variations, and accompaniments (MENC 2007)

**INSTRUCTIONAL OBJECTIVES:**  Students create/improvise music in response to another's music.

**ASSESSED BY:**  Observing children engaged in the conversation or listening to the recording of the conversations

## Mathematics Concepts and Objectives/Assessment

**STANDARDS ADDRESSED:**  Count with understanding and recognize how many in sets of objects (NCTM 2008)

**INSTRUCTIONAL OBJECTIVE:**  Students will be able to count and identify patterns in the improvisations.

**ASSESSED BY:**  Asking them to play the same number of beats in their reply to the teacher's conversation

## Time for Lesson

Duration: 5 minutes or more

## Materials/Resources

Many instruments can be used. One of the best is one or two Orff-type xylophones with one or two mallets for each player.

## Procedure

### Anticipatory Set (Attention Hook)

Demonstrate with one student how to initiate and continue a conversation on the instrument. Say to the student, "I'll say something with my instrument and you can answer with your instrument." It is also useful to discuss the idea that talking on the instruments is like talking on the telephone. Provide feedback with statements about the child's productions such as, "You played the same rhythm pattern I did and then something different." After constructing and decorating the instrument, play the instruments to the steady beat of live performed or recorded music.

## Evaluation

Students achieve the objective if they participate in the conversation and create rhythms and melodies. Ask question such as the following: Can you talk on the instrument as if you are talking on the phone? Can you repeat your partner's rhythm pattern using the same number of beats (strikes)? Can you repeat your partner's melodic pattern?

## Continuing the Lesson

Try conversations with three or four children.

## CREATING EXPERIENCE 2–IMPROVISING ON CHORDS

### Level

Grade 5 small group project

### Project/Activities

Improvise on three **triads**

## Previous Knowledge and Skills

Students previously learn the technique for playing bells or mallet instruments and concept of chords.

## Parallel Objectives

### Music Concepts and Objectives/Assessment

**STANDARDS ADDRESSED:** Performing on instruments, alone and with others, a varied repertoire of music; improvising melodies, variations, and accompaniments (MENC 2007)

**INSTRUCTIONAL OBJECTIVES:** Students improvise using three pitches of a triad and three different chords.

**ASSESSED BY:** Observing students or recording improvisations for later listening

### Mathematics Concepts and Objectives/Assessment

**STANDARDS ADDRESSED:** Count with understanding and recognize how many in sets of objects (NCTM 2008)

**INSTRUCTIONAL OBJECTIVE:** Students will be able to track the sounds of triads and triadic movement (movement using three pitches of the triad).

**ASSESSED BY:** Having students circle pictorial representations of how many pitches and chords they hear, and having them draw their own representations (lines, circles, other shapes) to represent a number of beats

## Time for Lesson

Duration: 10 minutes

## Materials/Resources

Instruments (3) for each group. Bells or mallet instruments are well designed for the lesson

## Procedure

### Anticipatory Set (Attention Hook)

Demonstrate a song on the instrument with three chords. For example, play chords on a piano or Autoharp to "When the Saints Go Marching In" using three chords.

In groups of students (three to five), each student will have an instrument such as bells or xylophone with triad pitches available for the chords of B♭, F, and G. Bells will be the simplest, with each student holding one bell for each chord. The pitches for each chord are in parentheses: (1) B♭ (B♭, D, F); (2) F (F, A, C); and (3) G (G, B, D). Notice that some pitches are in more than one chord. After each student is secure in playing each triad, the group can experiment with improvising together on one triad at a time and then move from triad to triad at the same time.

## Evaluation

Students achieve the objective if they participate in the improvisation and are able to improvise with pitches that correspond to the chord. Sample questions could include the following: Can you improvise on B♭? Can you improvise on F? Can you improvise on G?

**Continuing the Lesson**

Groups extend the improvisations into a composition in rondo form (ABACA, and so forth). The extension addresses the national standard of composing and arranging music within specified guidelines.

## COOPERATIVE LEARNING ACTIVITIES

Create an assessment model for creative experiences. Try analyzing the child's responses to creative experiences with Guilford's ideas of operations (what the child does), vehicle (the instrument or object used), and product (the forms in which the information is processed). Besides the quantity of ideas produced, look for divergent thinking, originality, and flexibility. Consider using tests of creativity found in resources.

## Chapter Conclusions

Creating music during the early years may include free exploration, guided exploration, and improvisation. The creativity research gives us descriptions of what to expect from children. Children naturally play, experiment, and create music. The children's environment is important in the development of musical creativity. No one creates music in a vacuum. Young children tend to create spontaneous song and free music play with instruments and movement. Later, between 3 and 5 years of age, they often try to reproduce familiar songs or music from their environment such as a television jingle or song sung at home. The children require rich experiences with music so that they will have skills and understanding with which to create. They require opportunities to experiment with music for an extended period of time.

## Resources

Biasini, A., R. Thomas, and L. Pogonowski. 1970. *MMCP interaction: Early childhood music curriculum.* Bardonia, NY: Media Materials, Inc.

Foshay, A., ed. 1970. *Manhattanville Music Curriculum Project (MMCP) synthesis.* Bardonia, NY: Media Materials, Inc.

For tests of creativity, see M. Hickey. 2002. Creativity research in music, visual art, theater, and dance. In *The new handbook of research on music teaching and learning,* eds. R. Colwell and C. Richardson, 398–415. New York: Oxford University Press.

# Playing Instruments

**This chapter addresses the following:**

## WHY PLAY INSTRUMENTS? NATIONAL STANDARDS

Children love to experiment with sound-making objects in their environment. If you offer bells, drums, or wood sticks to first grade children, they will be delighted to try making sounds on each instrument. Children learn from experimenting with sound-making objects. The experimentation can be in large groups, small groups, or individual experimentation. Teachers may guide experiences or may create an environment for free exploration. The national music standard specific to playing instruments is performing on instruments, alone and with others, and playing a varied repertoire of music (National Association for Music Education 2007).

## DEVELOPMENT AND PLAYING INSTRUMENTS

Consider the general developmental abilities of children when planning. Individual children exhibit large music skill differences; their skills generally improve with age, experience, and instruction. Table 9.1 milestones are set to approximate ages.

## STEPS TO SUCCESSFUL PLAYING EXPERIENCES

Pitfalls are avoided by careful attention to several steps before beginning playing experiences.

### How to Select an Appropriate Instrument

A child's ability to play an instrument is related to their physical development and co-ordination. Trying to teach a 3-year-old to play the trumpet would be useless because the child does not possess physical ability to control all the facial and breathing muscles involved. For each instrument you introduce, check Table 9.1, and then try out the instrument with the children to check if they are developmentally capable of playing the instrument.

### Dos and Don'ts

- *Be careful to have children take turns.* Many adults remember a time in their childhood when they wanted to play an instrument, but never had the opportunity. Children may remember that they did not get a turn playing the step bells. For children under the age of 4, use the same instrument for all children if possible (also same in color, shape, size) because the children commonly want what their friends are playing. It is common for a child to say, "I want a big drum like my friend."
- *Take care when asking younger children to wait and take turns.* Their concept of time is different from adults, and they may not understand waiting until the next class or waiting until it is their turn. Taking turns for 6-year-olds and older usually works well. Children aged 7 years and above understand waiting until tomorrow to get their turn.
- *Remember to select only those instruments or musical toys that are durable and safe.* Do not use unsafe instruments such as tambourines with metal disks that are attached

Student playing violin.

*Photo courtesy of Vernon and Judith Trollinger*

**TABLE 9.1** Milestones in Playing Instruments

| Month | Milestone |
|---|---|
| 2–5 | Simple play with rattle |
| 4–8 | Bangs in play; interested in sound production |
| 5–13 | Rings bell purposively |
| 8–17 | Pokes piano key with isolated index finger and listens, then pokes another key (Michel and Rohrbacher 1988) |
| 12 | Claps hands (pat-a-cake) in imitation of adult; is able to shake small maracas, jingle bells, and rattles; initiates music play |
| 18 | Enjoys shaking maracas to fast tempi (160+ bpm) (Loong 2002); may attempt striking many items in the environment—instruments, pots, pans, books, and so on; may play with instrument for several minutes |
| 24 | Is able to play sticks; and to strike xylophone and step bells (make sure children in a group are not close enough to strike each other); and chooses and plays a musical instrument independently |
| 30 | Has better motor control for playing rhythm instruments; and may be drawn to and experiment with other instruments such as piano, guitar, or Autoharp |

| Year | Milestone |
|---|---|
| 3 | Children are capable of playing many wood, metal, and drum percussion instruments (for example, woodblock, tambourine, claves, and triangle); are also able to strum Autoharp and dulcimer; may respond to call-and-response project with instruments; are able to control mallets on xylophone; and are also able to perform body percussion of clap, pat, and stomp. Many children start Suzuki violin or piano at 3 years (to start instruction, children should have attention skills, interest in instrument, and coordination skills for holding, standing for violin, and sitting for piano). |
| 4 | Children at 3 are capable of more control of mallets for xylophone; and are able to use boomwhackers and Autoharp with two hands. Simple patterns on xylophone are appropriate. |
| 5 | At age 5, guitar instruction is often appropriate; they are able to play a wide variety of indefinite pitched instruments including drum, tambourine, triangle, blocks, claves, finger cymbals, sleigh bell, and maracas; are able to perform with tone chimes. |
| 6 | Instruction on violin, piano, and guitar are appropriate for most children (see 36 months for violin and piano; 60 months for guitar). Children are able to take turns with instruments, and many are able to perform body percussion of snap. |
| 7 | Children at 7 years are able to physically control mallets for xylophones and bells including hand bells. |
| 8 | The recorder is often introduced in grades 4 and 5. Most children possess fine motor dexterity necessary for recorder fingering. |
| 9 | Ages for beginning orchestra and band programs are widely diverse in schools. Orchestral programs begin between third and seventh grade. The orchestra instruments can be found in sizes designed for children. For example, violins come in sizes that are a fraction of the adult size (1/16, 1/8, ¼, ½, ¾). Band programs begin between fourth and seventh grade. Not all children are ready for all band and orchestra instruments. |
| 10–11 | At this age, most children possess coordination skills necessary for beginning band and orchestra instruments. |

by nails because the nails can come loose. Maracas can crack and the beans or metal inside can prove dangerous. Other instruments such as sticks can injure a child other than the child playing the instrument.

• *Don't give a child an instrument that is difficult to handle.* Choose an instrument appropriate for the size and/or age of the child. For example, several sizes of maracas are available for the hand sizes of children.

• *Don't think that all children develop physically and musically at the same rate.* For example, many children are ready for recorder instruction in fourth grade, but some of the children may not possess the fine motor coordination to cover the little open holes of the recorder. Introducing an instrument that is developmentally inappropriate could easily be frustrating to children.

• *Check the resources in this book for quality instruments.* There is a difference in quality. For example, the Parent's Choice Award in 2001 was Bob McGrath's rhythm band set of eight instruments (McGrath 2001).

• *Don't forget to demonstrate each instrument, including how it is held, played, and how to take care of it.* Encourage children to experiment with different ways to play an instrument. For example, try playing at varying degrees of loud and soft, short and long, moving up and moving down, even and uneven, or fast and slow.

• *Standardize a way to pass out and collect instruments.* Passing out instruments without a standardized method can become a free-for-all. Ask children to show you the behavior you wish (for example, sitting quietly) to receive an instrument. When passing out sticks, make sure each child has enough space so that hitting each other is avoided. A good idea for mallets and sticks is to have the children put the sticks under their arms as soon as they get them—this keeps them from banging the sticks or mallets, hitting instruments, and hitting each other. When collecting instruments, try movement like a march around the room; have a box for collecting them. As the children march by, they place their instrument in the box.

Student playing euphonium.

*Photo courtesy of Vernon and Judith Trollinger*

Keeping the beat.

*Photo courtesy of Christine Stratton*

## PLAYING INSTRUMENTS

Playing instruments is very enjoyable for children. It is a high point for many children in the music class and can be utilized as a way to reward good behavior.

### Basic Ways of Playing

There are four basic ways to produce sound on instruments.

*Pluck.* Use fingers or other small items to pluck a string.

*Strike.* Use hands, feet, or mallets to strike an instrument.

*Toot* or *Whistle.* Creating sound by blowing air through an aperture or opening.

### Nonpitched Instruments

Nonpitched instruments do not have a set pitch such as C or D. They are often used to color the sound of the music with sound and rhythm patterns. Three types include woods, metals, skins, and body percussion. The following are the most common instruments for children.

#### WOODS

*Rhythm sticks.* Wooden sticks often painted and approximately one foot in length and ½ inches in diameter, and may be smooth or ribbed. They may be struck together or struck on the floor. If ribbed, they may be scraped against each other.

*Claves.* Short, hardwood sticks approximately six inches by one inch. One clave is held in a cupped hand to provide a resonating chamber for the sound. The other clave is tapped or struck on top of the clave in the cupped hand. They are Latin American in origin and are useful for loud accents.

Child playing temple blocks.

*Photo courtesy of Texas Woman's University, Joe Pinson*

Playing the cymbals.

*Photo courtesy of Christine Stratton*

A student shows how to play the triangle.

*Photo courtesy of Rountree Elementary, Texas*

*Sand blocks.* Small wooden rectangles covered with sandpaper, often made with small handles for children's hands. They make a pleasant "swish, swish" sound.

*Wood blocks.* A hardwood block approximately three inches by six inches with part of the middle of the block removed for a resonating chamber. The hollow piece of wood makes a horse hoof-type sound.

*Temple block.* They are usually a set of five hollow wood blocks. Different-sized blocks possess distinct higher and lower sounds.

## METALS

*Triangle.* A small diameter piece of metal in a triangle shape struck with a short metal mallet approximately five inches in length. It is similar to a dinner bell.

*Cymbal.* A cymbal is a brass disc of wound metal struck together or with a mallet. Cymbals come in many sizes including a small finger cymbal.

*Jingle bells or sticks.* Perfect for Santa Claus sounds or winter themes, the jingle bells are bells attached to a stick or a piece of cloth.

*Tambourine.* A round piece of wood with small metal discs attached that may be struck, shaken, or tapped.

A child experiments with sounds on a conga drum.

*Photo courtesy of Christine Stratton*

**SKINS/DRUMS**    Today, drums are often made from synthetic materials, but were originally made from animal skins and other available materials. Many instruments share the qualities of drums including instruments with a circle or circular wooden cylinder covered with a leather or plastic head. Drums for classroom use include bongo, hand drum, small tympani, and conga.

**BODY PERCUSSION**    Many percussive sounds may be made with one's own body. The most common body percussion is used in the Orff method. The four common sounds are snap, clap, pat, and stomp. Try the rhythm piece with body percussion in Figure 9.1.

**EXPERIENCING NONPITCHED PERCUSSION**    Try the rhythm piece with three instruments in Figure 9.2. Try using one made from wood, one made from metal, and one made from skin.

**FOUND INSTRUMENTS**    Children love to find objects and experiment with the sound-producing characteristics of those objects. If a wood, metal, and skin instrument are not available, try the previous rhythm example with some of these found instruments: pots and pans, pencils, pencil sharpeners on the wall, books, loose change, plastic tubes, or straws.

A child demonstrates how to muffle the cymbals.

*Photo courtesy of Christine Stratton*

Body Percussion

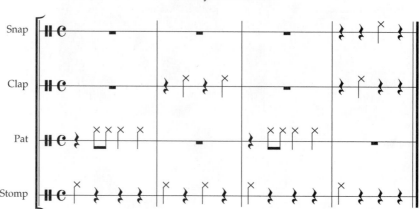

**FIGURE 9.1** Body Percussion

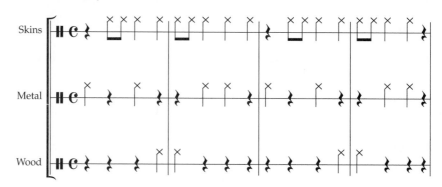

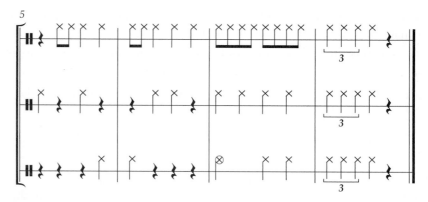

**FIGURE 9.2** Rhythm Piece for Nonpitched Percussion

## Pitched Instruments—Melody

**PIANO AND ELECTRONIC KEYBOARDS** The piano is classified as a percussion instrument because a hammer inside the piano strikes the string when the piano key is pushed. An electronic keyboard imitates the sound of a piano and other sounds with electronic synthesizers. Try the following piano experience.

**Experiencing the Piano.** The teacher or student faces the piano on the left. Play two pitches, such as G♭ and D♭, in a steady beat. Another student sits on the right side facing the keyboard and improvises or makes up music by playing only the black keys.

**MELODY BELLS** There are several types of bells for playing melody including step bells, resonator bells, handbells, and handheld chimes (see the following), and an instrument simply named melody bells. All produce sound by striking them with a mallet. Mallets come in various sizes and materials including rubber, plastic synthetics, wood, and metal. A special type of bell, mushroom bell, was developed for Montessori classrooms. The mushroom bells often are a set of black and a set of white bells. They look like mushrooms and all look alike unless viewed from the bottom where each is a different thickness to produce different pitches.

Child playing bells.

*Photo courtesy of Texas Woman's University, Joe Pinson*

**Experiencing Bells.**    One child plays the step bells. If she plays higher pitches, everyone moves high in space. For example, to indicate higher sounds, raise hands over the head. If she plays lower pitches, everyone moves lower in space. Also try experimenting with steps (go up each step) and skipping some steps (skip or hop).

**ORFF INSTRUMENTS: XYLOPHONE, GLOCKENSPIEL, METALLOPHONE**    The xylophone is a wooden bar instrument. In the 1920s, Carl Orff asked German instrument makers to construct beautiful sounding yet easy-to-play instruments for children. The result is a collection of instruments we now call the Orff Instrumentarium. The collection includes wood bar xylophones, metal bar glockenspiels, and metallophones. The wood bar xylophones are made for soft mallets rather than metal or wood mallets.

The following are special techniques for Orff instruments:

1. Rather than striking the mallet on the instrument, pretend you are drawing sound out of the bar. The drawing-out mallet technique produces a better sound and helps prevent children from striking a bar so hard that it bounces.
2. When removing bars, make sure to use two hands, one on each end of the bar. The bars fit on a small rod, and the rod may bend if the bar is pulled off with one hand.

**Experiencing Orff Instruments.**    Orff instruments are constructed so that you may take the bars off the instrument and reduce the number of pitches.

On one Orff instrument, take off all the bars with the exception of those marked F and C. On another Orff instrument, leave only bars marked F, G, A, C, and D on the instrument. A child or teacher plays the F and C, the other improvises a song with the F, G, A, C, and D.

**HANDBELLS AND HANDHELD CHIMES**    Handbells are very popular for school and church music groups. Moving the instrument through the air, causing a mallet to strike the bell, produces the handbell and handheld chime sounds. They may be used to play melodies or played simultaneously to produce harmony. Normally an individual classroom teacher does not have access to the expensive handbells. Another alternative is the less expensive handheld chimes that are marketed under different names such as Choirchimes® by Malmark and ToneChimes® by Suzuki (www.handbellworld.com).

**Experiencing Handbells and Handheld Chimes.**    If you are lucky to have access to either instrument, try using from two to four chimes to signal events in the classroom. For another experience, give three children the pitches E, D, and C. Point to them or make a chart on the board to indicate when to play the song "Hot Cross Buns."

E, D, C (Hot cross buns)

E, D, C (Hot cross buns)

CCCC, DDDD (One a penny, two a penny)

E, D, C (Hot cross buns)

**BOOMWHACKERS**    Boomwhackers are plastic tubes of different lengths and colors constructed to produce various pitches. Sound is produced when they are struck (whacked) on the floor or together. Children enjoy boomwhackers, and they are relatively inexpensive.

**Experiencing Boomwhackers.**    The experience under tone chimes and handbells with "Hot Cross Buns" also works with boomwhackers.

The melody instruments may also be used in combination to produce harmony. For more experiences, see the following harmony instrument experiences.

### Pitched Instruments—Harmony

Harmony is created when two or more pitches are played simultaneously. Most music heard on radios and in movies has many pitches performed at the same time, resulting

*C*

Mary had a little lamb,

*G7*

Little lamb,

*C*

Little lamb.

*C*

Mary had a little lamb, it's

*G7*

Fleece was white as

*C*

Snow.

**FIGURE 9.3** "Mary Had a Little Lamb"

in a rich harmonic texture. The following instruments are capable of playing two or more pitches simultaneously as well as single pitches. Melody instruments may also be used to produce harmony. A problem with all of the following string harmony instruments is that they go out of tune. The strings are sensitive to changes in temperature and jarring. To use them effectively, teachers must learn how to tune the instruments.

**ONE-CHORD SONG**   The following is an example of a song that can be harmonized with one chord. Other one-chord songs are "Make New Friends" from campfire experiences and "Are You Sleeping."

The key for "Hey, Ho!" contains low pitches that are somewhat low for younger children to sing, but it is a good simple key for guitar and Autoharp.

**TWO- (OR THREE-) CHORD SONG**

| *C* | *F* (can substitute G7) |
|---|---|
| Oh, when the saints | Number, when the |
| Go marching in | |
| Oh, when the saints | *C* |
| Go marching | Saints go |
| *G7* | *G7* |
| in | Marching |
| Oh I | *C* |
| *C* | In. |
| Want to be in that | |

**FIGURE 9.4** "When the Saints Come Marching In"

 **AUTOHARP AND OMNICHORD**   The **Autoharp's** name describes its sound and function. It is basically an automatic harp. Several bars are labeled for harmony; felt underneath the bars silences some strings while allowing others to sound. The bars are labeled for chords. Chords are standard harmonies such as the C or F. The C chord is comprised of the pitches C, E, and G. The electronic equivalent of the Autoharp is called the Omnichord. The advantage of the Omnichord is that it is electronic and does not go out of tune.

**Experiencing Autoharp.**   Strum the Autoharp while pressing the C bar and move to the G7 bar when the G7 appears in the Figure 9.3. Ask the children to sing the words while playing the Autoharp. For young children, try asking one child to strum across the strings while another child or the teacher presses the appropriate bar.

**DULCIMER**   The dulcimer or Appalachian dulcimer is one of the simplest string instruments to play. The player strums the four strings of the simple dulcimer while moving a round wood dowel up and down the fingerboard of the instrument to change pitches. The bottom strings make a droning sound.

**Experiencing Dulcimer.**   Try playing simple songs such as "Hot Cross Buns" or "Go Tell Aunt Rhody." One player may strum the strings while the other player moves the round wood dowel to change pitches.

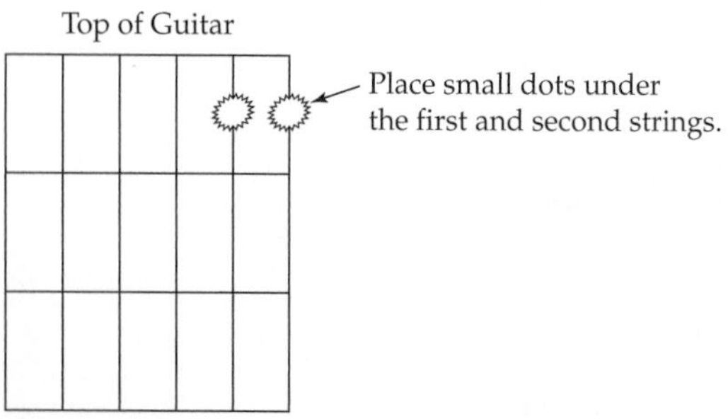

Top of Guitar

Place small dots under the first and second strings.

**FIGURE 9.5** Fret Markings for Guitar

**GUITAR**   The guitar is probably the most popular instrument of all. The guitar may be divided into three basic groups: nylon string, metal string, and electric. Within these groups are classical, folk, twelve-string, and Hawaiian guitars.

**Experiencing Guitar.**   To explore a simple experience with the guitar, first use small, colored red and green dots and place them under the first and second string by the first fret (see Figure 9.5). The song from Figure 9.1 for Autoharp also works well for guitar. The C chord is produced by strumming the top three strings while holding down the red dot at the second string with the left-hand index finger. The G7 chord is produced by strumming the top three or four strings while holding down the green dot at the first string with the left-hand index finger. The slash lines mean to strum the same chord again.

## SAMPLE PLAYING INSTRUMENT EXPERIENCES

Children love to experiment with instruments. We are fortunate to have many fascinating, colorful, and diverse musical instruments available from around the world. No music classroom should be without experiences with playing musical instruments.

## PLAYING INSTRUMENT EXPERIENCE 1—MAKING AND PLAYING INSTRUMENTS

### Level

Grade 1 individual project

### Project/Activities

Construct and play an instrument

### Previous Knowledge and Skills

Ability to work with supplies to make the instrument

### Parallel Objectives

#### Music Concepts and Objectives/Assessment

**STANDARDS ADDRESSED:** Performing on instruments, alone and with others, a varied repertoire of music (MENC 2007)

**INSTRUCTIONAL OBJECTIVES:** Students construct a small instrument and performs the steady beat alone and with others.

**ASSESSED BY:** Observing children playing the instrument

#### Science Concepts and Objectives/Assessment

**STANDARDS ADDRESSED:** Young students begin their study of matter by examining and qualitatively describing objects and their behavior. Important abstract ideas of science all begin with observing and keeping track of the way the world behaves (NSTA 2008).

**INSTRUCTIONAL OBJECTIVE:** The students examine and qualitatively describe instruments and sound making objects.

**ASSESSED BY:** Observing the students playing with sound and answering questions about the sound qualities

### Time for Lesson

Duration: 15 minutes

### Materials/Resources

1. Resource materials for each instrument choice
2. Drum: tape, oatmeal box, balloons or tubing from a bicycle, sticks
3. Shakers (maracas): film containers or plastic eggs, fill materials of different kinds (beans, small rocks), glue
4. Tambourines: paper plates, yarn for lacing, small bells

## Procedure

### *Anticipatory Set (Attention Hook)*

Show the children examples of the instruments that may be constructed.

Use found or simple materials to make instruments. For a drum, tape the top on an oatmeal box or remove both ends of a large can, cover both ends with a balloon or inner tubing from a bicycle, and use sticks for the drumsticks. Experiment with the sounds of different drumhead materials. Talk about the different sound qualities of the balloon, bicycle tube, and oatmeal top. For a shaker, use film containers or plastic eggs filled with different items. For tambourines, lace two paper plates together and tie small bells to the edges with yarn. For more ideas, see Richards and Richards (1974a; 1974b) and Turner and Schiff (1995).

After constructing and decorating the instruments, play the instruments to the steady beat of live performed or recorded music.

## Evaluation

Students achieve the objective if they participate alone and with others in the construction and playing of the instruments on the steady beat. Questions may include the following: Who can show us how to play an instrument softly? Who can show us how fast or slow the beat goes with this music?

## Continuing the Lesson

Give the children a choice to construct another instrument.

# PLAYING INSTRUMENTS EXPERIENCE 2—GUITAR WITH ONE CHORD

## Level

Grade 4 individual project

## Project/Activities

Strum the guitar to "Row, Row, Row Your Boat."

## Previous Knowledge and Skills

Singing the song and concept of steady beat

## Parallel Objectives

### *Music Concepts and Objectives/Assessment*

**STANDARDS ADDRESSED:** Performing on instruments alone and with others, a varied repertoire of music (MENC 2007)

**INSTRUCTIONAL OBJECTIVES:** Students strum the guitar with an open chord.

**ASSESSED BY:** Observing students strumming the guitar while others sing

### *Physical Education Concepts and Objectives/Assessment*

**STANDARDS ADDRESSED:** Demonstrates competency in motor skills and movement patterns needed to perform a variety of physical activities (NASPE 2004)

**INSTRUCTIONAL OBJECTIVE:** The students display competency in strumming and holding the guitar.

**ASSESSED BY:** Observing students playing the guitar

**Time for Lesson**

Duration: 15 minutes

**Materials/Resources**

One guitar is needed, but several can make the lesson move faster and give students longer turns.

**Procedure**

**Anticipatory Set (Attention Hook)**

Demonstrate the guitar or ask a guitarist to visit the class and demonstrate the guitar, including strumming to a song.

Take turns strumming the guitar(s) as the rest of the class sings the song.

**Evaluation**

Students achieve the objective if they participate in the strumming of the guitar with proper technique *and* sing while others strum the guitar.

**Continuing the Lesson**

Experiment with different strumming rhythms. Repeat with other one-chord songs such as "Are You Sleeping?" or "Hey, Ho!"

## COOPERATIVE LEARNING ACTIVITIES

See the DVD or the website at www.pearsonhighered.com/flohr for a section on guitar and prepare one two-chord song to play while the rest of the class sings the song (for example, "Mary Had a Little Lamb").

## Chapter Conclusions

There is a rich and varied resource of instruments from around the world that will fascinate elementary children. Learning about and experimenting with many instruments helps children prepare for choosing an instrument to study in orchestra or band.

## Resources

*Enriching the classroom with technology*

Generally we don't think of the computer as a musical instrument, but it is possible to use it to enhance playing situations. With computer programs, one can make simple accompaniments for students to play along with **classroom instruments.** The following are some simple ideas on how to use a computer in the classroom in relationship to playing:

1. Try a web search to find out about instruments of other world cultures. For example, because seeing a Gamelan in action in the United States is often difficult, view the Gamelan on the accompanying DVD (also available on the website at www.pearsonhighered.com/flohr) or go to websites that show video of Gamelan orchestras in Indonesia, Bali, and Malaysia that offer a real-life observation experience.

2. Computer programs allow music to be created on the computer without the knowledge of reading and writing music. Good software programs to try are: Apple's *Garage Band* (http://www.apple.com/ilife/garageband/) and Morton Subotnick's *Creating Music* (www.creatingmusic.com/).

3. Students and teachers who have musical training may enjoy composing using actual music notation software. One that can be downloaded for a minimal cost is Coda Technology's *NotePad* (http://www.makemusic.com/), which is a simpler version of the more robust Finale program.

## CHAPTER 10

# Reading
# and Writing

**This chapter addresses the following:**

- Why Reading and Writing Music? National Standards
- Development in Reading and Writing
  *Developmental Milestones*
- Research About Writing Music
- Steps to Successful Reading/Writing Experiences
  *Pitfalls to Avoid*
  *Steps*

*Tools*
*Rhythm–Mnemonics*
*Rhythm–Iconic Representation*
*Melody–Hand Signs and Syllables*
*Taxonomies*

- Sample Reading and Writing Experiences
- Cooperative Learning Activities
- Chapter Conclusions

## WHY READING AND WRITING MUSIC? NATIONAL STANDARDS

In learning English, French, or any other language, reading and writing are intertwined. It is the same in learning music—reading music and writing music are two parts of the process of associating symbols with sounds. Formal reading and writing of standard Western music often begins in first and second grade. Younger children's experiences are primarily pre-reading and pre-writing experiences. For example, a **pre-reading** experience is hearing, clapping, and moving to rhythm patterns that will later be used in reading (for example, **stick notation** or dashes and dots). Another pre-writing experience is using flat wooden sticks to represent rhythm patterns. Children less than 6 years of age are able to manipulate music notation. However, there is no reason to believe that reading and writing experiences before 6 years of age are necessary or desirable. Children taught standard music notation after they receive a substantial pre-reading base may catch up and surpass children who have learned to read earlier. The national standards addressed in reading and writing are reading and notating music (National Association for Music Education 2007). It is important to note that studies indicate that improvisation experiences transfer to a child's comprehension of music performed from notation (Azzara 1993; Montano 1983).

## DEVELOPMENT IN READING AND WRITING

How do children learn to read and write? What should be taught first, reading or writing? Neither question has firm answers. Reading language and reading music represent challenging perceptual tasks for young children. The process of learning to read and write is not fully understood, but there are principles such as emergent literacy (outlined in the following list) garnered from language research and practice. Reading symbols, or at least the awareness that sounds are related to symbols on the written page, appear to come before writing symbols, but some children using electronic composition programs may possibly try to write a sound or are able to write a sound before they are able to read any form of musical notation. Although reading music and reading language are different tasks, they have similarities, and the vast amount of literature on reading language may help understanding of music reading. The following are several ideas from reading language applied to music:

1. *Emergent literacy.* Children first learn about reading at home where they acquire emergent reading—hearing music, exploring instruments, singing, moving to music, and seeing written music in the home sets the stage for learning that the pitches on the page are related to particular sounds. The research base for emergent literacy is from language learning, and the transfer to music is theoretical and not thoroughly researched.

2. *Intermodal.* Reading is a complex task requiring children to attend to visual cues, sound cues, and when writing, apply physical coordination skills.

3. *Phonological awareness* (spoken words can be decomposed into basic sound units or phonemes). Children learning to read music need to understand that music can be decomposed into basic sound units of short patterns and notes.

4. *Emergent reading* (knowledge of letters—pitches and rhythms). Children learn pitch names by playing with tone bells marked with the pitches, hearing singing syllables (for example, sol, mi, la), and later decoding and sounding out musical symbols. In the same way, children learn rhythm durations and patterns by playing with rhythm instruments, hearing rhythm syllables (for example, ta, ta, titi, ta), and later decoding and sounding out rhythm syllables.

In language reading, two broad approaches are debated. The first, phonics, teaches children letter and sound relationships so they can decode new words by breaking them down into component sounds. The second, whole-language, teaches children to recognize whole words by sight and use the context of the sentence to figure out meaning. The phonics approach is analogous to teaching standard musical notation of quarter notes, eighth notes, and single pitches. The whole-language approach is analogous to teaching standard musical notation of rhythmic and tonal patterns. In music, there is support for a whole-language approach (Gordon 1997; Upitis 1992). Experienced music readers are found to read ahead of the music they are performing in units or chunks (Hodges 1992). Hodges summarizes that research shows (1) a high correlation between sight-reading rhythm patterns and sight-reading in general; (2) the advantage of one particular syllabic (for example, do, re, mi) or mnemonic device (for example, ta ti-ti) is unclear; (3) tonal pattern instruction is effective; and (4) the advantage of body movement in reading (for example, hand signs) is unclear.

### Developmental Milestones

The milestones in Table 10.1 are set to approximate ages. Individual children exhibit large music skill differences; their skills generally improve with age, experience, and instruction.

## RESEARCH ABOUT WRITING MUSIC

Several researchers examined children's writing of music and making symbolic representations of music (Bamberger 1994; Davidson and Colley 1987; Davidson and Scripp 1988; Domer and Gromko 1996; Gromko 1994; Upitis 1992). Bamberger found answers to several questions by asking children to listen to a clapped rhythm pattern and then to write it down on paper. She found children's responses could be placed into one of two general types of notation, which she labeled figural and formal (see Figure 10.1). By formal, Bamberger posited that the notations in some way indicate how each word or sound relates to the underlying steady beat. In figural, the notations show figures or chunks rather than the relationships between sounds (see Figure 10.1; notice the difference between the figural and formal representation). In Bamberger's research, children

**TABLE 10.1 Milestones in Reading and Writing Music**

| Years | Milestone |
| --- | --- |
| 0–5 | Children require musical experiences and training to prepare them for music reading. Hearing and seeing music in the home are important parts of emergent literacy (language research). |
| < 5 | Children have been shown to be able to manipulate music notation before the age of 5. However, ample experiences with music will aid future development more than emphasis on reading or writing. Use of figural or iconic notation is common. Children without music training respond to figural aspects of rhythm (Bamberger 1994). Reading and writing often accompany the experience of learning to play the violin or piano. |
| 5 | Pre-reading or emergent reading skills continue to be important skills to emphasize in preschool and kindergarten. |
| 6 | Children are able to recognize distinctive visual features of letters and are ready to identify visual features of quarter note, eighth note (two barred together), quarter rest, and pitch notation on two to three lines. They are able to use sticks to notate four-beat measures comprised of eighth and quarter notes; to use two-line notation to notate two pitches; and to read one- and two-line staff notation. |
| 7 | After 6 years, children may gradually add more to their reading and writing symbols, including more rhythm patterns, half notes, eighth notes standing alone, dotted notes, syncopation, **sixteenth notes,** sixteenth and eighth patterns, triple meter, 6/8 meter, compound meters, pitch names, and tonal patterns (sequence of presentation is important).<br><br>For example, 6- to 7-year-olds will not be able to read and write half and quarter notes if they have not studied steady beat earlier. |
| 8 | Sixteenth notes and syncopation are often introduced by second grade. |
| 9 | Triple meter, 6/8 meter, and standard notation writing are often introduced in third grade. |
| 10 | In third and fourth grade, children typically play recorders and identify pitches with their letter names. |
| 11 | Many children by fifth grade are able to use standard notation for their compositions. |

with prior music training usually responded to the metric or formal aspects of rhythm whereas children without prior music training usually responded to the figural aspects of the rhythm. An important element of the research is that children without training will usually respond to the figural aspects of rhythm. After pre-reading and writing experiences (emergent), the sequence of instruction may best move to figural representations rather than jump right to the metrical aspects of rhythm.

Different researchers describe the children's notations in somewhat different ways, from all note progression of scribbles or no representation to counting or units to groupings (metrical or figural) and finally to true metric or standard notation (Domer and

**FIGURE 10.1** Figural and Formal Notation

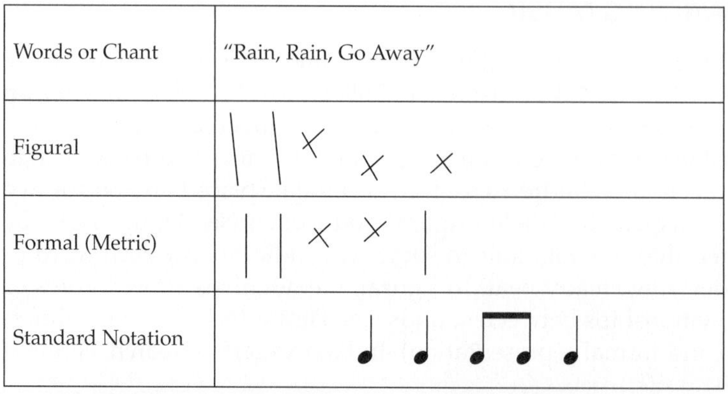

| Words or Chant | "Rain, Rain, Go Away" |
| --- | --- |
| Figural | |
| Formal (Metric) | |
| Standard Notation | |

Gromko 1996; Upitis 1992). Also, Gromko (1994) suggests that children notate pitch before rhythm. Walker (1978; 1981; 1987a; 1987b) notes similarities in the visual representations for sounds. He writes that humans "have an innate mechanism for processing, storing, and transferring across modalities information relating to auditory movements" (Walker 1987a, 492). He finds that children across cultures invent similar symbols to stand for musical sounds, although he finds in one study that, "Musical training is the most important single factor in choices of visual metaphor for sounds" (Walker 1987a, 500).

## STEPS TO SUCCESSFUL READING/WRITING EXPERIENCES

Techniques to enhance reading and writing experiences include a good foundation in doing music before writing music (providing sound experiences before symbols), using icons, manipulative tools, and common rhythm and tonal patterns.

### Pitfalls to Avoid

The chief pitfall to avoid is beginning music reading too early (for fear of possible burnout). Also, make sure they have ample emergent music reading experiences.

### Steps

Pitfalls are avoided by careful attention to several steps before beginning reading and writing experiences.

Child using traditional notation to write rhythm patterns.

*Photo courtesy of Jane Rivera*

1. Provide a firm foundation for reading and writing with many experiences in music. Include a wide variety of music. If the objective is to enable children to read quarter, eighth, and half notes by second grade, provide early experiences in moving, playing, singing, listening, and creating that use those rhythm durations.
2. Provide sounds before symbols. Provide pre-reading experiences. Include sound exploration, rhythm and tonal instruments for play, storybooks with music, examples of music notation, and, if at all possible, parent or other adult models of performing, reading, and writing music.
3. After pre-reading experiences, use pictures (see Figure 10.3).
4. Provide motivation to learn to read and write music. For example, ask the children to help you write out their composed music so that they can remember it for next week. There is no research base about how early music reading and writing might enhance or inhibit future development. Early emphasis on reading and writing without emergent literacy may cause less successful children to withdraw from the subject.
5. Provide experiences with rhythm and tonal patterns. For example, use felt boards or manufactured erasable slates for the notation of rhythm and melody.
6. Allow children to discover notation on their own with gentle teacher questions rather than telling them how to notate. For example, play a short rhythm pattern and ask the children to notate the pattern with wooden sticks.

### Tools

Several tools are used to help children to read and write music. It is not surprising to find many tools in the Kodály method because a major goal for the Kodály method is to promote music literacy.

**FIGURE 10.2** Examples of Mnemonic Representations

| Duration | Kodály | Gordon | Word | Number |
|---|---|---|---|---|
| ♩ | ta | du | walk | 1 |
| ♫ | ti ti | du-de | run, run | 1 & |
| ♬ | ti-ri-ti-ri or tika-tika | du-ta-de-ta | Miss-is-sip-pi | 1 e & a |

**FIGURE 10.3** Iconic
Representation of "Rain, Rain"

| Representation of the steady beat/pulse | |
|---|---|
| How can we make the picture fit the sound? Split the third umbrella! Oops, we will get wet! | |
| Make two little umbrellas for the third beat | |
| The two little umbrellas are holding hands! | |
| Remove the tops and the icons look similar to standard notation. | |
| Standard notation | |

### Rhythm–Mnemonics

Teachers often use mnemonics to help teach rhythm, but it is unclear if any particular system is better than another (Hodges 1992).

For more complex duration and rhythm pattern syllables applicable to older children, see Choksy et al. (2001) and Gordon (1994).

### Rhythm–Iconic Representation

Iconic representations are part of most teachers' tools. The representations are used for rhythm, pitch, and musical form, although the use of icons is based more on theory (for example, Bruner) than on research results. See Figure 10.3 for the sequence of icons for "Rain, Rain, Go Away." The teacher leads the students from representation of the steady beat to realization that the steady beat umbrellas do not match the way the words move. Many teachers find that students learn most efficiently if they are left to discover on their own or with gentle teacher questions such as, "Does the picture match the number of sounds?"

### Melody–Hand Signs and Syllables

For young children, use the hands to show the contour of pitch. For example, show the up, down, same, stepwise, and skipwise movement of the pitches. Two or three **hand signs** (for example, for sol, mi, and la) can be used successfully with children as young as 4 and 5 years. Figure 10.4 shows the hand signs for the major scale.

### Taxonomies

Taxonomies are used for reading and writing rhythmic and melodic patterns. For example, rhythm durations are listed in order of presentation beginning with quarter, two eighths, quarter rest, half, and six eighths in 6/8 meter. The next five duration elements are dotted quarter plus eighth, two dotted quarters in 6/8 meter, syncopation, eighth plus dotted quarter, plus quarter and eighth in 6/8 meter (Choksy et al. 2001, 93). Chosky lists melodic patterns beginning with sol, mi, and then adding la, re, and do.

Ti

La

Sol

Fa

Mi

Re

Do

**FIGURE 10.4** Hand Signs

The five pitches (do, re, mi, sol, and la) form a **pentatonic scale.** A standard progression of pitches on a staff is (1) iconic representation (no staff); (2) one-line staff notation; (3) two-line staff notation; and (4) three- to five-line or standard staff notation. Rhythm and tonal patterns are also sequenced (Choksy et al. 2001).

## SAMPLE READING AND WRITING EXPERIENCES

Reading music notation is an important musical skill for future musical opportunities and development. Music notation is a combination of abstract symbols and icons (see Bruner, Chapter 2). For example, letter and solfège names of pitches are abstract symbols. Pitch placement on the music staff is iconic in the way in which the placement of pitches on a staff corresponds to the highness and lowness of the pitches.

### READING AND WRITING EXPERIENCE 1—TWO-LINE NOTATION

#### Level

Grade 1 group project

#### Project/Activities

Move to the pitch movement of two-line notation. After practice, each child composes their own two-line notation comprised of five to ten pitches for the class to decipher by moving to the ways the pitches move.

#### Previous Knowledge and Skills

Experience with moving to express music and work with two pitches (high and low).

#### Parallel Objectives

#### *Music Concepts and Objectives/Assessment*

**STANDARDS ADDRESSED:** Composing and arranging music within specified guidelines; reading and notating music (MENC 2007)

**INSTRUCTIONAL OBJECTIVES:** Students compose a two-line notation example comprised of five to ten pitches for the class to decipher.

**ASSESSED BY:** Observing children moving arms in relation to the notation. Also assessed by the five- to ten-pitch composition

#### *Physical Education Concepts and Objectives/Assessment*

**STANDARDS ADDRESSED:** Demonstrates competency in motor skills and movement patterns needed to perform a variety of physical activities (NASPE 2004)

**INSTRUCTIONAL OBJECTIVE:** The students display competency in movement to the pitches.

**ASSESSED BY:** Observing students moving

#### Time for Lesson

Duration: 15 minutes

#### Materials/Resources

Make available one of the following types of notation boards: flannel board, magnetic two-line staff, SMART Boards, paper, and cutouts of quarter note heads for teacher and each child.

## Procedure

### Anticipatory Set (Attention Hook)

Sol-mi song material is to be sung first. Choose one song such as "Rain, Rain" to demonstrate how to move to show pitch movement (repeat with other Sol-mi songs until the children can demonstrate appropriate movement to the pitches). Demonstrate on a few songs.

Turn to notation examples and, while pointing to the notation, sing and move an arm with the pitch movement. Ask the children to imitate you and then move to one or more examples in which they show the movement without movement cues.

For the composition of a short two-line example, give each child the materials (magnetic board, paper, or other notation system manipulative) and give a demonstration on how to compose a five- to ten-pitch example. As the children compose, facilitate their work; move among them while helping them. After the children complete their examples, have each student show their example to the class and ask the class to move to the pitches (with or without singing). The moving responses may be arms only, whole body, feet only, and so forth.

## Evaluation

Children achieve the objective if they participate in the movement and composition, and demonstrate movements that correspond to the notation. Question could include the following: Who can show us which way this pitch moves? (While pointing to a pitch and the pitch following): Can you show me the whole pattern with your arm?

## Continuing the Lesson

Give the children a chance to compose another pattern.

## READING AND WRITING EXPERIENCE 2—WRITING RHYTHMS

### Level

Grade 1 group project

### Project/Activities

Write rhythm patterns using manipulatives; create notation patterns for the class to clap.

### Previous Knowledge and Skills

Experience in notating simple songs as in the first lesson of this chapter

### Parallel Objectives

### Music Concepts and Objectives/Assessment

**STANDARDS ADDRESSED:**   Composing and arranging music within specified guidelines; reading and notating music (MENC 2007)

**INSTRUCTIONAL OBJECTIVES:**   The students write rhythm patterns and compose new patterns.

**ASSESSED BY:**   Observing and checking the manipulatives for correct notation of rhythms and correct number of steady beats for the patterns

### Mathematics Concepts and Objectives/Assessment

**STANDARDS ADDRESSED:**   Count with understanding and recognize how many in sets of objects (NCTM 2008)

**INSTRUCTIONAL OBJECTIVE:**   The students will be able to count, identify, and notate sounds they hear in a pattern or song.

**ASSESSED BY:**   Asking students how many sounds they count in a pattern or song

**FIGURE 10.5** Quarter and Eighth Note Four-Beat Patterns

## Time for Lesson

Duration: 15 minutes

## Materials/Resources

Each child needs fifteen to twenty flat wooden sticks; also used in mathematics, these are available from craft and teacher stores.

## Procedure

### Anticipatory Set (Attention Hook)

The children should have sung and moved to music that includes all rhythm patterns used in this lesson. For example, if the pattern ta, ta, titi, ta is to be used, the children's experience would include songs such as "Rain, Rain, Go Away" that use that pattern.

Start with simple rhythms to notate such as ta, ta, titi, ta. There are sixteen four-beat rhythm possibilities for combinations of quarter notes and eighth notes (see Figure 10.5). Ask the children to compose their own pattern for the class to hear that uses eight or more steady beats. Demonstrate how two of the four-beat rhythms can be repeated or combined to make an eight-beat rhythm.

## Evaluation

Children achieve the objective if they correctly notate the rhythm patterns and compose a pattern within the guidelines. Question could include the following: How many sounds do you hear in this pattern? Who thinks they have the correct notation? Who can show us their pattern so we can clap it?

## Continuing the Lesson

Extend the number of steady beats and/or the rhythm durations.

## COOPERATIVE LEARNING ACTIVITIES

For both of the previous lessons, form groups of three to five students. The task of each group will be to construct rhythm examples for the class to notate (from two to eight measures). Later, each can construct pitch examples.

## Chapter Conclusions

Reading and writing music are intertwined. Reading music and writing music are two parts of the process of associating symbols with sounds. The sound-to-symbol approach is important to consider; the children should have experiences with songs, pitch movements, and rhythms they are learning to notate. Reading music notation is an important musical skill for future musical opportunities and development.

## CHAPTER 11

# Approaches to Music Learning

**This chapter addresses the following:**

- Introduction
- Traditional Methods
  *Dalcroze*
  *Montessori*
  *Orff*
  *Kodály*

*Suzuki*
*Gordon*
*Music Series*

- Chapter Conclusions
- Resources

## INTRODUCTION

There are many ways to teach young children. Being presented with many choices is not necessarily a bad situation. The choices affect teaching skills, preferences, and the individual learning differences in children. Individual teachers should decide which method is best for the children and themselves. Teachers may decide to specialize in one particular method or use ideas from several methods.

Methods do not stand apart from history, and the methods and educational thought have historical relationships. For example, the renowned eighteenth- and nineteenth-century Swiss educator Heinrich Pestalozzi contributed ideas of sequence, repetition, and rote learning during the nineteenth century. An influential nineteenth-century American educator, Lowell Mason, understood the value of Pestalozzi's work for children's music learning and applied Pestalozzi's ideas of sequence to music, that are still reflected in music series books used in the twenty-first century. The discovery method or "learning by doing" idea of John Dewey permeates many of the methods. The oldest method examined in this chapter is that of Émile Jaques-Dalcroze. Dalcroze influenced the work of both Montessori and Orff. Kodály incorporated techniques from many sources, including the solfège ideas of Glover and Curwen. The burgeoning number of methods for young children in the past twenty years may be traced to music methods and educational ideas discussed in Chapter 2.

A method includes many suggested experiences and provides a systematic and/or sequenced plan for achieving objectives. Normally, a method includes several experiences and objectives that may be thought of as a curriculum. What is a musical experience? For example, clapping the steady beat to music is an activity. When an objective is linked to the activity of clapping a steady beat, such as "the child will synchronize his/her clapping to steady music of 100 beats per minute," the activity becomes an experience. Experiences are teaching activities or strategies that are linked to an objective.

All the methods do not have the same degree of organization or body of pedagogy, and proponents of methods often prefer to refer to the method as a process or technique. The Kodály method or process, for example, is organized on the basis of the idea that all children can be musically literate, and Kodály pedagogy is sequenced to achieve specific literacy objectives. To fully understand a method, it is best to observe the method in action with children. There is no substitute for observing a method in action in addition to taking course work. This text's objective is not to critique methods on the basis of their organization or value. However, it is prudent to get firsthand knowledge of any method before enrolling in training or enrolling a child in a class. It is possible that a teacher or parent may decide to look further after watching a demonstration class of a method. It is a good idea to contact organizations or associations using the contact information at the end of this chapter to schedule time to observe classes and performances.

## TRADITIONAL METHODS

The traditional methods were all developed before 1960, but continue to be used by many educators. The following is a glimpse or taste of the methods created by Dalcroze, Montessori, Orff, Kodály, and Suzuki, as well as methods found in music series books.

Refer to Tables 11.1 and 11.2 for an overview of the methods. Five topic descriptors are used in Tables 11.1. *Fundamental idea* refers to the philosophy and/or basic idea of the approach. *Instructional goal* refers to the overall program goal. *Primary musical vehicle*

**TABLE 11.1** Methods for Teaching Music to Children

| Method | Fundamental Idea | Instructional Goal | Primary Musical Vehicle | Teacher Skills | Training |
|---|---|---|---|---|---|
| Dalcroze | Emphasis on rhythmically musical performance. For every musical sound, there is a movement gesture (preschool through college) | Good rhythm (eurhythmic) and ear training; improvisation; musical expression | Improvisation and movement | Piano skills; percussion or other instruments are also used. | Intensive; several course and levels |
| Gordon | Based on Gordon's music learning theory using eight-step process (birth through elementary age and above) | Audiation; sound before symbol; tonal and rhythm hearing; and performance | Listening, reading, singing | Singing and rhythmic sense; tonal and rhythm patterns from *Jump Right In!* | University courses |
| Kodály | Music literacy for all children (birth through upper elementary) | Music literacy | Singing (usually a cappella); moving with hand signals | Singing and ear training | Intensive; courses and levels |
| Montessori | Self-directed learning through sensory experience with teacher-prepared materials (preschool through high school); music integrated into total educational program | Materials for pitch discrimination, vocal training, listening, pulse of music | Sensory experiences with materials, singing, moving | Teacher provides environment and uses questions to help student discover | Intensive certification for total educational program |
| Music Series Books | Curriculum for preschool through elementary and beyond (K–8+) | Objectives by grade level; resource and curriculum for public school teachers | Singing, listening, creating, moving, reading, and writing | Assumes teacher can follow lessons and implement curriculum | Offered by publishers as short or weeklong workshops |
| Orff | Teach music to follow historic development; start with chant and simple rhythm instruments (preschool through upper elementary) | Improvisation; music creation | Percussive instruments; mallet instruments; voice is secondary | Rhythm, singing, and percussion instrument competency | Intensive; courses and certification levels |
| Suzuki | Humanitarian education and personality development; talent education (3 years through adulthood) | Performance skills and ear training | Violin, viola, cello, bass, piano, flute, guitar, harp, recorder | Violin (piano); group instrumental lessons for beginners | Intensive; certification levels and for different instruments |

*Note:* Methods are listed alphabetically. This table is not meant to be an exhaustive listing of all methods. Columns contain generalizations and are designed to give readers a broad and general overview. The particular teacher using the method may change the focus. For example, a teacher using the Orff method may modify the method by using singing or the voice rather than mallet instruments as the primary musical vehicle. For more detail on each method, please consult references in this text.

**TABLE 11.2  Methods: Experiences for 5-year-olds**

| Method | Singing | Creating | Moving | Playing | Listening | Concepts |
|---|---|---|---|---|---|---|
| Dalcroze | Sing simple three- to five-pitch songs | Create movements in response to music and stories | Movement is emphasized; change response to expressive characteristics of music | Play simple instruments and body percussion | Listen to express the music through movement | Movement expression of steady beat, slow/fast, accent, longer/shorter sounds, repetition, contrast |
| Gordon | Imitates the sounds of music in the environment (e.g., tonal patterns and rhythm patterns); this preparatory audiation stage is called "breaking the code." | Movement creativity through imitation and improvisation using audiation | Move to rhythm patterns | Clap and play rhythm patterns | Listening to patterns (preparatory audiation experiences) | Structured formal guidance where the parent/teacher plans but does not expect specific responses; tonal and rhythm patterns |
| Kodály | Emphasis is on participation in singing folk songs based on three to four pitches; match contour of melody | Creating not emphasized | Move while participating in singing games | Clapping to match steady beat | Listening to folk songs and examples from classical music | Steady beat, slow/fast, pitch movement, repetition. and contrast |
| Montessori | Sing simple three- to five-pitch songs | Creating while playing with and experimenting with instruments | Moving to the piano music (ala Dalcroze) | Cylinders, monochord | Experimenting with cylinders and monochord; discovery of sound properties | Same/different timbre, steady beat, matching pitch, listening skills |
| Music Series Books | Sing simple three- to five-pitch songs | | Moving to recorded music | Playing simple rhythm instruments (e.g., sticks) | Listening to recorded music for movement | Basic concepts of steady beat, movement of pitches, repetition, contrast, loud/soft |
| Orff | Chanting, singing simple three- to five-pitch songs | Create simple movements; improvise on xylophones | Moving to the beat | Play simple patterns on Orff xylophones, simple rhythm instruments | Listen to songs, chants, and instruments | Steady beat, slow/fast, matching pitch, movement of pitches, experimentation with timbre of voice during chanting, repetition and contrast |
| Suzuki | No singing usually; adaptation of Suzuki to singing is available | | Moving to emphasize performance skills such as bow use | Emphasis is on performance skills (violin, piano, or other instrument) | Listening to recordings of instrument and music from the curriculum | Emphasis on performance skills such as holding the violin, bow position and technique, production of sound, and playing by imitation |

refers to the way(s) in which the child experiences music. *Teacher skills* refer to musical skills emphasized in the method. Traditional and other methods require all or most of the following teacher skills, including an accurate, expressive, and pleasant singing voice; ability to lead movement and dancing activities; knowledge about music and movement development; ability to share songs and rhymes from memory; and ability to be personable and comfortable with both children and adults. *Training* gives a brief overview of the types of training available. Tables 11.2 summarizes what a 5-year-old would be expected to do in each method. Refer to the sources at the end of the chapter for further information.

## Dalcroze

Émile Jaques-Dalcroze (1865–1950) believed that humans feel emotions by various sensations produced at different levels of muscular contraction and relaxation. Abramson (in Chosky et al. 2001) explains that human emotions are translated into musical motion, the emotions are sensed in various parts of the body, and the emotions are felt by the various levels of muscular contraction and relaxation. Human emotion's contraction and relaxation moves in a way analogous to the way in which the tension and release of music moves. Both emotion and music are related to movement (see Figure 11.1).

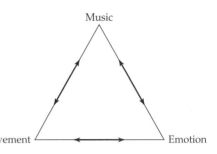

**FIGURE 11.1** Music, Movement, and Emotion

The child's ear and body are the primary focus of instruction. While teaching at a conservatory, Dalcroze found that many of his students could play technically very well but their performances were devoid of musical feeling and expression. Rhythm in their music was dry, lifeless, and mechanical. He spent the rest of his life developing ways to help his students play musically. Dalcroze believed that children should be able to express what they hear through movement before translating their physical sensations into forms of musical expression (singing, playing, and creating). Dalcroze's mother was a Pestalozzian music teacher who undoubtedly influenced him. The Dalcroze method is known for its emphasis on rhythm, and Abramson lists thirty-four Dalcroze elements of rhythm (Choksy et al. 2001, 53). The entire Dalcroze method includes not only eurhythmics, but also improvisation and solfège. Dalcroze categorized rhythmic performance into three types, two of which are incorrect (Caldwell 1992): (1) *arrhythmic* performance is spastic and offbeat; (2) *errhythmic* performance has all the notes in the right place but is dull and boring with no nuance of weight, motion, and time; and (3) *eurhythmic* performance balances motion and rhythm and solves the problem of how to make music move so that the audience and performer are emotionally moved. To perform in a eurhythmic way, musicians must be able to control their performance in an errhythmic, synchronized way. What Abramson (in Choksy et al. 2001) calls the missing link, kinesthesia or kinesthetic sense, makes sense with what is now known about the brain and human development (Flohr and Trevarthen 2008). Dalcroze saw the link between mind and body and how he might guide students to perform music expressively by involving them in movement experiences.

The early training for young children includes three steps: (1) expression of the music through movement, (2) simple and short experiences in learning to listen to music, and (3) movement in different ways to express the music. Experiences include singing games, finger play, playing percussion instruments (including body percussion), and stories with musical accompaniment usually improvised by the teacher.

**SAMPLE DALCROZE EXPERIENCE: RUNNING AND WALKING TEMPO**   A teacher asks the children to walk around the room while she begins to improvise on the piano or a percussion instrument to match the general or average walking tempo of the children. For control, it is important that the children learn to stop when the music stops. The teacher may say, "Get ready to stop," then stop playing the piano and say, "Stop." The same procedure can then be used to find the general or average running tempo for a particular group of children. The teacher may then introduce a song at a walking tempo such as "Twinkle, Twinkle, Little Star," and encourage the children to sing the song in the children's walking tempo (while standing still). Then the teacher may ask the children to walk their hands over their body while the song is played at the walking tempo. The same strategy is used for the running tempo. The teacher asks the children to run in a space cleared of obstacles. In these ways, the teacher begins at the children's walking or running tempo and the children, in general, feel comfortable moving. For more ideas, watch a class in action or view other publications about the Dalcroze method (Abramson 1973; 1998; Caldwell 1992).

## Montessori

Dr. Maria Montessori (discussed in Chapter 2), like Dalcroze, believed the best way for children to learn was by doing. The most well-known musical aspects of Montessori's method are the instruments. Suggested instruments include wooden cylinders and the monochord for children less than 5 years of age. Six wooden cylinders are used to develop children's listening skills, compare sounds, match sound, and study dynamics. A teacher or parent can make cylinders or purchase or construct objects so that three sets have the same sound-making material inside. For example, find six same-colored plastic eggs and fill two with beans, two with sand, and two with small rocks. As the children shake the eggs, there will be no clues as to the way in which they may be categorized other than the sound. The eggs will be shaped and colored the same. As the children play with and explore the eggs, they will begin to notice that some eggs sound alike.

The Montessori monochord looks like a small dulcimer with one string and is used to experiment with vibration (a child can see the string moving) and the way in which placing the finger on the instrument to shorten the string affects pitch. For children 5 years and older, Anna Maria Maccheroni, Montessori's music consultant, developed a double series of thirteen bells that became known as "mushroom bells." The bells are used to teach pitch discrimination by matching and sorting the double set of bells. The idea of discovery by experimentation and play that Montessori promoted is evident in many instructional approaches today.

There is also a book of music for the teacher to perform on the piano that was probably designed after the ideas of Dalcroze. Montessori was aware of Dalcroze's work and he is mentioned in several of Montessori's books (Faulmann 1980). The piano music is divided into categories for various types of movement such as marches, gallops, **skips,** and trots. Faulmann (1980) points out that Montessori initially recommended a series of small whistles developed by Pizzoli for pitch discrimination. Pizzoli prepared the Laboratory of Scientific Pedagogy and possessed talent for the construction of tools and instruments.

**SAMPLE MONTESSORI EXPERIENCE–LESSON OF SILENCE**    Montessori's *lesson of silence* is a very effective technique used to prepare children for listening (for example, listening to music to recognize and name compositions). She realized the children needed to be very attentive and good listeners to learn from the environment and the teacher. The teacher asks the children to listen to the sounds in the classroom during a count of ten (it is sometimes helpful to hold up ten fingers and silently lower them, one by one, for the count). At the end of the silence, ask the children what they heard. For example, one child may have heard an air conditioning sound, a bird, or a siren. Another child may remember someone talking in the hall. Children will often make up something they heard such as, "I heard a caterpillar crawling on a leaf." Use the lesson of silence to prepare the children to carefully and attentively listen to music experiences as well as other classroom experiences.

## Orff

*[This section was contributed by Pamela Stover, University of Southern Illinois.]*

The Orff-Schulwerk is an approach to teaching music through improvisation, creativity, speech, movement, drama, and playing instruments. It began in the 1920s, with the work of composer Carl Orff and his colleagues Dorothee Günther, Maja Lex, and especially Gunild Keetman. The Orff-Schulwerk approach was adapted for children in 1948, with radio broadcasts in Munich using simple folk songs and children's rhymes. Keetman and Orff published the materials from the radio shows as *Musik für Kinder* between 1950 and 1955. The Orff-Schulwerk approach has spread throughout the world and incorporates music and instruments from many cultures in child- and teacher-created pieces and dramatic productions. The popular group Stomp uses Orff-Schulwerk elements of body percussion and ostinato in their found-percussion stage creations.

The Orff-Schulwerk approach is used in elementary and middle school classrooms throughout the world, allowing students to experience and create music and movement. The Orff-Schulwerk approach is strong in meeting all of the national standards for music education and many of the standards for dance education. Although it

Children learning an ostinato.

*Photo courtesy of Jane Rivera*

is especially strong in standards concerning improvisation and composition, as well as playing instruments, it is weaker in the reading and writing music standard, as music literacy is not essential to create and experience music through the Orff-Schulwerk approach. In many of today's classrooms, teachers will include music literacy skills in addition to the Orff-Schulwerk approach to create a well-rounded program.

In the Orff-Schulwerk approach, it is important for students to experiment with sound and movement and to create culminating musical experiences. One sequence in the learning process could be: (1) exploration, (2) observation, (3) imitation, (4) experimentation, and (5) creation/improvisation. The teacher usually plays the role of the guide on the side or as the model for imitation, and will plant seeds of creativity that blossom with the children's musical discovery. Thus, the processes of making and discovering music are more important than the final product.

The modes of expression with the Orff-Schulwerk approach include the body, the voice, and instruments. The body is used in movement and also with body percussion. Singing and speaking are important in creating and experiencing music, as often rhymes or chants are the impetus for creating a piece. The resulting music may then be incorporated into a dramatic setting. Playing instruments, especially the Orff instruments, are obviously important in the Orff-Schulwerk approach.

Bodily or kinesthetic learning is crucial in the Orff-Schulwerk approach, as are the development of fine and gross motor skills. Natural movements such as walking, running, skipping, jumping, turning, kicking, and spinning are used as the first steps in experiencing movement in the Orff-Schulwerk approach. These movements can be organized into simple and complex folk dances from around the world or original dances that students create.

The body is used as a percussion instrument through snapping, clapping, patching (or patschen: patting your lap), and stomping. Body percussion is especially useful in rhythmic exercises in classrooms without many instruments. Students can imitate and echo patterns, or create new patterns as question and answers. Varying kinds of body percussion can be used in transferring rhythm patterns to instruments. For example, the bass part can be stomped while the glockenspiel part is snapped. Many Orff-Schulwerk teachers will ask students to patch an instrumental ostinato (a repeated pattern) before transferring it to the barred instruments. Students, who have the rhythm internalized in their body, will be more successful in playing it on an instrument.

The word is the basis of many rhythmic compositions, and many Orff-Schulwerk arrangements are based on folk songs from around the world. Thus, the word is an important medium for the Orff-Schulwerk approach. Student pieces can start with a saying, rhyme, or repeated text. Instrumental parts and tricky rhythms may be solidified and remembered by using text cues. Singing and speech add to the dramatic element of the Orff-Schulwerk approach. Songs using the pentatonic scale (do-re-mi-sol-la) are easy to accompany using an open-fifth drone (do-sol). Pentatonic songs with open-fifth accompaniments make up much of the repertoire for the beginning Orff-Schulwerk.

The instruments used in the Orff-Schulwerk approach include recorders, unpitched and pitched percussion instruments, as well as barred percussion instruments. The guitar has historically been used, but Orff did not like to use the piano. The recorders and barred instruments allow for melodic and harmonic experiences whereas other percussion instruments hone rhythmic skills. Most culminating musical experiences involve adding an instrumental accompaniment or improvisation.

Recorders come in various sizes and two keys. The full consort of recorders with their keys includes: kleine sopranino (C), sopranino (F), soprano (C), alto (F), tenor (C), bass (F), and great bass (C). The four most common recorders for consort playing are the soprano, alto, tenor, and bass. In today's classrooms, the soprano recorder is most commonly taught. Recorders come in two types of fingerings: German and baroque.  The main difference is in the right hand for fingering F—the German fingering is a single finger, whereas the baroque uses a "forked" fingering of the index, ring finger, and pinkie finger. Although it may be easier for students to play F on a German recorder, the tuning is not as stable, and most teachers use the standard baroque fingering in the long run. Wooden or plastic recorders are available for classroom use, and

Student performing an ostinato.

*Photo courtesy of Rountree Elementary, Texas*

plastic recorders are fine. It is best to keep one brand throughout the class for consistent tuning. To avoid contagion, each student needs to own a recorder; otherwise the teacher must disinfect the instruments after each use. Good sources for published recorder methods and consort music are the Beatin' Path Publications and the Sweet Pipes company.

Pitched and unpitched percussion instruments make up the bulk of the Orff Instrumentarium. Hand drums, conga drums, and tympani or rototoms are essential drums. Many wooden instruments such as temple blocks, claves, rhythm sticks, guiro, maracas, vibraslap, and others are used for sharp clicking or scraping sounds. Metal instruments add dings and jingles and include finger cymbals, tambourines, wind chimes, triangles, and gongs. Classrooms should have an assortment of instruments that are hit, scraped, or shaken, made of metal, wood, or skin/membranes for sound exploration.

Barred instruments are commonly thought of as "Orff instruments." There are several categories. The glockenspiels (German literal translation is bell play) are small high-pitched instruments with thin metal bars played by a hard rubber or wooden mallet. The metallophone also has metal bars, but they are thick and the resonator box is large, and it is played with a yarn or rubber mallet. The xylophone has the same large resonator box as the metallophone, but has wooden bars and is played with a yarn, rubber, or, less often, a soft wooden mallet. The metallophones and xylophones come in three main sizes: bass, alto, and soprano—sounding one octave higher respectively. The glockenspiel comes in two sizes: Alto sounds in the same octave as the soprano xylophone and soprano sounds an octave higher than the alto. Instruments (mostly xylophones) in the alto range should comprise the bulk of the Instrumentarium, with metallophones and high glockenspiels filling out the collection. A bass metallophone is not necessary until you have a full set of instruments.

To set up instruments in C pentatonic scale, remove the Fs and the Bs (the burgers and fries). The Cs and Gs play open-fifth drones of many types, either simultaneously in chords or broken apart (first one note, then the next, usually in an alternating fashion).

The rhythm is usually repeated as an ostinato (repeated pattern) and may vary depending on the student's skill, from playing a steady beat to a complex rhythm.

Melodic improvisations with the pentatonic scale can be added to one of the drone accompaniments. The pentatonic scale takes out bars that clash, giving everyone a chance for success. When setting up early improvisation experiences, students need a set number of beats and guidelines to end on C; limiting the number of pitches is also helpful. Instructions to students may be like the following: "Play for eight counts using quarter notes and rests, eighth notes, and half notes. End on beat nine with a C." Then the teacher lets the students experiment. A guided practice may have students playing improvisations at the same time, followed by individual playing or playing by instrument groups. If the students write improvisations, they have taken the first step in composition.

Orff-Schulwerk is a philosophy and approach to music education and not a prescribed method. New Orff-Schulwerk teachers need continuing experience to hone skills. One of the basic tenets is learning by experience. Many universities offer summer "levels" courses in Orff-Schulwerk that lead to certification. Local Orff-Schulwerk chapters also sponsor Saturday workshops in many cities. Orff-Schulwerk workshops are given at state music conferences and at universities. The American Orff-Schulwerk Association (www.aosa.org) holds an annual conference in November and also has a video library of past conference sessions available for rental.

Books are available to help teachers implement the Orff-Schulwerk approach. *Discovering Orff* and *Orff-Schulwerk Today* by Jane Frazee, *Exploring Orff* by Arvida Steen, *Orff-Schulwerk: Applications for the Classroom* by Brigitte Warner, and *Elementaria* by Gunild Keetman are very detailed and helpful in describing the teaching process. Original Orff-Schulwerk materials have two English translations. The British edition by Margaret Murray stays true to the original with text translations or adaptations in English. The Canadian edition, by Doreen Hall and Arnold Walter, simplifies and adapts many of the instrumental accompaniments so beginning students can play them. Also available are three volumes of the American edition of *Music for Children*, with completely new pieces, many based on American folk tunes, arranged in grade-level order. Over twenty authors compiled the American edition, which includes informative articles as well as teaching advice.

There are a plethora of Orff arrangements available in school textbooks and in published collections by experienced Orff-Schulwerk specialists. However, in the true Orff-Schulwerk approach, these materials are not needed; music exploration and culminating experiences grow from the creativity of the students.

**SAMPLE ORFF EXPERIENCE—IMPROVISATION ON "ARE YOU SLEEPING" (GRADE 1)**
Children experience playing instruments and improvising in this Orff experience in Figure 11.2. First, sing the song "Are You Sleeping." Then *layer* the sounds: Begin with the bass xylophone, adding in order the alto xylophone, wood block, finger cymbals. Finally, sing and play the song again with the instruments. For reinforcement, offer all children the opportunity to improvise on another xylophone (first remove the bars to build a pentatonic scale; pitches f, g, a, c, and d are present). The teacher may also encourage children to

Are You Sleeping

American folk song/arr. JWF

**FIGURE 11.2** Orff Arrangement of "Are You Sleeping"

improvise on rhythm instruments. Continue the song without stopping; giving turns to fifteen to twenty-five children does not take very much time! It is best to give all the children a turn playing the xylophones, woodblock, and finger cymbals as well as a turn to improvise.

### Kodály

The Kodály method emphasizes the development of musical literacy skills and total musicianship as part of human experience. Unlike the Orff-Schulwerk approach, the Kodály method is a clearly defined instructional strategy that is used primarily in the K-8 music curriculum, although much of it still continues in high school music programs. The actual method, although named after the Hungarian composer Zoltan Kodály (1882–1967), was not originated by him nor did he invent the various components. Kodály was able to collect a number of strategies together and promote them as a method to teach and preserve music in Hungarian schools, and it was the force of his philosophy of music as a part of every human life experience that further boosted its popularity. From there, it became better known at an international level, and has evolved into what it is today. Prior to the Kodály method, a number of musicians and teachers contributed pedagogical methods to teaching singing and music literacy. In music, we are unique in that we have a pedagogical method, Solmization, created by the Catholic monk Guido d'Arezzo (ca. 991–1033), that we still use, although it has changed quite a bit. Many teachers throughout Europe adapted solmization, and other strategies were also developed to help teach music literacy, among them the Paris-Cheve-Galin rhythm symbols, the Norwich Solfa, and the Curwen hand signals. What we call the Kodály method is a compendium of many strategies, altered as needed through the ages, with several of them several hundred years old.

This methodology is primarily used because many of the components have had such a long and successful life, no matter the incarnation through history. In its current form, there are some centerpieces that add to its success. Several critical components of the Kodály method are: (1) the use of authentic and high-quality music and folk songs; (2) the sequencing of instruction; (3) the use of **solfège**; (4) the emphasis on singing; and (5) the development of the total musician (Organization of American Kodály Educators 2004; http://www.oake.org). As in the Orff-Schulwerk approach, students need to experience personal interaction and engagement with the music.

The components of Kodály instruction include the following:

1. *The use of authentic and high-quality music and folk songs.* Folk songs should represent the culture and be age- and content-appropriate. High-quality music refers to music written by the masters (OAKE 2004), although is not limited to the greatest composers of the Western musical canon. Contemporary composers should be included in this mix. Teachers need quality education to present quality music. OAKE (2004) specifies the following: (1) teacher education needs to be as well rounded as possible, and (2) teachers need to develop musical and vocal skills to a high degree.

2. *Sequencing of instruction.* Three Ps of instruction are closely associated with the Kodály method: (1) preparation, (2) presentation, and (3) practice. Sequential instruction is based on child development. The three Ps, which should be part of any well-planned lesson from an instructional design view, are addressed in greater detail in Chapter 12.

3. *The use of solfège.* As stated earlier, Kodály did not create solfège; it was a pedagogical approach rich in history successfully used for nearly 1,000 years. It still works. In the Kodály method, solfège uses moveable *do* and Curwen hand signals. The use of moveable *do* is common in American public schools; however, many music conservatories around the world, including some in the United States, still rely upon the use of fixed *do* for teaching music theory. For practical applications, moveable *do* is less confusing, especially for children. The Curwen hand signals, attributed to the English musician and educator John Curwen, are seen in Chapter 10, Figure 10.4.

When using hand signals with students, make sure they are placed consistently and appropriately (low *do* is usually near the waist, high *do* is a bit higher than the head) to indicate reasonable distances between pitches. The remaining syllables should move in stepwise distances between the high and low *do*.

4. *Singing.* The primary performance vehicle of the Kodály method is the voice. However, the use of the voice in this method presupposes that children are able to sing (see Chapter 6 on Singing) while research on the child voice indicates that singing is not a simple skill, and using the Kodály method will not automatically teach healthy singing skills. Nevertheless, the voice is the best vehicle to develop the inner ear and should come before instrumental training (OAKE 2004).

5. *Development of the total musician.* OAKE (2004) states the following objectives of the Kodály method that lead to total musicianship:

   a. Kodály training is a complete and comprehensive approach to music education that meets the national standards for arts education as published by MENC (1994a).

   b. The development of all skill areas begins very early with simple tasks required of all the students. As knowledge grows, skills are developed further in a sequential manner.

   c. In addition to music reading and writing, which are begun at an early stage, the following skill areas are also developed: part-singing, part-hearing, improvisation, intonation, listening, memory, phrasing, and understanding of form.

   d. An awareness and knowledge of musical styles develops as skills become more proficient.

The Kodály method is a well-rounded approach to teaching music literacy and musicianship. For beginning teachers, becoming familiar with this method and receiving training in it will not only enable them to be better musicians but also much better educators. Using the Kodály method in conjunction with other music methods and approaches will also further the breadth of music education that teachers are able to offer.

One may briefly touch on the Kodály method in classes on teaching music. Actually, this is not enough to really help you know how it works in the field. Like the Orff-Schulwerk approach, a number of classes are available in summer; how far one wishes to go in levels of training depends upon needs, ability, and finances. There are three levels leading to certification. Many colleges and universities also offer weekend workshops and summer weeklong courses. Check into the Organization of American Kodály Educators (http://www.oake.org) for more information on workshops and certification.

A number of excellent materials are also available to help you. The primary books, *Kodály Concept I* and *Kodály Concept II*, written by the Kodály scholar Lois Choksy, are excellent foundations on this method. Finding an old set of the *Listen, Look and Sing* books by Aden Lewis (1976) will provide you with a good start on practical application and sequencing for instruction in the elementary classroom. These are out of print but copies are still available. A current and excellent resource is *An American Methodology* by Ann Eisen and Lamar Robertson (2002). For the Kodály method to be effective in the classroom, there needs to be solid sequential presentation. An occasional foray will destroy the important sequential presentation.

**SAMPLE KODÁLY EXPERIENCE: INTRODUCING STEADY BEAT NOTATION (TA) (GRADE 1)**
Because Kodály lessons are not designed to stand alone but as a part of an instructional sequence, teachers need to bear in mind that students would need to achieve the following in previous lessons: (1) accurate discrimination between music that has beat or no beat; (2) recognition of hearts and clock icons for indicating steady beat; and (3) ability to keep a beat by clapping, patting, or walking to music that moves in twos.

In preparation, the teacher puts the following on a magnetized chalkboard (using chalk): four rows of "ta" beats, four beats in each row, and evenly spaced. Over the chalk-written beats, the teacher puts cutouts of hearts or clocks with magnets on the back to cover the "tas." The icons need to be large enough to completely cover the "tas."

At the beginning of the activity, children should be seated on the floor in front of the prepared blackboard. Because the children already recognize that the hearts or clocks represent a steady beat, they can clap or pat the rows of beats. For variety, the teacher can exchange individual or rows of heart and clock icons; children clap for the hearts and pat for the clocks, reinforcing other ways to keep a steady beat.

When children accurately pat and clap steady beats, they are prepared to hypothesize (a preparation step). The teacher can ask students whether hearts and clocks would work well for other kinds of musical notation. Most will suggest that they would not, and from there, the teacher can show the students that there is another way to show steady beat, by using *ta*. Removing the first row of magnetized icons reveals the *tas* drawn underneath (a presentation step). Practice applying the new knowledge by gradually removing the icons while the children clap the steady beat. Children who already read music may ask, "Where are the note heads?" because they will think of quarter notes. This is easily handled by telling the students that the heads will be attached when they start indicating pitches and melodies, such as sol and mi. The heads don't need to be there to work with rhythm. In our past experience, children who already read music understand and are better able to help classmates who don't read music yet. From here, the activities to practice steady beat using *ta* continue; the next large step will be introducing the silent *ta*, otherwise known as a rest.

## Suzuki

The Suzuki method or Talent Education is named after Shinichi Suzuki (1898–1998). While in Germany studying violin, Suzuki experienced difficulty with the German language and began developing his ideas of the **mother tongue approach** to music learning. He noticed that children learn to speak their mother tongue with ease. He developed his music method by mirroring the way children learn language. The method uses daily listening and imitation, constant repetition, praise, and encouragement in a positive nurturing home and lesson environment. Children as young as 3 years develop their musical ear before they are introduced to music reading in the same way children speak their mother language before learning how to read. Major success of the method is evident when observing groups of Suzuki-trained children in performance (Morita, n.d.). The title of one of Suzuki's books, *Nurtured by Love,* underlines the importance of the nurturing environment (Suzuki 1969).

The major goal of the method is not to produce musical prodigies, but rather to foster the development of the total child. Suzuki's method and its mother tongue technique differ from traditional methods of teaching instrumental music. The following nine basic principles define the method.

1. Begin as early as possible. Suzuki recommended beginning training or ability development at birth. Formal training usually begins by age 3. A parent must play the instrument around the home, and the children decide on their own to play the instrument based on imitating a parent.
2. Teach in small steps so the children master the material and feel a sense of success. All children progress at their own paces.
3. Either the mother or father attends all lessons to understand the learning process and objectives, and can work with the children as a home teacher.
4. Listen daily to recordings of the Suzuki repertoire as well as to other music. This approach is based on the way children learn their spoken language through listening.
5. Postpone music reading until the children's aural and performance skills are well established in the same way children are taught how to read a language only after they can speak.
6. Follow Suzuki repertoire sequence (for the most part). It was designed and refined to produce the results that have come to be expected from the method.
7. Create an enjoyable learning environment so that the children will have enthusiasm for learning.
8. Group lessons and individual lessons are valuable. For younger children, place the emphasis on group lessons.
9. Foster the attitude of cooperation rather than competition among students.

Since the development of the Suzuki method, many other methods incorporate ideas from Suzuki. Although the method is traditionally instrumental, teachers in Finland have applied the ideas to vocal training (Matthews 1991). The Suzuki method began with violin instruction but now includes teacher training and materials for violin, viola, cello, bass, piano, flute, guitar, harp, and recorder.

## Gordon

Edwin E. Gordon developed a method and tests based on his sequential learning theory. His learning sequences in music form the basis of his method (Bolton et al. 1990; Gordon 1994). The learning sequences, at least in his earlier work, were based on the early work of Robert Gagné (Gordon 1971; Jordan-DeCarbo 1986). His work with children ages 1 to 4 helped develop and refine his techniques for beginning music instruction (Gordon 1997). Gordon modeled his early childhood ideas to be consistent with language development. In language development, children babble both with and without stimulus. Children younger than age 2 are encouraged to babble music as they babble with words. The teacher sings tonal and rhythm patterns to the children, and the children are encouraged to sing those patterns. In tonal babble, children sing with a speaking voice; in rhythm babble, children move without consistent tempo or discernible meter. In Gordon's view, children who have not yet emerged from music babble do not benefit from formal music instruction. They need *unstructured informal guidance* with no specific plan from a parent or teacher from birth to age 3. Musical thinking of children who have not emerged from music babble is in *preparatory audiation*. Gordon recommends that children in preparatory audiation should receive both unstructured and structured informal guidance in music. In *structured formal guidance*, a parent or teacher plans what to say and do, but does not expect specific responses from children age 3 to 5. Formal training begins after a child is able to audiate, usually around the age of 5.

Gordon's term *audiation* should not be confused with inner hearing. **Audiation** is the ability to hear and *understand* music without the sound being physically present. Inner hearing is simply hearing the sound without comprehension being necessary. "The simplest explanation of understanding through audiation are hearing the **tonic** before the music ends" (E. Gordon, pers. comm., August 9, 2002). Also included in audiation is hearing tonality and key modulations, implied harmonic functions, the meter of the music as being duple, triple, unusual, and hearing metric modulations. Gordon's *Tonal Register Books* and *Rhythm Register Books* 1 and 2 are used for organizing instruction. The register books contain tonal and rhythm patterns to sing and clap with the children. For detailed information, see Gordon (1997) and Runfola and Swanick (2002).

## Music Series

The roots of American music textbooks began over 100 years ago with singing books and public education. Today, there are several music series such as those published by G.I.A., Macmillan, and Silver Burdett. Each series is an effort to build a curriculum, often combining several methods with sequenced experiences. Texts usually include teacher manuals with lesson plans and recordings with attention to special education and multicultural music. Beginning teachers may organize teaching from these texts and, later, with more experience, develop a style and organization tailored to teach the students. Kindergarten is the earliest grade normally addressed by series text publishers. However, kindergarten and first and second grade materials are often useable with children ages 3 to 5.

Consider the following caveats:

- Just because children are in fifth grade does not necessarily mean they are ready for the fifth grade book.
- The books are not necessarily sequenced in terms of presentation and learning.
- Double-check to make certain the information is correct.
- The books are often visually overstimulating for children and may interfere rather than enhance instruction and learning.

## Chapter Conclusions

With so many choices, choosing one method for teaching music to young children is difficult. There are several issues to consider. First, it is best to form a system of beliefs leading to a personal philosophy of music education for children. After you have formed a personal philosophy, consider the follow key points when reviewing older methods and the newer methods that are being marketed every day.

1. The research studies on methods are not definitive. In fact, the question of what is better is subject to much discussion. What is better depends on philosophy, students, situation, objectives, instructional approach to learning, as well as the teacher's education and perception. It is easy to fall into the problem of comparing apples to oranges when comparing methods. It is probably better to center thoughts on present instructional strategies rather than spending time deciding how some methods are ineffective and some methods are effective.

2. Should a teacher concentrate on one method or use several methods? Method experts often think it best to choose one method. In a discussion about four methods, the authors of *Teaching Music in the Twenty-First Century* write "[N]o *combination* of methods can be as effective . . . as a knowledgeable use of any one of them in the hands of a teacher with sufficient training" (Choksy et al. 2001, 335.). Using techniques from more than one method may prove advantageous provided you have a firm personal philosophy of music education, link experiences with objectives, and organize experiences. If you use techniques from several methods, be sure to study those methods. Costanza and Russell (1992, 501) suggest that the most effective methods and experiences are those that the teacher knows best.

3. What is the teacher's level of musicianship? Some methods demand a much higher level of musicianship than others. For example, a certified Dalcroze teacher needs adequate improvisation and performance skills. A certified Kodály or Orff teacher must pass three levels of competency. See Table 11.1, on teacher skills, for the requirements of other methods.

4. What is the amount of necessary training? Is a teacher willing to devote time, energy, and money to that training?

5. How do the goals and techniques for understanding music fit with the teacher's musical skills and beliefs? Visit a recommended teacher successfully using the method to be considered.

6. Consider the demands of the school district or teaching situation. Some school systems base their curriculum on one particular method.

7. Consider the cultural issues and values. For example, the Kodály method uses indigenous folk songs whereas other methods may use recently composed songs. Does the teacher, the school, or family value singing more than being able to play the piano or violin? Development is best understood within the sociocultural context of the family, educational setting, community, and broader society.

8. Consider the individual differences among children. Some of the methods may accommodate special needs more readily than other methods. For example, the Orff method experiences have been widely used with individuals with handicaps.

9. Do you use a systematic or immersion approach? A systematic approach like the Kodály method uses a systematic design based on child development and sequence of learning. In an immersion approach, children are immersed in or exposed to music. For an immersion approach to work, the children would normally need to be immersed more than one or two times per week.

10. In a sense, all the various teaching methods can be divided into the categories of *teacher-centered* or *student-centered* methods (Colwell and Wing 2004). Is the method or the way in which you use the method more child-centered or is it more teacher-centered? Current thinking in early childhood education advocates a child-centered approach.

## Resources

Many of the methods and associations may be accessed through the web.

Feierabend, John. GIAmusic.com/feireabend or feireabend@aol.com

G.I.A. Publications-Jump Right In. GIA Publications, Inc., 7404 South Mason Avenue, Chicago, IL 60638

Gordon, Edwin E. GIA Publications, Inc., 7404 South Mason Avenue, Chicago, IL 60638

Dalcroze Society of America. Terry Boyarsky, Treasurer, 2812 Fairmount Boulevard, Cleveland Heights, Ohio 44118-4020

Kindermusik International, P.O. Box 26575, Greensboro, NC 27415

Organization of American Kodály Educators, 823 Old Westtown Road, West Chester, PA 19382, http://www.oake.org/

Lovenotes. Silver Lake College Publications, 2406 South Alverno Road, Manitowoc, WI 54220-9319

Macmillan Music Series. Macmillian/McGraw-Hill, 1221 Avenue of the Americas, New York, NY 10020

American Montessori Society, 150 Fifth Avenue, New York, NY 10011.

Music Together. Center for Music and Young Children, 66 Witherspoon Street, Princeton, NY 08542

Musikgarten. 507 Arlington Street, Greensboro, NC 27406

American Orff-Schulwerk Association, P.O. Box 391089, Cleveland, OH 44139, http://www.aosa2.org/

Silver Burdett Making Music Series. Silver Burdett Company (Pearson/Scott Foresman). 250 James Street, Morristown, NJ 07632

Suzuki Association of the Americas, Inc., P.O. Box 17310, Boulder, CO 80308

Weikart, Phyllis. High/Scope Educational Research Foundation, 600 N. River Street, Ypsilanti, MI 48198-2898

CHAPTER **12**

# Designing Instruction

**This chapter addresses the following:**

- Introduction to Curriculum
- Instructional Design for Music Educators: The ADDIE Model
  *In Detail: Analysis*
  *In Detail: Development*
  *In Detail: Design*
  *In Detail: Implementation*
  *In Detail: Evaluation*
  *The Hunter Model*

- Modifying Lesson Plans
- Assessment in Music
- Working with Rubrics
- Taxonomies
- Environment
- Cooperative Learning Activities
- Chapter Conclusions
- Resources

## INTRODUCTION TO CURRICULUM

When you get your first job teaching, you will probably be surprised to find out that your classroom is essentially a revolving door for at least your first year. Principals, parents, curriculum directors, and other people with a vested interest in the success of your classroom teaching will visit quite often. However, a number of people may not visit your classroom nor attend concerts, but will nonetheless have a say in what you teach and how you teach it in your classroom. These people are generally those associated with school boards, various cultural and special interest groups, and local, state, and national government. What you teach in your classroom is actually taken from the school, state, and national instructional guidelines or requirements, more commonly known as a curriculum.

A curriculum is an attempt at providing a systematic and sequential presentation and assessment of instruction. It includes objectives, materials, lessons, and sequencing information to help teachers. In some school districts, a curriculum is very strict whereas it may be very loose in others. However, with the implementation of "No Child Left Behind" and previous educational initiatives, loose curriculums are becoming a thing of the past.

Music teachers often must follow an official curriculum for music. New music teachers need to check the curriculum—often housed within several large notebooks in the district offices—to see what is required. What most curriculums will not provide are the specifics on how to design the instruction. This is where lesson design and lesson plans come in.

Contrary to what you may have experienced in previous education courses, lesson plans are only one component of designing instruction, not the only part of instruction, of importance. Designing effective instruction is an intensive process that requires much more planning than just jotting down what you want to teach the night before the class. The field of instructional design has long been in existence, since the time of

Comenius (Comenius 1638), and we haven't given it as much attention in music education as we need to, as it is really helpful.

## INSTRUCTIONAL DESIGN FOR MUSIC EDUCATORS: THE ADDIE MODEL

ADDIE is the acronym for the standard process in instructional systems development (ISD) design: *Analysis, Development, Design, Implementation,* and *Evaluation.* One book with information on the ADDIE model, *The Systematic Design of Instruction* (Dick, Carey and Carey, 2008), is a standard in the field of instructional design. The ADDIE model's actual origins are elusive, and Michael Molenda of Indiana University describes it as "a colloquial term used to describe a systematic approach to instructional development, virtually synonymous with instructional systems development" (Molenda 2003, 1). The idea goes beyond writing lesson plans, and lesson plans are not written until the implementation stage of the model.

If you think of the ADDIE model as a way to develop a menu in a fine restaurant that specializes in fixed-price offerings, you as the chef would want to have the dishes on the menu work together to pique the interests and taste buds of your targeted clientele and to enhance the entire dining experience. You want your customers to leave satisfied and interested in a return visit. However, you wouldn't just throw together a menu of unrelated or clashing dishes, such as an appetizer of steak tartare followed by a salad of pigs' knuckles, pomegranate seeds, and iceberg lettuce, followed by courses of soy burgers, prunes, and tripe, with a dessert course of chicken-flavored pound cake with a cheese and fruit course consisting of rambutan fruit and limburger cheese, all washed down with cheap wine. If this is your particular dream menu, you would still go out of your way to make these courses work together and subsequently thrill your customers. You would do a tremendous amount of research, testing, and trying out dishes and combinations of dishes, and making substitutions of ingredients before you would finally offer the full menu to the public. The ADDIE model illustrates this process. As a teacher, you will do a tremendous amount of preparation before you work with your students. You need to know who they are, their needs, and what they can learn versus what you want them to learn. The ADDIE model will help you make sure you address all this long before you plan the lessons (and to maintain the metaphor, to cook the final recipes, with substitutions needed to meet diners' needs, that you will serve to your entire dining clientele).

ADDIE can be broken down into five distinct areas of inquiry. The first area, *analysis,* is probably the most intellectually and research-oriented component, in that the teacher or curriculum designer needs to do a number of analyses to determine program content; needs of learners; psychological, affective, and psychomotor development of learners; outcomes; and special needs of students. Using the ADDIE model will be a big help in designing differentiated instruction in that you can apply various task analyses to working with students with special needs, who are English language learners (ELL), and who have different learning styles, which is becoming more of a requirement for teacher education programs. Luckily, much of the information obtained in this area can be applied to future curriculum development with additional information added as discovered or needed. In cooking, this would be the stage in which the chef would decide the courses for the menu, the necessary ingredients, the available ingredients, the cooking temperature versus altitude, kinds of cooking hardware needed, and the demonstrated desires of the customers or guests (for example, accommodating vegetarian, lactose-intolerant, picky eaters, or other special kinds of diets or requests).

*Development* is also an intensive step in which the teacher needs to investigate the kinds of instructional strategies to use, the kinds of audio and visual media, books, and computer programs required, and how to put these together or modify them to meet the needs of the students and the teacher. This is the stage at which the teacher makes decisions on what kind of teaching strategies will be the best for the students' learning of the materials (discovery methods, cognitive approaches, group work, critiques, and so on). This is the stage in which one would gather all the possible instructional materials and ideas, and include everything that is possible, based on the previous analysis.

In cooking, this is where the chef would gather ingredients and determine the cooking methods and materials, including optional recipes and ingredient substitutions.

The *design* process deals with testing materials and instructional strategies using a limited number of students or one class period that represents the larger target population of learners and by sharing it with content area specialists. For example, a teacher may not be sure if a group project is best for the students, but could do a trial run with one small fourth grade class to see if it works. Based on what is revealed, the teacher can fix problem spots before all the fourth grade students receive the instruction. In a general classroom setting, this step may be a bit awkward but, in practice, a teacher usually tries out several strategies and approaches while teaching and takes mental notes of what works and doesn't work and subsequently adjusts instruction. On another level, music textbook series rely on this part of the production process quite extensively, as they send their books out across the country to be piloted by a number of music teachers who answer questionnaires to help the book's authors fix problem areas before the final mass printing. In cooking, this is when a chef may test certain combinations of ingredients, cook them under different situations, and have several people try the dish—a connoisseur, a friend, and perhaps someone invited from off the street. The chef could also see if any odd things happen to ingredients as they are combined or cooked at different temperatures, as well as finding out if certain taste combinations among menu items are complementary or not. This is useful information to have before one prepares the menu items.

The *implementation* stage occurs when the entire unit is applied, in this case, as a sequence of lessons, under various or specific teaching circumstances, with information regarding the instructional efficiency collected and analyzed. In a general music situation, this occurs when a complete unit of instruction is presented to an entire grade level (for example, a unit in music theory and composition, or a unit about a particular period of music history or of a world culture). In cooking, this would be the actual creation and serving of the menu items in the best and most complementary order, which often happens at a restaurant opening or premiere.

The final *evaluation* process occurs when the teacher or curriculum developers critically assess the data concerning the program's effectiveness, and make changes as needed. In cooking, a chef may delete or adjust the menu items based on feedback from customers and reviews from food critics. The chef may also use feedback to try new and perhaps more effective and imaginative dishes. Hopefully the chef considers modifying the cooking choices in response to the feedback. Teachers can utilize the evaluation process in the same way. One pitfall should be avoided; it is unwise to abandon an approach receiving negative assessments when the approach shows promise of success if adjustments are made, especially in student-centered lessons that take more time to prepare than teacher-centered approaches such as lecturing. *Evaluation* is a positive—not a negative—part of the ADDIE model. Designing effective and meaningful instruction takes time, effort, and thought.

Although undertaking the ADDIE approach seems to be a lengthy process, it is useful and will create excellent results. Teachers need to know for whom they are developing instruction, which is why writing lesson plans for students you do not yet know can be very confusing. Also, being able to write curriculum is a skill that is required of teachers in today's educational climate, and although the ADDIE model may not be the one a school district specifically uses in name, it is often the one that others are based upon (Molenda 2003). The following details show how the ADDIE model can be applied to help you design your own classroom curriculum and learning units. Although the work at the analysis and development steps is intense, it really pays off when it is time to create, teach, and then evaluate the lesson plans. More importantly, the early work decreases as a teacher gets to know the students, because they will already have this information and will not need to keep doing it over and over. The following detailed information is from the article "ADDIE for Music Educators" (Trollinger 2001).

## In Detail: Analysis

The analysis component deals specifically with a number of analyses, with most emphasis placed on learner analysis, needs analysis, goal analysis, and content analysis.

*Learner analysis* refers to the applications of knowledge concerning psychomotor skills, intellectual skills, verbal information, attitudes, motivational strategies, context, and relevance. The teacher or curriculum designer needs to have information concerning all these areas at the entry levels of the learners to avoid making too many assumptions about what the children already know. For example, glaring examples of lack of application of learner intellectual and verbal analysis may be seen in Internet-available computer programs that are supposedly geared for preschool children, but when a youngster selects the "?" button, a screen full of words pops up. Attitudes of the students are important as well. It is useful to be familiar with research about music preference; social needs; psychological, cognitive, and physical development; and cultural expectations. Psychomotor skill knowledge of the students can be exhibited by the selection of tasks required of the learner, such as in playing Orff instruments or singing skills required. Other areas of learner analysis include entry behaviors (what are they already able to do?), prior knowledge of the topic or subject, attitudes toward the content and potential delivery system (lecture, discovery, cooperative learning), learning preferences and styles, and learning environment. However, analyses are not restricted to these particular areas.

*Needs analysis* is conducted to ascertain (1) the optimal desired level of performance or achievement that is required, and (2) what actual levels already exist in these areas. The difference between what is actual and what is optimal is considered the "need." For music teachers, the optimal level of performance may be for students to accurately identify all the notes of the bass and treble clef, whereas the actual level of the students may be no knowledge of the two clefs, lines, or spaces. Therefore, the need is indicated by the gap in between. At a more advanced level, a new teacher may inherit an elementary choral program as part of getting a job. The teacher diligently orders several two-part pieces for a holiday concert but, upon finally meeting the choir, finds students do not read music and that the previous teacher used word sheets with everyone singing in unison rather than written music. The analysis of the skills already present (the kids can sing, but not in two parts) and what the new teacher wants the chorus to do (read music and sing in two parts) would reveal a tremendous need; the new teacher could either modify the music or shelve it entirely until the children have learned how to read and sing with written music. The need, then, is generally determined to derive the instructional objectives that would have to be achieved for the students to be successful in performing the music in two parts and reading music.

*Task analysis* is another kind of analysis that needs to be considered in music education, because it deals with the development of psychomotor skills (singing, playing instruments). Task analyses are commonly done in the field of occupational therapy, in that therapists need to know every step that needs to be undertaken when an individual is learning how to brush one's teeth after suffering a brain injury and forgetting how that is done. In music education, understanding the sequential steps required for success on an instrument or in singing is a key to being able to teach these skills effectively. Unfortunately, this particular process hasn't been addressed as much as is necessary in music education, as evidenced by the increasing and alarming number of performance injuries that can be attributed to improper singing or instrumental performance activities (Bernstorf et al. 2004; Palac et al. 2004).

According to Dick et al. (2008), instructional goals are usually stated as skills, knowledge, and attitudes that some groups of learners must acquire to satisfy identified needs. These kinds of *goal analyses* usually use action verbs, such as identify, create, perform, sing, play, write, defend, and describe. With these goals, the focus is upon what learners will be able to do at the completion of the instruction. Unlike in many areas of instructional design, music educators also need to address the "fuzzy" or less assessable goals, such as learning to appreciate, like, and understand music. To address the systematic approach to fuzzy goal analysis, Mager (1997) suggests that the goal should first be written, and then the teacher needs to identify and write out what behaviors the students will demonstrate that indicate the goal has been met. These behaviors can be written as behavioral objectives, which cumulatively will theoretically result in the attainment of the fuzzy goal. For example, a student will indicate mastery of understanding the notes of the bass and treble clefs by writing the 100 percent correct note names under the treble staff notes as they are written on a worksheet. This objective would contribute to the goal of being able to sight-read a piece of music, or to read a score and hear the music in one's head.

*Content analysis* is another area that concerns the content of the proposed course or sequence of lessons. What particular activities, skills, and cognitive knowledge will most effectively represent and address mastery of the content? This area can be particularly tricky for music educators who may want to crowd as much material as possible into a music class, which in turn may cloud the view of the instructional goal or the behavioral objectives for the unit of study. Effective content analysis will help a teacher avoid this kind of problem. In addition, a content analysis will also reveal crucial steps in the instruction that must be included to avoid confusion. Content analysis may also be approached within the area of context, such as how relevant mastery of the material is to the child's continued success in music in general or in the unit of study in particular.

Other areas of analysis that also need to be addressed include identifying subordinate skills that must be included in the instruction and entry behaviors and knowledge that the learners need to have before instruction begins, such as the ability to discriminate between high and low before reading notes and associating them with pitches on a treble clef.

Overall, Dick et al. (2008) suggest that a complete goal description should include the following:

- Statement identifying the characteristics of the students, including students with special needs, remedial needs, and enrichment needs
- Statement of what the students will be able to do at the end of the learning experience
- Description of the context in which the skills will be applied
- Description of the materials that will be available to the students to aid their learning

When you are creating your own ADDIE model for a course or unit of study, a good sequence of thinking through the A process is to (1) identify your goals for the students and include strategies on how you will evaluate the students to see if the goals are met, (2) identify the objectives or steps that need to be achieved for the goals to be accomplished, (3) identify the characteristics and knowledge of your learners, (4) identify what the difference is between what the students know (Step 3) and the objectives you want them to meet (Step 2), which establishes the instructional need, and (5) decide what content, activities, and skill development you will include in the course or unit that will help you address the instructional need. When working with this ADDIE model, you will often need to come back to a section to see if you are consistent in designing instruction that meets your goals.

## In Detail: Development

The development process includes creating instructional materials, and selecting instructional delivery formats (for example, worksheets, videos, recordings, group activities, and so on), ways of instruction, and ways of evaluating student learning. Instructional materials contain the information that students will use to achieve the objectives. This includes materials for major objectives as well as for remedial (for students who need more help) or enrichment (for students who can zoom ahead) materials. This is also the stage in which teachers integrate developmentally appropriate practice (DAP) and chose instructional strategies. Table 2.1 lists instructional strategies including behaviorism (for example, teacher claps a pattern, students clap it back), cognitivism (students are required to complete essay questions concerning facts on a test), and constructivism (students make their own instruments, write their own pieces of music, or improvise, thus creating their own personal meaning of the musical experience). Learning styles and information processing styles are also considered. This stage also provides detail to learner analyses and needs analyses that are addressed in the analysis section. Although this may seem redundant, please know that repetition is built into the model and helps reinforce your strategies and overall instructional goals. The various approaches you include in this section of the ADDIE model later become the road maps for your instructional delivery via the lesson plans.

Overall, Dick et al. (2008) suggest addressing the following outline of components in depth during the process of developing instructional strategies:

1. Pre-instructional activities
   a. Motivation: How will the students maintain interest in learning the materials?
   b. Objectives: The skills and knowledge that the students need to achieve to be successful, and these should be observable. The objectives lead to attainment of the goals that you outlined in your analysis section.
   c. Entry behaviors: What knowledge or skills are required prior to the new learning? You never want to assume that they have the knowledge or skills. Much of this is will be revealed in your learner analysis.
2. Information presentation
   a. Instructional sequence: Small manageable steps are the best way to go. Will you include discovery activities? Videos? Webquests? These need to be developed to work in a sequence that isn't overwhelming or poorly interconnected. For example, if older students are expected to gain a lot of information via watching a video, they need a fill-in sheet to help them focus on the information presented in the video.
   b. Information: Needs to be relevant and in context; age-appropriate language and content is important. For example, having kindergarteners memorize all the major melodic themes of the Beethoven 6th Symphony aurally is not age appropriate; however, they are certainly able to aurally learn and identify the storm scene in this symphony, and engage in many creative activities concerning it. Conversely, older students are able to learn a number of musical themes and pieces that ultimately could be used in a tune-naming game.
   c. Examples of finished projects: If you are working on project-based activities, students benefit greatly from seeing and working with a finished exemplar of the project.
3. Learner participation: Ways to keep everyone engaged
   a. Practice: Allows for new knowledge and skills to be rehearsed, and eventually part of the student's long-term cognitive scaffolding. Examples of practicing include having students hold up flash cards in answer to questions, and having them work together on practice activities.
   b. Feedback/reinforcement: Provided after each practice activity. This can be provided by teachers or by classmates.
4. Testing and formative evaluation of the students: Use this to find out if the students learned, what they learned, and if your instruction worked.
   a. Pretest: Use this to check for previous knowledge.
   b. Posttest: To assess learning of the new knowledge. Please know that for pre- and posttesting, the worst strategy is to ask a question of the class and then call on one student for the answer. Although this is the simplest way to check for learning, you are actually just checking on the learning of one student, and that can give you an inflated sense of your instructional success. Pre- and post-evaluations need to be undertaken by every student.
5. Follow-through activities
   a. Remediation: Go back and readdress skills and knowledge that aren't mastered. You may need to use a different instructional strategy.
   b. Enrichment
   c. Memorization and transfer of what was learned to learning new skills or knowledge. For example, if your students learned to identify the perfect fourth melodic interval by connecting it with the opening motive to "Here Comes the Bride," then a next step (which can also serve as a practice activity) could be to play a number of intervals and ask them to identify perfect fourths versus other intervals. A further step for choir students would be to ask them to aurally and/or visually identify perfect fourths in their choir music.

## In Detail: Design

The design stage is a formative evaluation of material and approaches done on a small scale. This isn't as impossible as it may seem, as you can check to see if what you are planning will meet needs of students, school district, and overall music curriculum in many ways. With current educational emphasis on making sure that teachers are sequencing materials and keeping student needs at the forefront, it is suggested that you share some of your materials with a colleague at school, or at another school, to see if s/he understands them. Although running them by other music teachers is a good idea, it is also a good idea to share some of the materials with non-music teachers because they will look at them differently, and they may uncover some discrepancies or confusion that you may inadvertently overlook. This is also a method to garner support and interest in your subject, as other teachers may want to connect their lessons to what you are doing in your classes, or may wish to initiate a grade-level unit of study.

Other than teachers, you can also share your materials with colleagues who may be specialists in the particular field you are planning. For example, if the unit is on the music of India, then having your materials checked for accuracy by someone who really knows Indian music is a good idea. Your former college professors are also good people from whom to bounce these materials off. In a nutshell, you want to make sure that errors are caught early before you finish planning the entire unit of study.

## In Detail: Implementation

The implementation of the program usually occurs on a large scale. This is the stage in which you construct your lesson plans and then try them out with all the classes for whom you have planned. This is the actual time of instruction. What is especially important is that the teacher needs to refer back to the development section to make sure that the instructional approaches that were identified are actually used, as well as to the analysis section to make sure that the instruction being implemented actually addresses the goals and needs of the students.

## In Detail: Evaluation

During and after completing a unit, the teacher undertakes formative (in-progress) and summative (final evaluation) evaluations on the unit and its success. A teacher will know instruction is successful if students clearly meet the goals of instruction outlined in the analysis section. It is very normal, however, to find out after one has completed a unit that the lesson needs modifications for the next time; with that in mind, the teacher may go back to the analysis section and see what could be done differently. Being an efficient and effective teacher is a cyclical process.

**MODEL LESSON PLAN EXAMPLES**    The lesson plan is a road map that shows the sequence of instructional events. The format of a lesson plan depends upon information and materials defined and developed in the first three parts of the ADDIE model. Needless to say, the lesson undertakes numerous formats and designs to meet the needs of the teacher and students. Designing the sequence of instruction is crucial in creating a satisfying and effective learning experience (Brown and Green 2006). It is no wonder that writing lesson plans is a staple activity in education methods classes, but trying to do so without knowledge of the learners and their needs makes it difficult. Teachers aren't able to create truly effective lesson plans until they actually write for specific students.

With that in mind, this part of the chapter will present lesson plan models that are currently in use. These models, as well as the sample lesson plans presented in the next section of the book, all need to be modified to work with future students. Every child, every classroom, and every teacher and curriculum is unique, and those differences always need to be considered when planning instruction. By undertaking an ADDIE approach, all the plans can be modified to meet your future students' needs.

Instructional designers, past and present, have contributed many road maps to how instruction is presented. Although too numerous to name here, several come to the forefront, especially when music instruction is concerned. John Seely Brown, an eminent instructional designer who worked for many years in the Xerox Corporation, promotes a "situated cognition" setting that is very easily applied to music education; it is actually echoed in the praxial music education approach advocated by David Elliot, and tangentially by educational philosophers such as Maxine Greene and Michael Apple (Brown et al. 1989). The model advocates instructional events that take place in the situation in which they would be normally occurring. For example, sight-reading a new piece of music in a band rehearsal is an example of situated cognition—the students are learning the piece in the live situation of a rehearsal, applying a number of strategies and skills that they previously learned. Music rehearsals and dress rehearsals are also part of this strategy. However, situated cognition experiences are less considered in general music education classes. For example, a lecture or a video presented to sixth graders about music of the Classical period may not be as effective as having students experiment with compositional techniques of the Classical period (such as the sonata-allegro form) and playing with Mozart's Musical Dice Game (*Die Musicalisches Würfelspiel*). Preparing a lesson plan for a video or lecture is less work than planning a lesson plan for composition, because students need to have a wealth of prior music learning skills in the composition activity, such as being able to fluently notate and read music, so they are successful at the activity or objective.

The situated cognition approach also contributes to the constructivist approach in designing lesson plans in which students are encouraged to derive meaning and values from the activity. A video on the Classical period, simply by the content included, defines for students what is important and valuable to know about the Classical period. However, engaging in investigative activities, such as webquests, composing, and performing music of a Classical style allows students to use the found knowledge to form values and meanings. Although you as readers may be shaking your head and thinking that this may not be possible at an upper elementary level, rest assured that it certainly is and that elementary music teachers who do the background work and the planning required for this kind of success have achieved this. Designing these kinds of plans takes time and a strong knowledge of the students and their capabilities.

However, how does one go about designing these kinds of lesson plans? Robert Gagné (1985), the eminent educator and instructional scholar, proposed that nine sequenced events need to take place in the instructional process of a lesson plan. These events, paraphrased here with some examples as needed, are simply the following:

1. Gain the students' attention.
2. Inform the learners of the instructional objectives.
3. Help the learners recall prior learning.
4. Present the activity (singing, the song, rhythm patterns, video).
5. Provide guidance to the learners on how to process and respond to the activity (for example, "repeat after me," "echo-clap after me," "listen to the song and tell me what rhythms you hear").
6. Elicit the learners' responses (singing, clapping in response, describing what is new on the music staff).
7. Provide detailed feedback (What did we do well? What errors did we make? Did we find all the new things on the staff?).
8. Assess the learner performance (That was good, but how can we make it better?).
9. Enhance the retention and transfer of the knowledge (practice the rhythm or melodic patterns, drill the names of the notes, perform the patterns backwards or in rounds).

These events have been adopted into a number of instructional strategies that are actually used in planning music instruction. The most common model is the Hunter Model, attributed to the educator Madeline Hunter. The other model that we use frequently in music education is the 3-P model (preparation, presentation, and practice) used extensively in the Kodály method of instruction. Other models used less extensively in music education but often in general elementary education include those that are based on the theory of multiple intelligence, the discovery approach, the brainstorming approach, and a puzzle-solving approach. Most of these models are cognitively based, requiring students to problem-solve or discover based on a set of information provided. At the end of this chapter, you'll find resource information for investigating these kinds of lesson plan strategies; however, a caveat needs to be offered. Music learning is not only cognitively based, but is also skill-based and aesthetically based, and that requires music educators to consider the psychomotor development (especially for singing) that is often considered in physical education in addition to the aesthetic value and cognitive processing. This presents an interesting and unique hybrid situation for us, which is not often considered in traditional lesson planning.

## The Hunter Model

The Hunter Model is not terribly unique; however, it is the most standard planning format that is used in U.S. public schools. The following presents the model with current additions and modifications that are occurring in the public schools:

1. Objective(s) of the lesson (may also include the essential question of the lesson)
2. Knowledge and skills previously learned (that lead to success in achieving the objective(s)
3. State and national standards addressed (which national standards in music, which state standards in music)
4. The anticipatory set (also known as an "attention hook" to grab attention and focus learners)
5. Materials needed
6. Instructional process
7. Guided practice and monitoring
8. Evaluation of learning
9. Closure
10. Independent practice (homework)

This model is the simplest one to use, and is used as the foundation lesson plan format throughout this book, with adjustments for included parallel objectives.

Another lesson plan model is based on the Hunter Model, but is especially relevant to music education. The Kodály method lesson includes all that is included in the Hunter Model, especially in that the anticipatory set translates to the *Preparation*, and the lesson plan sequence translates into *Presentation* and *Practice*, but has special emphasis on elements that are to be included in every lesson.

The Kodály method elements include the following:

1. Singing
2. Creating
3. Inner practice
4. Reading
5. Writing
6. Moving
7. Ear training
8. Listening
9. Form
10. Part work

One can simply argue that these components should be included in all music lesson plans, but including all of them in the space of a thirty-minute lesson may be difficult. On paper, it looks difficult, because what is not indicated is that an effective teacher can design activities that will cover several of these simultaneously or can have the pacing down so that there are no lags in instruction.

The most efficient way to develop a set of sequential lesson plans is to remember that there are several avenues to music learning, including listening, singing, moving, creating, playing, reading, and writing (see Chapters 5 through 10). These avenues can be traveled down in many ways. For example, if we were to use the metaphor of a trip to San Francisco, we know we can travel there via many avenues. We can drive, fly, take a long trip by boat, go on horseback, go by balloon—and then there are virtual avenues to go: in our imaginations via space ship, by flying (not in an airplane), by looking at a travel book of San Francisco, by creating our dream itineraries to San Francisco, by talking to a friend on the phone in San Francisco, or by eating a dinner reminiscent of a trip there. In music, musical avenues can also be traveled down many ways, and the ten elements of instruction of the Kodály method are ten good ways to start. Imagine if you traveled to San Francisco the same way every time you went. As a result, you would really know only one way to experience the trip. In teaching, we run the risk of using the exact same approaches or avenues without testing new or different ones that may be equally effective and can then be added to a collection of successful teaching strategies. Varying approaches (after making sure they work) helps ensure that the students don't get bored and that you, as the teacher, don't get bored either. Children's songs are great fun at the beginning but they become awfully mind-numbing after a few years to the teacher. Varying your approaches is not unlike mixing up a regular workout routine at the gym so the muscles don't become acclimated to the activities and no longer need to work as hard.

To quickly review, a lesson plan is a map that guides the teacher through instructional events. An effective lesson plan needs to be written specifically for students, and attempting to create lesson plans without considering students' needs, differences, levels of knowledge and ability, previous learning, and overall curriculum requirements will likely result in a faulty plan. Lesson plans are also sequential in that each plan builds on knowledge and skills gained in previous lessons, with the links made clear to students.

## MODIFYING LESSON PLANS

Existing lesson plans in books or downloaded from the Internet can be modified to work with your students, as long as they fit into your curricular plans and also if there is enough detail for you to define the goals of instruction. We feel this is important to address due to the plethora of online teacher lesson plan websites, many of them created with good intentions, but with many plans written for specific students that are different from the students you teach. New teachers could download a number of these plans and try them in their classrooms, not realizing until it is too late that using plans designed for one teacher's class doesn't mean they will work for all students.

If you see a lesson plan that you think is interesting and believe may be useful for your students, you need to review it with a critical eye and ask the following questions:

1. What skills and knowledge do my students need to have already so they can be successful with this lesson plan?
2. What steps are missing?
3. What information is missing? Is the information there correct?
4. Is the process clear enough that I can replicate it, or do I essentially have to rewrite it so there is detail?
5. How are the students assessed to make sure they learned? Is this even included?
6. What other parts of my curriculum can this plan connect to? Or is it a one-shot plan with little chance for good follow-up?

## ASSESSMENT IN MUSIC

Assessment is a major buzzword in education. All academic fields are finding themselves in situations in which they need to devise tests or other evaluations that allow school district officials, parents, and state and federal governments to see if and what children really are learning. Statistics published in newspapers concerning reading, writing, math, and various achievement test scores attest to the great concern about assessment.

Assessment in the arts is also being considered, with arts teachers wondering how to assess objectively something that is inherently subjective. Arts educators now find themselves in situations where they need to objectively assess arts achievement, especially in situations where letter grades need to be included on report cards.

Historically, assessment was often accomplished in instrumental and choral music because competitions for performing ensemble included trophies to display in a trophy case, and thus validated that the students were achieving in music. The more trophies, awards, and citations students earned, the better they were learning about music—or so it was perceived. Of course, trophies don't give information on assessment of aesthetic value, nor do they give any indication that the students are learning health-based performance practices. General music classes are rarely engaged in competitive activities, so mass achievement is not displayed. However, general music teachers are finding that they are being required to provide objective assessment of their students' achievement. A caveat is that, to truly understand assessment, particularly in the numerical measurement that school administrators favor, music teachers will likely need to engage in a summer course or graduate class in educational assessment. These courses usually include statistics to make clearer the numbers and the true face of assessment (in addition to finding a practical use for all those years of algebra).

A teacher instructs a recorder class.

*Photo courtesy of Kelly Riccio*

Assessment activities in the arts run the gamut from simple observations of students engaged in arts creation, to students filling in blanks on a test, to playing a performance test, to more complex ones involving music creation at an advanced level and music criticism and evaluation. Many of these can be used from the elementary through the high school level. The following are examples of assessment activities:

*Electronic portfolios.* These are really not all that difficult to create and to maintain, and many schools are using these as a way to keep records of student work as they progress through school. Very simply in music, samples of the child's musical creations, writings, worksheets, performances, and projects can all be scanned or saved into the e-portfolio. Although teachers may not have time to do this, the task can be the responsibility of students or parent volunteers. The e-portfolio can remain online for the child's entire school career, and can be downloaded and burned onto a disc upon graduation.

*Performance tests.* These can run from having children perform by clapping, snapping, singing, or playing musical patterns as part of a test, to a full-blown recital performance. What is important for these kinds of tests—if they are to affect grades—is that a set of achievement guidelines (rubrics) is created to allow the children to see what level of performance will result in which grade. Rubrics can be used for straight grading or they can be used for self-assessment. For example, a fourth grade music teacher will often need to teach recorder to the entire fourth grade class, and one objective is to have them perform well enough for the spring concert. However, the teacher knows that some children have no interest in performing, whereas others really want to. Therefore, a rubric would be set up that would allow the students to see what they need to accomplish to perform in the concert, and what they need to accomplish to achieve an A or B in the unit. This is not as simple as it sounds, as a lot of planning needs to take place. The teacher may also be in a school district in which parents wish their child to perform whether the child wishes to or not (in one school at which one of the authors taught, the annual talent show lasted for two days). This is where an ADDIE model analysis comes in handy.

*Student assessment of each other's work.* Students are able to use rubrics to evaluate their own and others' work. This would work well with a classroom that emphasizes collaborative and/or peer teaching and learning. With a rubric provided, the students will likely not make hurtful or useless comments.

*Group projects.* Students can also work together in groups to create a project or a class presentation. One dimension that is added is that students will also assess each other in their (1) contribution to the group project, (2) being responsible for getting work done, and (3) communication with the group. Although this may be a new idea to the music classroom, it is a standard practice in instructional design. It pretty much guarantees that one person will not end up doing everything (in our experience, students have been very truthful in evaluating each other, as these evaluations are done anonymously, and only by the fellow group members). If students rate each other on a scale of one to five with points in this assessment, then the teacher would include the average of the points in grading.

For this to work, the teacher needs to be engaged in assessing in the *formative* stage (process of forming and shaping the learning experience) as well as in the *summative* stage (final evaluation of the learning experience). Formative feedback (such as conferencing, having progress checks, pop quizzes in class) allows teachers to provide helpful guidance information as students work on the projects or assignments. The summative evaluation is the final, culminating evaluation or assessment of the final project. For successful and honest assessment to work, these two approaches must both be used. This is also the kind of information a parent or other authoritarian figure should have access to, because grades on report cards cannot be handed out arbitrarily.

The National Association for the Education of Young Children outlines eight major guidelines for developmentally appropriate assessment practices. The following guidelines are appropriate for all of elementary education (although the association's definition of young children ends with 8 years of age):

1. Assessment of young children's progress and achievements is ongoing, strategic, and purposeful. The results of assessment are used to benefit children—in adapting curriculum and teaching to meet the developmental and learning needs of children, communicating with the child's family, and evaluating the program's effectiveness for the purpose of improving the program.

2. The content of assessments reflects progress toward important learning and developmental goals. The program has a systematic plan for collecting and using assessment information that is integrated with curriculum planning.

3. The methods of assessment are appropriate to the age and experiences of young children. Therefore, assessment of young children relies heavily on the results of observations of children's development, descriptive data, collections of representative work by children, and demonstrated performance during authentic, not contrived, activities. Input from families as well as children's evaluations of their own work are part of the overall assessment strategy.

4. Assessments are tailored to a specific purpose and used only for the purpose for which they have been demonstrated to produce reliable, valid information.

5. Decisions that have a major impact on children, such as enrollment or placement, are never made on the basis of a single developmental assessment or screening device but are based on multiple sources of relevant information, particularly observations by teachers and parents.

6. To identify children who have special learning or developmental needs and to plan appropriate curriculum and teaching for them, developmental assessments and observations are used.

7. Assessment recognizes individual variation in learners and allows for differences in styles and rates of learning. Assessment takes into consideration such factors as the children's facility in English, stage of language acquisition, and whether the children have had the time and opportunity to develop proficiency in their home language as well as in English. An advantage of music instruction in a bilingual situation is that language need not be a barrier (for example, music without words).

8. Assessment legitimately addresses not only what children can do independently but also what they can do with assistance from other children or adults. Teachers study children as individuals as well as in relationship to groups by documenting group projects and other collaborative work (NAEYC 1997).

## WORKING WITH RUBRICS

Rubrics, as mentioned previously, are a terrific way to work with assessment. They can be used to assess teaching, student learning, student participation, and student progress in learning a skill and final achievement. The key to an effective rubric is that the levels and what is required remain consistently defined and are easy to understand by the teacher and the students. The following is a simple rubric for singing that a teacher may use to find out where her students in first grade are in developing this skill.

Rubrics can be revised as needed to make sure they work properly under the prescribed circumstances. These are wonderful tools to help teachers solidify how to do

**TABLE 12.1** First Grade Singing Development Rubric

| | Excellent! | Getting There | OK (needs special help from music teacher) | Poor (needs intervention of voice specialist) |
|---|---|---|---|---|
| **Vocal Health and Phonation** | Sound is healthy and even, with no sign of vocal stress anywhere. | Sound is mostly healthy, but displays vocal pressing behavior at times. | Sound is somewhat healthy, but there is obvious evidence of much vocal distress. | Sound is dysphonic or aphonic in some areas, suggesting a vocal issue. |
| **Pitch-matching** | Student matches pitch with teacher and with other students. | Student matches pitch better with students instead of teacher. | Student matches pitch to some notes with teacher and/or student. | Child does not match pitch with anyone, or only matches one or two notes in a very restricted range. |
| **Range** | Range is healthy and easily achieved (middle C or D up to B or so). | Range is moderate to small size; student displays some vocal distress when at extremes. | Range is very narrow, and may be artificially too low due to vocal distress. | Range is very restricted due to possible vocal issues. |
| **Breathing and Breath Support** | Student has no breath distress, hyper- or hypofunction. No clavicular breathing evident. | Student has some hyper- or hypofunction of breathing, poor posture, some shoulder movement indicating clavicular breathing. | There is evidence of hyper- and/or hypo-breathing behavior; posture is rigid and unyielding, and child appears very tense. | There is evidence of hyper- and/or hypofunction, tenseness, and jutting out or pulling in of chin. |

assessment. A link to RubiStar, a very well-known teacher website that allows teachers to create and modify their own rubrics as well as see other rubrics, is included at the end of this chapter.

## TAXONOMIES

Effective instruction arranges objectives in a sequence that leads to mastery. Sequencing comes in several forms. Much of a young child's learning is through imitation and doing. Learning proceeds from the concrete to abstract, from old to new, obvious to subtle, rote to note, short to long, single to multiple, part to whole, simple to complex, and familiar to unfamiliar (Colwell and Wing 2004).

Colwell and Wing (2004) believe it is crucial for teachers to think about taxonomies. Taxonomies are helpful to classify, order, establish priorities or hierarchies, and to gain a reasonably complete idea of the scope of the field. Perhaps the most well-known taxonomy is known as Bloom's taxonomy. Taxonomies are developed to portray learning in many dimensions including psychomotor skills, affective or experiential objectives, and cognitive skills. Table 12.2 illustrates a simplified taxonomy for children's music learning based upon elements of music. Other taxonomies may be found in curriculum guides, series textbooks, and methods such as Kodály, Orff, and Dalcroze.

Objectives from standards, curriculum guides, or based on taxonomies need to be adjusted to the needs of individual students. For example, children in special education need fewer objectives or more experiences on each part of the taxonomy sequence. Children with visual impairments need adaptations using senses other than sight, and children with a physical challenge need instruments adapted to their physical abilities. Children with a rich home music environment, for example, Suzuki violin students, will have mastered many of the kindergarten objectives and will likely need enrichment activities.

**TABLE 12.2 Taxonomy Example**

### Rhythm

| Level | Concept |
|-------|---------|
| 1. | Music moves with a steady beat (like a heartbeat). Contrast with absence of steady beat. |
| 2. | Slower and faster beat |
| 3. | One sound or rest can be concurrent with a beat (quarter note and quarter rest). |
| 4. | Sounds and rests through beat; longer and shorter sounds |
| 5. | Two sounds or rests to one beat (and combinations such as short-short-long, long-short-short). There can also be more sounds on a beat (sixteenth notes). |
| 6. | Two and four beat durations (half and **whole notes** and rests) |
| 7. | Accents; meter grouping of beat into twos and threes |
| 8. | Sounds can be even or uneven. |
| 9. | Duple, triple, 6/8 meter (all part of our culture) |
| 10. | Accelerando and **ritardando** |

### Pitch

| Level | Concept |
|-------|---------|
| 1. | Indefinite pitch; exploration of sounds in environment |
| 2. | Definite pitch |
| 3. | Movement of pitches is melody (three-note melody). Melodies may move by steps, skips, or stay on the same pitch. |
| 4. | Pitches move up; pitches move down; pitches stay the same. |
| 5. | Higher-lower pitches |
| 6. | Pentatonic melody |
| 7. | Melody with **tonal center**; seven pitch melodies |
| 8. | Major/minor melodies |
| 9. | Two or more pitches sounded together make harmony. |

### Timbre (Tone Color)

| Level | Concept |
|-------|---------|
| 1. | Expressiveness through timbre choice |
| 2. | Contrast of timbre. You can change the sound of instruments depending on how you play them. |
| 3. | Combining timbre |
| 4. | Percussion, brass, woodwind, string timbres |
| 5. | Specific instrument timbres |

### Form

| Level | Concept |
|-------|---------|
| 1. | Overall form–expressive intent |
| 2. | Repetition |
| 3. | Contrast |
| 4. | Unity, variety/variation; phrase: ability to sing in phrases rather than one or two notes at a time |
| 5. | AB (two-part form) |
| 6. | Ostinato |
| 7. | Introduction and **coda** |
| 8. | Rondo |
| 9. | ABA (three-part form) |

### Dynamics and Expressive Devices

| Level | Concept |
|-------|---------|
| 1. | Louder-softer; **forte** (*f*) and piano (*p*) |
| 2. | **Crescendo-diminuendo** |
| 3. | Fortissimo (*ff*), pianissimo (*pp*), mezzo piano (*mp*) |
| 4. | Attack and release |
| 5. | Shaping with dynamics |
| 6. | The mood changes as the dynamics and rhythm change; identify the emotional tone (for example, sad or happy). |

## ENVIRONMENT

Building an environment conducive to learning is not easy. There is no cookbook for teaching. An erroneous idea that many beginning teachers have is that they will be the "magic" teacher. Magic teachers help *any* child learn; they will take the most difficult possible situation and turn it around to save the child. Magic teachers are able to leap tall insurmountable learning problems in a single flick of an instructional finger! The reality is that many forces act upon children's learning (Colwell and Wing 2004). Teaching is such a complicated enterprise that it is best viewed as an art or craft rather than a set of techniques to apply as in following an unvarying or unmodified recipe from a boxed cake mix. The learning environment is considered in the analysis and development of the ADDIE model and pervades the design, implementation, and evaluation sections as well.

There are at least six general dimensions or ingredients to consider when organizing instruction. First are the children and the forces influencing the children. Current thought clearly supports a child-centered classroom with developmentally appropriate practice. However, the children do not come to the classroom as a blank slate. Many forces influence children, including parents and other adults, emotional characteristics and the mood of the day, prior learning, how their needs are being met, and culture and the cultural context. The second ingredient is the teacher. The teacher brings to the situation a philosophy of music, beliefs about learning theory, knowledge of the subject, experience, and emotional characteristics and mood for the day. Third is the environment. Much is included in the environment such as temperature, weather patterns, physical space, safety, and equipment. Fourth is the social climate of the classroom and school. For example, what social interaction occurred in the last class? How does an individual child relate to other children as they engage in group music activities? Fifth, what are the instructional materials, including lesson plans, instruments, methodology, and techniques? Sixth is the instructional moment. What are the forces in place at the moment, and how does the teacher adapt the timing, sequence, and reinforcement of learning to best optimize all children's learning?

All six of the dimensions of instruction interact with each other in all instructional models. The teacher might wish to arrange a lesson so that a child will move from not being able to sing the pitches sol, mi, and la to the skill level of being able to sing those three pitches in tune; however, learning is not necessarily a straight line sequence of activities. All the dimensions of instruction—the child, teacher, materials, social climate, instructional moment, and environment—interact with the singing objective. Figure 12.1 illustrates a simplified matrix of interaction for dimensions of instruction (see Colwell and Wing [2004] for a discussion of Marzano's and Bloom's complete taxonomies). Notice how each dimension such as social climate interacts with all other dimensions to

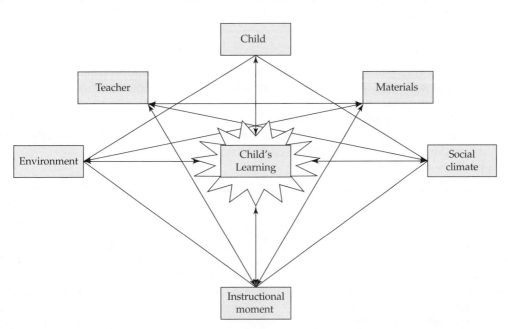

**FIGURE 12.1** Matrix of Interaction

influence the child's learning. The learning environment and interaction of elements within the environment can very easily scatter many clouds on a teacher's instructional goals; considering the environment as part of the ADDIE model can remove the clouds and allow the sun to shine on the teaching and learning process and interaction.

## COOPERATIVE LEARNING ACTIVITIES

Using your knowledge about lesson planning, sequencing instruction, and the ADDIE model, work through the following activities:

1. Design a grading rubric for a recorder unit. At one level, include the requirements necessary for playing in a spring concert, and on the remaining levels, include information on what children need to accomplish to receive a particular grade. Areas to be addressed may include fingering, note reading, memorization, pitch and intonation, and rhythm. Some ways to help you develop criteria are in the recorder video that accompanies this book. Create the rubric using your own resources or RubiStar.
2. Use the ADDIE model to develop a unit of study on an aspect of international music or jazz. Remember to create your lesson plans *after* you have done the analysis and the development sections, as they are part of the implementation section; as well, make sure your lesson plans address what you outlined in those first two sections. You also need to design evaluation activities (both formative and summative) that need to directly relate to all the sections of the ADDIE model.

Imagine that you are creating this unit of study for one of the following:

a. In a third grade class in a rural location, you meet with a class of fifteen students twice a week for thirty minutes. Of the children, 75 percent read at grade level, and the remaining 25 percent need special reading help. You also have five students with academic special needs mainstreamed into the classroom, and two children with Down syndrome, swelling your total class size to twenty-two. Overall, your students are able to read music and sing well, thanks to their training using the Kodály method.
b. In a sixth grade class in an urban location, you meet with a class of twenty students once a week for thirty minutes. Of the children, 55 percent read at grade level, while the remaining 45 percent need special reading help; in addition, two children are from the nearby classroom for children who are socially and emotionally disturbed (SED), and an aid accompanies each of those students. You also have six students with academic special needs mainstreamed into the classroom. Overall, your students are not able to read music and their singing is marginal, despite how hard you have worked on both these skills.

## Chapter Conclusions

The process of preparing to teach a lesson goes well beyond the scope of a simple set of lesson plans. The ADDIE model and many variations of it have been used for years to help instructional designers and teachers develop effective and efficient ways to deliver instruction. Applying it to developing curriculum and instruction in the music classroom will help savvy music teachers make sure that the instruction is first-rate and appropriate and that the students are providing evidence that they are learning about music. Assessment has become a very important consideration in arts education, and it behooves current music educators entering the field to be knowledgeable about how it is done in the arts.

## Resources

RubiStar: http://rubistar.4teachers.org/index.php

Lesson plan samples: http://www.uwsp.edu/education/lwilson/lessons/intro.htm (maintained by Professor Leslie Owen Wilson, University of Wisconsin-Stevens Point)

Center for Educator Development in Fine Arts Texas Essential Knowledge and Skills (TEKS) page for music: http://finearts.esc20.net/music/music%20teks/music_teks_home.html

Smaldino, S. Russell, J., Heinich, R., and Molenda, M. 2006. *Instructional technology and media for learning.* 8th ed. Upper Saddle River, NJ: Pearson Merrill Prentice Hall.

Brown, A., and T. Green. 2006. *The essentials of instructional design.* Upper Saddle River, NJ: Prentice Hall.

CHAPTER | **13**

# Special Areas

**This chapter addresses the following:**

- Special Learners
- Categories of Impairment
- Types of Skills and Impairments
  *Motor Skills*
  *Communication Skills*
  *Cognitive Skills*
  *Social-Emotional Skills*

- Guidelines
- Inclusion/Mainstreaming
  *Gifted or Outstanding Talents*
- Cooperative Learning and Group Activities
- Chapter Conclusions
- Resources

## SPECIAL LEARNERS

Over thirty years ago, parents and public officials designed legislation to give quality education to children with special needs. For the purposes of this brief overview, broad issues and terms are addressed including Public Law (PL) 94–142, least restrictive environment (LRE), individual educational program (IEP), mainstreaming, inclusion, and exceptional children. The Individuals with Disabilities Education Act (IDEA) of 1990 redefined disability as a physical or mental impairment that limits major life activities. Passage and implementation of PL 94–142, the Education for All Handicapped Children Act of 1975, mandated that students with all types of disabilities be educated in the LRE, meaning that their education would be as close to normal as possible while offering specialized instructional support. Since 1975, the laws have been refined and schools across the nation have implemented programs for preschool and older children.

Parents are not always happy with the term *special* when applied to an individual child. The term *special* works for special education or Special Olympics, but parents are often displeased with any term indicating that their child is different or not like other children.

## CATEGORIES OF IMPAIRMENT

Exceptional children include children with many and varied handicapping conditions. Four general diagnostic categories include:

1. Developmental disabilities such as autism and mental retardation
2. Psychiatric disorders such as bipolar disorder and social maladjustment
3. Physical disabilities such as paralysis and paraplegia
4. Behavior disorders such as hyperactivity and attention deficit disorder

Michel and Pinson (2005) recommend using the word *person* in front of the diagnostic terms as in a "person with hyperactivity" (see Stress and Developmental Skills Model of Music Therapy, p. 24). One resource to check for correct usage is the People First language site (www.disabilityisnatural.com).

## TYPES OF SKILLS AND IMPAIRMENTS

There are many types of impairments to consider when working with children. Impairments are often not a single impairment but a combination of disabilities in more than one skill. The following sections provide a general overview.

### Motor Skills

Motor skills include both fine and gross skills. A person with cerebral palsy may have difficulty with grasping and holding an object. For example, the person may be able to hold a mallet for a xylophone for up to ten seconds but then loose grasp for no apparent reason. Eye-hand coordination may also make it difficult for children to strike the correct note on a xylophone. A solution is to remove all bars except tones from the pentatonic scale needed for performance. The child may improvise on these tones and create a sound that is compatible. In Chapter 7, we learned about how music and movement are intertwined. For children with disabilities, the addition of movement will enhance a music strategy. In a singing experience of "She'll Be Comin' Round the Mountain," adding movements to words such as "whoa back" can help all children become more involved.

### Communication Skills

Basic skills in communication include visual, auditory, tactile, and speech/language skills. Michel and Pinson (2005) detail each skill in terms of reception, perception, and conception. Reception is the receiving of the stimuli (for example, the ability to hear). Perception is the ability to identify the stimuli. Conception includes comparison, understanding, and developing ideas from the perceived information.

**VISUAL SKILLS**  Visual skills include the ability to receive information and to express emotions with the eyes. Students with visual impairments often learn more quickly than those with auditory impairments. Imagine how much more you might understand from a television program if you were able to hear without seeing than if you were only able to see the images. The typical school district is not equipped to provide services for people with severe visual impairment. Specialized instruction is available at most state schools for the blind.

**AUDITORY SKILLS**  Auditory skills are the ability to receive, process, and interpret auditory stimuli. One common problem is being able to discriminate between the various frequencies for speech. Another is a focus problem where individuals are not capable of excluding certain sounds from their field of perception.

**TACTILE SKILLS**  Tactile skills include the ability to receive, process, and interpret information through touch. Two common problems are tactile defensiveness and loss of tactile discrimination. The term *tactile defensiveness* is used to describe a child who is hypersensitive to touch. Such children will withdraw their hand or whatever part of the body is involved in touching. The phrase *loss of tactile discrimination* is used to describe a child who does not have the ability to identify surfaces. For example, if you place five instruments in a bag and ask a child to pick out the tambourine using touch alone, a child with loss of tactile discrimination might not be able to do so.

### Cognitive Skills

*[This section was contributed by Joe Pinson, MT-BC, Texas Woman's University, Denton.]*

Michel and Pinson (2005) define cognitive skills as "the abilities that an individual has acquired to enable him/her to *access*, *interpret*, *modify*, and *retain* information." Cognition plays a significant part in everything we do, think, say, feel, taste, and smell—in short, every experience of life. If you have difficulty in any skill area, your problem is in many instances rooted in the function of the brain (that is, cognition). Those who are cognitively challenged are usually diagnosed with a numerical rating or descriptive term (mild, moderate, and so on) that describes the severity of their condition. This rating usually represents the ability of the individual compared to a norm. In the public schools, "cognitive skills" usually means "academic skills" (colors, numbers, letters, and so on).

Teachers in the regular or "mainstreamed" classroom may encounter the following conditions:

1. Attention deficit/hyperactive disorder (ADHD) is characterized by difficulty in focusing on one task for any length of time, which leads to actions that are perceived as "hyperactive."
2. Auditory discrimination disorder is characterized by the inability to discriminate similarities and differences in sound stimuli, sometimes causing difficulty in understanding or producing patterns of speech.
3. Auditory memory disorder is characterized by the inability to retain segments of sound, usually leaving the child at a significant loss in learning.
4. Auditory sequencing disorder is characterized by difficulty in repeating rhythmic patterns associated with the production of music and speech.
5. Down syndrome is characterized by a slow rate of learning and a limited spectrum of auditory frequencies, caused by a genetic defect.
6. Rett syndrome is characterized by a progressive decline in physical abilities and the ability to communicate.
7. Traumatic brain injury is characterized in many instances by actual damage to the brain (as in combat or accidental injuries) and also by recurring memories that inhibit an individual's ability to learn (as in child abuse).

Teachers in special education classes or in the institutional environment may also encounter the following conditions:

1. Behavior disorder is characterized by inappropriate, attention-getting behaviors that interfere with the learning process.
2. Conduct disorder is characterized by physical actions that may have the capacity to injure others or destroy property.
3. Epilepsy is characterized by seizures (many or most usually controlled by medication) that may be only a temporary loss of connection with the moment, or that may involve loss of motor control, falling, and a longer-lasting disconnection.
4. Oppositional defiant disorder is characterized by an unwillingness to follow instructions and a defiant attitude (quite similar to a behavior disorder).
5. Post-traumatic stress disorder is characterized by helplessness related to recurring memories of stressful situations (usually psychological in nature instead of actual damage to the brain).

## Social-Emotional Skills

Social-emotional skills may be divided into three categories of function that include physical-neurological, psychological-behavioral, and psychoses-neuroses. Delays in the area of social-emotional skills are often accompanied by delays in other skill areas. For example, speech delays often lead to less desirable social interaction. The following are three general categories of functioning and types of problems that may occur in elementary school.

**PHYSICAL-NEUROLOGICAL**   *Developmental disability* is a general term for lack of development in all skills areas. The disabilities usually occur at birth or in early childhood (see http://www.cdc.gov/ncbddd/).

*Autism* and the *autism spectrum* disorders are complex. Autism is a bio-neurological disability that generally appears before the age of 3, and impacts development in social interaction, communication skills, and cognitive function. It is diagnosed in boys four times more often than in girls, and an overwhelming majority of people working with people with autism are women (see http://www.nationalautismassociation. org/index.php).

*Asperger's syndrome* is a neurobiological disorder often included in the autism spectrum. Signs and symptoms include inappropriate or minimal social interactions, robotic or repetitive speech, obsession with complex topics such as puzzles or music, average to above-average verbal cognitive ability but less skill in nonverbal cognitive ability, and odd behaviors or mannerisms such as walking on tiptoes.

**PSYCHOLOGICAL-BEHAVIORAL**  Generalized *anxiety disorder* is characterized by constant worry. The child may feel anxious and worried about things both large and small, such as school, performance (physical or musical), natural disasters, and health. Several risk factors may contribute to the anxiety. Risk factors include child hardships or adversity, serious illness, stress, and some personality and genetic factors. Also included under this category are *behavior disorders* and *conduct disorders* that have been defined previously.

**PSYCHOSES AND NEUROSES**  Children with psychoses and neuroses such as bipolar disorder and schizophrenia problems would be in a hospital setting rather than the school setting. To some extent, children in the schools may exhibit personality disorders characterized by extreme and inflexible behaviors that cause problems in learning and social interactions.

Any handicapping event affects more than one part of a child's functioning (Michel and Pinson 2005).

## GUIDELINES

An individual educational program (IEP) is a program designed specifically for one child to meet that child's needs. Music teachers are sometimes, but not often enough, asked to be part of the IEP team that analyzes the child's needs, determines objectives, and organizes instruction. Examples of IEPs are available from sources directed at special education (Graham and Beer 1980; Wilson 1996).

A specialized field of music, music therapy, exists to address the ways in which music aids children with special needs. Music therapy is available for young children and often available through the public schools. Therapists such as Joe Pinson, MT-BC (music therapist-board certified), treat children with disabilities in four primary areas of (1) motor, (2) communication, (3) cognitive, and (4) social/emotional skills (Michel and Pinson 2005). As music therapists work with people with disabilities, they often encounter extraordinary individuals with well-developed music traits or *savant* skills. *Savants* in music have special gifts, but their mode of learning is often just as restricted as those people who do not possess these gifts. Pinson (2002) identifies several key points to consider when working with children with disabilities: (1) nontraditional students need nontraditional methods of music education (this is more true for children with severe disabilities); many instrumental programs (bands, choirs, and so on) successfully include children with disabilities); (2) in many cases, people with disabilities do not respond to traditional methods of music education; (3) consider using techniques that do not require academic skills; (4) parents of special learners are often not expecting their children to progress from their state of disability to become soloists or section leaders in the band or choir; (5) children with a disability, who have been rejected by most every public organization, will be very satisfied if they can be included in some small way (for example, a single strike of a suspended cymbal at the end of a composition).

## INCLUSION/MAINSTREAMING

*Mainstreaming* and *inclusion* are terms referring to integrating learners with disabilities or exceptional skills with nondisabled learners. "[M]ainstreaming, integration, and inclusion will refer to the placement of children with disabilities into general music education settings" (Wilson 1996, 334). In preschools, children are normally included in the mainstream because many children who will later become identified as disabled are often not so identified during the preschool years. In the elementary school, more school districts are mandating inclusion of or mainstreaming disabled learners into the music class, and some districts are mandating preschool education for those identified as disabled learners before elementary school. There are several positive outcomes from inclusion in music education, including reaching children in a nonverbal way, providing social interaction with children from the entire school, and adapting a single experience in music for a wide range of abilities. For example,

Orff instrumental experiences have been adapted to the wide range of abilities in special populations (Pinson 2001).

One important question for mainstreaming or inclusion is: Can the included children keep up with the class? The children mainstreamed are often done so into younger classes but still may have difficulty functioning in that classroom. The optimal placement is often difficult and can lead to the child being placed in an environment that is not least restrictive.

MENC lists good practices for mainstreaming students into music education. They encourage teachers to (1) be involved in the decision for a child attending music; (2) determine class placement by developmentally appropriate practice; (3) avoid exceeding standard class size in placement; (4) include music education in the special education classes for students not mainstreamed; (5) use aides to help the music teacher while students are attending music; (6) avoid placing a disproportional number of mainstreamed students in the music class (MENC 1986).

In addition to MENC and the federal government, other individuals and groups promote the use of music and other arts for exceptional children. For example, the CIVITAS Child Trauma Clinic of Houston enrichment activities include healing arts such as massage and music, music and movement, and creative arts such as dance, drama, painting, sculpting, and music (Miranda et al. 1998). The Tomatis method is another therapy using music. Elongating the vowels or filtering the frequencies changes music listening examples to provide a therapeutic reorganization of auditory-processing difficulties or speech problems to improve speech. Alfred Tomatis, the founder of this therapy, investigated many selections of music and suggests that Mozart's music provides the best therapeutic results for auditory-processing difficulties or speech problems. Tomatis also uses Gregorian chant because of its rhythmic similarity to the rhythm of the heartbeat (although the chants are usually performed slower than young children's heartbeats and Gregorian chant is normally not steady in rhythm as is the heartbeat). For more detail, consult special education sources listed in the resource and reference sections.

## Gifted or Outstanding Talents

What is it to be gifted or have outstanding talents? The Jacob Javits Gifted and Talented Students Education Act passed Congress in 1988, to support talent development in the schools. The U.S. Department of Education definition of outstanding talent includes:

> Children and youth with outstanding talent perform or show the potential for performing at remarkably high levels of accomplishment when compared with others of their age, experience, or environment. Outstanding talents are present in children and youth from all cultural groups, across all economic strata, and in all areas of human endeavor. (U.S. Department of Education 1993)

Four questions about outstanding talents are important to ask for elementary education. First, are children born musically talented? Although a child may possess qualities of outstanding talent at birth, the interaction of environment with talents is of import. Potential alone will not result in outstanding talent; the child requires a rich musical environment to nurture talent. Second, is outstanding musical talent or musical giftedness an unchanging quality? Young children often exhibit talent, but tests of music abilities show developmental gains at least to the age of 9 years (Flohr 2004). Third, does outstanding talent in music go hand in hand with intelligence? Certainly not! Anyone who knows many musicians knows that this cannot be the case. Guilford and Gardner's ideas of multiple intelligence outline how a person may have talent in one area and not another. Fourth, what can the elementary teacher do for the outstandingly talented child? Teachers can take at least four important steps: (1) Seek to identify outstanding talent by observation and musical assessments; (2) supply the parents and child with resources for their development (for example, sources for music instruction in violin); (3) make an effort to be sure that the child is not bored in the classroom; and (4) give the child opportunities to develop the talents in class (Flohr 1987).

### ENGLISH AS A SECOND LANGUAGE: BUILDING LANGUAGE, INCORPORATING CULTURE; MAKING CONNECTIONS WITH MUSIC AND LITERATURE IN THE ELEMENTARY SCHOOL CLASSROOM

*[This was contributed by Melinda Cowart and Phap Dam, Texas Woman's University, Denton.]*

The real world of school in the United States includes a burgeoning student population whose members speak a first language other than English. Known as English language learners (ELLs), their numbers increased by 104 percent during the 1990s (National Clearinghouse for Bilingual Education 1999). Continued immigration and refugee resettlement add substantially to the variety of first languages represented in the public school classroom. A total of 53,725 refugees were resettled in the United States during 2005 alone. They arrived from many countries, including Somalia, Iran, Burma, Sudan, Ethiopia, and Vietnam. The five states that received the greatest numbers of new arrivals were Florida, Minnesota, Texas, California, and Washington (World Refugee Survey 2006). Green (2006) notes that, because more than 10 percent of students in grades pre-K through 12 in U.S. public schools are in the process of learning English as a second language, it is imperative to specifically attend to the unique and substantial needs of ELLs. If language minority students are to receive an effective and equitable education so that they may become all that they may be, it is essential that the teachers of culturally and linguistically diverse students possess the knowledge and skills necessary for creating a welcoming and stimulating classroom environment.

Many ELLs are newcomers to this country whereas others were born into families that have lived here for generations (Ovando et al. 2006). Whatever the circumstances may be, English language learners are always students in transition. Law and Eckes (2000) note that ELLs frequently encounter some of the following changes as they endeavor to learn English as a second or third language:

1. A change in geography or climate
2. A change from rural to urban settings
3. A change in the size of the living environment and or the economic situation
4. A change in the culture of school
5. A change in social status or opportunities or goals
6. The change itself—traumatic and frequently life-threatening
7. A change in the language
8. A change in the way language is used
9. A change in their relationship with their parents

At the same time ELLs are making significant adjustments within the school setting, they necessarily encounter additional challenges in adapting to changes that most certainly occur at home and in society. If the ELLs are newcomers, they have experienced what Igoa (1995) refers to as an uprooting experience. This experience is characterized by six stages, including mixed emotions during a time when the child feels sad to leave all that is familiar behind, but excitement about going to a new place. The second stage is a time of either excitement or fear about the journey to the new place. Although some children of newcomers may experience a journey that is marked by anticipation, the journey of refugees to a new location may be an escape that is full of danger. Curiosity defines the third stage, which is a time of inquisitiveness regarding what the new place may be like. The first three stages generally occur prior to arrival in the new host country. The last three stages occur once the child begins to attend school in a new land and encounters the challenges inherent to learning in an unfamiliar language.

When newcomers first enter school in the United States, they may experience a time of culture shock that includes homesickness, loss, further poverty, anxiety, and isolation as they try to adjust (Cowart 2007). The fifth stage of uprooting is a time in which newcomer ELLs face a choice to assimilate or abandon the heritage language and culture to fit in or to positively embrace both the heritage and new languages and cultures through a more positive acculturation experience.

The final stage involves entering the mainstream of school and society as a culturally and linguistically diverse student who has either turned away from what was once meaningful and valued or has been shown by an informed and caring educator how to participate fully in both languages and cultures. Teachers as well as the school environment have the greatest influence on a student's adjustment during the last three stages of the uprooting experience.

Linguistically diverse students are faced with unique challenges, including the need to learn the English language simultaneously with content area information. They also possess critical needs along with their culturally diverse counterparts. These needs include the invitation to participate, acceptance by teachers and other students, and seeing not only themselves, but also their experiences included in the school curriculum. Additional needs include experiencing success in school and realizing that they don't need to abandon the home culture and language to belong at school. Using culturally relevant materials, music, songs, and literature helps culturally and linguistically diverse students to believe that school is a welcoming and accepting environment in which to learn. Gay (2000) defines culturally relevant or culturally responsive teaching as utilizing students' cultural knowledge and previous experiences and knowledge to facilitate learning that is meaningful and effective for culturally and linguistically diverse students. When children hear, sing, or perform music from their own heritage culture, they feel welcomed by school in this new land and in experiences with second or third languages. Music that includes rhythms, instruments, words, or melodies from such countries as China, Afghanistan, Rwanda, Vietnam, Burma, and Mexico will validate the heritage cultures of ELLs, including the newest refugees and immigrants. Additionally, students of other cultures will have the opportunity to learn about certain musical aspects of a variety of cultures in a respectful, positive, nonthreatening manner.

Thematic teaching that leads students to make cross-curricular connections is effective in building language and comprehension of related content area instruction. When language development and literacy concepts are taught in tandem with key musical concepts through the use of children's literature and related music and songs, the cognitive and linguistic results are frequently surprising. Mathis (2007) has noted that multicultural children's literature has become a well-respected and established resource, promoting culturally responsive and culturally relevant teaching and learning. The affective impact of utilizing culturally relevant literature and music woven together in interdisciplinary lessons is critical to overall school success. For example, when teaching about instruments that were and still are used in music from Old China, such as the ehru, the music teacher might set the stage by reading aloud *Ruby's Wish*, a story of a young Chinese girl from Old China. When teaching some of the rhythms that are associated with various Latin American cultures, the music educator could read *Prietita y La Llorona*, a story of a ghostly woman who is found weeping and looking for her children near rivers and lakes. This book is a familiar scary story that most Latino children have heard and is available in English and Spanish. When a music educator combines the study of musical concepts with multicultural children's literature, the result is that all children, including ELLs, are able to learn musical content such as rhythm, repetition, keeping a steady beat, and high and low pitch. Simultaneously, the ELLs learn critical aspects of the English language such as pronunciation, vocabulary, idioms, and less familiar expressions while sensing that school is a welcoming place.

The music class offers every child the opportunity to participate in a safe environment where the expectations for everyone are the same and can be accomplished. It is not necessary for students to understand each word of a song that is being learned. In fact, in many instances, even children whose first and only language is English who are learning some of the more traditional tunes will not comprehend all of the words and their meanings. Children learn to sing the traditional Christmas carol "Silent Night" without fully understanding the line "Round yon virgin . . . ," and are still able to sense the overall gist of the song. English language learners have a similar experience. A former teacher of English as a second language has shared the story of an ELL who kept asking to sing the song about "Round John." Later, the teacher learned that the student was requesting to sing "Silent Night" and had simply misunderstood the familiar previously mentioned line. However, if the music educator provides enough modeling and guided practice of first the entire song, and then small segments of the song, the ELLs will be able to sing and participate even when much of the language is not yet comprehensible. Visual aids will further assist the students in learning music and musical concepts.

It is important to note that every teacher, not only a music teacher, can employ the suggestions in this section. If the music teacher is actually the regular classroom teacher who teaches music in addition to reading, science, social studies, and math, musical concepts and aspects of the English language may still be taught at the same time. Using the same strategies, the regular education teacher can use instruments and recordings along with culturally relevant children's books to achieve the same results.

For culturally and linguistically diverse students to experience the promise of democracy, they must feel included in the school setting, and they need to see themselves reflected in the curriculum. Knowledgeable and caring educators of diverse populations will embark on a journey of discovery about self and others, developing a sense of intercultural understanding that guides perception and critical educational decisions. Intercultural understanding involves a motivation to be a student of diverse cultures and their component languages, behaviors, values, and beliefs. When students perceive that a teacher has chosen to learn about their unique life experiences and to incorporate them into the curriculum, they sense that they are welcome in the classroom. Similarly, students who see themselves and their experiences reflected in the school curriculum tend to believe that school is a place for them. The expectation is that, as intercultural understanding increases for both teacher and students, academic achievement in music as well as English as a second language will be enhanced. The music class offers an excellent opportunity to promote intercultural understanding while accomplishing curricular goals and objectives.

## COOPERATIVE LEARNING AND GROUP ACTIVITIES

1. Take any lesson plan in this book and modify it to work with children with the following impairments: (1) communication skills, (2) motor skills, and (3) visual skills.
2. What would you identify as nontraditional methods of music education? Using the lesson plans in Part III as a basis, create a list of strategies that you believe would be helpful in working with children with cognitive skill impairments for several of those plans.
3. Using the plans in Part III, take at least four of them and design enrichment activities that you could use for your students who are more musically advanced than others in the class. For the same lessons, design remedial activities for students who may need some extra help.
4. Visit an English as a second language (ESL) class near you, and observe how music is used in the classroom. Interview the teacher and the students to find out what music means to them; then, using the lesson plans in Part III as a starting point, develop alternate activities to work with ESL students.
5. Research the CIVITAS and Tomatis programs (music therapy) and other music therapy programs. Are any strategies presented in music therapy adaptable to the music classroom?

## Chapter Conclusions

Teachers find children with many and often multiple impairments and special needs in the schools. Knowledge of the ramifications of the special needs and impairments are important when addressing the learning issues resulting from the impairment(s), to accommodate children with disabilities mainstreamed into the classroom, and to construct individual education programs. Language differences are also important considerations for teachers. For culturally, linguistically diverse students to experience the promise of democracy, they must feel included in the school setting, and they need to see themselves reflected in the curriculum.

## Resources

National Autism Association: http://www.nationalautism association.org/index.php

National Association for Gifted Children: http://www.nagc.org/resourcedirectory.aspx

Centers for Disease Control and Prevention National Center on Birth Defects and Developmental Disabilities (NCBDDD): http://www.cdc.gov/ncbddd/

The Center for Applied Linguistics at www.cal.org

National Association for Bilingual Education at www.nabe.org

Teachers of English for Speakers of Other Languages at www.tesol.org

PART III

# Musical Experiences

essons are grouped according to the avenues of learning music from Part II. Each chapter includes four lessons grouped into the categories of pre-K through K, grades 1 and 2, grades 3 and 4, and grades 5 and 6. These lessons are cumulative from K through sixth grade. The lesson sequence from year to year illustrates how concepts may be taught and reinforced over a continuum of seven years (K–6 grades), as well as how many of the same pieces of music can be used to help reinforce these concepts. For example, *Carnival of the Animals* may be used to teach many aspects of music throughout elementary school. The procedure sections of the lesson plans are in a narrative style so you can see in your mind's eye how the lesson would progress in class. It is recommended that you use less narrative and more short, to-the-point, student-centered steps in your own lesson plans.

## CHAPTER 14

# Listening Lessons

## LESSON 1

Higher and lower sounds

### Level

Prekindergarten to K

### Project/Activities

Class activity: Students will identify, play, sing, and discriminate between high and low sounds; they will be able to explain how and why they can be used to indicate or illustrate animals.

### Previous Knowledge and Skills

Ability to discriminate aurally between extreme high and low sounds of the piano

### Music Concepts and Objectives/Assessment

**STANDARDS ADDRESSED:** Performing on instruments, alone and with others, a varied repertoire of music; improvising melodies, variations, and accompaniments; composing and arranging music within specified guidelines; and listening to, analyzing, and describing music (MENC 2007)

**INSTRUCTIONAL OBJECTIVES:** The students will discriminate aurally between high and low sounds, as indicated by using appropriate bodily gestures. They will also create and improvise high and low accompaniments to particular animals portrayed in the *Carnival of the Animals*.

**ASSESSED BY:** Observing the students improvising either vocally or on available classroom instruments (with long and short melody bars, if available)

### Science Concepts and Objectives/Assessment

**STANDARDS ADDRESSED:** Life science, physical science (NSTA 2008)

**INSTRUCTIONAL OBJECTIVE:** The students describe characteristics of the elephant and the fish, and their native environments. Students also identify that a short or small instrument makes high sounds, whereas large instruments make low sounds.

**ASSESSED BY:**   Having students identify, from a list, characteristics of the two animals; having students aurally identify instruments as large or small by the sounds they make; having students make vocal sounds (which will be high) and comparing them with a grown male voice (which will be low), because the vocal mechanisms of the children are small and will sound high when compared to the voice of an adult male

## Time for Lesson

Duration: 30 minutes

## Materials/Resources

1. Recording of Saint-Saens's *Carnival of the Animals*: "The Elephant" and "Aquarium." The chamber version was used for this lesson (from Sony Essential Classics, SBK 47655, Camille Saint-Saens's Symphony No. 3, *Carnival of the Animals,* and "Danse Macabre," Philadelphia Orchestra with Eugene Ormandy and others)
2. Classroom instruments of various sizes
3. Drawing paper, pencils, or crayons
4. Pictures of various kinds of fish
5. Pictures of elephants

Children can feel and hear the string bass vibrate in the "The Elephant" from *Carnival of the Animals.*

*Photo courtesy of Union City School District, Pennsylvania*

## Procedure

**ANTICIPATORY SET (ATTENTION HOOK)**   Start with the hook/anticipatory set. Ask, "How many of you have been to the zoo? What animals do you see in the zoo? Do they all live in places of the same size? How big are they?" Ask the students to imagine how an animal may be portrayed in music (for example, slow, fast, flying, swimming, running, furry, hairless, and so on). The teacher can improvise animal sounds using an instrument or vocally. Students may also do this, if they are permitted. Come up with a list of how the class thinks small animals would sound in music and how large animals would sound in music. Use simple terms (for example, *slow, fast, high, low, loud, soft*).

After the students have experimented with different kinds of sounds for different kinds of animals, tell them that they are going to listen to a piece of music that is about fish swimming in an aquarium (if the school has one, this would be a good time for a visit). Ask the students to hypothesize and demonstrate, with vocal or instrumental sounds, the kinds of music they think various animals might make. Would the music be made of high or low sounds? Or both? How might the water sound?

Make a list of the hypothesized sounds (either using pictures or words, depending upon the students' literacy skills). Say, "Listen for a sound you thought might sound like an animal as you hear this piece. Be certain to remember what it was like and be able to tell about sound and the animal."

Play *Aquarium* from the CD or audio file (approximately 2:05 minutes). After the piece is finished, help the students to see if any of their hypotheses were true. They can even add sounds to the list that they didn't expect to hear. If the students are familiar with some instruments, they may also be able to name the ones they hear. Play the piece one more time, while the students pretend to be fish swimming in an aquarium.

Then tell the students you will play another piece, but they have to figure out what animal it may be. Play "The Elephant" from the CD (approximately 1:24 minutes). After the recording finishes, help the students find out if the instrument that played the melody played high or low sounds (answer: low), if the speed of the beat was fast or slow (answer: slow, but not too slow), and ask them to suggest possible animals it may be. Play the piece one more time so the students can hear everything (they may come up with some other ideas). After the piece is finished, students can add to the list and then vote on which animal it was. After they find out it is the elephant, they may wish to imitate elephants as they hear the piece one more time. A story about what the elephants are doing could also be generated.

Next, if there is time, the students may be able to go back to their seats and color pictures of fish or elephants (this is where the other pictures may come in handy).

Before leaving class, you can play excerpts of the two pieces heard in class, and have the students hold up their pictures if it matches the music.

## Evaluation

Look for movements that indicate high sounds (waving arms over the head), low sounds (waving arms closer to floor). Also look and listen for physical indications of vocal stress if students try to make sounds that are too high or too low when vocalizing.

Questions could include: Who can play high sounds on their instruments? Who can play low sounds? Which ones would go with which animal? Can you show me if you hear high or low sounds with your arms as I play the piano? How does a fish differ from an elephant? Which is usually larger? How do they move?

## Continuing the Lesson

Students who have pets at home may wish to create a piece of music on whatever instruments they have available to them at home (for example, a piano or some play instruments). They can perform their pieces for the class.

They may also find it interesting to go through their own song collections about animals and see if high and low sounds are used to indicate small and large animals. They may be invited to bring these recordings to class as examples. These pieces may be used to help prepare students to learn about fast and slow in a later lesson.

## LESSON 2

Higher and lower sounds

## Level

Grades 1 and 2

## Project/Activities

Students will identify, play, sing, and discriminate between higher and lower pitches and how they can be used to indicate or illustrate particular animals (in this case, the cuckoo bird).

## Previous Knowledge and Skills

Ability to aurally discriminate between the extreme high and low sounds played on flute, clarinet, and low instrument like a tuba (the clarinet is used as the cuckoo), and also between higher and lower sounds in a continuum of a melody. Students also need to be familiar with the do-mi and mi-do intervals (major third, ascending and descending). Being able to identify melodic movement from high to low and low to high (getting higher, getting lower) in a melody is a much more difficult discrimination task than only identifying high and low sounds.

## Music Concepts and Objectives/Assessment

**STANDARDS ADDRESSED:**  Performing on instruments, alone and with others, a varied repertoire of music; improvising melodies, variations, and accompaniments; composing and arranging music within specified guidelines; and listening to, analyzing, and describing music (MENC 2007)

**INSTRUCTIONAL OBJECTIVES:**  The students will aurally discriminate between higher and lower sounds, using appropriate bodily gestures. They will also create and improvise high and low accompaniments to particular animals portrayed in the *Carnival of the Animals*.

**ASSESSED BY:**  Observing the students improvising either vocally or on available classroom instruments (with long and short melody bars, if available)

## Science Concepts and Objectives/Assessment

**STANDARDS ADDRESSED:**   Life science, physical science (NSTA 2008)

**INSTRUCTIONAL OBJECTIVE:**   The students describe characteristics of birds (local to exotic), and their native environments. Students also identify that short or small instruments and birds make higher sounds, whereas larger instruments and birds make lower sounds.

**ASSESSED BY:**   Having students identify, from a list, characteristics of the cuckoo and other birds; having students aurally identify instruments as large and small by the sounds they make; and having students make vocal sounds (which will be high) and comparing them with a grown male voice (which will be low), because the vocal mechanisms of students are quite small. It would be interesting to have students compare the sounds they made from the previous year, to see if their own voices are starting to get lower (some of them will be).

## Time for Lesson

Duration: 30 minutes

## Materials/Resources

1. Recording of Saint-Saens's *Carnival of the Animals:* "The Cuckoo in the Depths of the Woods." For this particular lesson, the chamber version was used (from Sony Essential Classics, SBK 47655, Camille Saint-Saens's Symphony No. 3, *Carnival of the Animals,* and "Danse Macabre," Philadelphia Orchestra with Eugene Ormandy and others)
2. Classroom instruments of various sizes
3. Drawing paper, pencils, or crayons
4. Picture of various kinds of birds (small and large) including a cuckoo

## Procedure

**ANTICIPATORY SET (ATTENTION HOOK)**   What birds do you know? What kinds of sounds do they make? Describe the ones you like the most. Can you make some of their sounds? You can also play the "Aquarium" and "Elephant" from *Carnival of the Animals* to reinforce high and low, and from there, move to working on higher and lower. Also, you can reinforce the mi-do descending relationship if students are familiar with solfège. Continue to have the students hypothesize how a bird may be portrayed in music (for example, slow, fast, flying, swimming, running, pecking, swooping, and so on). You can improvise these sounds on a piano, moving from high sounds to lower sounds, especially for swooping behaviors, and students may do so, also, if they are permitted. Come up with a list of how the class thinks small birds would sound in music and how large *large* would sound in music. Review simple terms (*slow, fast, high, low, loud, soft,* and so on).

If using the song "Cuckoo, Where Are You" to prepare for this activity, please note that the interval for that song is a descending minor third (sol-mi), whereas Saint-Saens uses the descending major third (mi-do) for this piece. Saint-Saens uses the concert C# to A pitches. This can cause confusion if you don't catch this right away. Changing the minor third to a major third in the "Cuckoo, Where Are You" song is not all that difficult to do, and is recommended in this situation.

After the students have experimented with different kinds of sounds for different kinds of birds, and you have moved them into identifying and imitating a cuckoo bird, tell them that you are going to play a piece of music for them about a cuckoo bird in the woods. What sound would they expect to hear the cuckoo make? Have the students hypothesize about what kinds of music they may hear that would indicate the forest. Would it be made of high or low sounds? Or both? At this point, you may wish to make a list of the hypothesized sounds (either using pictures or words, depending upon the students' literacy skills).

Play "Cuckoo in the Depths of the Woods" from the CD or audio file (approximately 45 seconds). After the piece finishes, help the students to find out if any of their hypotheses were true. They can even add to the list sounds they didn't expect to hear. If the students are familiar with some instruments, they may also be able to name the ones they hear (the clarinet is prominent in this piece, as is the piano). Play the piece one more time, and the students can pretend to be a cuckoo resting and calling in the woods. They could also be solfège cuckoos in that, when they hear the cuckoo, they make the appropriate hand signal (mi-do) or a simple higher-to-lower hand motion if they do not know the hand signals. They can also be sleepy cuckoos, baby cuckoos, lost cuckoos, and angry cuckoos. This would allow them to experiment with many expressive ways to perform the same two pitches.

Next, if there is time, the students may be able to go back to their seats and color pictures of a cuckoo to add to the fish and elephants they drew earlier (if you are keeping a music portfolio from K-6). Before leaving class, you can play excerpts of the three pieces already heard in class ("Aquarium," "Elephant," "Cuckoo"), and have the students hold up their picture if it matches the music. These can be turned into puppets for later use, if desired. If students have a music folder that moves with them from year to year, then these pictures would add to their collection.

## Evaluation

Look for movements that indicate higher sounds (arms moving upward), lower sounds (arms moving downward). Also look and listen for physical indications of vocal stress if students try to make sounds that are too high or too low when vocalizing.

Questions could include: Who can play high sounds on their instrument? (Or who can sing high sounds?) Who can play low sounds? Can you play a melody that moves from high to low? How does a small bird, like a cuckoo differ from a large bird, like an eagle? Where do they each live? What do they eat? How do they move? If we were to use a clarinet to make sounds like a cuckoo, where would it play the sounds, in the higher or the lower notes of the instrument? What about if a tuba was going to play the cuckoo? Where would it toy the sounds?

## Continuing the Lesson

Students may wish to create a piece of music about a bird of their choice (chickens, eagles, condors, robins, crows, and so on) on whatever instruments they have available to them at home (for example, a piano or some toy instruments). They can perform their pieces for the class.

## LESSON 3

ABA and ABACA form

## Level

Grades 3 and 4

## Project/Activities

Students will use listening sheets to help them discover the musical characteristics of the sections of one piece of music. They will also identify music that is already familiar to them, and see if music taken from one piece of music and put into another makes it better, worse, funny, or sad (Grade 4).

## Previous Knowledge and Skills

Students should have mastered the concepts of pitch in that it moves higher and lower, and that notes strung together create melodies. They also need to be able to discriminate between sections of music that are the same or different, and identify simple musical forms (AB and ABA by Grade 3) with perhaps the rondo being new (Grade 4). They should also know that sections differ not only by melody (which is often the main indication) but also by other characteristics that may include differences in rhythms used, instruments, and texture. Students will already be familiar with using listening sheets (see Chapter 5 on listening for a sample).

## Music Concepts and Objectives/Assessment

**STANDARDS ADDRESSED:**   Performing on instruments, alone and with others, a varied repertoire of music; improvising melodies, variations, and accompaniments; composing and arranging music within specified guidelines; and listening to, analyzing, and describing music (MENC 2007)

**INSTRUCTIONAL OBJECTIVES:**   The students will identify and list musical characteristics of sections of music (A, B, and C) to indicate form in a piece from the *Carnival of the Animals*.

**ASSESSED BY:**   Students listing and describing the characteristics of each section, and also by showing physical hand motions or holding up labeled flash cards (A, B, C) to indicate sections as they hear them.

## National Science Concepts

**STANDARDS ADDRESSED:**   Life science, physical science (NSTA 2008)

**INSTRUCTIONAL OBJECTIVE:**   The students identify characteristics of fossils of various dinosaurs and other prehistoric life. Comparing and contrasting previous with current beliefs about how prehistoric life behaved reinforces how knowledge can change over time.

**ASSESSED BY:**   Having students identify from or generate a list of characteristics of the T-rex, velociraptor, triceratops, or other prehistoric life forms they are familiar with; having them describe, draw, create a story about fossils; and finally, having them research online about "living" fossils to see what they find, and compile a class list (in this case, you would need to select websites for students to study. *Living fossils* are generally creatures that are very much like their ancient predecessors.).

## Time for Lesson

Duration: 30 minutes

## Materials/Resources

1. Recording of Saint-Saens's *Carnival of the Animals: Fossiles*. For this particular lesson, the chamber version was used (from Sony Essential Classics, SBK 47655, Camille Saint-Saens's Symphony No. 3, *Carnival of the Animals,* and "Danse Macabre," Philadelphia Orchestra with Eugene Ormandy and others)
2. Drawing paper, pencils, or crayons
3. Flash cards or index cards

## Procedure

**ANTICIPATORY SET (ATTENTION HOOK)**   So far, we have listened to "Aquarium," "The Elephant," and "The Cuckoo" from the *Carnival of the Animals*. What other animals do you think he wrote about? Why do you think he called it a carnival? After brief hypothesizing by students, indicate that the animals to be listened to today include fossils and a swan. Fossils may get particular interest because they are not generally regarded as being currently living, but are remains of creatures that previously lived. A discussion on fossils will lead to hypothesizing to what kinds of fossils there are; for this piece, Saint-Saens uses musical fossils.

*and/or*

Review what musical form is (at the level they are familiar: either same-different comparisons or by the letter names).

*and/or*

Play any of the earlier pieces, or part of them, to see if students can identify the forms (as they are pieces with which are already familiar).

**Historical Note for Teacher**   Saint-Saens uses fossils in this piece to indicate his satirical treatment of older pieces of music and old compositional techniques. He includes his own "Danse Macabre," "Twinkle Twinkle Little Star," and a bit of "Una Voce Poco Fa" (Rosina's aria) from Rossini's opera *The Barber of Seville,* among others. "Twinkle Twinkle" will be the most recognized, and if the students are familiar with "Danse Macabre," they will recognize that too. If listening for the "A" only (Grade 3), then the "Danse Macabre" quote is indicative of that particular section.

After the students have provided evidence that they are able to discriminate between same and different sections in music, or use the appropriate terminology, hand out the listening sheets (see the sample in Chapter 5, modified as needed for this activity).

Play an excerpt of the A section in "Fossiles" (for now, the three short phrases at the beginning will work well enough). Play again as needed. Check to make sure they get it by perhaps playing several other three-phrased melodies on the piano and then playing the one you want them to listen for. Remember, they need to be familiar with the melody on many levels before playing the recording.

When students indicate that they are familiar with the theme (A), then play the piece and have them either (1) raise their hands, or (2) hold up flash cards with A on it when they hear the main theme.

Have the students listen again, this time using their worksheets and circling what they hear in terms of instruments, melodic characteristics, meter, tempo, and so on. They may listen as many times as needed. If continuing with an extended activity (see the following), having them circle these characteristics in one color (markers or crayons) will be especially effective. Have the students trade papers and check them. The classroom shares answers, and generates a list of what constitutes the A section. From here, they can continue on or save the rest for the next class.

## Evaluation

Look for correct card holding, listing, and checking. Having students help each other will be useful. Allow for multiple listenings to encourage students to listen constructively and to identify what they hear.

Questions could include: What is a living fossil? What are they made out of? Where do we find fossils? What songs are musical fossils to you?

## Continuing the Lesson

Compare and contrast with the section in between the first two A sections—using the listening sheets. In this first contrasting section, the students will hear "Twinkle Twinkle Little Star." Circling what they hear in a different crayon or marker color will help them visually identify the differences in the sections. If students are doing well at this, then have them continue with the second contrasting section, using a different color. The colors will indicate to them that they are hearing three different sections. Listen to the entire piece again to find out how many times they hear each section (A section is three times, B and C sections are each once, although you may refer to them by colors, such as the red, green, and yellow sections, for example).

At this point, if students are familiar with using the letters to indicate forms, then they can discover this is an ABACA form. If they are only working on hearing the same sections and differentiating them from contrasting sections, then they discover that sections can be repeated. Students can bring in to the next class a recording of their favorite music that is either rondo form (difficult to find) or that uses repeated sections. Listening sheets could be used with these in the next class as well, to practice the activity.

Listening for form on these shorter scales will help them develop the listening and discrimination skills to listen to larger forms of music as well.

## LESSON 4

Identifying musical parody and satire

### Level

Grades 5 and 6

### Project/Activities

Students will identify musical practices, such as quoting previously written music in a new piece, as part of musical satire and parody. In turn, they will create their own pieces of music to illustrate the same. Classical music is often presented in the guise of being serious, and that it should be taken seriously. However, many composers from the medieval period to the present had terrific senses of humor, and it showed in their music. The key was to be able to pick up the humor, and that requires a higher level of sophisticated listening skills.

### Previous Knowledge and Skills

Everything listed in the previous lesson plans needs to be mastered for this lesson. Students need to be attentive and critical listeners by this time, and should also have a working and applicable knowledge of musical terminology (meter, tempo, melody, and so on). Students may already be familiar with the terms *irony, parody,* and *satire,* depending upon their reading level and preferences.

### Music Concepts and Objectives/Assessment

**STANDARDS ADDRESSED:** Performing on instruments, alone and with others, a varied repertoire of music; improvising melodies, variations, and accompaniments; composing and arranging music within specified guidelines; and listening to, analyzing, and describing music (MENC 2007)

**INSTRUCTIONAL OBJECTIVES:** The students will identify, list musical characteristics of several pieces of music that indicate the music is being satirical or a parody. Students will create their own pieces of music to illustrate satire and/or parody.

**ASSESSED BY:** Students listing and describing the characteristics of each section, and by creating their own pieces of music

### Language Arts Concepts and Objectives/Assessment

**STANDARDS ADDRESSED:** Students read a wide range of literature from many periods in many genres to build an understanding of the many dimensions (for example, philosophical, ethical, aesthetic) of human experience; students apply knowledge of language structure, language conventions (for example, spelling and punctuation), media techniques, figurative language, and genre to create, critique, and discuss print and nonprint texts; students participate as knowledgeable, reflective, creative, and critical members of a variety of literacy communities (NCTE).

**INSTRUCTIONAL OBJECTIVES:** The students will identify literary satire and create their own example of literary satire.

(As suggested resources, please review books by Jon Scieszka and Lane Smith: *The True Story of the Three Little Pigs, The Stinky Cheese Man and Other Fairly Stupid Tales, Science Verse, Math Curse,* and *Cowboy and Octopus,* all published by Viking Press. The words as well as the pictures communicate parody at a level these younger students will understand.)

**ASSESSED BY:** Having students identify literary satire and create their own literary satire.

## Time for Lesson(s)

Duration: 90 minutes (two 45-minute class periods, or three 30-minute periods)

## Materials/Resources

1. Recording of Saint-Saens's *Carnival of the Animals:* "Fossiles," "Tortoises," "Pianistes," and "Personnages with Long Ears." For this particular lesson, the chamber version was used (from Sony Essential Classics, SBK 47655, Camille Saint-Saens's Symphony No. 3, *Carnival of the Animals,* and "Danse Macabre," Philadelphia Orchestra with Eugene Ormandy and others)
2. Index cards with musical terms on them (for example, *high melody, low melody, fast tempo, slow tempo, major key, minor key, simple texture, complex texture*).
3. Recording of the "Infernal Galop" (more commonly known as the cancan) by Jacques Offenbach (from the opera *Orpheus in the Underworld*). If a recording is not available, you can play the melody on the piano.

You can add more if desired, depending upon classroom instruments available, styles, and songs students already know from their years of music class.

## Procedure

**ANTICIPATORY SET (ATTENTION HOOK)**    So far, we have listened to "Aquarium," the "Elephant," the "Cuckoo," and "Fossiles" from the *Carnival of the Animals*. Let's listen to them again to see if Saint-Saens was trying to be funny. How would the music be funny? How do you think composers would try to make music sound funny? Do you read the funnies in the newspaper? Which ones do you like the best? Why? Do any of you listen to music that you think is funny? Who? Why is it funny to you? What about television shows? Do you find any of them particularly funny? Why?

Some students may be familiar with more adult TV programs, such as *South Park, The Simpsons,* and *Family Guy.* You would need to monitor carefully any references to these shows in class, because some students may be offended.

The students listen to each selection to discover if any of the pieces were funny. Some students may think they are all funny, whereas some may think they are not funny. However, most will remember the intended humor of the "Fossiles." After each piece, vote on whether the piece was funny or not, and list characteristics on the blackboard that contributed to the funniness. It is important to point out that what is funny to one person is not always funny to another, so having differences of opinion is fine.

Because the "Fossiles" are generally considered funny, have the students listen again and identify what they hear particularly that makes it funny. Most will note the use of "Twinkle Twinkle Little Star." You can point out the others (the Rossini quote and Saint-Saens's use of his own "Danse Macabre").

At this point, introduce the topic of musical parody. Many composers wrote this way, usually by taking a piece of music written by someone else (or themselves) and putting it in their own new pieces, but changing it so it would sound out of place or funny. This was often done not to necessarily be mean-spirited, but to instead poke fun at an outdated compositional style or a popular song.

Play an excerpt of the Offenbach "Infernal Galop" (more commonly known as the cancan melody) from the opera *Orpheus in the Underworld* on the piano, or on a recording. Most students will recognize the melody. Ask them to describe the song musically by tempo, melody, and tonality. Next, for students who recognize the song, they will often be familiar with the dance that goes with it (the high leg kicking in a line, often exemplified by the Rockettes chorus line at Radio City Music Hall). Have the students describe, and if they are game, form a kick line. Have them start slowly and then try to get faster and stay in sync with each other.

After they have tried to do this dance (and may be a bit tired out), ask them to describe characteristics and provide adjectives of the dance (*high-kicking, energetic, tiring, fast*). Next, have them list any animals that are the total opposites from those adjectives (for example, sloths and turtles).

Have them hypothesize and demonstrate how a turtle or sloth would dance the cancan. Next, have them list how the music would be changed to accommodate the sloth or turtle or any other slow-moving animal. List the characteristics on the board (for example, slower, lower melody, and so on).

Listen to "Tortoises" from *Carnival of the Animal,* and have students check their hypotheses. Have a brief discussion with the students on why the tortoise doing the cancan is a silly thing. Having them draw an illustration would further reinforce the idea.

**Historical Note for Teacher**   The original French version of the cancan dance is very risqué, but the form in the United States has been changed over time to be much more family-friendly. Saint-Saens wrote this particular parody because Offenbach's "Infernal Galop" was so popular that it was played all over France, and this was one way to poke fun at that popularity.

Saint-Saens didn't stop with parodying turtles and the cancan. He did several more in the *Carnival of Animals*. Another approach is parodying the exercises, which we call etudes in music, which young piano students need to practice over and over.

See how many students in the class take piano lessons. Ask them if they practice scales and arpeggios. If students in the class can demonstrate this, have them do so. If not, you can demonstrate (the ones used in "Pianistes" are easy to replicate on the piano, starting on C).

It is important to note to the students that these kinds of exercises are important on all instruments to help develop technique and to keep musicians' hands in shape (in the same way athletes need to stay in shape). However, the drawback is that they can get boring, especially after one has been doing them for twenty years or more. How would one's attitude be when sitting down at the piano to play these etudes after all that time? Have students hypothesize about attitudes and behaviors after many years of practicing the same thing over and over (bored, can't stand it, angry, daydreaming, and so on).

Play the recording of "Pianistes." Ask the students if they get the impression that the piano player is having fun or is bored (piano students will more likely pick up on the very pedantic and painful way the pianists are deliberately playing).

If the students are sophisticated enough, then you can play the most scathing piece of the *Carnival of Animals*, "Personnages with Long Ears." Ask students to describe what animals have long ears, and perhaps aren't very smart (many may come up with donkeys, rabbits, and so on). Play the piece, and ask the students to identify what animal the violin is imitating (it is obviously a donkey). Ask the students whom they think Saint-Saens may have been poking fun at (you may get many answers, or none at all). Officially, Saint-Saens was making fun of music critics.

To move the students into creating their own musical parodies, you may wish to play two other examples (that have words) that parody recipes or menus:

1. John Rutter's "Let me tickle your fancy, Toad" from *The Wind in the Willows*. (*Three Musical Fables*, Collegium Records, 1983. Also available via iTunes). You may need to translate the British English and describe the food (tripe, bloaters in brine, sweetmeats, pig's trotters, and so on) to help the students understand these traditional English dishes.
2. William Bolcom's "Lime Jello Marshmallow Cottage Cheese Surprise." Many recordings are available; however, there is a streamed version of the composer and his wife, Joan Morris, performing the piece at http://www.carlinamerica.com/titles/titles.cgi?MODULE=DETAIL&ID=625&terms=19. Students can list the ingredients and menu items in the song (which are truly nauseating) and then analyze the music to see how the music helps add to the parody.

## Evaluation

Look for indications of senses of humor, and make sure the students laugh during these particular classes.

Questions could include: So far, you have learned about how composers create parody in music. How may we do that in writing? Are there any stories you know that would be good if they were redone as a parody?

## Continuing the Lesson

At this point, students can compose their own parodies, either individually or as a class. You can have the students select a song they already know (that lends itself to parody) from a predesigned list. Going back to songs they learned when very young are good materials with which to start. Next, using the index cards with the musical characteristics on them (high melody, low melody, fast tempo, and so on), they can select the characteristics they wish to change in the music to create a parody. Finally, if allowable, words can be changed, or other performance aspects added to embellish the parody. Students can also come up with their own menu or recipe parody songs.

Students can create their own musical parodies for homework (make sure the directions are very clear as on how to do this so there is no confusion). If students are able, they can perform their parody in the next class (or classes), and have students see if they can figure out what is being parodied.

CHAPTER | **15**

# Vocal Lessons

## LESSON 1

Exploring and using the voice healthfully

### Level

Prekindergarten to K

### Project/Activities

Students (individually and in groups) engage in activities to discover and define the healthy parameters of their voices. They investigate and create a number of vocal sounds and ways to keep their voices healthy. Students will create their own water cups, and "I'm on Vocal Rest" buttons.

### Previous Knowledge and Skills

Students need to be able to talk and phonate healthfully; the activity may reveal that students have vocal issues that may not have been documented yet.

### Music Concepts and Objectives/Assessment

**STANDARDS ADDRESSED:**  Singing alone and with others, a variety of music (MENC 2007)

**INSTRUCTIONAL OBJECTIVES:**  Students will demonstrate using their voices to make many sounds, and will be able to delineate between healthy sounds and unhealthy sounds.

**ASSESSED BY:**  Listening, watching, and observing student vocal behaviors

### Science National Standards

**SCIENCE NATIONAL STANDARDS ADDRESSED:**  Standard F—Science in personal and social perspectives: Personal health (NSTA 2008)

**INSTRUCTIONAL OBJECTIVES:**  Students will demonstrate healthy vocal behaviors and provide answers on how to take care of their voices.

**ASSESSED BY:**  Students complete vocal health projects and demonstrate healthy vocal behaviors.

### Time for Lesson

Duration: 20–30 minutes

## Materials/Resources

1. Recordings of animal sounds (many available online)
2. Paper water cups
3. Paper buttons with "I'm on vocal rest" or a mouth with a line drawn through it to signify "not talking," or simply, a mouth with "No" over it
4. Button maker (optional, but recommended)
5. Safety scissors, crayons
6. Stencil or traceable image of a water drop
7. Pictures of animals and their mouths
8. Pictures of humans yawning, talking, singing, and calling

## Procedure

**ANTICIPATORY SET (ATTENTION HOOK)** "I am talking to you right now using my what? Yes, my voice. Do you all have voices? Does anyone else you know have a voice? Do any animals have voices? What are the ways we can use our voices?" At this point, you could entertain a number of answers, such as we talk, sing, yell, whisper, bark, sigh, yawn, and so on. We use them to call someone, to give directions, and to talk to each other.

Students experiment with different vocal sounds, using the pictures of animals and humans as guides. What you need to watch for is that the students don't get carried away and get too loud or too high in their vocalizations. This is also where you can monitor and identify students who may be experiencing vocal problems. Conduct a sound tapestry of various animal voices in concert, or other kinds of vocal sounds.

Next, ask, "Has your throat ever hurt when you talk? What about when you have a cold? What about when you are tired? What if you yell too much?" Most of the students have likely experienced some vocal distress; however, it is important to let those who have not experienced distress know that this is a very good thing.

Ask the students what they do when their voices hurt. For most, it will mean they don't talk. Students are to be praised for that.

Reinforce that there are three behaviors needed to take care of voices: (1) don't yell or scream, (2) drink lots of water, and (3) be quiet when our voices hurt, because they need to heal. From here, they can go to the next activity of making special drinking cups (they can be stenciled or have a few water drops on them, with the child's name on it) and they can make their "I'm on vocal rest" buttons that they can wear when their throats feel bad and they don't want to talk. Vocal rest buttons can be laminated, and can be held on with tape or another sticky material. Students may take two home and keep one at school in their cubbies, along with their special drinking cups.

**Special Notes to Teachers** Whispering is actually very stressful to the voice, so whispering when the voice hurts can make it worse in the long run. Overuse is also another problem, especially diagnosed in students who talk far too much and often mistake yelling for singing.

## Evaluation

Have students remind you of the three behaviors they need to do to keep their voices healthy, and of all the different ways voices can be used.

## Continuing the Lesson

It is expected that at this point, students will be more careful about how they use their voices and in monitoring their own vocal behaviors. This should continue for the remainder of music classes the students have in their education.

## LESSON 2

Extending Vocal Range Healthfully

## Level

Grades 1 and 2

Bow Wow Wow

Bow wow wow    Whose dog art thou?

Lit - tle Tom-my Tuck-er's dog.    Bow wow wow. Wooof!

**FIGURE 15.1** "Bow Wow Wow"

## Project/Activities

Students sing the song "Bow Wow Wow" by rote, and play the game (see Figure 15.1). They demonstrate healthy vocal singing by singing with a larynx in resting position, breathing properly, starting and ending sounds healthfully, and singing at a healthy dynamic level.

## Previous Knowledge and Skills

Students should already be able to discriminate moving upward (higher) and downward (lower) vocally. They need to be able to comfortably sing in the range of F4 to D5 with no evident vocal stress. By this time, they should have had some simple instruction in breathing efficiently for singing and singing with a resting larynx (a resting larynx is one that does not move excessively vertically when singing). They need to already know some very basic vocal anatomy (larynx, lungs, tongue, mouth, and so on).

## Music Concepts and Objectives/Assessment

**STANDARDS ADDRESSED:**  Singing alone and with others, a variety of music (MENC 2007)

**INSTRUCTIONAL OBJECTIVES:**  Students will demonstrate using their voices to make many sounds, and will be able to delineate between healthy sounds and unhealthy sounds.

**ASSESSED BY:**  Listening, watching, and observing student vocal behaviors

## Science National Standards

**SCIENCE NATIONAL STANDARDS ADDRESSED:**  Standard F—Science in personal and social perspectives: Personal health (NSTA 2008)

**INSTRUCTIONAL OBJECTIVES:**  Students will demonstrate healthy vocal behaviors and provide answers on how to take care of their voices.

**ASSESSED BY:**  Students complete vocal health projects and demonstrate healthy vocal behaviors.

## Time for Lesson

Duration: 20–30 minutes cumulative

## Materials/Resources

1. "Bow Wow Wow" (see Figure 15.1)
2. Game directions (available at www.pearsonhighered.com/flohr)
3. Pictorial poster of singing process (breathing in, making sound, stopping sound)

## Procedure

**ANTICIPATORY SET (ATTENTION HOOK)**   "Why don't we start with a favorite song that you pick today? Can you demonstrate to me healthy singing posture and breathing?" After the song is sung, continues: "Did we sing healthfully? Do we need to fix some things to make our singing better? What do we need to fix?" If necessary, the students can sing again to fix what they may not have liked.

At this point, introduce the new song by having the students listen for the direction of the melody to the words *bow wow wow* at the very end of the song (the melody goes downward at the end). The students can also listen for, and draw the contour of, the melody of the song (it goes up, then goes down, looking like an angle). (The song is taught by rote method; four phrases can be collapsed into two shorter ones.)

After you teach the song, you need to investigate that the highest note (C) may be a little higher than where students usually sing. Find out if any of the students had difficulty reaching the C (some will have). There is a trick to help get out high notes that you will demonstrate: "When we sing higher in our voices, we want to keep our larynxes as relaxed as possible, because we don't want them moving upwards." Demonstrate this by drawing on the blackboard.

Have everyone put two fingers on their own throat, and then swallow. They should move their fingers to where they feel the bulk of the swallowing energy happen (this will be close to where the neck joins the torso, but is variable for each child. You can help by gently helping students find this area).

With their fingers placed correctly, the students sing the first three words of the song on F. They will feel the vibrations under their fingers. Next, have them sing the next three notes—all As. They will still feel the energy and vibrations concentrated there. Next, have them sing the part of the song "Little Tommy Tucker's dog," which uses Cs and a D. Students who are able to sing these pitches comfortably with no obvious vocal stress will likely still feel the energy. However, if you see children sticking out their chins, raising their chins, and perhaps grimacing, those are classic examples of hyperactivity in the voice, and it is likely the larynx is being forced upward. Those children will not feel the vibrations in the same place.

Indicate to the student that they can sing the same higher notes without raising their larynxes, and with a trick to help. When singing the higher notes, have students step out to the front and lunge, and then return to regular standing position when singing the rest of the song.

Although there is no research concerning raised larynxes and singing specific to children, there is a plethora of it at the adult level, and voice specialists usually see it as an undesirable vocal behavior, as it puts undue stress on the larynx. This is a learned behavior and has its roots, like all other vocal behaviors, in childhood. Both pedagogical strategies presented here are used in vocal training: the placing of the fingers in the laryngeal notch area and the lunging activity. The lunging activity somehow helps singers keep the larynx from moving upward, probably because of the downward motion of the entire body. The goal here is to be able to sing higher in range but to get the notes more by breath support and vocal control rather than raising the larynx. Raising and lowering the larynx will not allow for a great increase in vocal range, although we know from behavioral studies in adults that there seems to be a belief that it will. Learning to sing with a resting larynx also has implications for retention between elementary and middle school choirs, and can help children transition from child to adult voices.

Have the students do the experiment again, this time lunging when they get to the higher notes. Most of them will notice that they feel the vibrations better when they lunge. This is an example of singing with a resting larynx, and that is desirable for vocal health. Sing the song through a few times, lunging on the higher notes. As they get better at singing the higher pitches more relaxed, they can lunge less.

When students can sing the song with no evident stress, with good intonation and diction, then they can play the game that goes with it. The singing quality should not be compromised while playing the game.

## Evaluation

Students are evaluated by how comfortably they are able to sing the song. If necessary, students with vocal problems can be identified as well.

## Continuing the Lesson

This song can be used to practice and reinforce (1) the do-mi-sol triad, (2) melody moving downward by step, (3) eighth and quarter note rhythms, (4) rest, and (5) steady beat. Students can also change the animal from a dog to cat, cow, or chick, for example.

## LESSON 3

Singing in Parts and Texture: Monophony, Polyphony

## Level

Grades 3 and 4

## Project/Activities

Students practice singing, with good tone quality, intonation, and healthy phonation, songs in rounds, partner songs, and songs with ostinato to investigate texture. Students also create a texture art project to present a visual example of what they did vocally.

## Previous Knowledge and Skills

Students need to be able to talk and phonate healthfully; the activity may reveal that some students have vocal issues that have not yet been documented. Students should be able to demonstrate singing in a nonstressful and relaxed manner, and should also be able to sing about an octave comfortably in their range. They should already have experiences in singing very simple rounds. They also should be reading and writing music using standard notation, and they should be able to draw contours of melodies.

## Music Concepts and Objectives/Assessment

**STANDARDS ADDRESSED:**   Singing alone and with others, a variety of music (MENC 2007)

**INSTRUCTIONAL OBJECTIVES:**   Students will demonstrate using their voices to make many sounds, and will be able to delineate between healthy sounds and unhealthy sounds. Students will be able to aurally identify and sing monophonic and polyphonic music.

**ASSESSED BY:**   Listening, watching, observing student vocal behaviors, creating a texture collage, and singing the appropriate textures

## National Science Standards

**SCIENCE NATIONAL STANDARDS ADDRESSED**:   Standard F—Science in personal and social perspectives: Personal health (NSTA 2008)

**INSTRUCTIONAL OBJECTIVES:**   Students will demonstrate healthy vocal behaviors and provide answers on how to take care of their voices.

**ASSESSED BY:**   Observing students demonstrating healthy phonation habits

## Time for Lesson

Duration: 20–30 minutes cumulative

### Materials/Resources

1. Simple songs to start ("Frère Jacques," "Row, Row, Row Your Boat," and "Mary Had a Little Lamb," but you can certainly choose other ones from your own repertoire)
2. Construction paper (white preferred)
3. Glue, glitter, crayons, cotton, pencils, and any other materials that can provide texture

### Procedure

**ANTICIPATORY SET (ATTENTION HOOK)** "We have been working on singing healthfully the last few years, and your voices and singing ability have really improved, so now we are going to make things more interesting! Do you remember what a 'round' is?" Most students will be able to identify "Frère Jacques" ("Brother John") as a round, and singing it through in the key of D Major to review it would be helpful. If another round is selected, that will work, too.

"If we sing 'Brother John' all together, and not in a round, we sing in a style that is called monophonic, with 'mono' meaning '1' and phonic meaning sound. This is what we call a musical texture. Can you think of anything else that has texture?" Students will come up with things like fur, clothing hair, skin, and so on. "When we sing only one melody, all alone and by ourselves, then we are singing in a thin texture, since it's just one melody. However, what if we sing the song 'Brother John' again in a round? Do we still have a thin texture?" (Answer: no).

Ask the students to sing "Frére Jacques" in a round. They will notice that, although they are singing the same melody, they are singing it at different times, and this makes the texture thicker. Instead of hearing only one melody, they hear many melodies —even if it is the same one repeated. This is called polyphonic, with poly meaning "many" and phonic meaning sound.

After the students discover the difference between monophonic texture and polyphonic texture, then they can try experimenting with hearing a totally different song along with "Frère Jacques." "London Bridge" will work with it, as long as it is sung through twice, as will "Row, Row, Row, Your Boat." It is important that they are all in the same key. Students sing "Frére Jacques" while the teacher sings one of the other two songs at the same time. What texture is created? (Answer: Polyphony.) How would we turn this into monophonic music? (Answer: Sing only one song at a time.)

If the students are really good at this or have prior experience singing in parts, then it can be made more interesting in a number of ways:

1. The students alternate in singing every other line of the song (so it's still monophonic, but two different songs blended together).
2. They can create an ostinato with instruments or their voices, from extracting a part of the song (for example, "Din Dan Don" in "Frère Jacques" can make a simple ostinato for both songs to be sung with in a round).
3. They can add another song into the mix: "Row, Row, Row Your Boat" (sung in the same key) also works.

From here, the students can illustrate the texture of the music via a simple art project. They will have two pieces of white construction paper. On one, they can either (1) freehand draw the melodic contour to "London Bridge" and "Frére Jacques," or (2) you can provide a notated paper of both songs. Students blacken the back of the paper, and then place it on the construction paper, blackened side down, and on the front, draw lines connecting the note heads of the music. This will transfer as contour on the white construction paper.

The students illustrate monophonic in their picture; then on the second one, they can overlap the melody lines of "Frére Jacques" and "Row, Row, Row, Your Boat." These lines can be further illustrated by being outlined in different colors, or with glitter and sequins, and even bits of cotton or yarn. The final projects indicating monophony and polyphony (and how each child can interpret them a bit differently) can be mounted on a classroom bulletin board, and can serve as a reinforcement of the terms.

## Evaluation

Evaluation is completed by finishing the projects in respect to the objectives.

## Continuing the Lesson

Because part work is an important skill for singing in choirs and also for being able to play in ensembles, this is a skill that can be built upon for the remainder of music classes, as it will transfer well to band, orchestra, and chorus. Introducing other textures (for example, homophony) also can come out of this. Because the focus of the class was using the voice to help discover texture, then a reinforcement of healthy singing behaviors should always be present.

# LESSON 4

Changing Voices (Boys and Girls)

## Level

Grades 5 and 6

## Project/Activities

Students work in pairs to find information online on a webquest that will help them compose a project on their own changing voices. Students create a voice log so they can keep track of what happens with their voice and how they can work with it as it changes and evolves into a new voice.

There is a lot of information available online to help you with this activity, and the information changes regularly as new information is discovered. Be careful to get information from a source such as a voice care center. We are providing links here that are part of professional health services.

## Previous Knowledge and Skills

Students need to be able to talk and phonate healthfully; the activity may reveal to a teacher that students have vocal issues that have not yet been documented. Students should be able to demonstrate singing in a nonstressful and relaxed manner, and should also be able to sing about an octave comfortably in their range. They should already have experiences in singing in parts. They should be familiar with their own basic vocal anatomy. They should know how to do research on the Internet to find reputable information.

## Music Concepts and Objectives/Assessment

**STANDARDS ADDRESSED**: Singing alone and with others, a variety of music (MENC 2007)

**INSTRUCTIONAL OBJECTIVES:** Students will demonstrate using their voices healthfully, and how to take care with it as it changes. Students will construct a model of a human larynx.

**ASSESSED BY:** Listening, watching, and observing student vocal behaviors

## Science Concepts

**SCIENCE NATIONAL STANDARDS ADDRESSED:** Standard F—Science in personal and social perspectives: Personal health (NSTA 2008)

**INSTRUCTIONAL OBJECTIVES:** Students will demonstrate healthy vocal behaviors and provide answers on how to take care of their voices. Students will construct a model of a human larynx.

**ASSESSED BY:**   Students demonstrate healthy phonation habits and an understanding of their voice and how it will change, and demonstrate changes using a self-constructed tilting larynx.

## Time for Lesson

Duration: 50 minutes

## Materials/Resources

1. Computers with Internet access
2. Worksheets to guide the webquest
3. Manila paper or other heavy card stock, scissors, glue, small paper fasteners (four for each person)
4. The template (from http://www.vocalprocess.co.uk/resources/build_your_own_tilting_larynx.pdf to build a tilting larynx)

## Procedure

**ANTICIPATORY SET (ATTENTION HOOK)**   "We have been working on singing healthfully the last few years, and your voices and singing ability have really improved, so now we are going to make things more interesting! Some of you are noticing about now that your voices aren't the same as they used to be. They are very strong at this point, but soon your voices are going to start changing. Over the next several classes, we are going to look at how the voices change, both for boys and girls. This is a normal transition for all humans, and you can't avoid it. Our goal here is to help you get through it so you can come out on the other side of the change singing just as much as you have before."

Allow students to work with a partner on the webquest. Each student gets a copy of the guide sheet and fills in the answers. At the end of the class, they can share as an entire class what they found out about the changing voice.

## Webquest Guide Sheet

The goal of this webquest is to help you discover information and answer the following questions about your changing voices.

First weblink: http://kidshealth.org/teen/sexual_health/guys/voice_changing.html

1. What happens to a boy's larynx when the voice changes?
2. Why does the voice crack or break?
3. When does a male voice mature (finish growing up?)

Second weblink: http://kidshealth.org/kid/grow/boy/changing_voice.html

4. Do girls' voices change, too?
5. Who has a bigger Adam's apple after the voice changes? Why does an Adam's apple appear?

(After students complete the answers, they may share them with the class.)

## Construction of the Larynx (This Is a Model of an Adult Larynx)

By constructing these, students can use the model to help better illustrate and understand how voices work, and how they will change. Also, by building this model, they will become familiarized with the names of the cartilages. Later on, students can attach strings or cords that would act as ligaments within the larynx (with the ends protruding) to show how the processes move.

This will be an activity you will need to show the students how to do.

## Evaluation

Evaluation is completed by finishing the webquest and the larynx model.

## Continuing the Lesson

The next lesson can include some more investigation into the anatomy of the larynx and how it functions. The reason for saving this activity until later years (upper elementary) is because very young voices are very different from adult voices, and consideration must be taken to teach students about the vocal processes they are growing into. Resources you may wish to peruse to further flesh out your own knowledge and instructional ideas are available in Chapter 6 on singing.

Also, some students who are experiencing vocal changes may wish to start a log or journal to keep track of how their voices feel and behave on certain days. These journals will be interesting to compile and to share with the younger students as they age, and many older students like to share their experiences with younger students. The point of this activity is to get students to understand (1) their own vocal anatomy, (2) how to work with the voice as it changes—it doesn't mean the end to singing!—and (3) that this is normal and can be spoken about freely.

Young boys will sing quite readily.

*Photo courtesy of Vernon and Judith Trollinger*

## CHAPTER 16

# Movement Lessons

The music and dances from Ireland and Africa for the entire sample sequence show how the same materials may be used and modified at different grades

*[The dance and movement material was contributed by Gladys M. Keeton, Texas Woman's University, Denton. Percussion music was contributed by John Osburn, music major at Texas Woman's University, Denton.]*

## LESSON 1

Cultural dance movement and creating movement with music

### Level

Prekindergarten to K

### Project/Activities

Small group project: Students move to African and Irish music and create their own dance.

### Previous Knowledge and Skills

Ability to stop and start with the music

### Music Concepts and Objectives/Assessment

**STANDARDS ADDRESSED:**  Respond through movement to music of various tempos, meters, dynamics, modes, genres, and styles to express what they hear and feel in works of music (MENC 2007)

**INSTRUCTIONAL OBJECTIVES:**  The students will move to African and Irish music and create their own dance to music.

**ASSESSED BY:**  Observing the students moving

### Social Studies or Physical Education Concepts and Objectives/Assessment

*Social Studies*

**STANDARDS ADDRESSED:**  Social studies programs should include experiences that provide for the study of culture and cultural diversity (NCSS 1994)

**INSTRUCTIONAL OBJECTIVE:**  The students identify differences in the music culture of Ireland and Africa.

**ASSESSED BY:** Asking questions about the music and musical instruments of each country

*Physical Education*

**STANDARDS ADDRESSED:** Demonstrates competency in motor skills and movement patterns needed to perform a variety of physical activities (NASPE 2004)

**INSTRUCTIONAL OBJECTIVE:** The child demonstrates competency in fundamental movement patterns and proficiency in a few specialized movement forms.

**ASSESSED BY:** Observing the students moving to the two types of music

## Time for Lesson

Duration: 10 minutes

## Materials/Resources

1. Recording of "Sitimela ga puma e Rhodesia" (African) and "Johnny's Favorite/ Thrush in the Morning" (Irish medley) available as download from http:// www.smithsonianglobalsound.org/
2. Optional pictures of instruments and dancers

## Procedure

**ANTICIPATORY SET (ATTENTION HOOK)** Play the African music example, "Sitimela ga puma e Rhodesia."

Have you ever heard African music before? What animals live in Africa? Which ones are your favorites? Why? Describe the ones you like the most. What kind of food do Africans eat? Can you show me how to plant a seed?

Have you ever heard Irish music? Play the Irish music example, "Johnny's Favorite/Thrush in the Morning" (medley).

Allow the students to make up their own movements to the music.

Match the students' movements with the following types of body movements for each culture. Try out each movement with the students (my turn, your turn, procedure works well for demonstrations).

## Irish

- Upright torso
- Arms beside body

After trying the movements, play the music again, try out the movements, and encourage the students to create their own dance.

## African

- Torso flexed forward at hip
- Arms freely moving
- Flat feet

After trying the movements, play the music again, try out the movements, and encourage the students to create their own dance.

## Evaluation

Evaluate the movement by observation using the objectives. Look for differences in movement types for the differences in the music.

## Continuing the Lesson

After the initial experience, encourage the students to extend the experience.

A "country center" (for example, Africa) may be set up in the classroom. The center could include a listening station with headphones, pictures, African animal puppets, and more.

## LESSON 2

Cultural dance movement and creating movement with music

### Level

Grades 1 and 2

### Project/Activities

Small group project: Students move to African and Irish music. They perform simple rhythm accompaniments and create their own dance.

### Previous Knowledge and Skills

The pre-K Lesson 1 included the ability to respond through movement to music of two tempos, meters, dynamics, modes, genres, and styles to express what they hear and feel in works of music.

### Music Concepts and Objectives/Assessment

**STANDARDS ADDRESSED:**   Respond through purposeful movement to selected prominent music characteristics or to specific music events while listening to music, and perform easy rhythmic, melodic, and chordal patterns accurately and independently on rhythmic, melodic, and harmonic classroom instruments (MENC 2007)

**INSTRUCTIONAL OBJECTIVES:**   The students will move to African and Irish music, perform simple rhythm patterns, and create their own dance to music.

**ASSESSED BY:**   Observing the students moving and performing on the instruments

### Social Studies or Physical Education Concepts and Objectives/Assessment

*Social Studies*

**STANDARDS ADDRESSED:**   Social studies programs should include experiences that provide for the study of culture and cultural diversity (NCSS 1994)

**INSTRUCTIONAL OBJECTIVE:**   The students identify differences in the music cultures of Ireland and Africa.

**ASSESSED BY:**   Asking questions about the music and musical instruments of each country

*Physical Education*

**STANDARDS ADDRESSED:**   Demonstrates competency in motor skills and movement patterns needed to perform a variety of physical activities (NASPE 2004)

**INSTRUCTIONAL OBJECTIVE:**   The child demonstrates competency in fundamental movement patterns and proficiency in a few specialized movement forms.

**ASSESSED BY:**   Observing the students moving to the two types of music

### Time for Lesson

Duration: 15 minutes

### Materials/Resources

1. Recording of "Sitimela ga puma e Rhodesia" (African) and "Johnny's Favorite/ Thrush in the Morning" (Irish medley) available as download from http://www.smithsonianglobalsound.org/
2. Music
3. Optional pictures of instruments and dancers

**4.** African and Irish instruments (kidi, sogo, spoons, and bodhran) or substitute available classroom instruments

## Procedure

**ANTICIPATORY SET (ATTENTION HOOK)**    Play the Irish music example, "Johnny's Favorite/Thrush in the Morning" (medley).

Do you remember this music? Today we will play a game with movement and we will play instruments, too. Match the students' movements with the following types of body movements for each culture.

### Irish

- Upright torso
- Arms beside body
- Footwork: sevens and threes
- Extended feet; on balls of feet

After trying the movements, show them the Irish instruments. Give students turns playing the two instruments (or multiple sets of the instruments), along with "Johnny's Favorite / Thrush in the Morning" (medley).

Encourage the students to create their own dance while others perform the Irish music in Figure 16.1 (without the recorded example).

### African

- Torso flexed forward at hip
- Arms freely moving
- Flat feet
- Angular designs

After trying the movements, show them the African instruments. Give students turns playing the two instruments (or multiple sets of the instruments), along with "Sitimela ga puma e Rhodesia." Encourage the students to create their own dance while others perform the African music in Figure 16.1 (without the recorded example).

### Evaluation

Evaluate the moving by observation using the objectives. Look for differences in movement types for the differences in the music. Also evaluate their playing of the music examples in Figure 16.1.

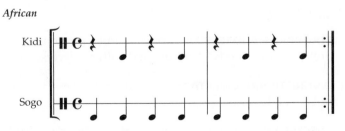
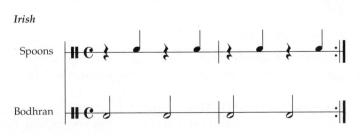

**FIGURE 16.1** African and Irish Two-Part Rhythm

## Continuing the Lesson

After the initial experience, encourage the students to extend the experience.

Dance music from other countries can be found on the Smithsonian website. Start with choosing music from countries represented by the students in the class.

## LESSON 3

Cultural dance movement and creating movement with music

### Level

Grades 3 and 4

### Project/Activities

Small group project: Students move to African and Irish music. They perform simple rhythm accompaniments and create their own dance.

### Previous Knowledge and Skills

Ability to respond through purposeful movement to selected prominent music characteristics or to specific music events while listening to music and performing easy rhythmic, melodic, and chordal patterns accurately and independently on rhythmic, melodic, and harmonic classroom instruments.

### Music Concepts and Objectives/Assessment

**STANDARDS ADDRESSED:** Describe in simple terms how elements of music are used in music examples from various cultures of the world; identify and describe roles of musicians in various music settings and cultures (MENC 2007)

**INSTRUCTIONAL OBJECTIVES:** The students will move to African and Irish music, perform simple rhythm patterns, and create their own dance to the music. They will use simple terms to describe the two examples of music and answer questions about the role of musicians in those cultures.

**ASSESSED BY:** Observing the students moving and asking questions about the elements of music and the cultures

### Social Studies or Physical Education Concepts and Objectives/Assessment

*Social Studies*

**STANDARDS ADDRESSED:** Social studies programs should include experiences that provide for the study of culture and cultural diversity (NCSS 1994)

**INSTRUCTIONAL OBJECTIVE:** The students identify differences in the music culture of Ireland and Africa.

**ASSESSED BY:** Asking questions about the music and musical instruments of each country

*Physical Education*

**STANDARDS ADDRESSED:** Demonstrates competency in motor skills and movement patterns needed to perform a variety of physical activities (NASPE 2004)

**INSTRUCTIONAL OBJECTIVE:** The child demonstrates competency in fundamental movement patterns and proficiency in a few specialized movement forms.

**ASSESSED BY:**   Observing the students moving to the two types of music

## Time for Lesson

Duration: 20 minutes

## Materials/Resources

1. Recording of "Ko" (translated as "Forest") (Ghana, African) and "The Ash Plant/ Merry Harriers/Hut in the Bog" (Irish medley) available as download from http://www.smithsonianglobalsound.org/
2. Music
3. Optional pictures of instruments and dancers
4. African and Irish instruments (kidi, sogo, kagan, spoons, bones, and bodhran) or substitute available classroom instruments

## Procedure

**ANTICIPATORY SET (ATTENTION HOOK)**   Play the Irish music example, "The Ash Plant/ Merry Harriers/Hut in the Bog" (medley). What instruments do you hear (accordion, fiddle, pipes)? Do you remember the other Irish music we moved to?

Play the music again and add the following movements.

## Irish

- Same movements as lesson 2 (upright torso; arms beside body; footwork in sevens and threes; extended feet and on balls of feet)
- Couple position
- Using leg from hip

After trying the movements, show them the Irish instruments. Give students turns playing the three instruments (or multiple sets of the instruments), along with "Ash Plant/Merry Harriers/Hut in the Bog" (medley).

Encourage the students to create their own dance while others perform the Irish music (without the recorded example). Simple forms such as AB or ABACA (rondo) provide a framework.

## African

- Same movements as lesson 2 (torso flexed forward at hip; arms freely moving; flat feet; angular designs)
- Isolated body parts
- Bound movement

After trying the movements, show them the African instruments. Give students turns playing the three instruments (or multiple sets of the instruments), along with the music "Ko." Encourage the students to create their own dance while others perform the African music in Figure 16.2.

## Evaluation

Ask questions using simple terms to describe the two examples of music and about the role of musicians in those cultures. Also evaluate their performance of the music in Figure 16.2.

## Continuing the Lesson

After the initial experience, encourage the students to extend the experience.

Choose dance music from other countries on the Smithsonian website. Encourage the students to construct a presentation for a school assembly with instruments and dance movements that they create.

**FIGURE 16.2** African and Irish
Three-Part Rhythm

## LESSON 4

Cultural dance movement and creating movement with music

### Level

Grades 5 and 6

### Project/Activities

Small group project: Students move to African and Irish music. They perform rhythm accompaniments, improvisations, and create their own dance.

### Previous Knowledge and Skills

Ability to describe in simple terms how elements of music are used in music examples from various cultures of the world; identify and describe roles of musicians in various music settings and cultures.

### Music Concepts and Objectives/Assessment

**STANDARDS ADDRESSED:**  Perform music representing diverse genres and cultures, with expression appropriate for the work being performed; describe distinguishing characteristics of representative music genres and styles from a variety of cultures (MENC 2007)

**INSTRUCTIONAL OBJECTIVES:**  The students will move to African and Irish music, perform rhythm patterns, and create their own dance to music. They will use simple terms to describe distinguishing characteristics of representative music genres and styles.

**ASSESSED BY:**  Observing the students moving and asking questions about the elements of music and the cultures

## Social Studies or Physical Education Concepts and Objectives/Assessment

### Social Studies

**STANDARDS ADDRESSED:**   Social studies programs should include experiences that provide for the study of culture and cultural diversity (NCSS 1994)

**INSTRUCTIONAL OBJECTIVE:**   The students identify differences in the music culture of Ireland and Africa.

**ASSESSED BY:**   Asking questions about the music and musical instruments of each country

### Physical Education

**STANDARDS ADDRESSED:**   Demonstrates competency in motor skills and movement patterns needed to perform a variety of physical activities (NASPE 2004)

**INSTRUCTIONAL OBJECTIVE:**   The child demonstrates competency in fundamental movement patterns and proficiency in a few specialized movement forms.

**ASSESSED BY:**   Observing the students moving to the two types of music

## Time for Lesson

Duration: 20 minutes

## Materials/Resources

1. Recording of "Ko" (translated as "Forest") (Ghana, African) and "The Ash Plant/ Merry Harriers/Hut in the Bog" (medley) (Ireland) available as download from http://www.smithsonianglobalsound.org/
2. Music
3. Optional pictures of instruments and dancers
4. Instruments of Ireland (see http://www.world-beats.com/Instru.htm)
5. Instruments of Africa (see http://www.brooklynx.org/neighborhoods/panafrican/ african_instrumentstext.htm)
6. African and Irish instruments (kidi, sogo, kagan, talking drum, spoons, bones, guitar, and bodhran), or substitute available classroom instruments

## Procedure

**ANTICIPATORY SET (ATTENTION HOOK)**   Play the Irish music example, "The Ash Plant/ Merry Harriers/Hut in the Bog" (medley). Do you remember this Irish music we moved to? Can you describe the music in terms of music elements (pitch, rhythm, harmony, dynamics, timbre, texture, form)?

Play the music again and add the following movements.

## Irish

- Same movements as Lesson 3 (upright torso; arms beside body; footwork in sevens and threes; extended feet and on balls of feet; couple position; using leg from hip)
- Progressive footwork

After trying the movements, show them the Irish instruments. Tune the guitar to a G chord (strings tuned from largest or lowest to highest = D, B, D, G, B, D). Give students turns playing the four instruments (or multiple sets of the instruments), along with "Ash Plant / Merry Harriers / Hut in the Bog" (medley).

Encourage the students to create their own dance while others perform the Irish music (without the recorded example). Simple forms such as AB or ABACA (rondo) provide a framework.

**FIGURE 16.3** African and Irish Three-Part Rhythm with Talking Drum

*Optional improvisation with talking drum

*Optional improvisation on bones

## African

- Same movements as Lesson 3 (torso flexed forward at hip; arms freely moving; flat feet; angular designs; isolated body parts; bound movement)
- Combinations: call-and-response

After trying the movements, show them the African instruments. Give students turns playing the three instruments (or multiple sets of the instruments), along with the music "Ko." Encourage the students to create their own dance while others perform the African music in Figure 16.3. Also encourage improvisations on the talking drum.

## Evaluation

Ask questions using simple terms to describe the two examples of music, the role of musicians in those cultures, and the distinguishing characteristics of representative music genres and styles from a variety of cultures. Also evaluate their performing the music in Figure 16.3.

## Continuing the Lesson

Choose dance music from another country on the Smithsonian website. Encourage the students to construct a presentation for a school assembly with instruments and dance movements that they create with a performing ensemble.

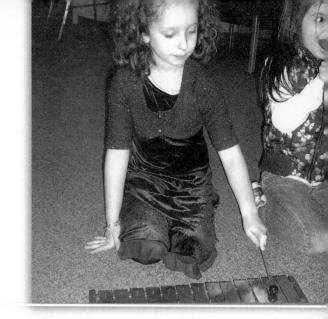

# CHAPTER 17

# Creating Lessons

## LESSON 1

Music story and magnets

### Level

Prekindergarten to K

### Project/Activities

Free exploration with instruments and magnets

### Previous Knowledge and Skills

Care in handling small magnets and music instruments

### Music Concepts and Objectives/Assessment

**STANDARDS ADDRESSED:**   Improvise instrumental accompaniments to songs, recorded selections, stories, and poems (MENC 2007)

**INSTRUCTIONAL OBJECTIVES:**   The students play and experiment with several instruments and use those instruments to improvise an accompaniment to a story.

**ASSESSED BY:**   Observing the students playing and creating during the story

### Science Concepts and Objectives/Assessment

**STANDARDS ADDRESSED:**   Physical science: Magnets attract and repel each other and certain kinds of other materials (NSTA 2008)

**INSTRUCTIONAL OBJECTIVE:**   By experimenting with light, heat, electricity, magnetism, and sound, students begin to understand that phenomena can be observed, measured, and controlled in various ways.

**ASSESSED BY:**   Observing the students experimenting with magnets

### Time for Lesson

Duration: 20 minutes for free exploration and 5 minutes for the story

### Materials/Resources

1. Story of "The Fox-the Crow-the Cheese" from J. W. Flohr and R. B. Smith. 2008. *Storytelling with music: Sing, play, dance and act.* Allen, TX: Troost Press.

2. Fox and crow puppets with yellow box for the cheese (puppet website: http://www.folkmanis.com. See the *Storytelling with Music* book for other visuals).
3. Several small magnets
4. Several classroom instruments such as sticks, maracas, tambourine, wood block
5. Storyboard for the story (see Resources for construction notes). Figures of the fox, crow, and cheese with magnets attached so that they can be mounted on the storyboard and moved.

## Procedure

**ANTICIPATORY SET (ATTENTION HOOK)**   Start by telling the story with a storyboard and figures with magnets. The story is included in this lesson. Tell them that you will need their help to tell a story about the fox, the crow, and the cheese. Ask them to clap their hands when they hear, "The handsome red ____," and stomp their feet when they hear "The shiny black ____." Ask the students to decide on a sound they can make with their mouth for the big piece of yellow cheese (say, "The big piece of yellow ____").

**THE STORY**

**"The Fox-the Crow-the Cheese"**[1]   A handsome red (fox) lived in a beautiful green forest.

*(Ask the students to help by clapping their hands in place of the word* fox.*)*

One day the handsome red (fox) was very, very hungry and had no food to eat. He began walking in circles, thinking very hard and tapping his head. Tapping his head helped him think. While he was walking and tapping, he thought he heard a sound. He stopped and listened. He heard the sound again, very soft and quite far away.

*(Make a cawing sound at this point and ask the students to help with this soft sound.)*

The handsome red (fox) thought to himself, "Perhaps there is food where that sound is. I will walk toward the sound and try to find something to eat." So the handsome red (fox) began to walk toward the sound. He was so hungry he began to rub his stomach. He walked and walked through the beautiful green forest until he heard the sound again. This time it was louder.

*(Together with the students, make another cawing sound. This time, it should be a little louder.)*

The handsome red (fox) became more excited and more hungry. He knew he was moving in the right direction and began to walk faster and faster. He finally reached an open space in the beautiful green forest and saw a large tree in the middle of the space. He looked up into the large tree and saw a shiny black (crow) with a big piece of yellow (cheese) in her mouth.

*(Ask the students to help by stomping their feet in place of the word* crow.*)*

How could he get that big piece of yellow (cheese) away from the shiny black (crow)? He walked in a circle round and round the tree and thought and thought, tapping his head to help him think.

Finally he had an idea. He walked up to the tree and said to the shiny black (crow), "I have heard that you are the smartest creature in the forest. Please say something smart for me." The shiny black (crow) was very pleased that everyone thought she was so smart. She started to open her mouth to say something wise but, just in time, she remembered the big piece of yellow (cheese) in her mouth. So she simply kept her mouth closed, bowed to the handsome red (fox), and flapped her wings. The handsome red (fox) was very mad. He had tried to trick the shiny black (crow) and it hadn't worked. So he walked around the big tree again, thinking and tapping his head.

Then he had another idea. He walked back to the tree, looked up at the shiny black (crow) with the big piece of yellow (cheese) in her mouth, and said, "I have heard you have the most beautiful singing voice in the forest. Please sing for me." The shiny black (crow) was so pleased with this compliment that she forgot about the big piece of

---

yellow (cheese) and opened her mouth to sing her most beautiful song. The big piece of yellow (cheese) fell to the ground, and the handsome red (fox) grabbed it and ate it.

The shiny black (crow) suddenly stopped singing. She knew the handsome red (fox) had tricked her and stolen her food. So she left the tree and flew home to her nest, very sad and very hungry.

*(Have the students caw again. Each caw will get softer as the crow flies farther away.)*

The handsome red (fox) was not sad at all. He was very happy as he walked slowly home. He had fooled the shiny black (crow), and he had also eaten a good meal.

**FREE EXPLORATION AND IMPROVISATION**    After the story is told at least once, place magnets and instruments in the students' play area. Allow them to freely explore the sounds of the instruments and the properties of the magnets. After the students play with both instruments and magnets, ask them to help with the story again. This time, encourage the students to improvise music on the instruments for each character. For example, rather than clapping for the fox, improvise music on the tambourine.

Child playing a melody on a metallophone.

*Photo courtesy of Union City School District, Pennsylvania*

## Evaluation

Evaluate both objectives by observation. Look for participation in the improvisation and play with magnets.

## Continuing the Lesson

After the initial experience, encourage the students to extend the experience by improvising music to other stories.

## LESSON 2

Improvising with instruments and describing sound

## Level

Grades 1 and 2

## Project/Activities

Play with sound objects and describe the qualities

## Previous Knowledge and Skills

A few musical terms such as *loud, soft, timbre, higher, lower*

## Music Concepts and Objectives/Assessment

**STANDARDS ADDRESSED:**  Improvise short songs and instrumental pieces, using a variety of sound sources, including traditional sounds, nontraditional sounds available in the classroom, body sounds, and sounds produced by electronic means; use appropriate terminology in explaining music, music notation, music instruments and voices, and music performances (MENC 2007)

**INSTRUCTIONAL OBJECTIVES:**  The students improvise short pieces using many sound sources including instruments and found objects.

**ASSESSED BY:**  Observing the students creating and answering questions about the sound qualities of the sound-making objects and instruments

## Science Concepts and Objectives/Assessment

**STANDARDS ADDRESSED:**  Young students begin their study of matter by examining and qualitatively describing objects and their behavior. The important but abstract ideas of science all begin with observing and keeping track of the way the world behaves (NSTA 2008)

**INSTRUCTIONAL OBJECTIVE:**   The students examine and qualitatively describe instruments and sound-making objects.

**ASSESSED BY:**   Observing the students playing with sound and answering questions about the sound qualities

## Time for Lesson

Duration: 15 minutes

## Materials/Resources

1. Several music instruments such as tambourine, African talking drum, sticks, maracas
2. Found objects and materials such as pots, pans, rug remnants, and anything found in the classroom. One way to organize sound sources for a center is to attach several different materials to a board (such as carpet, tin foil, spoon, plastic).

## Procedure

**ANTICIPATORY SET (ATTENTION HOOK)**   Demonstrate the sounds from a few instruments and sound sources in the classroom. Ask the students to describe the sounds they hear with adjectives such as *louder, softer, higher, lower, thicker, thinner,* and so forth.

Place several instruments and sound sources around the room in groups (four is usually good) or in a music center area. Ask the students to play with the instruments and sound sources. Encourage them to construct short improvisations using the sound sources.

## Evaluation

Evaluate their improvisations by participation and use of the sound sources. Evaluate the descriptions of sound by asking questions about sound qualities.

## Continuing the Lesson

After the initial experience, encourage the students to describe and categorize music instruments and sound sources in the environment.

# LESSON 3

Improvisation and metronome

## Level

Grades 3 and 4

## Project/Activities

Create a musical composition or improvisation of a train in small groups

## Previous Knowledge and Skills

Students require free exploration time with the instruments to be used during improvisation (see Chapter 8).

## Music Concepts and Objectives/Assessment

**STANDARDS ADDRESSED:**   Create and arrange short songs and instrumental pieces within specified guidelines; improvise short songs and instrumental pieces, using a variety of sound sources (MENC 2007)

**INSTRUCTIONAL OBJECTIVES:**   The students compose or improvise short songs to illustrate the sound of a train.

**ASSESSED BY:** Observing the students improvising and asking questions about their musical decisions

## Science Concepts and Objectives/Assessment

**STANDARDS ADDRESSED:** An object's motion can be described by tracing and measuring its position over time (NSTA 2008)

**INSTRUCTIONAL OBJECTIVE:** The child uses a metronome to measure their musical creation and apply the beats to a train's motion.

**ASSESSED BY:** Asking questions about the beats and the train's motion

## Time for Lesson

Duration: 20 minutes

## Materials/Resources

1. Instruments (for example, Orff instruments, as in Chapter 11, or drums)
2. Metronome
3. Small train with tracks or video of trains

## Procedure

**ANTICIPATORY SET (ATTENTION HOOK)** Observe a small train and track in the classroom or watch a video of trains moving. Talk about the sounds the train makes and if the sounds are in a steady rhythm (at a constant speed, the rhythm is more likely to be steady).

Ask small groups of students to create or improvise a short piece of music with a steady beat like a train (and they may use the sound of a train as a stimulus). Use a metronome to measure the beats per minute (bpm) of their created piece (a clock with a second hand could also be used).

Determine the position over time or distance traveled in a straight line of a train that would travel at 30 mph for the duration of their composition. For example, if their composition lasted 2 minutes, the following formula could be used:

$$30 \text{ mph} = \tfrac{1}{2} \text{ mpm (mile per minute } 30/60) \times 2 \text{ minutes} = 1 \text{ mile of travel}$$

If using the metronome, another formula would be used if, for example, the metronome reading of their music was 120 bpm and there were the following:

$$30 \text{ mph} = \tfrac{1}{2} \text{ mpm (mile per minute } 30/60)$$
$$\times$$
$$(240 \text{ beats}/120 \text{ bpm} = 2 \text{ minutes}) = 1 \text{ mile of travel}$$

The formulae can be used for any speed of the train and bpm of the compositions.

## Evaluation

Ask questions about the characteristics of the created music and about the observations leading to the answer for the train's miles of travel.

## Continuing the Lesson

After the initial experience, encourage the students to use the metronome and the clock to measure music and other items in their environment.

# LESSON 4

Composition with musical forms ABA, rondo, and variation

## Level

Grades 5 and 6

### Project/Activities

Small group project: Students create music that demonstrates qualities of energy.

### Previous Knowledge and Skills

Motor ability with instruments and prior experiences with improvisation and composition

### Music Concepts and Objectives/Assessment

**STANDARDS ADDRESSED:** Compose short pieces within specified guidelines, demonstrating how the elements of music are used to achieve unity and variety, tension and release, and balance (MENC 2007)

**INSTRUCTIONAL OBJECTIVES:** The students compose short pieces of music that illustrate qualities of energy in some parts or all of the composition.

**ASSESSED BY:** Observing the students creating and recording the compositions

### Science Concepts and Objectives/Assessment

**STANDARDS ADDRESSED:** The understanding of energy in grades 5 through 8 will build on the K-4 experiences with light, heat, sound, electricity, magnetism, and the motion of objects; kinetic energy and potential energy (NSTA 2008)

**INSTRUCTIONAL OBJECTIVE:** The students experiment with qualities of energy using their voices, a roller coaster, bouncing ball, a mallet instrument, and/or websites.

**ASSESSED BY:** Observing the students experimenting with energy and asking questions about kinetic and potential energy

### Time for Lesson

Duration: 20 minutes

### Materials/Resources

1. Mallet instrument(s), website access, and/or bouncing ball such as tennis balls
2. Roller coaster (a model or student-made roller coaster would be helpful). Manufactured models are usually found while searching Amazon.com
3. Websites about energy; for example, see the following:
   http://jersey.uoregon.edu/vlab/PotentialEnergy/index.html
   http://www.glenbrook.k12.il.us/gbssci/Phys/mmedia/energy/ce.html
   http://science.howstuffworks.com/roller-coaster3.htm
4. Instruments for each group of students to use for compositions
5. Writing material for map of compositions or music notation

### Procedure

**ANTICIPATORY SET (ATTENTION HOOK)** Start with the voice. Ask the students to inhale and hold their breath; after a count of five, have them release the air by singing a tone such as *doh*. Ask them if they think holding their breath represented kinetic or potential energy. Use a ball or a mallet instrument and demonstrate holding the ball, for example, over the ground and then dropping the ball. Which part was kinetic energy? (The vocal sound making is the kinetic energy, as it illustrates the Bernoulli effect in physics. The pressure waves through the vocal bands create the sound.)

Show at least one website about energy and/or ask for helpers to play or demonstrate the roller coaster (you may wish to work with the science teacher, for example, as many science classes construct roller coasters out of simple materials). Experiment, discuss, and ask questions about the type of energy the roller coaster is showing in different parts of the track (the websites are very good for this).

Ask the groups of students to create a short musical example that in some way illustrates different types of musical energy (for example, faster, slower, louder, softer, accented, fermata). Some groups may wish to illustrate the energy of a roller coaster in part of their composition.

## Evaluation

Ask questions using musical and scientific terms to describe the compositions.

## Continuing the Lesson

Encourage more compositions by groups or individuals with experimentation with music energy.

# Playing Lessons

### LESSON 1

Perform body percussion to a story

### Level

Prekindergarten to K

### Project/Activities

Large group project: Perform on cue to a story with body percussion.

### Previous Knowledge and Skills

Ability to listen and perform on cue

### Music Concepts and Objectives/Assessment

**STANDARDS ADDRESSED:** Experiment with a variety of instruments and other sound sources (MENC 2007)

**INSTRUCTIONAL OBJECTIVES:** The students perform body percussion to a story.

**ASSESSED BY:** Observing the students playing and playing on cue

### English Concepts and Objectives/Assessment

**STANDARDS ADDRESSED:** Students apply a wide range of strategies to comprehend, interpret, evaluate, and appreciate texts (NCTE 2004)

**INSTRUCTIONAL OBJECTIVE:** The students listen to a story and play body percussion on cue.

**ASSESSED BY:** Observing the students' performance

### Time for Lesson

Duration: 5 minutes

### Materials/Resources

Story of "The Fox-the Crow-the Cheese" from *Storytelling with Music: Sing, Play, Dance, and Act* (Chapter 17).

## Procedure

**ANTICIPATORY SET (ATTENTION HOOK)**   Show the puppets to the students. Tell them that you will need their help to tell a story about the fox, the crow, and the cheese. Ask them to clap their hands when they hear, "The handsome red _____," and stomp their feet when they hear, "The shiny black _____." Ask the students to decide on a sound they can make with their mouth for the big piece of yellow cheese (say, "The big piece of yellow_____").

"The Fox-the Crow-the Cheese" story can be found in Chapter 17.

## Evaluation

Evaluate the playing by observing the students during the story. Look for correct body percussion for the different word cues.

## Continuing the Lesson

After the initial experience, encourage the students to extend the experience.
The students enjoy becoming the characters with puppets and masks.

Storytelling using music and puppets helps build creative thinking.

*Photo courtesy of Christine Stratton*

## LESSON 2

Adding instruments to a story

## Level

Grades 1 and 2

## Project/Activities

Add a number of found or instrumental sounds to the story *The Stinky Cheese Man*.

## Previous Knowledge and Skills

Ability to play on cue (see previous lesson: pre-K Lesson 1)

## Music Concepts and Objectives/Assessment

**STANDARDS ADDRESSED:**   Performing on instruments, alone and with others, a varied repertoire of music; improvising melodies, variations, and accompaniments (MENC 2007)

**INSTRUCTIONAL OBJECTIVES:**   The students choose instruments and improvise simple patterns to accompany the story.

**ASSESSED BY:**   Observing the students moving and performing on the instruments

## English Concepts and Objectives/Assessment

**STANDARDS ADDRESSED:**   Students read a wide range of literature from many periods and in many genres to build an understanding of the many dimensions (for example, philosophical, ethical, aesthetic) of human experience (NCTE 2004)

**INSTRUCTIONAL OBJECTIVE:**   The students are able to answer discussion questions about what happens to the stinky cheese man as an ethical and aesthetic character. Students are able to demonstrate playing of instruments to reinforce listening and comprehension skills of the story.

**ASSESSED BY:**   Observing students in discussion and performance

## Time for Lesson

Duration: 10 minutes

### Materials/Resources

1. Classroom instruments including drums, rhythm sticks, and jingle bells are fun if the story is read during winter; otherwise, use maracas or whatever can be found and made into an instrument.
2. J. Scieszka and L. Smith. 2002. *The stinky cheese man and other fairly stupid tales.* New York: Viking Books.

### Procedure

**ANTICIPATORY SET (ATTENTION HOOK)**   Read the story *The Stinky Cheese Man.* During the reading, the students will enhance repeated text ("Run, run, run!") by playing rhythm instruments at a fast tempo to illustrate running.

Settle the students on the floor, on a carpet, in front of you, and proceed to hand out instruments. It is best that the instruments remain on the floor in front of the seated students, and the students can pick them up when directed.

Prepare the students for the story by asking them to describe cheese they like, cheese they don't like, what cheese smells like, and where cheese comes from. From there, say this is a special story about special cheese, cheese that was made into a man. Continue by telling them that this cheese man likes to run, and whenever the students hear you say the words, "Run, run, run," they should raise their hands and wave them in the air, like they are making their hands and arms run. Finally, ask them to listen to find out whom the cheese man meets, and what happens to him at the end.

Read the story, while the students respond to the "Run, run, run." Discuss whom the cheese man meets on the way (old man, old lady, little boy, little girl, a cow, and then a fox) and what happens to him at the end (he falls in the river and comes apart.)

The second time you read the story, direct them to play their instruments fast only on the words "Run, run, run," but not to play on other words.

Read this story on another day, and encourage the students to create instrument sounds for each of the characters. Students may also act out the story as they become more familiar with it.

### Evaluation

Evaluate by discussing with the students what happens to the stinky cheese man as an ethical and aesthetic character.

### Continuing the Lesson

This activity can be recreated and revised at more advanced levels as the students become more adept and comfortable improvising on instruments. Sounds can be added for repeating verbs or appearances by specific characters, for example. Suggested stories include the remainder of *The Stinky Cheese Man and Other Fairly Ridiculous Tales, The True Story of the Three Little Pigs*—also by Jon Scieszka and Lane Smith—and *Stellaluna* by Janell Cannon. Students can also work in small groups and make their own stories or select another favorite story to act out using instruments.

## LESSON 3

Making a reed instrument from a straw

### Level

Grades 3 and 4

### Project/Activities

Individual project: Make an oboe from a common plastic straw.

### Previous Knowledge and Skills

Ability to handle scissors in a safe manner

## Music Concepts and Objectives/Assessment

**STANDARDS ADDRESSED:** Performing on instruments, alone and with others, a varied repertoire of music (MENC 2007)

**INSTRUCTIONAL OBJECTIVES:** The students construct a straw oboe and perform various pitches by changing the length of the straw.

**ASSESSED BY:** Observing the students playing

## Science Concepts and Objectives/Assessment

**STANDARDS ADDRESSED:** Students should develop understanding and abilities aligned with the following concepts and processes: (1) evidence, models, and explanation; (2) constancy, change, and measurement (NSTA 2008)

**INSTRUCTIONAL OBJECTIVE:** The students discover explanation of changes in sound using measurement in the length of the instrument.

**ASSESSED BY:** Observing students working with the straw oboe and asking questions about the pitches produced

## Time for Lesson

Duration: 10 minutes

## Materials/Resources

1. Plastic straws (three to four per child)
2. Blunt end scissors to cut plastic straws

(Try this before class so that you can demonstrate how it is done for the students.)

## Procedure

**ANTICIPATORY SET (ATTENTION HOOK)** Cut the end of the straw to make a letter V shape similar to an oboe reed. As you place the straw in your mouth, the straw should look like an upside down letter V. Flatten one inch at the end of the straw and cut along each side (experiment with the cutting to produce the sound. The best shape is usually achieved by cutting approximately ¾ inch on each side of a flattened straw while leaving the tip about half the size it was before cutting).

Place the flat and cut end in your mouth so that the cut part is inside the lips, and blow. Make additional cuts to the straw to achieve a sound. Next, make another straw oboe and cut it to half the length. Play each and notice the difference in sound.

## Evaluation

Ask questions about the length of the oboes and the differences in pitch. "If you cut the straw to half of the present length, how does the sound change?" Also, observe the students measuring the straw oboe and cutting it in half.

## Continuing the Lesson

Form groups of four and use different length straws playing at the same time to create harmony.

# LESSON 4

Music for space aliens

## Level

Grades 5 and 6 (can be split across the grades)

## Project/Activities

Students in small groups create (1) a music notation system for a specified space culture, and/or (2) musical instruments for a specified space culture (these aliens are created from a list that is provided). In Chapter 5 on listening, we discussed the use of music in the *Voyager* expedition. The purpose of sending music along with *Voyager* was to share our earthly music with any other space culture that they would find and listen to the disc. In this lesson, the tables are turned.

## Previous Knowledge and Skills

Students need to already be familiar with standard musical notation and traditional and nontraditional musical instruments.

## Music Concepts and Objectives/Assessment

**STANDARDS ADDRESSED:** Reading and notating music; understanding relationships between music, the other arts, and disciplines outside the arts; understanding music in relation to history and culture (MENC 2007)

**INSTRUCTIONAL OBJECTIVES:** Students create musical notation systems and invent musical instruments (and models, if time) for the space aliens, based on the characteristics provided in this lesson.

**ASSESSED BY:** Completion of projects and evaluation by peers

## Science Concepts Objectives and Assessment

**STANDARDS ADDRESSED:** Content Standard E—Abilities of technological design and understanding about science and technology; Content Standard F—Populations, resources, and environments; natural hazards, risks, and benefits; and science and technology in society (NSTA 2008)

**INSTRUCTIONAL OBJECTIVES:** To design a musical instrument and/or a notational system based on a set of given criteria about aliens who do not reside on Earth

**ASSESSED BY:** Completion of projects and evaluation by peers

## Time for Lesson

Duration: 120 minutes over several class days or weeks

## Materials/Resources

1. Heavy-duty drawing paper
2. Magic markers
3. Pencils
4. Sketching paper
5. Pens or fine tip markers
6. Glue
7. Other materials that the students find or create by their own means
8. Other art supplies: glitter, cotton, scissors, and so on
9. List of characteristics of space aliens (see the following: they will be mixed and matched)

## Physical Characteristics of Space Aliens

(Select one from each of the following categories to construct a space alien.)

### HEAD AND HEARING

- Giant head, so large that they can't stand up and need to sit all the time. They have one ear that hears only low sounds, and it's located at the front of the head.
- Size of head is just like earthlings, but with three ears that hear very low to very high sounds

- Two heads and four ears that turn (like dog ears do) to hear sound
- One head and one ear that rotates to hear sound. It is very keen and picks up very high sounds down to very low sounds.
- One head, three ears. The two on either side of the head hear high sounds, but the one in front hears low sounds.
- No ears at all. They sense their music through vibrations.

## MOUTH AND BREATHING

- One mouth, and they inhale and exhale
- One mouth, but they do not breathe
- Two mouths, two sets of lungs for breathing
- No mouth and no lungs!

## SIGHT

- Eyes are on hands (they have two hands); they see only in black and white.
- One eye that sees in color
- Two eyes that see in color in middle of the belly
- No eyes at all

## EXTREMITIES

- Two arms, one on each side of the body, with one hand on each with three fingers and no thumb
- Three arms, one on each side of the body and one at the chest level, each with one hand, with three fingers and a thumb
- One arm with two hands at the chest level of the body, four fingers on each hand, and two thumbs, one on each hand
- Two arms with two fingers, and one centralized leg and foot, with eight toes

## PERSONALITY AND INTELLIGENCE

- They have a great sense of silliness and like silly sounds. They like things simple, not complex, and very silly.
- They have a large brain and are very intelligent. They love attention to detail and work hard to get just the right kinds of sounds that they want.
- They don't talk, so they communicate with their instruments and music. They like sounds that are very expressive, and their instruments need to have a wide range to make the sounds they want.
- They are very lazy and don't like any work at all, so they like to keep things as simple as possible so they don't have to spend time thinking things out.

## MATERIALS AVAILABLE

- Their planet is overrun with three-legged pink *nubbies* (like bunnies) and purple giant spotted *lurterts* (like turtles), which means they have lots of fur and shells available (only after animals have passed on after living long lives, as they would never hurt an animal). There is water available on the planet, and they have many bamboo trees, not unlike the ones on planet Earth. There are no other kinds of trees.
- The planet is all rock. Everything is rock. There are no trees. Because of this, the residents of the planets have devised a lot of tools to drill and carve rocks and use them in unusual ways. They also have plenty of water, but it is mostly salt water. The animals that live on this planet are mostly aquatic; however, they are able to communicate vocally with the other planet inhabitants. They are called *phlindops* (like dolphins).
- The planet is wood and water. There is no rock. All animals grow special fur coats, so their coats are covered in plastic-type material to protect them (just like the ones we put on furniture). When the coats are struck with rain or snow—if they are uncovered—they make sounds like little high bells and can get a bit noisy. The wood is mostly like our pine, maple, or walnut woods (so it ranges from soft to hard). Of special significance, this planet is governed by four-legged creatures, not

unlike dogs on this planet, which walk upright and have very sensitive hearing, so they don't really like very loud or high music. These four-legged creatures are called *pussopoms*.
- The planet is made of a plastic material, lots of metal, crystal, and has water. It was originally a satellite set adrift millions of years ago, and the inhabitants kept adding on to it as they developed materials in their laboratories. Everything is alien-made. There are no animals other than ones who are computerized.

### Procedure

**ANTICIPATORY SET (ATTENTION HOOK)**    "The musical instruments that humans invented had a lot to do with how human bodies were made. For example, we need two arms to play instruments of the string family. How do we play those instruments? What other instruments do we play and what body parts or physical skills do we need to play them? Would we be able to play these instruments with our feet? Would we be able to read music visually if we had no eyes? What if we had three arms instead of two? How could we change instruments to be playable for us if we had an extra arm and hand?"

After gathering hypotheses during the opening construction, perhaps with some drawing on the board to further illustrate, start the activity. First, the students will need to be divided into at least five groups. Then, a member of each group will go to the five plastic bags that have previously been individually filled with cut strips of paper describing each alien characteristic. You can either define the alien, or the students can mix and match their own, picking one characteristic from each plastic bags (which is more fun). When the groups are together, they have to piece together their alien and the circumstances under which it lives, and will do both or either of the following:

1. Design a musical instrument that this alien can play. They would need to develop how it will be constructed, how the sound will be produced, the kind of sound it will make, and then they will illustrate it on a sheet of heavy construction paper;
2. Design a notation system of reading music. They would create not only the system, but they would need to illustrate it and describe how the alien would read it, with special emphasis that it would need to be read while an instrument is being played.

Past experience with this activity has taught us that the students really like to spend time brainstorming to come up with a number of ideas; through this activity, they develop a better understanding of why we have the instruments we have and why we have our notation system. The final projects are excellent for a class exhibition. Sample projects have included instruments for aliens with three arms and a mouth but with no vision, so the extra hand reads the music, and also for instruments that included live animals helping create the sounds (without them getting hurt or abused in any way). You can take as many liberties as possible with the characteristics, as we include only a sample list.

### Evaluation

Students can evaluate each other on this project, and this is commonly done with group projects. The students will rate each other (anonymously, of course) on a scale of 1 to 5 (with 5 being good and 1 being not good) on the following: (1) contributing to the design, (2) getting tasks done responsibly, and (3) communicating with group members. This kind of evaluation helps students realize that they are being held responsible for the work, and it also helps to avoid having one person doing all of the work. Students are also evaluated on the quality of the project. You are strongly advised to use a rubric to help evaluate this.

### Continuing the Lesson

Students can investigate world musical instruments to see how they became what they became (for example, refer to Chapter 4 in this book). They can also develop their own instruments that may be different from traditional ones.

CHAPTER **19**

# Reading and Writing Lessons

## LESSON 1

Beat and no beat, keeping a steady beat, using iconic representations to indicate beat

### Level

Prekindergarten to K

### Project/Activities

Class activity: Students will identify, play, and discriminate among sounds and music that have a beat. They will also create their own representations of ways to keep a beat.

### Previous Knowledge and Skills

Students need to know how to count up to eight.

### Music Concepts and Objectives/Assessment

**STANDARDS ADDRESSED:**   Performing on instruments, alone and with others, a varied repertoire of music; improvising melodies, variations, and accompaniments; composing and arranging music within specified guidelines; moving to music; and listening to, analyzing, and describing music (MENC 2007)

**INSTRUCTIONAL OBJECTIVES:**   The students will aurally discriminate among numbers of beats, using appropriate bodily gestures. They will also create and improvise ways to keep the steady beat.

**ASSESSED BY:** Observing the students improvising either vocally or on available classroom instruments (with long and short melody bars, if available)

### Mathematics Concepts and Objectives/Assessment

**STANDARDS ADDRESSED:**   Count with understanding and recognize "how many" in sets of objects (NCTM 2008)

**INSTRUCTIONAL OBJECTIVE:**   The students will be able to count and identify how many beats they hear in a song.

**ASSESSED BY:**   Having students circle pictorial representations of how many beats they hear, and having them draw their own representations (lines, circles, other shapes) to represent a number of beats

Students improvise on Orff instruments.

*Photo courtesy of Union City School District, Pennsylvania*

## Time for Lesson

Duration: 20 minutes

## Materials/Resources

1. "Nanny Goat" (song) (Figure 19.1)
2. Classroom instruments of various sizes
3. Drawing paper, pencils, or crayons
4. Large drawing easel

## Procedure

**ANTICIPATORY SET (ATTENTION HOOK)**   Start with the hook/anticipatory set. Say, "Let's put our hands over our hearts, and be really still for a moment . . . what do you feel happening under your hand?" Students respond that they feel a heartbeat. Have students gently tap their own chests to their own heartbeats.

Continue by asking the students if they can think of anything else that has a beat, like a heart. Students will come up with clocks, and may also come up with windshield wipers, someone chopping vegetables, snow shoveling, walking, and so on. It is important to have the students identify and also imitate these behaviors to reinforce the sense of beat.

Tell students that all music has a beat, too, and that we are able to hear and feel it many times. When the beat stops, the music also stops.

Sing the song, "Nanny Goat," and pat the beat to the song. There are eight beats in this song, so ask the students how many times you pat the beat on your legs. When the students are able to pat the eight beats, then teach the song to the students by rote.

Students may also come up with other ways to keep a steady beat; for example, they can pat their heads, clap their hands, and snap their fingers. They may also do so on instruments.

You may also play a game in which you tap a certain number of beats and the students have to count how many were tapped. The students can also be the ones to tap beats and have the rest of the class count how many were tapped.

Students may also draw or color their own iconic representations of beats on paper or on a large drawing easel, and point to the beat and have the rest of the class clap or pat along.

Finally, the students can play the game that goes with "Nanny Goat," which is a chase game like "Duck, Duck, Goose." The students sit in a circle, and one child gets to walk outside the circle and gently tap the other students' heads to the beat while walking around the outside. On the eighth beat, the end of the song, the seated child will get up and chase the other child around the circle and back to the spot just vacated.

## Evaluation

Look for movements that indicate steady beat (clapping, patting, tapping) on instruments or on the body, or of drawings of iconic representations of beat (hearts, clocks, lines, circles, and so on).

Questions could include: How many steady beats am I clapping? How many steady beats is Sam (or any other student) tapping? What are things that move to a beat?

**FIGURE 19.1** "Nanny Goat"

Nanny Goat

Nan - ny goat, Nan - ny goat, You can't catch a bil - ly goat.

Game: Play nanny goat like duck, duck goose. Children sit in a circle; one child (the billy goat) walks around the outside and taps heads to the beat as song is sung (one pat per head). The last head patted is the one that belongs to the child (the nanny goat) who gets up to chase the billy goat back to the empty spot in the circle.

## Continuing the Lesson

The next lesson, reinforce beat with more rhythm games, and also move discriminating between music with a beat and music without a beat.

## LESSON 2

Lines and spaces of the treble clef using the hand staff

### Level

Grades 1 and 2

### Project/Activities

Students will use their hand staffs to name lines and spaces of the treble clef, to count steps, and to help create words and small melodies.

### Previous Knowledge and Skills

Students should already be familiar with what a full staff looks like (five lines, four spaces) and the solfège relationships between pitches of do, re, mi, sol, and la. Students also need to know the alphabet and be able to recite it. This lesson is best at the end of first grade or at the beginning of second grade (especially useful if the string instrumental program starts in the summer after second grade). Students should also be able to recognize a treble clef, and the difference between lower and higher.

### Music Concepts and Objectives/Assessment

**STANDARDS ADDRESSED:** Performing on instruments, alone and with others, a varied repertoire of music; improvising melodies, variations, and accompaniments; composing and arranging music within specified guidelines; moving to music; and listening to, analyzing, and describing music (MENC 2007)

**INSTRUCTIONAL OBJECTIVES:** The students will be able to name lines and spaces of the treble clef, using a hand staff (on the board and their own). They will be able to put the line and space names together to make words and melodies. If the students are not familiar with the whole staff, they can use part of the hand staff, like their first two fingers if they are only familiar with two lines and one space, and the following lesson can be adjusted and simplified as needed.

**ASSESSED BY:** Observing the students improvising melodies on a hand staff with correct names

### Mathematics Concepts and Objectives/Assessment

**STANDARDS ADDRESSED:** Count with understanding and recognize how many in sets of objects (NCTM 2008)

**INSTRUCTIONAL OBJECTIVE:** The students will be able to count and identify how many steps are used in moving from one note to another on a hand staff.

**ASSESSED BY:** Having students count on their fingers (held sideways) to show how many steps

### Time for Lesson

Duration: 30 minutes

### Materials/Resources

1. A drawing of a hand staff on the blackboard, with finger and spaces labeled. This should be a picture of a left hand, with the hand held sideways and with the thumb at the top.
2. Clean hands on the students
3. Melody bells and/or a piano

## Procedure

**ANTICIPATORY SET (ATTENTION HOOK)**   Ask students, "What do we call the five lines and four spaces that music notes live on?" Most students will recognize it as a staff. "Today will be different because now we are going to learn the official names of the lines and spaces on the treble clef staff."

Most students will recognize the staff on the board, but what they may not realize is that they carry a staff with them at all times, on their hands (as hands have five lines/fingers and four spaces). Model the hand staff using your right hand, while the students mirror using the left hand.

First, start with the spaces from the bottom up—F, A, C, and E. You can model and reinforce where the spaces are, and finally, a student can model instead and lead the students. As an extra activity, a child or two can play the corresponding bars on a barred instrument (make sure they are clearly marked so they are the ones in the right register) that will help reinforce the sound with the note, and reinforce direction (higher, lower).

Students can also create word melodies using the F-A-C and E letters, and if you allow for an extra letter, like a T, then more words can be created. This will likely work better for second graders than for first graders, depending upon spelling ability.

When the names of the spaces are learned, then the students can learn the names of the lines/fingers: E, G, B, D, and F, with emphasis on the letters being alphabetically in order between the spaces, so they realize that space-line-space-line sequence is always in alphabetical order.

At this point, there can be more spelling games, using the hand staff, and you and students can play the corresponding pitches on instruments if desired. After the students are familiar with the hand staff, then they can start to count steps between lines and spaces, say from A to C (three steps), making sure that they count the line or space they start on as step one and also include the line or space where they end. This will be helpful in learning intervals later on.

## Evaluation

Make sure students are pointing to the correct fingers or spaces when naming them, and have them help each other as needed.

Questions could include: Who can spell FACE with the hand? Who can spell BAD? What is the highest line on the staff? What is the lowest line on the staff?

## Continuing the Lesson

Students can create melodic patterns using words they create from the hand staff. Connecting the sounds of the notes with the names is important so they associate the particular sound mentally, which helps aural training.

## LESSON 3

Writing minimalist music

## Level

Grades 3 and 4

## Project/Activities

Students will create eight sixteen-measure pieces of music, using a tone box and a set of small melodic and rhythmic motives. This activity can be adjusted or modified to work with whatever materials are available in the classroom.

## Previous Knowledge and Skills

Students should be familiar with and able to read basic musical notation on the treble clef at the minimum, and bass clef is optional but encouraged. They should have experience playing melodies on tone bells or Orff instruments, and also in singing using solfège syllables *do, re, mi, fa, sol, la,* and *do.* They should also be able to internalize a steady beat and perform rhythms using instruments or body percussion that include but are not limited to the syllables *ta* (quarter note), *ti-ti* (two eighth notes), *ta-ah* (half note), *rest* (quarter, half), and the sixteenth-dotted eighth combination (see samples at www.pearsonhighered.com/flohr). Students should have experience creating and improvising music.

## Music Concepts and Objectives/Assessment

**STANDARDS ADDRESSED:**  Performing on instruments, alone and with others, a varied repertoire of music; improvising melodies, variations, and accompaniments; composing and arranging music within specified guidelines; and listening to, analyzing, and describing music (MENC 2007)

**INSTRUCTIONAL OBJECTIVES:**  The students will create a sixteen-measure minimalist piece of music, using their voices and available classroom instruments. They will also listen how a composer (John Adams) takes the same motives and creates a longer piece of music out of them ("The Chairman Dances").

**ASSESSED BY:**  Students listing, describing, and comparing the differences and similarities among and between their own versions of the music and the composers

## Language Arts Concepts and Objectives/Assessment

**STANDARDS ADDRESSED:**  Students employ a wide range of strategies as they write and use different writing process elements appropriately to communicate with different audiences for a variety of purpose (NCTE 1996)

**INSTRUCTIONAL OBJECTIVE:**  The students will create their own poetry (for example, cinquains and haiku) to show minimalism in writing.

**ASSESSED BY:**  Having students compose their own haiku or cinquains

## Time for Lesson

Duration: 30 minutes

## Materials/Resources

1. Recording of "The Chairman Dances" from the opera, *Nixon in China,* by John Adams
2. Tone box (on board) showing at least eight measures
3. Drawing paper, pencils, colored chalk
4. Tone boxes as handouts
5. Classroom instruments

## Procedure

**ANTICIPATORY SET (ATTENTION HOOK)**    Ask the students what elements of music they know about that are necessary to compose a piece of music (rhythm, melody, and so on)? Help students realize that these elements can be very complex or very simple: "For this class, we are going to look at the simple version. There are composers that use only a few elements to create a piece of music that can actually go on for a long time. These kinds of pieces are 'minimalist' pieces, and today the class will create one, and then hear how a composer uses the exact same elements in a piece of music. The elements for this piece will consist of several melodic and rhythmic motives, and some percussion instruments keeping a steady beat."

First, familiarize the students with the four motives (of course, depending upon the students' abilities, more may be used). Figure 19.2 illustrates the four patterns:

**FIGURE 19.2** The Chairman Dances Musical Motives

It is best to show each one on the blackboard or on large cards, and then to have the students sing them, repeating them over and over, layering them upon one another to build up a particular piece. This can be done by having one group sing pattern one, then bringing in pattern 2, then three, removing 1, bringing 4, and so on. Students may also conduct this kind of sound piece, cueing students when to sing and when not to sing. It is important to add a rhythm instrument to keep a steady beat constantly once things really get going (Adams is known for the use of the wood block to maintain the sense of a steady beat because the meters constantly change throughout the piece).

Students may also wish to create their own two-beat patterns and add them to the mix. As the patterns build, it is important to make sure that they are not all going at the same time for extended periods: certain ones can be brought out and emphasized as solos, for example.

The next step is to compose a piece of music using a tone box, such as is shown in Figure 19.3, that can be drawn on a blackboard.

| | 1 | 2 | 3 | 4 | 5 | 6 | 7 | 8 |
|---|---|---|---|---|---|---|---|---|
| **La-la (1)** | | | | | | | | |
| **m-m-r-r (2)** | | | | | | | | |
| **Do do do do (3)** | | | | | | | | |
| **mi-la (4)** | | | | | | | | |
| Rhythm Insstument: | | | | | | | | |
| Rhythm Instrument: | | | | | | | | |

**FIGURE 19.3** Tone Box

Each box indicates a measure. The students can draw the patterns into corresponding boxes to create their own pieces of music. Again, it is important to emphasize that not all boxes need to be filled: those that are empty indicate measures of rest. The tone box pattern can also be used to create a class ostinato, and other students may improvise over it, using other patterns that they make up and repeat over and over.

After the students have composed their own pieces, and the class has performed the pieces, then they can listen for the same patterns (at least the first four) in the opening of "The Chairman Dances" by John Adams. Patterns 1 and 2 are in from the beginning, pattern 3 joins in after about eight measures, and then pattern 4 is used as more of an exclamatory point rather than a repeated pattern.

Students may listen to the first minute or so several times to find out how Adams used the patterns, what instruments are used, perhaps other ones added, and so on, and to investigate the compositional process. What this piece illustrates is that one does not need a lot of fancy melodies or rhythms to make an engaging and exciting piece of music.

"The Chairman Dances" is from the part of the opera, *Nixon in China*, where Madame Chiang Kai-Shek dances in a traditional Chinese Cheongsam dress on a table. The piece moves into a traditional 1940s foxtrot dance, written primarily in pentatonic, before moving back to the style of the beginning section.

## Evaluation

Evaluation will take place by having the students create, improvise, and perform a piece of minimalist music, and by connecting in the listening part of the lesson how many of the elements they used in their piece were also used in "The Chairman Dances."

## Continuing the Lesson

Many people find minimalist music addictive to listen to, primarily because of the pervasive rhythms, strong beat, and simplicity to grasp. Other pieces that may interesting to investigate include Terry Riley's "In C," pieces by Steve Reich, and more pieces by John Adams, who currently combines minimalist techniques with other compositional devices and formal structures. Students may also engage in setting their haiku or cinquains to minimalist accompaniments, perhaps having an instrument playing the rhythm of the words as opposed to the words always being spoken. Students may also engage in minimalist art and movement activities as well.

## LESSON 4

Composing a piece of music using tone rows

## Level

Grades 5 and 6

## Project/Activities

Students will create one or several simple pieces based on a class-derived tone row in both original and retrograde (others are optional if you wish to go that far). The suggested length of the piece is thirty-two measures, but there can be more depending upon the abilities of the students.

## Previous Knowledge and Skills

Everything listed in the previous lesson plans needs to be mastered for this lesson. Students need to be able to read and write in standard musical notation (both melodic and rhythmic), be able to identify and apply formal structures in composition (for example, AB, ABA), and to compose either with pencil and paper or on a computer using a notation program.

## Music Concepts and Objectives/Assessment

**STANDARDS ADDRESSED:** Performing on instruments, alone and with others, a varied repertoire of music; improvising melodies, variations, and accompaniments; composing and arranging music within specified guidelines; and listening to, analyzing, and describing music (MENC 2007)

**INSTRUCTIONAL OBJECTIVES:** The students will compose pieces of music based on tone rows.

**ASSESSED BY:** Student compositional success

## Language Arts Concepts and Objectives/Assessment

**STANDARDS ADDRESSED:** Students read a wide range of literature from many periods in many genres to build an understanding of the many dimensions (for example, philosophical, ethical, aesthetic) of human experience; students apply knowledge of language structure, language conventions (for example, spelling and punctuation), media techniques, figurative language, and genre to create, critique, and discuss print and nonprint texts; students participate as knowledgeable, reflective, creative, and critical members of a variety of literacy communities (NCTE 1996)

**INSTRUCTIONAL OBJECTIVES:** Students create palindromes. Samples include:

> *A nut for a jar of tuna.*
> *A Santa at NASA.*

**ASSESSED BY:** Student success at creating palindromes

## Time for Lesson(s)

Duration: 90 minutes (two 45-minute class periods, or three 30-minute periods)

## Materials/Resources

1. Chalkboard and chalk
2. List of pitches in chromatic scale
3. Manuscript paper and pencils

## Procedure

**ANTICIPATORY SET (ATTENTION HOOK)** Up to this point, we have experimented with a number of ways to compose music. Can you remind us what they were (using tone boxes, improvising rhythms, using minimalist techniques, for example)? Today we are going to experiment with a very different kind in which we will create a list or row of twelve notes that need to stick to these rules:

1. Each note/pitch can only appear once in the list or row, and this is true for enharmonic notes (notes that sound the same but have different names, like B flat and A sharp).
2. The pitches must be played in the order they appear, either from the left to right or the right to left. You can have multiple pitches as a chord, as long as they are in the correct order.
3. Pitches that are in different octaves are permissible.

At this point, the students can create a tone row as a class, by calling out pitches that you (or a student) can write on the blackboard in the order they are mentioned. A tone row, perhaps similar to the following, may result:

A C# G D D# F B Ab E C D Gb

You can then play this row frontward, then backward on a piano, or the students can play them on bells to illustrate how a tone row works and also how following the sequence chords can be added. Usually, one melody line with a piano accompaniment works best, but if the students are able, they can write the piece for a small ensemble instead.

Some students may be able to work with the row in inversions, and if that is the case, an enrichment opportunity in developing inverted rows can be created for them. These can also be developed and added to the original row on the blackboard so more students can use them in their pieces.

Finished pieces may be performed within the class, using whatever instrumentation is available. Having a student recital showcasing their compositions is also a great classroom activity as well as a formal concert activity.

## Evaluation

One characteristic that really shows up with this activity is that, even though everyone starts with the exact same ingredients, they all come up with pieces that are totally different. Looking for these differences brings out individuality in the compositional process.

## Continuing the Lesson

This activity works well in conjunction with a listening lesson on serial writing, so introducing them to the works of Schoenberg, Berg, and Webern would help them see how this type of composition developed, and consequently perhaps why many composers of the later twentieth century went back to more of a melodic emphasis. In a different application, students can take any melodies they already know (previous compositions or known songs), and give them the same frontward and backward treatment in a composition.

A verbal activity that also works is to have students create palindromes (sentences or phrases that read the same whether read left to right or right to left). These could be set to an accompanying tone row and perhaps turned into a piece of performable music for the school chorus.

# APPENDIX 1: LIST OF SONGS

# APPENDIX 2:  LIST OF FIGURES

# APPENDIX 3: LIST OF TABLES

Table 2.1    Overview of Theories Relating to Children's Education

Table 4.1    Listening Similarities and Contrasts

Table 5.1    Milestones in Listening

Table 5.2    Listening Chart, Grade 6

Table 6.1    Vocal Development Milestones for Birth—Prior to Onset of Puberty

Table 6.2    Observed Singing Ranges of Children

Table 7.1    Milestones in Motor Skill Development

Table 7.2    Basic Moving Repertoire

Table 8.1    Milestones in Creating

Table 9.1    Milestones in Playing Instruments

Table 10.1    Milestones in Reading and Writing Music

Table 11.1    Methods for Teaching Music to Children

Table 11.2    Methods: Experiences for 5-year-olds

Table 12.1    First Grade Singing Development Rubric

Table 12.2    Taxonomy Example

# GLOSSARY

**A capella:** Singing without accompaniment.

**Accelerando:** Steady beat gradually gets faster.

**Accent:** Louder beat with emphasis.

**Audiation:** Ability to hear without the sound being physically present.

**Autoharp:** Stringed instrument used to accompany songs.

**Beat:** see steady beat.

**Blues scale:** One example in the key of C is C, D, E (E♭), F, G (G♭), A, B♭. Many variations of blues scales exist.

**bpm:** Beats per minute. Similar to m.m. (metronome marking).

**Call-and-response:** Form of singing or chanting. Soloist sings a phrase and is answered by the group.

**Chant:** Words spoken in rhythm.

**Chord:** The sounding together of three or more notes.

**Classroom instruments:** Typical instruments include recorders, recorder-type instruments, Autoharps, mallet instruments, simple percussion, fretted (for example, guitar, banjo), keyboards, and electronic instruments.

**Clef:** Symbol at beginning of staff to indicate where the pitches are on the staff. Commonly used clefs are treble and bass.

**Coda:** Italian for ending. A section at end of a piece of music.

**Crescendo:** Gradually becoming louder.

**Cricothyroids (CT):** Muscles that control how long and stiff the vocal bands become.

**Decrescendo:** See diminuendo.

**Diatonic:** Scale comprised of eight tones (for example, C, D, E, F, G, A, B, C).

**Diminuendo:** Gradually becoming softer.

**Dulcimer:** String instrument with three to four strings usually held across the lap (often in hourglass shape); also call Appalachian or mountain dulcimer.

**Duration:** Relative longness or shortness of sound.

**Dynamics:** The nuance or degrees of loudness and softness.

**Echo-singing, Echo-playing:** Group or person sings or plays back what is sung or played.

**Eighth note:** A rhythmic value 1/8 the duration of a whole note.

**Elements of music:** Rhythm, pitch, timbre, harmony, dynamics, texture, and form.

**Experience:** A purposeful activity based upon an objective or objectives.

**Expression or expressively:** With nuances of dynamics, phrasing, style, and interpretation. Related to emotion.

**Falsetto:** High-pitched voice.

**Form:** Overall structural organization of music. For example, a section (A), a contrasting section (B), and section A is ABA form (ternary). Other simple forms include AB (binary) and rondo (for example, ABACA, ABACADA).

**Forte:** Loud.

**Glissando:** Playing or singing a series of consecutive pitches (usually fast).

**Half note:** A rhythmic value half the duration of a whole note.

**Half step:** Smallest interval on keyboard instrument (for example, C to C#).

**Hand signs:** A sign language for pitches (for example, do, re, mi).

**Harmony:** Two or more tones played simultaneously.

**Improvisation:** Performing music spontaneously from imagination; to make up music on the spot rather than from a written score or from memory.

**Interval:** Distance from one pitch to another pitch.

**Key:** See tonal center.

**Legato:** Smooth, connected.

**m.m.:** Metronome marking; similar to bpm.

**Macrobeat:** The larger overall steady beat.

**Major scale:** An ordering of pitches. C, D, E, F, G, A, B and any transposition of the half- and whole-step arrangement of W W H W W W H.

**Measure:** The area between two vertical bars (bar lines) in music notation.

**Melisma:** Several pitches sung on the same syllable of text.

**Melody:** Arrangement of pitches into a sequence; linear aspect of music.

**Meter:** Grouping of steady beats; duple, triple, or a combination of twos and threes.

**Metronome:** A device to produce various tempi (speeds of steady beat).

**Microbeat:** The smaller steady beat; faster than the macrobeat.

**Middle C:** The C nearest to the midpoint of the piano keyboard.

**Minor scale:** An ordering of pitches. C, D, E♭, F, G, A♭, B♭, and any transposition of the half- and whole-step arrangement of W H W W H W.

**Mnenomics:** Speech sounds assigned to rhythm durations.

**Mother tongue approach:** An approach to learning music as you would learn language (Suzuki and Kodály).

**Note:** See pitch. Common note durations in common time include eighth (1/2 count), quarter (1 count), half (2 counts), and whole (4 counts).

**Orff instruments:** The collection of melodic percussion bar instruments developed by Carl Orff in the 1920s.

**Ostinato:** (Ostinati, pl.). Repeated harmony, rhythm, and/or melodic patterns.

**Pedal tones:** A held out or repeated tone on the tonic (key center).

**Pentatonic scale:** Scales comprised of five tones. The most common in folk songs is the gapped pentatonic scale.

**Percussion:** Unptiched are instruments such as triangle, finger cymbal, or woodblock that sound an indefinite pitch; and pitched instruments that sound a definite pitch such as middle C.

**Phrase:** A musical thought or idea. Similar to a sentence in language.

**Piano:** Soft; also a musical instrument.

**Piggyback songs:** Songs with the same melody but different words.

**Pitch:** Name for a musical tone; used interchangeably with note; also the highness or lowness of a sound.

**Pre-reading:** Used to refer to experiences that prepare children for later reading experiences.

**Program music:** Music that depicts or suggests nonmusical incidents, ideas, or images, e.g., *Peter and the Wolf* is based on a story.

**Pulse:** See steady beat.

**Quarter note:** A rhythmic value 1/4 the duration of a whole note.

**Range:** Highest and lowest notes of a piece of music, voice, or instrument.

**Register:** A range of pitches of a voice or instrument.

**Rest:** A music symbol indicating silence.

**Ritardando:** Gradually slower.

**Root:** Also tonic, home tone. Lowest pitch of a chord.

**Scale:** A series of pitches (see diatonic, pentatonic).

**Sixteenth note:** A rhythmic value 1/16 the duration of a whole note.

**Skip:** Interval of pitches more than one alphabet letter name away from another (for example, C to F).

**Solfa:** See solfège. Sometimes called tonic solfa.

**Solfège:** Also solfa, solmization. Using do, re, mi, fa, sol, la, ti for pitches.

**Solmization:** See solfège.

**Staccato:** Crisp, detached manner. Short sound.

**Staff:** Music notation system (five spaced horizontal lines); can be one or two horizontal lines in percussion music.

**Steady beat:** Also beat, pulse, heartbeat, tempo; recurring pulse of the music.

**Stick notation:** Simple shorthand for rhythmic notation.

**Syncopation:** Accent on a beat or part of beat not ordinarily accented.

**Tempo:** Speed of the steady beat.

**Thyroarytenoids (TA):** Muscles that control the amount of opening between the vocal bands.

**Timbre:** Tone color; quality of tones.

**Time signature:** Two numbers at beginning of music that indicate the number and note value of a measure.

**Tonal center:** The first pitch of a scale or the home pitch; melodies often gravitate toward the tonal center. Also key center.

**Tonic:** The pitch that is the tonal center.

**Transposition:** Process of moving pitches higher or lower than the original with the half- and whole- step relationships intact. Moving music from one key to another.

**Triad:** Three pitches sounded simultaneously. Types include major, minor, and augmented. Each type has a distinctly different sound.

**Vocal ligament:** Part of the vocal apparatus required to develop singing range; also referred to as the true vocal cord structure.

**Vocal register:** Term used to describe what we think is physically happening inside the larynx when we hear changes in the quality of tone in a voice. Also called registration events, shifts, or breaks.

**Whistle register:** The highest vocal register in the human voice. This register is used occasionally in singing due to the excessive vocal tension it causes.

**Whole note:** A rhythmic value consistently used in traditional notation. Usually four steady beats. Equals four quarter notes or two half notes.

**Whole step:** An interval (two pitches in sequence) comprised of two half steps.

**Zither:** Also called concert, alpine, Austrian zither, the traditional modern zither has four to five melody strings. It uses frets similar to the guitar. Open strings provide bass and chord accompaniment. Many forms of fretless zithers do not have fretted strings.

# REFERENCES

Abel-Struth, S. 1981. Frankfurt studies on musical audiation of five- to seven-year-old children. *Bulletin of the Council for Research in Music Education* 66–67:1–7.

Abramson, R. M. 1973. *Rhythm games for perception and cognition*. Hialeah, Florida: Columbia Pictures Publications.

Abramson, R. M. 1998. *Feel it*. Miami: Warner Bros.

Alborough, J. 1994. *It's the bear!* Cambridge, MA: Candlewick Press.

Alford, D. L. 1971. Emergence and development of music responses in preschool twins and singletons: A comparative study. *Journal of Research in Music Education* 19:222–27.

Amabile, T. M. 1989. *The social psychology of creativity*. New York: Springer-Verlag.

Anderson, L., D. Krathwohl, P. Airasian, K. Cruickshank, R. Mayer, P. Pintrich, J. Raths, and M. Wittroch. 2000. *A taxonomy for learning, teaching, and assessing: A revision of bloom's taxonomy of educational objectives*. Abridged ed. New York: Allyn & Bacon.

Andrews, M. 1999. *Manual of voice treatment: Pediatrics through geriatrics*. San Diego, CA: Singular Publishing.

Andrews, M., and A. Summers. 2001. *Voice treatment for children and adolescents*. San Diego, CA: Singular Publishing.

Ansell, G. 2004. *Soweto blues: Jazz, popular music and politics in South Africa*. New York: The Continuum International Publishing Group Inc.

Appelman, D. R. 1967. *The science of vocal pedagogy*. Bloomington, IN: Indiana University Press.

Ayotte, J., I. Peretz, and K. Hyde. 2002. Congenital amusia. *Brain* 125(2):238–51.

Azzara, C. D. 2002. Improvisation. In *The new handbook of research on music teaching and learning,* ed. R. Colwell and C. Richards, 171–87. New York: Oxford University Press.

Azzara, C. D. 1993. Audiation-based improvisation techniques and elementary instrumental students' music achievement. *Journal of Research in Music Education* 41(4):328–42.

Backus, J. 1977. *The acoustical foundations of music*. New York: Norton.

Ballantine, C. 1993. *Marabi nights: Early South African jazz and vaudeville*. Braamfontein: Raven Press.

Bamberger, J. 1994. Coming to hear in a new way. In *Musical perceptions,* ed. R. Aiello, 131–51. New York: Oxford University Press.

Bandura, A. 1977. *Social learning theory*. Englewood Cliffs, NJ: Prentice Hall.

Barbe, W., and R. Swassing. 1979. *Teaching through modality strengths: Concepts and practices*. Columbus, OH: Zaner-Bloser.

Barrett, M. 1998. Researching children's compositional processes and products: Connections to music education practice? In *Musikpedagogik: Children composing,* eds. B. Sundin, G. E.

McPherson, and G. Folkestad, 10–34. Malmo, Sweden: Lunds University.

Bella, S. D., I. Peretz, L. Rosseau, and N. Gosselin. 2001. A developmental study of the affective value of tempo and mode in music. *Cognition* 80(3):B1–10.

Bentley, A. 1973. Technical problems in group measurement of pitch discrimination and an apparent subjective preference for downward tonal movement. *Psychology of Music* 1(2):31–38.

Bernstorf, E., P. Bennett, J. W. Flohr, R. Fuelberth, J. Kerchner, G. McGraw, et al. 2004. Report from the vocal health work group. Paper presented at the Health Promotion in Schools of Music Conference, Denton, TX. from http://www.unt.edu/hpsm/index.htm.

Biasini, A., R. Thomas, and L. Pogonowski. 1970. *MMCP interaction: Early childhood music curriculum*. Bardonia, NY: Media Materials, Inc.

Blacking, J. 1967/1995. *Venda children's songs: A study in ethomusicological analysis*. Chicago: University of Chicago Press.

Blake, J., and R. Fink. 1987. Sound meaning correspondences in babbling. *Journal of Child Language* 14:229–53.

Blank, L., Producer. 1994. *Appalachian fiddle, my old fiddle: A visit with Tommy Jarrell in the Blue Ridge*. (Motion Picture). Flower Films.

Bloom, B., and D. Krathwohl. 1956. *Taxonomy of educational objectives: The classification of educational goals, handbook I: Cognitive domain*. New York: David McKay.

Boardman, E. 1988a. The generative theory of musical learning. Part I: Introduction. *General Music* 2(1):4–5, 26–31.

Boardman, E. 1988b. The generative theory of musical learning. Part II. General music. *General Music* 2(2):3–6, 28–32.

Boardman, E. 1989. The generative theory of musical learning. Part III: Planning for learning. *General Music* 2(3):11–16.

Bolton, B. M., C. C. Taggart, A. M. Reynolds, W. H. Valerio, D. G. Woods, and E. E. Gordon. 1990. *Jump right in: General music series*. Chicago: G.I.A.

Boseley, M., and C. J. Hartnick. 2006. Development of the human true vocal fold: Depth of cell layers and quantifying cell types within the lamina propria. *Annals of Otology, Rhinology and Laryngology* 115(10):784–88.

Bosma, J. F. 1975. Anatomic and physiologic development of the speech apparatus in the nervous system, vol. 3. In *Human communication and its disorders,* ed. D. B. Tower. New York: Raven.

Bresler, L. 2002. *Across music and other disciplines*. Bergen, Norway: International Society for Music Education.

Bresler, L. 1995. The subservient, co-equal, affective, and social integration styles and their implications for the arts. *Arts Education Policy Review* 96(5):31–37.

Briggs-Myers, I., and M. McCaulley. 1992. *A guide to the development and use of the Myers-Briggs type indicator*. Mountain View, CA: Consulting Psychologists Press.

Bronfenbrenner, U. 1989. Ecological systems theory. In *Annals of child development: Theories of child development: Revised formulations and current issues,* ed. R. Vasta, 187–251. Greenwich, CT: JAI Press.

Brophy, T. S. 2000. *Assessing the developing child musician: A guide for general music teachers.* Chicago, IL: G.I.A. Publications.

Brophy, T. S. 1999. The melodic improvisations of children ages six through twelve: A developmental perspective. Doctoral dissertation, University of Kentucky. *Dissertation Abstracts International* 59 (9):3386A.

Broudy, H. S. 1972. *Enlightened cherishing: An essay on aesthetic education.* Urbana, IL: University of Illinois Press.

Brown, A., and T. Green. 2006. *The essentials of instructional design.* Upper Saddle River, NJ: Prentice Hall.

Brown, J. S., A. Collins, and P. Duguid. 1989. Situated cognition and the culture of learning. *Educational Researcher* 18(1): 32–42. Brown, O. L. 1996. *Discover your voice.* 4th ed. San Diego, CA: Singular Publishing Group, Inc.

Bruner, J. 1996. *The culture of education.* Cambridge, MA: Harvard University Press.

Bruner, J. 1983. *Child's talk: Learning to use language.* New York: Norton.

Bruner, J. 1966. *Toward a theory of instruction.* Cambridge, MA: Harvard University Press.

Butler, S. 1992. *The musician's guide to cognition and perception.* New York: Schirmer.

Byerly, I. 1996. *The music indaba: Music as a mirror, mediator and prophet in the South African transition from apartheid to democracy.* Unpublished doctoral dissertation, Duke University.

Caldwell, R., and J. Wall. 2001. *Excellence in singing: Multilevel learning and multilevel teaching.* Redmond, WA: Caldwell Publishing Co.

Caldwell, T., with Robert M. Abramson. 1992. *Dalcroze eurhythmics.* Chicago: G.I.A. Publications.

Calogero, J. M. 2002. Integrating music and children's literature. *Music Educators Journal* 88(5):23–30.

Campbell, P. S., and A. Beegle. 2003. Middle Eastern expansions on cultural diversity in music education. *Music Educators Journal* 90(1):21–30.

Central Intelligence Agency. 2008. *The world factbook.* https://www.cia.gov/library/publications/the-world-factbook (accessed May 15, 2009).

Chang, H. W., and S. E. Trehub. 1977a. Auditory processing of relational information by young infants. *Journal of Experimental Child Psychology* 24:324–31.

Chang, H. W., and S. E. Trehub. 1977b. Infants' perception of temporal grouping in auditory patterns. *Child Development* 48:1666–70.

Charlton, A. 1997. *Cloggers shuffle and skip to save Appalachian tradition.* http://www.aldha.org/clogging.htm (accessed January 18, 2008).

Chen-Hafteck, L. 1998. Pitch abilities in music and language of Cantonese-speaking children. *International Journal of Music Education* 31:14–24.

Chesky, K., G. Kondraske, M. Henoch, J. Hipple, and B. Rubin. 2002. Musicians' health. In *The new handbook of research on music teaching and learning,* ed. R. Colwell and C. Richardson, 1023–39. New York: Oxford University Press.

Chew-Sanchez, M. I. 2003. Cultural memory in the rituals of the Mexican diaspora in the United States: The role of the corridos about immigration played by conjuntos norteños and the aesthetics of the bailes norteños. The Interpretation and Representation of Latino Cultures: Research and Museums Conference at the Smithsonian Institute, Washington, DC.

Choksy, L., R. M. Abramson, A. E. Gillespie, D. Woods, and F. York. 2001. *Teaching music in the twenty-first century.* 2nd ed. Englewood Cliffs, NJ: Prentice Hall.

Chomsky, N. 1957. *Synactic structures.* The Hague: Mouton.

Cleall, C. 1970. *Voice production in choral technique.* London: Novello.

Cohen, V. 1980. The emergence of musical gestures in kindergarten children. Doctoral dissertation, University of Illinois.

Colwell, R., and C. Richardson, eds. 2002. *The new handbook of research on music teaching and learning.* New York: Oxford University Press.

Colwell, R., and E. Wing. 2004. *The context for music education.* Upper Saddle River, NJ: Prentice Hall.

Comenius, J. A. 1638. In *The great didactic,* ed. and trans. M. W. (1967 ed.). New York: Russell & Russell. http://core.roehampton.ac.uk/digital/froarc/comgre/.

Commons, M. L., and F. A. Richards. 2002. Organizing components into combinations: How stage transition works. *Journal of Adult Development* 9(3):159–77.

Coplan, D. B. 2007. *In township tonight: Three centuries of South African black city music and theatre.* Chicago: University of Chicago Press.

Costanza, P., and T. Russell. 1992. Methodologies in music education. In *Handbook of research on music teaching and learning,* ed. R. Colwell, 498–508. New York: Schirmer Books.

Cowart, M. 2007. Loss and hope: Challenges in acculturation for refugee children in the United States. In *Intercultural understanding,* ed. P. Dam and M. T. Cowart, 1–20. Denton, TX: Federation of North Texas Area Universities.

Csikszentmihalyi, M. 1990. *Flow: The psychology of optimal experience.* New York: Harper and Row Publishers, Inc.

Csikszentmihalyi, M. 1975. *Beyond boredom and anxiety.* San Francisco: Jossey-Bass, Inc.

Darrow, A. A. 1989. Music and the hearing impaired: A review of the research with implications for music educators. *Update* 7:10–12.

Davidson, L., and B. Colley. 1987. Children's rhythmic development from age 5 to 7. In *Music and child development,* eds. J. C. Peery, I. W. Peery, and T. W. Draper, 107–36. New York: Springer-Verlag.

Davidson, L., P. McKernon, and H. Gardner. 1981. The acquisition of song: A developmental approach, 301–317. Ann Arbor Symposium on the Applications of Psychology to the Teaching and Learning of Music, Ann Arbor, MI.

Davidson, L., and L. Scripp. 1988. Young children's musical representations: Windows on music cognition. In *Generative processes in music: The psychology of performance, improvisation, and composition,* ed. J. A. Sloboda, 195–230. Oxford: Claredon Press.

Davies, C. 1992. Listen to my song: A study of songs invented by children aged 5–7 years. *British Journal of Music Education* 9(1):19–48.

Davies, E. 2001. *Beyond dance: Laban's legacy of movement analysis.* Santa Ana, CA: Seven Locks Press.

de Bono, E. 1993. *Teach your child how to think.* New York: Penguin.

de Boysson-Bardies, B., P. Halle, L. Sagart, and C. Durand. 1989. A cross linguistic investigation of vowel formants in babbling. *Journal of Child Language* 16:1–17.

de Jager, F. 2005. *Music instruments from the Philippines.* http://www.kipas.nl/MainMenu.html (accessed January 18, 2008).

Deasy, R., ed. 2002. *Critical links: Learning in the arts and student academic and social development.* Washington, DC: Arts Education Partnership.

Deliège, I., and J. A. Sloboda, eds. 1996. *Musical beginnings: Origins and development of musical competence.* New York: Oxford University Press.

DeMente, B. L. 1995. *Chinese in plain English.* Chicago: Contemporary Publishing Group.

DeVries, R., and L. Kohlberg. 1987. *Constructivist early education: Overview and comparison with other programs.* Washington, DC: National Association of the Education of Young Children.

Dewey, J. 1966. *Democracy and education.* (Reprint of 1929 Macmillian Co. publication ed.). New York: The Free Press.

Dick, W., L. Carey, and J. Carey. 2008. *The systematic design of instruction.* 7th ed. New York: Allyn & Bacon.

Dick, W., L. Carey, and J. Carey. 2004. *The systematic design of instruction.* 6th ed. New York: Allyn & Bacon.

Domer, J., and J. E. Gromko. 1996. Qualitative changes in preschoolers' invented notations following music instruction. *Contributions to Music Education* 23:62–78.

Dowling, W. J. 1988. Tonal structure and children's early learning of music. In *Generative processes in music,* ed. J. A. Sloboda, 113–28. Oxford: Clarendon Press.

Dowling, W. J. 1984. Development of musical schemate in children's spontaneous singing. In *Cognitive processes in the perception of art,* eds. W. R. Crozier and A. J. Chapman, 145–63. Amsterdam: Elsevier.

Duke, R. A. 1989. Musicians' perception of beat in monotonic stimuli. *Journal of Research in Music Education* 37(4):61–71.

Dunn, R., and K. Dunn. 1984. Learning style: State of the science. *Theory into Practice* 23(1):10–19.

Eilers, R. E., and D. K. Oller. 1988. Precursors to speech: What is innate and what is acquired? In *Annals of child development,* 5th ed., ed. R. Vasta. Greenwich, CT: JAI Press.

Eisen, A., and L. Robertson. 2002. *An American methodology: An inclusive approach to musical literacy.* Lake Charles, Louisiana: Sneaky Snake Publications.

Elliot, D. 1997. *Music matters: A new philosophy of music education.* New York: Oxford.

Erlmann, V. 1996. *Nightsong: Performance, power and practice in South Africa.* Chicago: University of Chicago Press.

Farmer, H. G. 1978. *Historical facts for Arabian musical influence.* Manchester, NH: Ayer Publishing.

Faulmann, J. 1980. Montessori and music in early childhood. *Music Educators Journal* 66:41–43.

Feierabend, J. M. 2000. *The book of bounces.* Chicago: G.I.A.

Feierabend, J. M. 1996. Music and movement for infants and toddlers: Naturally wonder-full. *Early Childhood Connections,* Fall:19–26.

Fletcher, H., and W. A. Munson. 1933. Loudness, its definition, measurement, and calculation. *Journal of the Acoustical Society of America* 5:82–108.

Flohr, J. W. 2006. Enriching music and language experiences. *General Music Today* 19(2):12–16.

Flohr, J. W. 2004. *Musical lives of young children.* Upper Saddle River, NJ: Prentice Hall.

Flohr, J. W. 2001. Music listening for young children: An interactive music listening project. *Early Childhood Connections: Journal of Music and Movement-Based Learning* 7(1):24–9.

Flohr, J. W. 2000. *Rhythm performance test—Revised manual.* Champaign, IL: Electronic Courseware Systems, Inc.

Flohr, J. W. 1987. Parenting the musically gifted: Assumptions and issues. *The Creative Child and Adult Quarterly* 12(1):62–65.

Flohr, J. W. 1985. Young children's improvisations: Emerging creative thought. *The Creative Child and Adult Quarterly* 10(2):79–85.

Flohr, J. W. 1981. Short-term music instruction and young children's developmental music aptitude. *Journal of Research in Music Education* 29(3):219–23.

Flohr, J. W. 1979. Musical improvisation behavior of young children. Doctoral dissertation, University of Illinois.

Flohr, J. W., D. Atkins, T. G. R. Bower, and M. Aldridge. 2000. Infant music preferences: Implications for child development and music. *Music Education Research Reports:* Texas Music Educators Association.

Flohr, J. W., and J. Brown. 1979. The influence of peer imitation on expressive movement to music. *Journal of Research in Music Education* 29(3):143–48.

Flohr, J. W., and D. Hodges. 2006. Music and neuroscience. In *MENC handbook of musical cognition and development,* ed. R. Colwell, 3–39. New York: Oxford University Press.

Flohr, J. W., and D. C. Miller. 1995. *Developmental quantitative EEG differences during psychomotor response to music.* Paper presented at the Texas Music Educators Convention, San Antonio, Texas: ERIC Document PS025653.

Flohr, J. W., D. C. Miller, and R. deBeus. 2000. EEG studies with young children. *Music Educators Journal* 87(2):28–32.

Flohr, J. W., D. C. Miller, and D. C. Persellin. 2000. Recent brain research on young children. *Music makes the difference: Music, brain development, and learning,* 37–43. Reston, VA: MENC.

Flohr, J. W., and R. B. Smith. 2008. *Storytelling with music: Sing, play, dance and act.* Allen, TX: Troost Press.

Flohr, J. W., L. Suthers, and S. Woodward. 1998. Cross cultural study of rhythm performance in early childhood. In *8th international seminar of the early childhood commission of the international society for music education,* ed. S. Woodward, 111–16. Stellenbosch, South Africa: ISME.

Flohr, J. W., and C. Trevarthen. 2008. Music learning in childhood: Early developments of a musical brain and body.

In *Neurosciences in music pedagogy,* ed. W. Gruhn and F. Rauscher, 53–99. Hauppage, NY: Nova Science Publishers.

Folkestad, G. 1998. Music learning as cultural practice: As exemplified in computer-based creative music-making. In *Musikpedagogik: Children composing,* eds. B. Sundin, G. E. McPherson, and G. Folkestad, 97–134. Malmo, Sweden: Lunds University.

Forrai, K. 1974. *Music in preschool.* 2nd ed., trans. J. Sinor. Budapest: Franklin Printing House.

Fostnot, C., ed. 2005. *Constructivism: Theory, perspectives, and practice.* 2nd ed. New York: Teachers College Press.

Fox, D. B. 1990. An analysis of the pitch characteristics of infant vocalizations. *Psychomusicology* 9(1):13–24.

Fraisse, P. 1982. Tempo and rhythm. In *The psychology of music,* ed. D. Deutsch, 149–80. New York: Academic Press.

Frassinetti, F., N. Bolognini, and E. Ladavas. 2002. Enhancement of visual perception by crossmodal visuo-auditory interaction. *Experimental Brain Research* 147:332–43.

Frega, A. L. (1979). Rhythmic tasks with 3-, 4-, and 5-year-old children: A study made in argentine republic. *Bulletin of the Council for Research in Music Education* 45:1–20.

Frego, R. J. D. 1996. Determining tempo preference in elementary-aged children through gross motor movements. *Southeastern Journal of Music Education* 8:138–45.

Fung, C. V. 1995. Music preference as a function of musical characteristics. *The Quarterly Journal of Music Teaching and Learning* 6(3):30–45.

Gagne, R. 1985. *The conditions of learning and the sequence of instruction.* New York: Holt, Rhinehart & Winston.

Gallahue, D. L. 1982. *Developmental movement experiences for children.* New York: John Wiley & Sons, Inc.

Gallese, V. 2003. The roots of empathy: The shared manifold hypothesis and the neural basis of intersubjectivity. *Psychopathology* 36(4):171–180.

Garcia, M. 1841. *A complete treatise on the art of singing (Parts I and II),* trans. D. Paschke, 1984. New York: Da Capo Press.

Gardner, H. 1999a. *The disciplined mind.* New York: Penguin Books.

Gardner, H. 1999b. *Intelligence reframed: Multiple intelligences for the twenty-first century.* New York: Basic Books.

Gardner, H. 1993. *Frames of mind: A theory of multiple intelligences.* 10th ed. New York: Basic Books.

Gardner, H. 1983. *Frames of mind: A theory of multiple intelligences.* New York: Basic Books.

Gardner, H. 1982. *Art, mind and brain: A cognitive approach to creativity.* New York: Basic Books.

Gay, G. 2000. *Culturally responsive teaching: Theory, research, and practice.* New York: Teachers College Press.

Gelfand, S. A. 2004. *Hearing: An introduction to psychological and physiological acoustics.* New York: Marcel Dekker.

Gibson, P., E. Norris, and P. Alcock. 1992. *Music: The rock classic connection.* London: Oxford University Press.

Glaze, L. E., D. M. Bless, P. Milenkovic, and R. D. Susser. 1988. Acoustic characteristics of children's voices. *Journal of Voice* 2(4):312–19.

Godfroy, M., C. Roumes, and P. Dauchy. 2003. Spatial variations of visual-auditory fusion areas. *Perception* 32(10):1233–45.

Godfroy, M., C. Roumes, and P. Dauchy. 2003. Spatial variations of visual-auditory fusion areas. *Perception* 32(10):1233–45.

Goetze, M., N. Cooper, and C. Brown. 1990. Recent research on singing in the general music classroom. *Bulletin of the Council for Research in Music Education* 104:16–37.

Goetze, M. 1985. Factors affecting accuracy in children's singing. Doctoral dissertation, University of Colorado at Boulder: 8528488, 169.

Gordon, R. G., Jr., ed. 2005. *Ethnologue: Languages of the world.* 15th ed. Dallas, TX: SIL International.

Gordon, E. E. 1997. *A music learning theory for newborn and young children.* Chicago: G.I.A.

Gordon, E. E. 1994. *Learning sequences in music: Skill, content, and patterns.* Chicago: G.I.A.

Gordon, E. E. 1979. *Primary measures of music audiation.* Chicago: G.I.A.

Gordon, E. E. 1971. *The psychology of music teaching.* Englewood Cliffs, NJ: Prentice Hall.

Gould, A. O. 1968. *Finding and learning to use the singing voice: A manual for teachers.* No. ED025531.

Graham, R. M., and A. Beer. 1980. *Teaching music to the exceptional child.* Englewood Cliffs, NJ: Prentice Hall.

Green, C. 2006. Major demographics and schooling trends for English language learners and their teachers. In *Cultural and linguistic issues for English language learners,* eds. P. Dam and M. T. Cowart, 26–55. Denton, TX: Federation of North Texas Area Universities.

Greene, B. 2003. *The elegant universe: Superstrings, hidden dimensions, and the quest for the ultimate theory.* New York: W. W. Norton & Company.

Greer, D., L. Dorrow, and A. Randall. 1974. Music listening preferences of elementary school children. *Journal of Research in Music Education* 22:284–91.

Gromko, J. E. 1994. Children's invented notations as measures of musical understanding. *Psychology of Music* 22:136–47.

Grout, D. J., C. V. Palisca, and P. J. Burkholder. 2005. *History of western music.* 7th ed. New York: W.W. Norton & Company.

Guilford, J. 1967. *The nature of human intelligence.* New York: McGraw-Hill.

Haack, P. 1992. The acquisition of music listening skills. In *Handbook of research on music teaching and learning,* ed. R. Colwell, 451–65. New York: Schirmer Books.

Hansen, D., E. Bernstorf, and G. M. Stuber. 2004. *The music and literacy connection.* Reston, VA: MENC.

Hargreaves, D. J. 1982. The development of aesthetic reaction to music. *Psychology of Music* (Special Issue): 51–54.

Harkey, B. L. (1978/1979). The identification of and the training of the vocal range of three-year-old preschool children. Doctoral dissertation, Louisiana State University and Agricultural and Mechanical College, AAT 7911572, 147.

Hartnick, C. J., and M. Boseley. 2008. *Pediatric voice disorders.* San Diego, CA: Plural Publishing.

Hartnick, C. J., R. Rehbar, and V. Prasad. 2005. Development and maturation of the pediatric human vocal fold lamina propria. *Laryngoscope* 115(1):4–15.

Hasek, C. S., S. Singh, and T. Murry. 1980. Acoustic attributes of preadolescent voices. *Journal of the Acoustical Society of America* 68(5):1262–65.

Hast, M. 1985. Comparative anatomy of the larynx: Evolution and function. In *Vocal fold physiology: Biomechanics, acoustics and phonatory control*, ed. I. Titze. Denver, CO: The Denver Center for the Performing.

Hayes, J. R., ed. 1992. *The genius of Arab civilization: Source of renaissance.* New York: New York University Press.

Hedden, S. K. 1981. Music listening skills and music listening preferences. *Bulletin of the Council for Research in Music Education* 65:16–26.

Hedden, S. K. 1980. Development of music listening skills. *Bulletin of the Council for Research in Music Education* 64:12–22.

Hetland, L. 2000a. Learning to make music enhances spatial reasoning. *Journal of Aesthetic Education* 34(3–4): 179–238.

Hetland, L. 2000b. Listening to music enhances spatial-temporal reasoning: Evidence for the "Mozart effect." *Journal of Aesthetic Education* 34(3–4): 105–48.

Hodges, D. 1992. The acquisition of music reading skills. In *Handbook of research on music teaching and learning*, ed. R. Colwell, 466–71. New York: Schirmer Books.

Hodgkinson, H. 2006. *ASCD releases analysis of U.S. education data as it relates to the "whole child".* http://www.ascd.org (accessed April 15, 2006).

Holst, G. 1990. In *The planets*, ed. Levine J., Chicago Symphony Orchestra. Hamburg, Germany: Deutsche Grammophon.

Hu, J. P., and S. C. Lee. 1992. *Basic Chinese vocabulary.* Chicago: Contemporary Publishing Group.

Igoa, C. 1995. *The inner world of the immigrant child.* Mahwah, NJ: Lawrence Erlbaum Associates.

Inscoe, J. C., ed. 2005. *Appalachians and race: The mountain south from slavery to segregation.* Rev. ed. Lexington, KY: University Press of Kentucky Press.

Ishii, K., K. Yamashita, M. Akita, and H. Hirose. 2000. Age related development of the arrangement of connective tissue fibers in the lamina propria of the human vocal fold. *Annals of Otology, Rhinology and Laryngology* 109(11):1055–64.

Israel, S., C. Block, and K. Kinnucan. 2005. *Metacognition in literacy learning.* Mahwah, NJ: Erlbaum.

Janowsky, J. S., and R. Carper. 1996. Is there a neural basis for cognitive transitions in school-age children? In *The five to seven year shift: The age of reason and responsibility*, eds. A. J. Sameroff and M. M. Haith, 33–60. Chicago: University of Chicago Press.

Jansma, P., and R. French. 1994. *Special physical education.* Englewood Cliffs, NJ: Prentice Hall.

Jaques-Dalcroze, E. 1921. *Rhythm, music and education.* New York: Putnam's Sons.

Jersild, A. T., and S. F. Bienstock. 1934. A study of the development of children's ability to sing. *The Journal of Educational Psychology* 25(7):481–503.

Joachim, H. 1932. Milestones in the history of violin playing. *The Musical Times* 73(1078):1079–82.

Jones, M. R., M. Bolz, and G. Kidd. 1982. Controlled attending as a function of melodic and temporal context. *Perception and Psychophysics* 32:211–18.

Jordan-DeCarbo, J. 1986. A sound-to-symbol approach to learning music. *Music Educators Journal* 72(6):38–41.

Joyner, D. R. 1971. Pitch discrimination and tonal memory and their association with singing and the larynx. Master's thesis.

Joyner, D. R. 1969. The monotone problem. *Journal of Research in Music Education* 17(1):115–24.

Kahane, J. 1975. The developmental anatomy of the human prepubertal and pubertal larynx. Doctoral dissertation, University of Pittsburgh. *Dissertation Abstracts International, B36* (10), 4964. (UMI No. ATT7608806).

Kalmar, M., and G. Balasko. 1987. 'Musical mother tongue' and creativity in preschool children's melodic improvisations. *Bulletin of the Council for Research in Music Education* 91:77–86.

Kamii, C., and J. Ewing. 1996. Basing teaching on Piaget's constructivism. *Childhood Education* 72(5):261–64.

Katz, L. 1989. *Engaging children minds: The project approach.* Norwood, NJ: Ablex.

Katz, L., and S. Chard. 1995. *Talks with teachers of young children: A collection.* Norwood, NJ: Ablex.

Keating, P., and R. Buhr. 1977. Fundamental frequency in the speech of infants and children. *Journal of the Acoustical Society of America* 63(2):567–71.

Kent, R. D. 1981. Articulatory-acoustic perspectives on speech development. In *Language behavior in infancy and early childhood*, ed. R. E. Stark, 105–26. New York: Elsevier.

Kostka, M. J. 1984. Effects of practice and vocal range preference on the singing performance of four and five year olds. Music Educators National Conference, Chicago, IL.

Krumhansl, C. L., and F. C. Keil. 1982. Acquisition of the hierarchy of tonal functions in music. *Memory and Cognition* 10: 243–51.

Kratus, J. 2001. Effect of available tonality and pitch options on children's compositional processes and products. *Journal of Research in Music Education* 49(4):294–306.

Kratus, J. (1995a). A developmental approach to teaching music improvisation. *International Journal of Music Education* 26: 27–38.

Kratus, J. 1995b. The effect of composing tempo on the musical characteristics of children's compositions. *Contributions to Music Education* 22: 40–48.

Kratus, J. 1991. Growing with improvisation. *Music Educators Journal* 78(4):35–40.

Kratus, J. 1989. A time analysis of the compositional processes used by children ages 7 to 11. *Journal of Research in Music Education* 37(1):5–20.

Kratus, J. 1985. The use of melodic and rhythmic motives in the original songs of children aged 5–13. *Contributions to Music Education* 12:1–8.

Kuehn, G. B. A. 1985. Discrimination and identification of Chinese and English infant vocalizations. Doctoral dissertation, Washington University, ATT852085, 154.

Laczó, Z. 1981. A psychological investigation of improvisational abilities in the lower and higher classes of the elementary school. *Bulletin of the Council for Research in Music Education* 66–67:39–45.

Lau, F. 2008. *Music in China.* New York: Oxford University Press.

Law, B., and M. Eckes. 2000. *The more-than-just-surviving handbook: ESL for every classroom teacher.* Winnipeg, Canada: Portage and Main Press.

LeBlanc, A. 1981. Effects of style, tempo, and performing medium on children's music preference. *Journal of Research in Music Education* 29:143–56.

LeBlanc, A., and R. Cote. 1983. Effects of tempo and performing medium on children's music preference. *Journal of Research in Music Education* 31(3): 57–66.

LeBlanc, A., and J. McCrary. 1983. Effect of tempo on children's music preference. *Journal of Research in Music Education* 31(4): 283–94.

Lefrancois, G. 1994. *Psychology for teaching.* 8th ed. Belmont, CA: Wadsworth.

Letts, R. 1997. Music: Universal language between all nations? *International Journal of Music Education* 29(1):22–31.

Leonhard, C., and R. House. 1972. *Foundations and principles of music education.* New York: McGraw-Hill.

Levine, L. 2005. *The Drum Café's traditional music of South Africa.* Johannesburg: The Drum Café.

Lewis, A. G. 1976. *Listen, look, and sing.* Morristown, NJ: Silver Burdett.

Lewis, B. E. 1989. The research literature in movement-based instruction with children: Implications for music teaching and learning. *Update* 7:13–17.

Lindsay, J. 1990. *Javanese gamelan: Traditional orchestra of Indonesia.* Singapore: Oxford University Press.

Loong, C. 2002. The effects of tempo in rhythm of young children under five years old. Music Educators National Convention, Nashville.

Loots, A. G. J. 1997. *A critical approach to rock music from a cultural-historical and theoretical perspective.* Unpublished dissertation, University of Port Elizabeth, South Africa.

Lornel, K. 1993. *Introducing American folk music,* Smithsonian Institution ed. New York: Brown & Benchmark Publishers.

Mager, R. F. 1997. *Preparing instructional objectives.* Atlanta, GA: Center for Effective Performance.

Malbrán, S. 2002. Tapping in time: A longitudinal study at the ages of three to five years. Paper Presented at the International Society for Music Education Conference, Bergen, Norway.

Malm, W. P. 1977. *Music cultures of the Pacific, the Near East and Asia.* Englewood Cliffs, NJ: Prentice Hall.

Maslow, A. 1998. *Toward a psychology of being.* 3rd ed. New York: Wiley.

Mathis, J. 2007. Contemplating community through multicultural children's literature. In *Intercultural understanding,* eds. P. Dam and M. T. Cowart, 92–113. Denton, TX: Federation of North Texas Area Universities.

Matthews, S. 1991. Suzuki singing in Finland. *American Suzuki Journal* (Spring), 23–24.

Matusky, P., and S. B. Tan. 1997. *Muzik malaysia: Tradisi klasik, rakyat dan sinkretik.* Malaysia: The Asian Centre.

McClatchy, D. 2000. *Appalachian traditional music: A short history.* http://www.mustrad.org.uk/articles/appalach.htm (accessed January 18, 2008).

McDonald, D. T., and G. M. Simons. 1989. *Musical growth and development: Birth through six.* New York: Schirmer Books.

McKernon, P. 1979. The development of first songs in young children. In *Early symbolization: New directions for child development,* ed. H. Gardner and D. Wolf, 43–58. San Francisco: Jossey-Bass, Inc., Publishers.

McKinney, J. 2005. *The diagnosis and correction of vocal faults.* Long Grove, IL: Waveland Press.

MENC. (1994a). *Opportunity-to-learn standards for music instruction: Grades preK-12.* Reston, VA: The National Association for Music Education.

MENC. (1994b). *The K-12 national standards, PreK standards, and what they mean to music educators.* Reston, VA. The National Association for Music Education.

MENC. 2009. *MENC position statement on early childhood education: Beliefs about young children and developmentally and individually appropriate musical experiences.* http://www.menc.org/about/view/early-childhood-education-position-statement (accessed July 11, 2009).

MENC. 1986. *The school music program: Description and standards.* Reston, VA: The National Association of Music Education.

Merriam, A. 1964. *The anthropology of music.* Evanston, IL: Northwestern University.

Michel, P. 1973. The optimum development of musical ability in the first years of life. *Psychology of Music* 1: 14–20.

Michel, D. E., and J. Pinson. 2005. *Music therapy in principle and practice.* IL: Charles C. Thomas.

Michel, D. E., and M. Rohrbacher, eds. 1988. *The music therapy assessment profile (MTAP)* (research edition ed.) Available from authors.

Miller, R. 2004. *Solutions for singers: Tools for performers and teachers.* New York: Oxford University Press.

Miller, R. 2000. *Training soprano voices.* New York: Oxford University Press.

Miller, R. 1996. *The structure of singing.* New York: Schirmer.

Miller, S. D. 1973. Guido d'Arezzo: Medieval musician and educator. *Journal of Research in Music Education* 21(3):239–45.

Miller, T., and A. Shahriari. 2006. *World music: A global journey.* London: Routledge.

Mills, J. I. 1989. Some developmental aspects of aural perception. *Bulletin of the Council for Research in Music Education* 85:140–45.

Miranda, L., A. Arthur, T. Milan, O. Mahoney, and B. D. Perry. 1998. The art of healing: The CIVITAS healing arts project. *Early Childhood Connections* 4(4):35–40.

*MMCP synthesis,* ed. A. Foshay. 1970. Bardonia, NY: Media Materials, Inc.

Molenda, M. 2003. In search of the elusive ADDIE model. *Performance Improvement Journal* 42(May/June):34–36.

Monsaas, J. A., and G. Engelhard. 1990. Home environment and the competitiveness of highly accomplished individuals in four talent fields. *Developmental Psychology* 26(2):264–68.

Montano, D. R. 1983. The effect of improvising in given rhythms on piano students; sight reading rhythmic accuracy achievement. Doctoral dissertation, New York University. *Dissertation Abstracts International, 44* (6), 1720A.

Moog, H. 1976. *The musical experience of the pre-school child.* London: Schott (original work published in German in 1968).

Moore, B. C. J. 2004. *An introduction to the psychology of hearing.* 5th ed. London: Elsevier Academic Press.

Moore, B. C. J. 1986. *Frequency selectivity in hearing.* London: Elsevier Academic Press.

Moore, R. S., and M. Staum. 1987. Effect of age and nationality on auditory/visual sequential memory of English and American children. *Bulletin of the Council for Research in Music Education* 91:126–31.

Moorehead, G. E., and D. Pond. 1978. *Music of young children.* Santa Barbara, CA: Pillsbury Foundation for Advancement of Music Education.

Morita, N. (n.d.). *Nurtured by love: The life and work of Shinichi Suzuki.* Cleveland: Telos Productions, Inc.

Morrison, G. S. 2006. *Early childhood education today.* 10th ed. Upper Saddle River, NJ: Prentice Hall.

Morrison, M., and L. Rammage. 1994. *The management of voice disorders.* San Diego, CA: Singular Publishing Group.

Murch, G. 1984. Physiological principles for the effective use of color. *IEEE Computer Graphics and Applications* 4(11): 49–54.

Murr, L. E., E. Ferreyra, G. Maldonado, E. Trillo, S. Pappu, C. Kennedy, J. De Alba, M. Posada, D. P. Russell, and J. L. White. 1999. Materials science and metallurgy of the Caribbean steel drum. Part 1: Fabrication, deformation phenomena and acoustic fundamentals. *Journal of Materials Science* 34(5):967–79.

*Music of Southeast Asia.* 2007. http://www.cartage.org.lb/en/themes/arts/music/Worldmusic/msoueastasia/msoueastasia.htm (accessed January 18, 2008).

Nasuruddin, M. G. 2003. *Muzik tradisional Malaysia.* Kuala Lumpur, Malaysia: Dewan Bahasa dan Pustaka.

National Academy of Recording Arts and Sciences (NARAS). (1999). *Smart symphonies.* Santa Monica, CA: National Academy of Recording Arts and Sciences Foundation, Inc.

National Association for the Education of Young Children. 1997. *Developmentally appropriate practice in early childhood programs serving children from birth through age 8.* National Association for the Education of Young Children.

National Association for Music Education. 2007. *National standards for music education.* http://www.menc.org/publication/books/standards.htm (accessed September 10, 2007).

National Association for Music Education (MENC). 2007. *The K-12 national standards, PreK standards, and what they mean to music educators.* http://www.menc.org/publication/books/prek12st.html (accessed September 10, 2007).

National Association for Sport and Physical Education (NASPE). 2004. *Moving into the future: National standards for physical education.* 2nd ed. http://ezproxy.twu.edu:2535/naspe/publications-nationalstandards.html (accessed February 7, 2008).

National Clearinghouse for Bilingual Education. 1999. *The growing numbers of limited English proficient.* Washington, DC: U.S. Department of Education.

National Council for the Social Studies (NCSS). 1994. *The curriculum standards for social studies.* http://www.socialstudies.org/standards (accessed February 7, 2008).

National Council of Teachers of English (NCTE). 2009. *Standards for the English language arts.* http://www.ncte.org/standards (accessed July 11, 2009).

National Council of Teachers of Mathematics (NCTM). 2008. *Principles and standards for school mathematics.* http://standards.nctm.org/ (accessed February 22, 2008).

National Science Teachers Association (NSTA). 2008. *National science education standards contents.* http://www.nap.edu/readingroom/books/nses/html/ (accessed February 20, 2008).

Nelson, C. A., and F. E. Bloom. 1997. Child development and neuroscience. *Child Development* 68(5):970–87.

Nettl, B. 2000. An ethnomusicologist contemplates universality in musical sound and musical culture. In *Origins of music,* eds. H. Wallin, J. Merke, and S. Brown, 463–72. Cambridge, MA: MIT Press.

Nettl, B. 1954. North American Indian musical style. *The Journal of American Folklore* 67(263):44–56.

Nettl, B., D. Capwell, I. Wong, T. Turino, P. Bohlman, and T. Rommen. 2008. *Excursions in world music,* 5th ed. Upper Saddle River, NJ: Prentice Hall.

*Norton recorded anthology of Western music.* 2005. New York: W.W. Norton & Company.

Organization of American Kodály Educators (OAKE). 2004. *Organization of kodály educators (OAKE).* http://www.oake.org/ (accessed January 28, 2008).

Ott, D. 1996. Effects of musical context on the improvisations of children as a function of age, training, and exposure to music. Doctoral dissertation, University of Alabama. *Dissertation Abstracts International* 57(2):1469B.

Ovando, C., M. C. Combs, and V. Collier. 2006. *Bilingual and ESL classrooms: Teaching in multicultural contexts.* 4th ed. Boston: McGraw-Hill.

Palac, J., K. Horvath, J. Jensen, G. Klickstein, L. Scott, and D. Sogin. 2004. Music education liaison report/neuro-musculoskeletal health. Paper presented at the Health Promotion in Schools of Music Conference, Denton, TX. www.unt.edu/hpsm/index.htm.

Patrick, L. 1998. A comparison of young childrens' movements to music with and without props. Music Educators National Conference, Phoenix, AZ.

Paul, P. 2003. *Children's emotional responsiveness to music as measured by the continuous response digital interface and verbal response.* Unpublished doctoral dissertation, Florida State University, Tallahassee, FL.

Peery, J. C., and I. Peery. 1986. Effects of exposure to classical music on the musical preferences of preschool children. *Journal of Research in Music Education* 34(1):24–33.

Peery, J. C., I. W. Peery, and T. W. Draper, eds. (1987). *Music and child development.* New York: Springer-Verlag.

Persellin, D. 1993. Responses to rhythm patterns when presented to children through auditory, visual, and kinesthetic modes. *Journal of Research in Music Education* 40(4):315–23.

*Philippine arts: Indigenous music.* http://filipinoheritage.zxq. net/arts/phil-music/pre-colonial-indigenous-music.htm (accessed December 24, 2007).

Phillips, K. 1996. *Teaching kids to sing.* New York: Schirmer.

Phillips, K. H. 1992. *Teaching kids to sing.* New York: Schirmer Books.

Piaget, J. 1962. *Play, dreams, and imitation in childhood.* New York: W.W. Norton.

Piaget, J. 1952. *The psychology of intelligence.* London, England: Routledge & Kegan Paul.

Pinson, J. 2002. *Assessing the needs of persons with disabilities.* Unpublished manuscript.

Pinson, J. 2001. *Mallet magic.* Rev. ed. Denton, TX: Pinson.

Plumridge, J. M. 1972. The range and pitch levels of children's voices, in relation to published material for children's voices. Doctoral dissertation, Advanced Study of Education.

Pond, D., ed. 1978. *Music of young children (reprint of studies, 1941–1951).* Santa Barbara, CA: Pillsbury Foundation for Advancement of Music Education.

Porter, S. Y. 1977. The effect of multiple discrimination training on pitch-matching behaviour of uncertain singers. *Journal of Research in Music Education* 25(1):68–91.

Racy, A. J. 1998. Improvisation, ecstasy and performance dynamics in Arabic music. In *In the course of performance: Studies in the world of musical improvisation,* eds. B. Nettl and M. Russell. Chicago, IL: University of Chicago Press.

Rainbow, B., and G. Cox. 2007. *Music in educational thought and practice: A survey from 800 BC.* London: Boydell Press.

Rainbow, E. L. 1981. A final report on a three-year investigation of the rhythmic abilities of pre-school aged children. *Bulletin of the Council for Research in Music Education* 66:69–73.

Reimer, B. 2002. *A philosophy of music education: Advancing the vision.* 3rd ed. Upper Saddle River, NJ: Prentice Hall.

Richards, E., and C. Richards. 1974a. *Making music around the home & yard.* New York: Award Music Co.

Richards, E., and C. Richards. 1974b. *Making music in mommy's kitchen.* New York: Award Music Co.

Riddle, A. 1970. *Book of ballads.* Baton Rouge, LA: Louisiana State University Press.

Ries, N. L. L. 1987. An analysis of the characteristics of infant-child singing expressions: Replication report. *The Canadian Journal of Research in Music Education* 29(1): 5–20.

Rockmore, T. 2005. *On constructivist epistemology.* Lanham, MD: Rowman & Littlefield Publishers.

Rose, S. E. 1995. The effects of Dalcroze eurhythmics on beat competency performance skills of kindergarten, first, and second-grade children. University of North Carolina at Greensboro.

Runfola, M., and K. Swanick. 2002. Developmental characteristics of music learners. In *The new handbook of research on music teaching and learning,* eds. R. Colwell and C. Richardson, 373–97. New York: Oxford University Press.

*Russian adoption statistics.* 2006. http://www. adoptionknowhow.com/russia/statistics (accessed September 29, 2007).

Rutkowski, J., and L. Chen-Hafteck. 2001. The singing voice within every child: A cross-cultural comparison of first graders' use of singing voice. *Early Childhood Connections: Journal of Music- and Movement-Based Learning* 7(1):37–42.

Rutkowski, J., L. Chen-Hafteck, and C. Gluschankof. 2002. *Children's vocal connections: A cross-cultural study of the relationship between first graders' use of singing voice and their speaking ranges.* ISME Early Childhood Conference: Copenhagen, Denmark.

Santos, R. P. 2007. *Traditional forms of music.* http://www. ncca. gov.ph/about-culture-and-arts/articles-on-c-n-a/ article.php?igm=1&i=161 (accessed July 12, 2009).

Saracho, O., and B. Spodek, eds. 2007. *Contemporary perspectives on socialization and social development in early childhood education.* Charlotte, NC: Information Age Publishing.

Sasaki, C. T., M. Suzuki, and M. Horiuchi. 1977. The effect of tracheostomy on the laryngeal closure reflex. *Laryngoscope* 87:1428–33.

Sataloff, R. T. 1998. *Vocal health and pedagogy.* San Diego, CA: Singular Publishing Group.

Sataloff, R. T. 1997. *Professional voice: The science and art of clinical care.* 2nd ed. San Diego, CA: Singular Publishing Group.

Sataloff, R. T., J. Spiegel, and D. C. Rosen. 1998. The effects of age on the voice. In *Vocal health and pedagogy,* ed. R. Sataloff, 123–33. San Diego, CA: Singular Publishing Group.

Sato, K., T. Nakashima, S. Nonaka, and Y. Harabuchi. 2008. Histopathologic investigations of the unphonated human vocal fold mucosa. *Acta Oto-Laryngologica* 128(6):694–701.

Schellenberg, E. G., A. Krysciak, and R. J. Campbell. 2000. Perceiving emotion in melody: Interactive effects of pitch and rhythm. *Music Perception* 18(2):155–71.

Schellenberg, E. G., and S. E. Trehub. 1996. Natural musical intervals: Evidence from infant listeners. *Psychological Science* 7:272–77.

Schilbach, L., A. M. Wohlschläger, A. Newen, N. Krämer, N. Shah, G. R. Fink, et al. 2006. Being with others: Neural correlates of social interaction. *Neuropsychologia* 44(5): 718–30.

Schleuter, S. L., and L. J. Schleuter. 1985. The relationship of grade level and six differences to certain rhythmic responses of primary grade children. *Journal of Research in Music Education* 16:110–27.

Schrade, L. 1947. Music in the philosophy of Boethius. *The Musical Quarterly* (33): 194.

Schutz, M., and S. Lipscomb. 2007. Hearing gestures, seeing music: Vision influences perceived tone duration. *Perception* 36(6):888–97.

Scieszka, J. 1999. *The true story of the 3 little pigs!* New York: Viking.

Seeger, M. 2003. *Music of the southern Appalachian mountains.* http://mikeseeger.info/html/1_sgcov.html (accessed January 18, 2008).

Serafine, M. L. 1988. *Music as cognition: The development of thought in sound.* New York: Columbia University Press.

Shehan, P. 1986. Music instruction for the live performance. *Bulletin of the Council for Research in Music Education* 88: 51–57.

Shelley, S. 1981. Investigating the musical capabilities of young children. *Bulletin of the Council for Research in Music Education* 68:26–34.

Simons, G. M. 1964. Comparisons of incipient music responses among very young twins and singletons. *Journal of Research in Music Education* 12: 212–26.

Sims, W. L. 2005. Effects of free versus directed listening on duration of individual music listening by prekindergarten children 53(1):78–86.

Sims, W. L., ed. 1995. *Strategies for teaching prekindergarten music*. Reston, VA: MENC.

Sims, W. L. 1991. Effects of instruction and task format on preschool children's music concept discrimination. *Journal of Research in Music Education* 39(4):298–310.

Sims, W. L. 1988. Movement responses of preschool children, primary grade children, and pre-service classroom teachers to characteristics of musical phrases. *Psychology of Music* 16:110–27.

Sims, W. L. 1986. The effect of high versus low teacher affect and passive versus active student activity during music listening on pre-school children's attention, piece preference, time spent listening, and piece recognition. *Journal of Research in Music Education* 34:173–91.

Sims, W. L., and B. Nolker. 2002. Individual differences in music listening responses of kindergarten children. *Journal of Research in Music Education* 50(4): 292–300.

Sinor, E. 1984. The singing of selected tonal patterns by preschool children. Doctoral dissertation, Indiana University, 8501456, 188.

Sloboda, J. A. 1985. *The musical mind: The cognitive psychology of music*. Oxford: Clarendon Press.

Smith, R. B., and C. Leonhard. 1968. *Discovering music together early childhood*. Chicago: Follett Educational Corporation.

Smithrim, K. L. 1997. Free musical play in early childhood. *Canadian Music Educator* 38(4):17–24.

Smoll, F. L., and R. W. Schutz. 1978. Relationships among measures of preferred tempo and motor rhythm. *Perceptual and Motor Skills* 46:883–94.

Standing, E. 1957. *Maria Montessori: Her life and work*. London: Hollis and Carter.

Standley, J. 2002. A meta-analysis of the efficacy of music therapy for premature infants. *Journal of Pediatric Nursing* 17(2):107–13.

Stathopoulos, E. T., and C. M. Sapienza. 1991. *Comparison of child and adult mechanisms for varying vocal intensity*. American Speech, Language and Hearing Association Conference: Seattle, WA.

Sternberg, R. J., and T. I. Lubart. 1996. Investing in creativity. *American Psychologist* 51:677–88.

Stillman, R. 1978. *The Callier-Azusa scale G edition*. Dallas, TX: Callier Center for Communications Disorders.

Strybel, T. Z., and A. Vatakis. 2004. A comparison of auditory and visual apparent motion presented individually and with crossmodal moving distractors. *Perception* 33(9):1033–48.

Sundberg, J. 1987. *The science of the singing voice*. Dekalb, IL: Northern Illinois University Press.

Sundin, B., G. E. McPherson, and G. Folkestad, eds. 1998. *Musikpedagogik: Children composing*. Malmo, Sweden: Lunds University.

Suzuki, S. 1969. *Nurtured by love*. New York: Exposition Press.

Swanick, K., and J. Tilman. 1986. A sequence of musical development: A study of children's compositions. *British Journal of Music Education* 3(3):305–39.

Taylor, E. 1990. *Musical instruments of Southeast Asia*. New York: Oxford University Press.

Taylor, M. 1985. Music in the daily experience of grade six children: An interpretive study. *Psychology of Music* 13(1): 31–39.

Thatcher, R. 1998. EEG database guided neurotherapy: Practical applications presentation at the annual conference of the society for the study of neuronal regulation, September 11. Presentation at the Annual Conference of the Society for the Study of Neuronal Regulation.

Thompson, L. 2001. *A history of South Africa*. 3rd ed. New Haven, CT: Yale University Press.

Thompson, W. F. 1994. Sensitivity to combinations of musical parameters: Pitch with duration, and pitch pattern with durational pattern. *Perception and Psychophysics* 56:363–74.

Thompson, W. F., and E. G. Schellenberg. 2002. Cognitive constraints on music listening. In *The new handbook of research on music teaching and learning*, eds. R. Colwell and C. Richardson, 461–86. New York: Oxford University Press.

Thurloway, L. 1977. An investigation into children's ability to sing through the study of playground songs. Doctoral dissertation, Froebel Institute.

Tilman, J., and K. Swanick. 1989. Towards a model of development of chldren's musical creativity. *Canadian Music Educator* 30(2):169–74.

Titon, J.T., ed. 2009 *World of music: An introduction to the music of the worlds peoples*. 5th ed. New York: Schirmer Books.

Titze, I. 1996. Why do we have a vocal ligament? *Journal of Singing* 53(1):31–32.

Titze, I. 1994. *Principles of voice production*. Englewood Cliffs, NJ: Prentice Hall.

Titze, I. 1992. Critical periods in vocal change: Early childhood. *The NATS Journal* 48:16–18.

Tonkova-Yampol'skaya, R. V. 1973. Development of speech intonation in infants during the first two years of life. In *Studies of child language development*, eds. C. A. Ferguson and D. I. Slobin, 128–38. New York: Holt, Rinehart and Winston, Inc.

Touma, H. 2003. *The music of the Arabs*. Rev. ed. New York: Amadeus Press.

Trainor, L. J., and S. E. Trehub. 1994. Key membership and implied harmony in Western tonal music: Developmental perspectives. *Perception and Psychophysics* 56:125–32.

Trainor, L. J., and S. E. Trehub. 1992. A comparison of infants' and adults' sensitivity to Western musical structure. *Journal of Experimental Psychology: Human Perception and Performance* 18:394–402.

Trehub, S. E. 2004. Music perception in infancy. In *Musical lives of young children*, ed. J. W. Flohr, 24–29. Upper Saddle River, NJ: Prentice Hall.

Trehub, S. E., D. Bull, and L. A. Thorpe. 1984. Infants' perception of melodies: The role of melodic contour. *Child Development* 55:821–30.

Trehub, S. E., E. G. Schellenberg, and S. B. Kamenetsky. 1999. Infants' and adults' perception of scale structure. *Journal of Experimental Psychology: Human Perception and Performance* 25:965–75.

Trehub, S. E., and L. A. Thorpe. 1989. Infants' perception of rhythm. categorization of auditory sequences by temporal structure. *Canadian Journal of Experimental Psychology* 43:217–29.

Trehub, S. E., L. A. Thorpe, and B. A. Morrongiello. 1987. Organizational processes in infants' perception of auditory patterns. *Child Development* 58:741–49.

Trollinger, V. L. 2007a. Pediatric vocal development and voice science: Implications for teaching singing. *General Music Today* 20(2):19–25.

Trollinger, V. L. 2007b. Technology for musicians: Review of the singing coach and singing coach Kidz Software. *General Music Today* 20(2):39–41.

Trollinger, V. L. 2006. Reconciliation of world vocal traditions and vocal health in music education: Does such a possibility exist? Paper presented at the 27th World Conference of the International Society for Music Education, Kuala Lumpur, Malaysia.

Trollinger, V. L. 2004. Preschool children's pitch-matching accuracy in relation to participation in Cantonese-immersion preschools. *Journal of Research in Music Education* 52(3):218–33.

Trollinger, V. L. 2003. Relationships between pitch-matching accuracy, speech fundamental frequency, speech range, age and gender in American English-speaking pre-school children. *Journal of Research in Music Education* 51(1):78–94.

Trollinger, V. L. 2001. ADDIE for music educators. Paper presented at the *Technological Directions in Music Learning*, San Antonio, TX. http://music.utsa.edu/tdml/conf-VIII/VIII-Trollinger.html.

Trollinger, L. 1978. A study of biographical and personality factors of creative women in music. D.M.A. Dissertation, Temple University.

Turino, T. 2001. The music of sub-Saharan Africa. In *Excursions in world music*, 3rd ed., eds. B. Nettl, C. Capwell, I. Wong, P. V. Bohlman, and T. Turino. Upper Saddle River, NJ: Prentice Hall.

Turner, J. B., and R. S. Schiff. 1995. *Let's make music! Multicultural songs and activities*. Milwaukee: Hal Leonard.

Updegraff, R., L. Heiliger, and J. Learned. 1938. The effect of training upon the singing ability and musical interest of three-, four-, and five-year-old children. *University of Iowa Studies in Child Welfare* 14: 83–131.

U.S. Department of Education. 2003. *No child left behind*. http://www.nochildleftbehind.gov/ (accessed February 10, 2003).

U.S. Department of Education. 1993. *National excellence: A case for developing America's talent*. http://www.ed.gov/pubs/DevTalent/part3.html (accessed November 08, 2007).

Upitis, R. 1992. *Can I play you my song?* Portsmouth, NH: Heinemann Educational Books.

Vaughan, M. M. 1981. Intercultural studies in children's natural singing and walking tempo. *Bulletin of the Council for Research in Music Education* 66–67:96–101.

Vennard, W. 1967. *Singing: The mechanism and technique*. 4th ed. New York: Carl Fisher.

Vihman, M. M., and R. Miller. 1988. Words and babble at the threshold of language acquisition. In *The emergent lexicon: The child's development of a linguistic vocabulary*, eds. M. D. Smith and J. L. Locke. San Diego, CA: Academic Press.

Vygotsky, L. S. 1978. *Mind in society*. Cambridge, MA: Harvard University Press.

Vygotsky, L. S. 1962. *Thought and language*. Cambridge, MA: MIT Press.

Walker, R. 1987a. The effects of culture, environment, age, and musical training on choices of visual metaphors for sound. *Perception and Psychophysics* 42(5):491–502.

Walker, R. 1987b. Some differences between pitch perception by children of different cultural and musical backgrounds. *Bulletin of the Council for Research in Music Education* 91:166–70.

Walker, R. 1981. The presence of internalised images of musical sounds. *Bulletin of the Council for Research in Music Education* 66–67:107–12.

Walker, R. 1978. Perception and music notation. *Psychology of Music* 6:21–46.

Walters, D. L. 1983. The relationship between personal tempo in primary-aged children and their ability to synchronize movement with music. Reviewed by M. Vaughan (1986) in *Bulletin of the Council for Research in Music Education* 88:85–89.

Watkins, R. 1993. Nonperformance time use in middle and junior high school choral rehearsals. *Update* 4(Spring):4–7.

Webster, P. 1992. Research on creative thinking in music: The assessment literature. In *Handbook of research on music teaching and learning*, ed. R. Colwell, 266–80. New York: Schirmer Books.

Webster, P. 1990. Creativity as creative thinking. *Music Educators Journal* 76(9):22–28.

Webster, P. 1987. Conceptual bases for creative thinking in music. In *Music and child development*, eds. J. Peery, I. Peery, and T. Draper, 158–74. New York: Springer-Verlag.

Wendrich, K. A. 1981. Pitch imitation in infancy and early childhood: Observations and implications. Doctoral dissertation, *Dissertation Abstracts International* 41(12), 5019A), ATT 8111923, 69.

Williams, J. A. 2002. *Appalachia: A history*. Chapel Hill, NC: University of North Carolina Press.

Willoughby, D. 1993. *The world of music*. 2nd ed. Madison, WI: Brown and Benchmark.

Wilson, B. L., ed. 1996. *Models of music therapy interventions in school settings: From institution to inclusion*. Silver Springs, MD: National Association for Music Therapy, Inc.

Wilson, D. K. 1987. *Voice problems of children*. 3rd ed. Baltimore, MD: Williams and Wilkins Co.

Wilson, D. S. (1973). A study of the child voice from six to twelve. *Bulletin of the Council for Research in Music Education* 34:54–60.

Wilson, J. T. L. 1987. Interaction of simultaneous visual events. *Perception* 16(3):375–83.

Witkin, H. A., P. K. Oltman, E. Raskin, and S. A. Karp. (1971). *A manual for the embedded figures tests (#3001)*. Mountain View, CA: Consulting Psychologists Press.

Wolfe, C. K. 1977. *Tennessee strings: The story of country music in Tennessee*. Knoxville, TN: Tennessee University Press.

Wood, L. 1994. *Bowmar orchestral library*. Van Nuys, CA: Alfred Publishing.

Woodward, S. C. 1994. The impact of current functions of music in children's lives on music education philosophies. In *Musical connections: Tradition and change*, ed. H. Lees, 194–200. Auckland, New Zealand: International Society for Music Education.

U.S. Committee for Refugees and Immigrants. World refugee survey 2006—Risks and rights. Retrieved 06/22, 2009, from http://www.refugees.org/article.aspx?id=1565&subm=19&ssm=29&area=Investigate&.

Young, W. T. 1971. *An investigation of the singing abilities of kindergarten and first-grade children in east Texas*. ERIC Document Reproduction Service No. ED 069 431 No. PS-006-178. Nacogdoches, TX: Stephen F. Austin State University.

Zemlin, W. R. 1988. *Speech and hearing science: Anatomy and physiology*. 3rd ed. Upper Saddle River, NJ: Prentice Hall.

Zimmerman, M. P., and L. Sechrest. 1968. *How children conceptually organize musical sounds*. Cooperative Research Project 5-0256, Northwestern University.

# INDEX